Federalism and the Welfare State

In this unique and provocative contribution to the literatures of political science and social policy, ten leading experts question the prevailing view that federalism *always* inhibits the growth of social solidarity. Their comparative study of the evolution of political institutions and welfare states in the six oldest federal states – Australia, Austria, Canada, Germany, Switzerland and the USA – reveals that federalism can facilitate as well as impede social policy development. Development is contingent on several time dependent factors, including the degree of democratization, the type of federalism, and the stage of welfare state development and early distribution of social policy responsibility. The reciprocal nature of the federalism–social policy relationship is also made evident: the authors identify a set of important bypass structures within federal systems that have resulted from welfare state growth. In an era of retrenchment and unravelling unitary states, this study suggests that federalism may actually protect the welfare state, and welfare states may enhance national integration.

HERBERT OBINGER is Assistant Professor at the Centre for Social Policy Research, University of Bremen, and principal investigator at its TranState Research Centre.

STEPHAN LEIBFRIED is Professor of Public and Social Policy in the Department of Political Science at the University of Bremen and co-initiator of the Bremen TranState Research Centre.

FRANCIS G. CASTLES is Professor of Social and Public Policy at the University of Edinburgh.

Federalism and the Welfare State

New World and European Experiences

Edited by

HERBERT OBINGER, STEPHAN LEIBFRIED
and FRANCIS G. CASTLES

CAMBRIDGE
UNIVERSITY PRESS

CAMBRIDGE UNIVERSITY PRESS
Cambridge, New York, Melbourne, Madrid, Cape Town, Singapore, São Paulo

Cambridge University Press
The Edinburgh Building, Cambridge CB2 2RU, UK

Published in the United States of America by Cambridge University Press, New York

www.cambridge.org
Information on this title: www.cambridge.org/9780521611848

© Cambridge University 2005

This book is in copyright. Subject to statutory exception
and to the provisions of relevant collective licensing agreements,
no reproduction of any part may take place without
the written permission of Cambridge University Press.

First published 2005

Printed in the United Kingdom at the University Press, Cambridge

A catalogue record for this book is available from the British Library

Library of Congress Cataloguing in Publication data
Federalism and the welfare state: new world and European experiences / Herbert Obinger, Stephan Leibfried, and Francis G. Castles, editors.
  p. cm.
Includes bibliographical references and index.
ISBN 0 521 84738 9 (hbk) – ISBN 0 521 61184 9 (pbk)
1. Social policy – Case studies. 2. Federal government – Case studies. 3. Democracy – Case studies. I. Obinger, Herbert, 1970– II. Leibfried, Stephan, 1944–
III. Castles, Francis Geoffrey.
HN17.5.F375 2005
320.6 – dc22   2004051187

ISBN-13 978-0-521-84738-4 hardback
ISBN-10 0-521-84738-9 hardback
ISBN-13 978-0-521-61184-8 paperback
ISBN-10 0-521-61184-9 paperback

Cambridge University Press has no responsibility for the persistence or accuracy of URLs for external or third-party internet websites referred to in this book, and does not guarantee that any content on such websites is, or will remain, accurate or appropriate.

Contents

List of figures	*page* viii
List of tables	ix
List of contributors	xi
Preface	xii
Note on illustrations	xiv

1 Introduction: federalism and the welfare state   1
Herbert Obinger, Francis G. Castles and *Stephan Leibfried*

Federalism and social policy	2
Varieties of federalism	8
Varieties of welfare states	23
How federalism affects the welfare state: theoretical approaches	29
The book at a glance	46

Part 1   New World experiences

2 Australia: federal constraints and institutional innovations   51
Francis G. Castles and *John Uhr*

Introduction	51
The federal settlement	53
Why no 'old politics' in Australia?	62
A dialectic of old and new?	81
The end of the Australian model?	86

3 Canada: nation-building in a federal welfare state   89
Keith Banting

Introduction	89

vi Contents

Territorial politics and Canadian federalism	90
Federalism and the expansion of the welfare state	95
The impact of the welfare state on federalism	129
Conclusions	134

4 **The United States: federalism and its counter-factuals** 138
Kenneth Finegold

Evaluating the effects of federalism	138
The American federal system	145
An overview of US social policies	152
The trajectory of US social policies	160
Conclusion	175

Part 2 European experiences

5 **Austria: strong parties in a weak federal polity** 181
Herbert Obinger

Introduction	181
The birth of the welfare state: the Habsburg monarchy	182
The German-Austrian Republic (1918–1919) and the First Republic (1920–1933/34)	188
Austro-fascism and National-Socialist rule (1934–1945)	195
The Second Republic (1945 onwards)	196
Federalism and the 'new politics' of the welfare state	209
Conclusion	219

6 **Germany: co-operative federalism and the overgrazing of the fiscal commons** 222
Philip Manow

Introduction	222
Bismarckian social legislation as a federalist compromise	225
Weimar and the conflict over resources and competencies	231
The Federal Republic's welfare state and fiscal joint decision traps	242
Conclusion	260

Contents

7 **Switzerland: the marriage of direct democracy
 and federalism** 263
 Herbert Obinger, Klaus Armingeon, Giuliano Bonoli and
 Fabio Bertozzi

 Introduction 263
 Switzerland: a multi-tiered welfare state 264
 The long road to a federal welfare state 269
 Varieties of cantonal welfare regimes 292
 Conclusion 300

Part 3 Conclusion

8 **'Old' and 'new politics' in federal welfare states** 307
 Stephan Leibfried, Francis G. Castles and *Herbert Obinger*

 What the case studies say 308
 The impact of federalism in comparative perspective 317
 Beyond 'old' and 'new politics': federalism as a laboratory
  for social experimentation 340
 Feedback effects: the intended and unintended
  consequences of the welfare state 343
 The future of the federal welfare state 353

 Index 356

Figures

Introduction

1.1 Clusters of social spending at the turn of the millennium   *page* 29

Canada

3.1 Union density: unionized workers as a percentage of the non-agricultural labour force (1921–2002)   96
3.2 Federal and provincial/local governments' share of total public revenues according to the National Accounts   103
3.3 Consolidated public debt as a percentage of GDP, all levels of government (1977–2001)   117
3.4 Ratio of UI/EI beneficiaries to total unemployed (1976–2002)   120
3.5a Provincial average Social Assistance benefits, single employable (1989–2002)   127
3.5b Provincial average Social Assistance benefits, total income, single parent, one child (1989–2002)   127

USA

4.1 Federal, state and local spending (1929–2003)   152
4.2 Federal percentage share of domestic expenditures (1840–1962)   153

Germany

6.1 Absolute volume of contribution payments of employers and employees as a percentage of GDP (1975–2002)   252
6.2 Total tax revenue, the relative shares of central, state, local government and social security funds, Germany (1973–2002)   253

Switzerland

7.1 Unemployment rate in Switzerland (1920–2001)   284
7.2 Social insurance expenditure as a percentage of GDP (1948–1998)   285

Tables

Introduction

1.1	Basic political and economic features of six OECD federations	*page* 7
1.2	Constitutional courts in six federations	16
1.3	Second chambers in six federations	18
1.4	The partisan complexion of central government, interest group pluralism and trade union membership over the post-war period (1945–2001)	22
1.5	The introduction of core welfare state programmes at the national level	24
1.6	Distribution of legislative authority for social provision as between state and central government	25
1.7	Welfare states spending patterns and funding at the turn of the millennium	28
1.8	Potential federalism effects on social policy contingent upon contextual factors	45

Australia

2.1	Australian welfare state spending (1900–1979)	63
2.2	Australian social expenditure levels and changes as a percentage of GDP (1980–2001)	82

Canada

3.1	Average monthly provincial benefit levels (1942, 1949)	98
3.2	Federal transfers for health care as a percentage of provincial health expenditures (1975–2000)	124
3.3	Health services and expenditures by province (2001)	132

USA

4.1	State variation in social programme benefits (1999)	142
4.2	Structural features of the House of Representatives and the Senate	146

4.3	Party control and social policy in the United States (1933–2003)	149
4.4	Federalism and United States social policy (2003)	155
4.5	Application of Tetlock and Belkin's criteria for counter-factuals to a unitary United States	164

Austria

5.1	Vetoes of the Federal Council against National Council legislation (1920–2002)	204

Germany

6.1	The position of the federal chamber in Wilhelmine Germany, the Weimar Republic and the Federal Republic	234
6.2	Percentage tax revenue shares of national, regional and local government (1885–1970)	237
6.3	West–East transfers in billion DM, central and regional governments and social insurance funds (1991–1999)	251
6.4	Total social expenditures as a percentage of GDP in eleven countries (1950–1970)	260

Switzerland

7.1	Responsibilities of the cantons and the federation for social security	265
7.2	Social expenditure by administrative level as a percentage of total spending for each category (1990–1998)	266
7.3	Partisan complexion of the federal government (1848–2004)	280
7.4	Operationalization of variables for the different aspects of cantonal welfare regimes	296
7.5	Worlds of welfare in Switzerland: classification of the twenty-six Swiss cantons by taxation and social security	298
7.6	Lag effect of obligatory and optional referenda on the introduction of core branches of social insurance	301

Conclusion

8.1	Distribution of legislative authority for social provision as between state and central government 1920, 1950 and today	320
8.2	Bypass structures	349

Contributors

KLAUS ARMINGEON, Professor of Political Science, Department of Political Science, University of Bern, Switzerland

KEITH BANTING, Queen's Research Chair in Public Policy, School of Policy Studies and Department of Political Studies, Queen's University, Kingston, Canada

FABIO BERTOZZI, Research Associate, Department of Social Work and Social Policy, University of Fribourg, Switzerland

GIULIANO BONOLI, Assistant Professor, Department of Social Work and Social Policy, University of Fribourg, Switzerland

FRANCIS G. CASTLES, Professor of Social and Public Policy, University of Edinburgh, United Kingdom

KENNETH FINEGOLD, Senior Research Associate, Urban Institute, Washington, DC, USA

STEPHAN LEIBFRIED, Professor of Public and Social Policy, Centre for Social Policy Research, University of Bremen, Germany

PHILIP MANOW, Senior Fellow, Max Planck Institute for the Studies of Societies, Cologne, Germany

HERBERT OBINGER, Assistant Professor, Centre for Social Policy Research, University of Bremen, Germany

JOHN UHR, Senior Fellow, Research School of Social Sciences, Australian National University, Australia

Preface

The idea for this volume stems from the observation that, somewhere between the literatures of political science and social policy, there is an unexplored territory where federalism and the welfare state meet, a no man's land without even a conceptual map to guide us. *Hic sunt leones!* is the warning etched on the uncharted regions of ancient maps, but for us it serves as enticement, an invitation to explore the unknown.

In some OECD federal nations almost one-third of the GDP is tied up in the welfare state, but scholars of the state and federalism typically ignore the welfare constituent of this spending and focus their attention almost entirely on *non*-welfare public agendas. For these political scientists, the state is always spelled with a capital S, and welfare, if mentioned at all, with lower-case w. As the majority shareholder of public expenditures at the federal level, the welfare state is not just a passive recipient of federalism's multi-tiered policy-making, but a key player in shaping those policies and, indeed, in shaping the functioning of the federal structure itself. Its size, its indispensability, and the large segment of the voting population it affects make the welfare state a force to be reckoned with. In many instances, it also provides a mechanism for coping with problems the normal federal process has no means of dealing with, as was so clearly demonstrated in the process of German reunification. Scholars of the Welfare state – capital W, small s – have likewise ignored the differences between welfare state development in decentralized and centralized polities, although quantitative charts suggest that they have quite different terrains and profiles. The Welfare state and the federal State have thus been treated as separate hemispheres subject to different academic suzerainty. This may have to do with the implicit and morally grounded assumption that the welfare state is, by its nature, a single and indivisible entity, to be preserved from contamination by the discordant and fickle forces of politics.

As we all know, successful expeditions into no man's land require funding. The Hanse-Wissenschaftskolleg (HWK) in Delmenhorst, Germany and the Volkswagen Foundation have been crucial for this volume's development and completion. A small workshop at the HWK in May 2002 brought the authors, welfare state scholars, together with experts on federalism from around the world, thereby creating the platform to launch a successful research project. Our thanks to those experts: to Martha Derthick and R. Kent Weaver, who played a vital role in framing the project and several of its chapters; to Jonathan Rodden, Arthur Benz and Fritz W. Scharpf for their on-going participation and support; and to Juan Linz, Alfred Stepan, Manfred G. Schmidt, Richard Simeon and Dietmar Braun for their input to the workshop. We appreciate their generosity with their time and their insights. The HWK also supported Francis Castles' work in the final stages of academic production.

Without on-going support from Bremen University, work on the volume would surely not have gone so smoothly. Thanks are due to the Centre for Social Policy Research, to Chancellor Gerd-Rüdiger Kück, and to Rectors Wilfried Müller and Jürgen Timm. A special contribution was made by the new Research Centre on Transformations of the State (TranState), funded by the Deutsche Forschungsgemeinschaft. TranState identifies four thematic threads in the unravelling of the 'golden age' State after the Second World War: internationalization, nationalization, socialization (*Vergesellschaftung*), and – the subject of this volume, and least studied of the four – sub-nationalization (see Stephan Leibfried and Michael Zürn, eds., *Transformations of the State?* (Cambridge: Cambridge University Press, 2005)). We are also grateful to Francis Castles' colleagues at the University of Edinburgh for generously allowing him the not inconsiderable time required for his editorial tasks on this volume.

There are others who should also be mentioned. Without John Haslam's on-going editorial encouragement, tactful advice and gentle prodding we might long ago have abandoned our journey. We also wish to acknowledge a number of individuals who helped with everything from suggesting chapter authors and offering intellectual input into chapter revisions, to correcting some thousand foreign quotation marks and wayward commas, not to mention providing much needed moral support. They include Jacob S. Hacker, Hugh Heclo, Paul Pierson, Arthur Benz, Tanja Börzel, Paul E. Peterson, Monika Sniegs, Susan M. Gaines, Stefanie Henneke, Hanna Piotter, Frank Vandenbroucke, Ana Guilen, Gitta Klein, Gerhard Roth, Ingeborg Mehser, Dörthe Hauschild and two anonymous referees who evaluated the manuscript for Cambridge University Press.

Mistakes and unruly lions are, as ever, the responsibility of the writers, but fresh insights and new discoveries will, we hope, be the reader's reward for accompanying this team of political science and social policy scholars on their joint expedition into the unkown territory where federalism and the welfare state consort.

Note on illustrations

The coins and seals depicted on the cover and in the chapter headings illustrate the rich tradition of federalist heraldry (for sources see below). Symbols for the welfare state, on the other hand, are rarely deemed worthy of the national currency, but its insatiable financial need is notorious.

In the oldest federalist nations, the US and Switzerland, symbols for federalism are often used on the common currency, making them part of everyday life. On US coins some variation of the Great Seal of the United States shown in the heading of the concluding chapter has been used since 1782. The national bird, an eagle, is depicted clutching thirteen arrows representing the colonies in one talon, and holding a scroll that proclaims *e pluribus unum* – out of the many, one – in its beak. Above the eagle there may be a 'glory' with thirteen clouds or thirteen five-pointed stars, and around the edge of the coin there is often a ring of stars, with one for each state of the Union at the time of minting. The shield on the eagle's breast shows a band of horizontal lines, unifying and supported by a series of vertical stripes, the former symbolizing Congress, the latter, the founding thirteen states. Similar motifs were used on the 1908 Barber half-dollar, shown at the beginning of the introduction and of chapter 4, and employed in the Seal of the President on the 1967 Kennedy half-dollar on the cover. Like many Swiss coins, the two-franc piece on the cover and in the chapter heading show *Helvetia*, the eighteenth-century symbol of Swiss nationhood, with one hand resting on a shield that bears the white Swiss Cross, which dates from the thirteenth century, and the other holding a lance. Switzerland's twenty cantons and six half-cantons are represented by twenty-three five-pointed stars around the edge. The common five-franc piece shown at the beginning of the introductory chapter portrays the legendary founding figure of the Swiss federation, the *Confoederatio Helvetica*, Wilhelm Tell (see Georg Kreis, *Mythos Rütli* (Zurich: orell füssli, 2004)).

In Germany and Austria, as in the federations chartered by the Crown, i.e., Australia and Canada, federalism is represented only on coins minted for special occasions. The 1928 Austrian *Gedenkausgabe* series of two-schilling coins portrays famous historical figures on one side and the coat of arms of the nine Länder plus the Republik situated above the 2 on the other. The 1989 ten-DM silver coin, which celebrates the fortieth anniversary of Germany's post-World War Two refounding, bears the coats of arms of the German Länder, eleven at the time. The design on Canada's 2004 collector's gold dollars displays the combined arms of the founding provinces, Ontario, Quebec, New Brunswick and Nova Scotia. It is derived from the Great Seal of 1868, which was never actually used as a seal, but was, rather, adopted as a national coat of arms. Attempts to add new provinces as they joined the Confederation, however, resulted in a design that was deemed too complex, and in 1921 the Canadian government requested a new arms. The British sovereign assigned a design with royal symbols from Great Britain and France and a sprig of maple leaves to replace their homespun federal theme. For its Centenary of Federation in 2001, Australia minted a special coin set. The fifty-cent piece on the cover shows the Australian coat of arms, which includes the coats of arms of the six founding states with a kangaroo and an emu on either side. The one-dollar piece in the chapter heading bears a symbolic representation of the federated continent.

The multi-tiered nature of the European Union, explored in the conclusion, was reflected in the images on national mintings even before the introduction of the euro. In 1987 Germany celebrated the thirty-year anniversary of the Rome Treaty with the ten-DM coin shown in the conclusion; this depicts twelve horses pulling one cart, a typically federal motif. For the euro, national mints have produced various commemorative coins that emphasize deepening European integration and multi-tier themes, with the French being particularly prolific.

We are grateful to the mint authorities of Australia (Royal Australian Mint), Austria (Austrian-Mint AG), Canada (Royal Canadian Mint), Germany (Deutsche Bundesbank), Switzerland (Swiss Mint) and the United States of America (US Mint) for permission to reproduce their coin images.

Every effort has been made to trace the copyright holders and to obtain their permission for the use of copyright material. We apologize for any error or omissions in the above list and would be grateful if notified of any corrections that should be incorporated in future reprints or editions of this book.

On US coins see Mort Reed, *Cowles Complete Encyclopedia of US Coins* (New York: Cowles Book Co., 1970), pp. 6–10, 29, 31f. *et passim*; Walter H. Breen, *Walter Breen's Complete Encyclopedia of US and Colonial*

Coins (Garden City, NY: Doubleday, 1988); Günther and Gerhard Schön, *Weltmünzkatalog 2004. 20. Jahrhundert von 1900 bis heute*, 32nd edn (Augsburg: Battenberg Verlag, 2003); Chester L. Krause and Clifford Mishler, *The Standard Catalogue of World Coins, 1901–present*, annual publication (Iowa, WI: Krause Publications, 2003).

1 Introduction
Federalism and the welfare state

HERBERT OBINGER, FRANCIS G. CASTLES
AND STEPHAN LEIBFRIED*

Now let us take the oath of this new federation. We will become a single land of brothers, nor shall we part in danger or distress.
   Friedrich Schiller (1759–1805), *Wilhelm Tell* 1804, part 2, scene 2 – founding oath of the Swiss confederacy, attributed 1291**

The federalism I have in mind – *real* federalism – aims to provide citizens with *choices* among different sovereigns, regulatory regimes, and packages of government services . . . The citizens' ability to vote with their feet and to take their talents and assets elsewhere will discipline government in the same way in which consumer choice, in nonmonopolistic markets, disciplines producers.
   Michael S. Greve, *Real Federalism: Why it Matters, How it Could Happen* (Washington, DC: AEI Press, 1999), pp. 2f.

The ideal that all citizens share responsibility for the welfare of their fellows, and the impulse to unite in federations have, on occasions, been historically conjoined. The founding myth of Swiss federalism, as recounted in Schiller's *Wilhelm Tell*, literally makes solidarity 'in danger or distress' a proviso for membership in a budding thirteenth-century federation.

---

* We thank Martha Derthick, Susan Gaines, Hugh Heclo, Paul Pierson and R. Kent Weaver for their valuable comments and help.
** 'Laßt uns den Eid des neuen Bundes schwören. Wir wollen sein ein einzig Volk von Brüdern, in keiner Not uns trennen und Gefahr.' Based on the translation by Willam F. Wertz, Jr, Internet Modern History Sourcebook. Schiller's play about the founding myth of Swiss federalism helped to popularize federalist thinking in the German-speaking world. According to the story, Wilhelm Tell liberated Switzerland from the Habsburg tyrant, Hermann Gessler, using just an apple, a crossbow and his son's steady nerve.

Federalism and social policy

Recent comparative welfare state research has acknowledged the importance of state structures in explaining cross-national variation in both the level and the dynamics of social policy formation. And yet the precise nature of this co-evolution of federalism and the welfare state, and the particular national combinations of state structures and social policy to which it gave rise, have not been subject to systematic, comparative investigation. As Paul Pierson noted in 1995, 'comparative work on federalism is rare and comparative research on the impact of federalism on social policy is non-existent'.[1] This volume bridges the gap by analyzing how the six major democratic federations of the 'OECD world' have organized their welfare states and how they manage their social policy.

More specifically, we explore the impact federalism has had on the development of their welfare states and patterns of welfare provision. Did the prior existence of federal institutions impede the early adoption and subsequent growth of welfare programmes, as economists and political scientists have maintained whenever they have touched upon the theme? And has this also been the case in the modern era of expenditure retrenchment and social policy reform? By analyzing how federal institutions in different countries have affected social policy development in the past, and the extent to which the growth of the welfare state has, in turn, influenced the form and functioning of federalism, we hope to provide a basis for understanding how political decentralization and social policy are likely to interact in the future. Our working premise is that the impacts of federalism on welfare state development are multiple, time dependent, and contingent on a number of contextual parameters, including, most conspicuously, the design of federal institutions and the power resources of social and political actors.

At first glance, the institutional arrangements of contemporary federalism and welfare states seem to fulfil antithetical functions. Federalism is an institutional device designed to secure unity by allowing a certain degree of diversity, whereas the primary goal of the welfare state is normally to enhance equal social rights for all citizens. Federalism and the welfare state thus seem to be at the opposite ends of a diversity–uniformity continuum. In federal polities, 'citizens within the same federal state will enjoy and experience different benefits and burdens'.[2]

---

[1] Paul Pierson, 'Fragmented Welfare States: Federal Institutions and the Development of Social Policy', *Governance*, vol. 8 (1995), no. 4, pp. 449–78, p. 450.
[2] Juan J. Linz, 'Democracy, Multinationalism and Federalism', in Wolfgang Merkel and Andreas Busch, eds., *Demokratie in Ost und West* (Frankfurt-on-Main: Suhrkamp, 1999), pp. 382–401, p. 398.

Central to the idea of social protection is the provision of nation-wide uniform social rights that supplement basic civil and political rights.³ Admittedly, social insurance states historically included a number of schemes for a vast range of occupationally differentiated social strata, but this differentiation typically diminished as welfare states matured. Hence one may assume that social policy in federal states generates multiple tensions and is prone to conflicts over who should get what, which tier of government should be entrusted to set up social programmes and – probably most important – which level of government should bear the costs of the spending involved.

In this book we examine how the act of sharing (social) policy responsibilities between central and sub-governments affects the process of social policy-making and social policy outcomes at different stages of welfare state development and vice versa. Since federalism and the welfare state have undergone considerable transformation over time, we distinguish early welfare state consolidation and the expenditure growth of the 'golden age', collectively labelled the 'old politics of the welfare state', from the welfare state development of more recent decades, described by Paul Pierson as the 'new politics of the welfare state'.⁴

With regard to the 'old politics', there is a consensus in the comparative literature that federalism is an impediment to welfare state expansion: 'In fact, one might point to the federalism/social policy linkage as one of the very few areas of unanimity in the literature, with writers from all the main competing explanatory paradigms arguing that federal institutions are inimical to high levels of social spending.'⁵ This is a far cry from the brotherly spirit of early federalism's founding myths, immortalized by Schiller. Rather, the consensus is one which is, seemingly, consistent with what Michael Greve calls 'real federalism', which, in the spirit of the twenty-first century, reinvents federalism as just another private market, where choice and competition are supposed to keep the government under control, and the citizens healthy, wealthy and wise.

The conclusion that federalism is inimical to high levels of social spending comes from the macro-quantitative literature.⁶ The studies that have

---

³ T. H. Marshall, *Class, Citizenship, and Social Development* (Garden City, NY: Doubleday, 1964), especially his essay 'Citizenship and Social Class', pp. 65–122 (first published 1949).
⁴ Paul Pierson, 'The New Politics of the Welfare State', *World Politics*, vol. 48 (1996), no. 2, pp. 143–79; Paul Pierson, ed., *The New Politics of the Welfare State* (Oxford: Oxford University Press, 2001).
⁵ Francis G. Castles, *Comparative Public Policy. Patterns of Post-War Transformation* (Cheltenham: Edward Elgar, 1999), p. 82.
⁶ See Harold L. Wilensky, *The Welfare State and Equality. Structural and Ideological Roots of Public Expenditures* (Berkeley: University of California Press, 1975), p. 52; David

matured in this literature provide empirical evidence that federal countries *ceteris paribus* spend less on social policy objectives than do unitary states. Employing a technique called Qualitative Comparative Analysis (QCA), Kittel and colleagues also find that democratic federalism has delayed the introduction of social security programmes at central state level.[7] Thus, the picture that emerges from comparative macro-quantitative and macro-qualitative research is that federalism limits the growth of the welfare state. But does an analysis of social policy in individual federal states support this conclusion? Federal states appear to spend less on social programmes than do non-federal states – but is there evidence that federal mechanisms have actually retarded welfare growth? Here, rather than focussing exclusively on outcomes, we seek to identify processes and historical conjunctures in particular countries. If federalism has indeed hindered the development of welfare states, then *how* has it done so? Are similar mechanisms at work in different countries, and is there any pattern to those mechanisms?

The 'new politics' paradigm refers to a new logic of social policy-making in an era which some have described as 'an age of austerity' and others as a 'silver age' of welfare state containment and cutbacks.[8] Rising

---

[1] R. Cameron, 'The Expansion of the Public Economy: A Comparative Analysis', *American Political Science Review*, vol. 72 (1978), no. 4, pp. 1243–61, p. 1253; Alexander M. Hicks and Duane H. Swank, 'Politics, Institutions, and Welfare Spending in Industrialized Democracies, 1960–82', *American Political Science Review*, vol. 86 (1992), no. 3, pp. 658–74, p. 666; Markus L. Crepaz, 'Corporatism in Decline? An Empirical Analysis of the Impact of Corporatism on Macroeconomic Performance and Industrial Disputes in 18 Industrialized Countries', *Comparative Political Studies*, vol. 25 (1992), no. 2, pp. 139–68; Evelyne Huber, Charles Ragin and John D. Stephens, 'Social Democracy, Christian Democracy, Constitutional Structures, and the Welfare State', *American Journal of Sociology*, vol. 99 (1993), no. 3, pp. 711–49; Alexander Hicks and Joya Misra, 'Political Resources and the Growth of Welfare in Affluent Capitalist Democracies, 1960–1982', *American Journal of Sociology*, vol. 99 (1993), no. 3, pp. 668–710; Manfred G. Schmidt, 'Determinants of Social Expenditure in Liberal Democracies: The Post World War II Experience', *Acta Politica*, vol. 32 (1997), no. 2, pp. 153–73; Francis G. Castles, 'Decentralisation and the Post-War Political Economy', *European Journal of Political Research*, vol. 36 (1999), no. 1, pp. 27–53; Duane H. Swank, 'Political Institutions and Welfare State Restructuring: The Impact of Institutions on Social Policy Change in Developed Democracies', in Pierson, *New Politics*, pp. 197–237, pp. 222–23; Evelyne Huber and John D. Stephens, *Development and Crisis of the Welfare State. Parties and Policies in Global Markets* (Chicago: University of Chicago Press, 2001); Duane H. Swank, *Global Capital, Political Institutions, and Policy Change in Developed Welfare States* (Cambridge: Cambridge University Press, 2002).

[7] Bernhard Kittel, Herbert Obinger and Uwe Wagschal, 'Die gezügelten Wohlfahrtsstaaten im internationalen Vergleich: Politisch-institutionelle Faktoren der Entstehung und Entwicklungsdynamik', in Herbert Obinger and Uwe Wagschal, eds., *Der gezügelte Wohlfahrtsstaat* (Frankfurt-on-Main: Campus, 2000), pp. 329–64.

[8] The latter usage is from Peter Taylor-Gooby, 'The Silver Age of the Welfare State: Perspectives on Resilience', *Journal of Social Policy*, vol. 31 (2002), no. 3, pp. 597–621.

unemployment rates, increasing public debt, declining economic growth, globalization and changing demographics, as well as shifting occupational structures, have increased pressure on advanced welfare states, prompting social policy reform in many countries. Paul Pierson argues that the politics of welfare state retrenchment in what he describes as an era of 'permanent austerity' is quite distinct from the political processes underpinning earlier welfare state expansion – the old politics of the welfare state. Consequently, 'research on the "golden age" of social policy will provide a rather poor guide to understanding the current period'.[9] In other words, an understanding of the forces that facilitate and hinder the growth of programmes in the 'golden age' of welfare capitalism will not help us understand social policy-making in hard times.[10] Indeed, Pierson argues that a new logic of politics is responsible for the remarkable resilience of the welfare state over the last two decades. This logic is driven by a politics of blame avoidance[11] that has restrained politicians from trying to retrench the welfare state, given that such efforts invite electoral retribution. Politicians seeking office or re-election either refrain from welfare state retrenchment altogether, or pursue strategies of retrenchment by stealth. Central to this new politics approach is a focus on strategies of blame avoidance, including obfuscation; division and compensation; and excessively complex policy reform packages designed to diffuse responsibility for unpopular retrenchment initiatives and reduce the visibility of painful benefit cuts.[12]

With respect to this new politics of the welfare state, the question is whether federalism supports or hampers retrenchment policies. There is no consensus in the theoretical literature on this issue, and – compared with the findings for the 'golden age' period – the empirical evidence is far less clear cut. While some studies still locate the expenditure retarding effect of constitutional veto points over the past two decades,[13] others suggest that this effect disappears in times of austerity.[14] Given a

---

[9] Paul Pierson, 'Introduction. Investigating the Welfare State at Century's End', in Pierson, *New Politics*, pp. 1–14, p. 2.
[10] Giuliano Bonoli, Vic George and Peter Taylor-Gooby, *European Welfare Futures. Toward a Theory of Retrenchment* (Cambridge: Polity Press, 2000), pp. 23–24.
[11] R. Kent Weaver, 'The Politics of Blame Avoidance', *Journal of Public Policy*, vol. 6 (1986), no. 3 (Oct.–Dec.), pp. 371–98.
[12] See Paul Pierson, *Dismantling the Welfare State? Reagan, Thatcher and the Politics of Retrenchment* (Cambridge: Cambridge University Press, 1994), pp. 19–26.
[13] Swank, 'Political Institutions and Welfare State Restructuring'; Nico A. Siegel, *Baustelle Sozialpolitik. Konsolidierung und Rückbau im internationalen Vergleich* (Frankfurt-on-Main: Campus, 2002).
[14] See Klaus Armingeon, Michelle Beyeler and Harmen Binnema, 'The Changing Politics of the Welfare State – A Comparative Analysis of Social Security Expenditures

theoretically ambiguous impact of federalism on retrenchment policies and empirically inconsistent findings, the contributions in this volume use their analyses of policy development in individual countries to investigate the possibility of a distinct federalism effect. One hypothesis, derived from research on both the 'old' and 'new politics' of the welfare state is that federalism consistently exercises an institutional 'ratchet effect', hindering the development of new welfare states and hindering retrenchment initiatives in mature welfare states.

Another major theme of this study is the *reciprocal* relationship between federalism and the welfare state. Analyzing Canadian social policy in recent decades, Michael Prince reports that 'changes in social policy have changed Canadian federalism'.[15] We are interested in both aspects of the feedback loop: not just the way politics shapes the growth of social policy, but also how the development of social policy modifies the growth of the state. The welfare state is often seen as the source of a growing centralization of government and of an increasing complexity of inter-governmental relations with respect to funding arrangements across, and the division of labour between, different branches of government. In Germany, for instance, the growth of the welfare state and a developed 'financial equalization' (revenue sharing) scheme have been held responsible for triggering the transformation from inter-state to intra-state federalism.[16] It is also possible that, in multi-ethnic federations, social policy may serve as the cement for reducing the depth of political cleavages. Here the welfare state, by generating mass loyalty, might contribute to the containment or reduction of centrifugal forces endangering social and political cohesion. Such feedback effects have not been widely addressed in the comparative literature to date.

This book employs a 'most similar' systems design, focussing on six democratic and affluent federations. In alphabetical order they are: Australia, Austria, Canada, Germany, Switzerland and the United States of America. Table 1.1 identifies the basic political and economic attributes of these six countries.

in 22 OECD Countries, 1960–1998', unpublished ms (Bern: Institute of Political Science, University of Bern, 2001); Bernhard Kittel and Herbert Obinger, 'Political Parties, Institutions, and the Dynamics of Social Expenditure in Times of Austerity', *Journal of European Public Policy*, vol. 10 (2003), no. 1, pp. 20–45.

[15] Michael J. Prince, 'From Health and Welfare to Stealth and Farewell: Federal Social Policy, 1980–2000', in Leslie A. Pal, ed., *How Ottawa Spends 1999–2000* (Oxford: Oxford University Press, 1999), pp. 151–96, p. 152.

[16] Ernst Wolfgang Böckenförde, 'Sozialer Bundesstaat und parlamentarische Demokratie', in *Staat, Nation, Europa. Studien zur Staatslehre, Verfassungstheorie und Rechtsphilosophie* (Frankfurt-on-Main: Suhrkamp, 1999; 1st edn 1980), pp. 183–207; Konrad Hesse, *Der unitarische Bundesstaat* (Karlsruhe: Müller, 1962).

Table 1.1 Basic political and economic features of six OECD federations

	Australia	Austria	Canada	Germany	Switzerland	USA
Democratic federation since	1901	1920–34/1945	1867	1919–33/1949	1848	1789
Type of state	Monarchy	Republic	Monarchy	Republic	Republic	Republic
Regime type	Parliamentary	Parliamentary	Parliamentary	Parliamentary	Directoral	Presidential
Population 2003 (millions)	19.73	8.19	32.21	82.40	7.32	290.34
Real GDP per capita 2002 (ppp)	25,900	27,900	29,300	26,200	32,000	36,000
Society	Homogeneous	Homogeneous	Heterogeneous	Homogeneous	Heterogeneous	Heterogeneous
Number of constitutional units	6 states and 2 territories	9 Länder	10 provinces and 3 territories	16 Länder	26 cantons	50 states
EU membership	No	Yes	No	Yes	No	No

Legend: ppp = puchasing power parities.
Source: Data for GDP per capita are measured in purchasing power parities and are from the *CIA World Factbook* (Washington, DC: CIA, 2003; accessible on the web).

These countries are not only amongst the wealthiest nations in the world, but also exhibit – Germany and Austria excepted – a long democratic *and* federal record. According to Arend Lijphart and Hans Keman,[17] they form a distinct cluster within the OECD world, because they are both federal *and* relatively fiscally decentralized. Other democratic federations, such as India and Venezuela, are excluded because of their low levels of economic development, while Spain and Belgium, although interesting cases in various ways, are not examined here because their federalisms are of too recent a vintage to have had an impact on the 'old politics' of the welfare state.[18]

In the next section we provide an overview of the varieties of federal institutions and welfare states in the countries featuring in this study. We then review a range of public choice and institutionalist theories, and use them to derive hypotheses concerning the impacts of federalism on welfare state development. Examining these theories and the variety of federalisms in conjunction, we develop our main argument that federalism does *not* affect welfare states *uniformly* across time and space. We conclude the section by identifying the contextual factors that make these hypothesized impacts more or less likely to come about.

Varieties of federalism

What is federalism?

According to Ivo Duchacek there is 'no accepted theory of federalism. Nor is there agreement as to what, exactly, federalism is. The term itself is unclear and controversial.'[19] However, all existing federations exhibit several common institutional characteristics,[20] which allow us to classify them more readily. Taking a broader view we may describe federalism as

---

[17] Arend Lijphart, *Patterns of Democracy. Government Forms and Performance in Thirty-Six Countries* (New Haven: Yale University Press, 1999), p. 189; Hans Keman, 'Federalism and Policy Performance. A Conceptual and Empirical Inquiry', in Ute Wachendorfer-Schmidt, ed., *Federalism and Political Performance* (London: Routledge, 2000), pp. 196–226, p. 209.

[18] Spain and Belgium may, however, be a model for the future, since the federalisms of the twenty-first century are likely all to be fragmenting unitary states rather than original federal start-ups. We will return to this point in the conclusion.

[19] Ivo D. Duchacek, *Comparative Federalism. The Territorial Dimension of Politics* (Lanham, MD: University Press of America, 1987), p. 189; see also Robert P. Inman and Daniel P. Rubinfeld, 'Rethinking Federalism', *Journal of Economic Perspectives*, vol. 11 (1997), no. 4, pp. 43–64.

[20] Daniel J. Elazar, *Federal Systems in the World. A Handbook of Federal, Confederal and Autonomy Arrangements* (Harlow: Longman, 1992); Ronald L. Watts, *Comparing Federal Systems*, 2nd edn (Montreal: McGill-Queen's University Press, 1999).

Introduction

1. a set of institutional arrangements and decision rules at central government level for incorporating territorially based interests; these arrangements vary in the degree to which they provide veto powers to subordinate branches of government
2. a set of territorially based actors with ideas and interests who vary greatly in number and heterogeneity
3. a set of jurisdictional arrangements for allocating policy responsibilities between different levels of government; this refers to both policy-making and policy implementation
4. a set of inter-governmental fiscal transfer arrangements
5. a set of informal arrangements – both vertical and horizontal – between governments

This categorization of federal arrangements makes clear that federalism is a very complicated form of government.[21] There are at present twenty-three federal states comprising about 40 per cent of the world's population.[22] Approximately half the population of the world's most advanced (OECD) welfare states live under federal rule. Despite divergent terminologies employed and a lively debate over the appropriate demarcation between federations and other forms of government, federalism is generally acknowledged as an institutional device for the vertical separation of powers, which splits jurisdiction along territorial lines. According to Riker's famous definition, 'the activities of government are divided between regional governments and a central government in such a way that each kind of government has some activities on which it makes final decisions'.[23] This definition has some potentially interesting implications for particular areas of policy, including the welfare state. If, in a given area of policy, there is no such division of decision-making power, is it federal in respect of that policy area? In a similar vein, Duchacek emphasizes the non-centralization of power as the crucial element of federal polities. In his view, a federal system is 'a constitutional division of power between one general government (that is to have authority over the entire national territory) and a series of sub-national governments (that individually have their own territories, whose sum total represents almost the whole national territory)'.[24]

---

[21] Linz, 'Democracy, Multinationalism and Federalism', p. 383.
[22] Watts, *Comparing Federal Systems*, p. xi.
[23] William S. Riker, 'Federalism', in Fred I. Greenstein and Nelson W. Polsby, eds., *Handbook of Political Science*, vol. V, *Governmental Institutions and Processes* (Reading, MA: Addison-Wesley, 1975), pp. 93–172, p. 101.
[24] Duchacek, *Comparative Federalism*, p. 194.

To enforce such a vertical separation of power and to keep a system of shared responsibilities working, all federations have established a set of secondary federal institutions.[25] First, all federations have a written constitution that is difficult to amend. Second, a supreme court acts as an umpire to settle conflicts between different branches of government. Third, the constitutional units participate in the federal policy process. With respect to legislation, most federations have a bicameral legislature with a strong second chamber representing the constitutional units, granting them – or, in certain instances, their populations through the ballot box – veto and deadlock powers. Finally, there are many formal and informal inter-governmental networks of co-operation addressing common problems that affect different levels of government and/or several constituent units.

Federalism has distinct functions. One, which is articulated in the Federalist Papers (Federalist No. 51), involves the establishment of a system of checks and balances designed to prevent the concentration of political power and to secure political and economic freedoms. Wherever this idea prevailed – as it did in most of the British colonies of settlement – institutions of inter-state federalism emerged to constrain the Leviathan. A second function of the territorial division of power, which is primarily relevant for large states, is to bring government closer to the people.[26] Finally, federalism can be seen as an institutional device for successfully managing societal and ethnic cleavages by giving minorities a large degree of autonomy, as is the case in Switzerland and Canada.[27] On the whole, Switzerland and the USA represent the extreme limits in respect of the functions attributed to federalism. Whereas federalism in the USA strongly emphasizes competition between the states, Switzerland's federalism is an institutional arrangement originally designed to settle conflicts resulting from multi-dimensional societal cleavages and to protect minorities. As a consequence, the Swiss variant of federalism rests upon local autonomy rather than on regional competition.[28]

Families of nations and types of federalism

The six countries under scrutiny can be seen as members of two distinct 'families of nations', with common cultural, historical and geographical attributes productive of quite similar public policy patterns.[29] The

---

[25] Lijphart, *Patterns of Democracy*, p. 187.
[26] See Duchacek, *Comparative Federalism*, p. 198.
[27] Linz, 'Democracy, Multinationalism and Federalism'.
[28] Wolf Linder, *Schweizerische Demokratie* (Bern: Haupt, 1999).
[29] Francis G. Castles, ed., *Families of Nations: Patterns of Public Policy in Western Democracies* (Aldershot: Dartmouth, 1993); Castles, *Comparative Public Policy*.

United States, Canada and Australia belong to an English-speaking family of nations that is united by language, by close historical ties with Great Britain and by common legal, denominational and political traditions. Germany, Austria and Switzerland form a sub-group within the so-called continental western European family of nations. These nations grew out of the Holy Roman Empire, share a common language, a common legal tradition, and their welfare states bear the imprint of nineteenth-century Catholic social doctrine. Arguably, the location of Switzerland in family-of-nations terms is more ambiguous than that of the other countries discussed here. Nevertheless, the country shows many affinities to its German-speaking neighbour countries, which justifies its inclusion in this wider family grouping.[30]

This designation of federal countries into distinct families of nations is supported by the fact that the six federal OECD countries cluster into two groups differing in respect of both the character of their federal arrangements and their welfare states. The three Anglo-Saxon nations have a strong tradition of *inter*-state federalism. This type of federalism[31] is characterized by a well-established vertical power separation, a distribution of competencies between different branches of government based on policy responsibilities (and not on functions such as legislation and implementation) and the congruence of legislative and executive competencies across different tiers of government. The social policy provision in the English-speaking countries is generally characterized as 'residual'. Esping-Andersen describes their welfare state regimes as 'liberal',[32] and Castles, more recently, has argued that they may be regarded as 'poverty alleviation'[33] states.

In Germany and Austria *intra*-state federalism is the dominant form.[34] This designation refers to a functional distribution of responsibilities. Here the sub-state units regularly implement federal legislation, while

---

[30] See also the discussion in Francis G. Castles, *The Future of the Welfare State: Crisis Myths and Crisis Realities* (Oxford: Oxford University Press, 2004), which shows that Switzerland's recent expenditure trends have made it progressively more like other members of the continental Western European grouping.

[31] This typology is taken from Rainer-Olaf Schultze's contrast of 'interstaatlicher Föderalismus' versus 'Verbundföderalismus' or 'intrastaatlicher Föderalismus' ('Föderalismus', in Dieter Nohlen, ed., *Kleines Lexikon der Politik* (Munich: Beck, 2001), pp. 127–34, p. 130).

[32] Gøsta Esping-Andersen, *The Three Worlds of Welfare Capitalism* (Cambridge: Polity Press, 1990); Gøsta Esping-Andersen, *Social Foundations of Postindustrial Economies* (Oxford: Oxford University Press, 1999).

[33] Castles, *Future of the Welfare State*, chapter 3.

[34] Rainer-Olaf Schultze, 'Föderalismus', in Manfred G. Schmidt, ed., *Lexikon der Politik*, vol. III, *Die westlichen Länder* (Munich: Beck, 1992), pp. 95–110; and Watts, *Comparing Federal Systems*.

legislation itself is overwhelmingly concentrated at the central state level. Intra-state arrangements are also to be found in certain policy domains in both Australia and Switzerland. Co-operation between different tiers of government in administrative and financial affairs, as well as shared legislation and implementation, have – especially in Germany – contributed to the emergence of a system of interlocking politics and joint decision-making.[35] With regard to social policy, Austria and Germany are widely seen as prototypes of Esping-Andersen's 'conservative' regime type, while, historically, Switzerland has manifested affinities to both the liberal and conservative worlds of welfare capitalism. Switzerland's variant of federalism is also a hybrid since it combines traits that are characteristic of both intra-state and inter-state federalism.

The historical trajectories of the English-speaking and the German-speaking federations also differ sharply. All the English-speaking federations are former British settler colonies. The formation of federalism was accelerated by external military threats, and in the case of the United States, by its struggles for independence from the mother country. Federation building was thus closely tied to creating defensive alliances and to pooling power to avert imminent military threats. In the United States, even the anti-federalists agreed to delegate defence powers to a federal government, given that all the foreign superpowers of that period had military forces in North America.[36] For their part, the Canadians feared an invasion of US troops – then one of the largest armies in the world – in the wake of their nextdoor neighbours' civil war, a fear already fed by earlier conflicts, such as the War of 1812, when US forces moved north and tried to take British-held territory. The adoption of federal constitutions in Australia and Canada was also inspired by efforts to improve inter-colonial commerce and transportation. In order to bridge the vast distances characterizing these areas of colonial occupation, it was necessary to remove trade barriers, which, in turn, required the formation of a centralized national government. Canada also needed a common framework for settling conflicts between its French and English communities, sharply divided not only by language, but also by religion and legal systems.[37]

---

[35] Arthur Benz, 'From Unitary to Asymmetric Federalism in Germany: Taking Stock after 50 Years', *Publius: The Journal of Federalism*, vol. 29 (1999), no. 4, pp. 55–78.
[36] John Kincaid, 'Federalism in the United States of America: A Continual Tension Between Persons and Places', in Arthur Benz and Gerhard Lehmbruch, eds., *Föderalismus. Analysen in entwicklungsgeschichtlicher und vergleichender Perspektive* (Wiesbaden: Westdeutscher Verlag, 2002), pp. 134–56, p. 135.
[37] Ronald L. Watts, 'Federal Evolution: The Canadian Experience', in Benz and Lehmbruch, eds., *Föderalismus*, pp. 157–76, p. 159.

Despite much older quasi-federal traditions, the formative moment for both the Austrian and German federations was the disintegration of the huge empires of central Europe in the aftermath of World War One. As was also true of Switzerland, these nations grew out of the Holy Roman Empire, and the history of some German and Austrian Länder and some Swiss cantons dates back to the Middle Ages. Following the Napoleonic Wars and the reconstruction of the anciens regimes in Europe at the Congress of Vienna, the German Confederation (Deutscher Bund) founded in 1815 constituted a confederation encompassing much of the territory that today constitutes Germany and Austria. In Switzerland a similar development had been cemented by Napoleon's *Mediationsakte*, which restored the old Swiss confederation of twenty-five formerly independent cantons. The year 1848 was critical for the future of all three nations. Following a short civil war between Protestant and Catholic cantons, Swiss liberal forces established the first democratic federation in Europe. However, unsuccessful revolutions in Berlin and Vienna, and the failure to bring about German unification (*großdeutsche Lösung*) at the constitutional convention in Frankfurt, increased antagonism between Prussia and Austria, culminating in the war of 1866 and the dissolution of the German Confederation.

Prussia's victory paved the way for the creation of the German Empire (Deutsches Reich) in 1871, which now also included the southern German territories. Imperial Germany was, like the Northern German Confederation (Nordeutscher Bund), which replaced the German Confederation in 1866, a highly asymmetric federation under Prussian domination. Austria, in defeat, shifted the balance of its imperial ambitions to the east, and the *Ausgleich* with Hungary in 1867 established the Austro-Hungarian dual monarchy. Military defeat in World War One finally destroyed imperial Germany and the Habsburg Empire and paved the way for the establishment of democratic federal republics in both countries.

This strong divide within our sample – which would be even more pronounced if other political and cultural variables were included in the comparison – raises the question of whether there is a systematic relationship between different types of federal systems and different types of welfare states. At first glance, *inter*-state federalism and liberal welfare regimes form a single cluster, while *intra*-state federalism and the conservative regime type are nearly as strongly linked. However, as is true of many classifications of federalism, and not least the currently popular distinction between competitive and co-operative federalism, this dichotomy becomes blurred when federal systems and their embeddedness in the general government structure are examined more closely.³⁸ This is a topic taken up in greater detail in the next section.

The pluralism of federalism

Despite common historical trajectories and similar institutional characteristics, federal systems differ in many ways. To begin with, constituent units in the six countries under consideration vary in size and number, and also differ in the extent to which competencies are allocated to regional governments. They also exhibit different degrees of horizontal asymmetry. Canada is the only country in our sample in which a nation-wide linguistic and religious minority is regionally concentrated and forms a majority in one constituent unit. Constitutionally, this is mirrored in horizontal asymmetry. In order to contain centrifugal forces, Quebec enjoys a special status, which enables it to opt in and out of certain policies. Although Switzerland's society is even more heterogeneous, cross-cutting cleavages dampen such centrifugal tendencies. Locally concentrated linguistic majorities do not coincide with particular denominational or political hegemonies. Minority protection is guaranteed by the device of giving smaller constituent units a greater weight in the federal decision-making process and not by opt-out clauses.

The degree of societal homogeneity is also important for the distribution of jurisdictions between different branches of government in federal nations. The more homogeneous a society is, the stronger the power of the central government and vice versa.³⁹ The countries we look at also exhibit varying degrees of centralization and decentralization. Judging by the tax revenues received by the central government, highly decentralized (Switzerland, Canada) and weakly decentralized (Austria, Australia) federal states can be distinguished, with Germany and the USA somewhere in between.⁴⁰

There is also a bewildering variation in the range of mechanisms relied on to preserve the continuing integrity of the federal form of government as such. Although all federal nations have a written constitution, amendment procedures and constitutional rigidities differ substantially from country to country. The US constitution is extraordinarily rigid, requiring a two-thirds majority in both houses of Congress and the consent of three-quarters of the states for alteration. In Australia and Switzerland constitutional amendments are subject to a mandatory referendum and

---

[38] Arthur Benz, 'Themen, Probleme und Perspektiven der vergleichenden Föderalismusforschung', in Benz and Lehmbruch, eds., *Föderalismus*, pp. 9–50, p. 19.
[39] Watts, *Comparing Federal Systems*, p. 35.
[40] See Castles, 'Decentralisation and the Post-War Political Economy'.

change requires a popular majority and support in a majority of states or cantons. In Germany a two-thirds majority of both houses is needed, while Canada has different amendment procedures with varying majority thresholds depending on the issue at stake. Most parts of the constitution – including changes in the division of powers – require the assent of two-thirds of the provinces, representing 50 per cent of the population. Canada is *sui generis* in other ways. Until 1982, which includes the period of the expansion of the welfare state in Canada, the British government retained a formal role in constitutional amendments, and the operating convention was that unanimous provincial approval was required for shifting social policy competencies to the central state. Barriers to constitutional revision are lowest in Austria. In normal circumstances, alteration of the constitution only requires a two-thirds majority in the lower house. Since 1984, however, approval by a two-thirds majority of the upper house has been required for a redistribution of competencies affecting Länder powers. Only where a fundamental constitutional principle is to be modified is a referendum mandatory.[41]

A comparison of the difficulty of the amendment process in thirty-two democracies reveals that constitutional rigidity is highest in the United States, followed by Switzerland, (Venezuela) and Australia. Austria's constitution is among the easiest to modify and constitutional rigidity is also below the sample average in Germany.[42] This variation in the rigidity of federal constitutions clearly demonstrates that politicians in federal states face obstacles of quite different dimensions when they seek to change the status quo.

There are also striking differences regarding constitutional courts (see table 1.2). Basically, there are two systems of judicial review in our sample. In the Anglo-Saxon countries, the Supreme or High Court is respectively the apex of the court hierarchy, serving as the appellate court of last resort for all issues, including constitutional ones. In the aftermath of the US Supreme Court's famous *Marbury* v. *Madison* decision (1803), a system of decentralized judicial review – in which constitutional issues were not monopolized by one court – emerged that later was adopted by many English-speaking countries. In contrast, many European countries set up centralized systems of judicial review of a kind first established in Austria in 1920. Today, the German Bundesverfassungsgericht is one of the most powerful constitutional courts of this type.

---

[41] The only referendum of this kind was held in 1994 when the Austrians had to decide whether or not to join the EU.
[42] Donald S. Lutz, 'Toward a Theory of Constitutional Amendment', *American Political Science Review*, vol. 88 (1994), no. 2, pp. 355–70, p. 369. Canada was excluded from this study.

Table 1.2 *Constitutional courts in six federations*

	Australia	Austria	Canada	Germany	Switzerland	USA
Name	High Court	Verfassungs-gerichtshof	Supreme Court	Bundesver-fassungsgericht	Bundesgericht	Supreme Court
Established in	1901	1920	1875	1949	1848/1874	1789
Location	Canberra	Vienna	Ottawa	Karlsruhe	Lausanne	Washington, DC
Number of judges	7	14	9	16	30	9
Tenure/age of retirement	70	70	75	12 years, 68	6 years	Lifetime
Recruitment by	Governor-General	President (government, parliament)	Prime Minister	Election	Election	President
Influence of constitutional units on appointment via	Consultation	Bundesrat (3 judges)	Consultation	Bundesrat (8 judges)	Ständerat via Bundes-versammlung	Senate
Judicial review	Yes	Yes	Yes	Yes	No (federal legislation)	Yes

While judicial review is a key element in almost all systems of federal government, Switzerland's Bundesgericht is not empowered to rule on whether federal legislation is in conflict with the Swiss Constitution. Instead, each parliamentary act is subject to a referendum if sufficient signatures have been collected. Hence 'not judges, but only the sovereign people of Switzerland can question the validity of federal laws'.[43] The Swiss Bundesgericht, which like the Supreme or High Court in the Anglo-Saxon nations is the highest appellate court in all fields except social insurance,[44] has the power to invalidate cantonal legislation and – like all other constitutional courts – to settle jurisdictional conflicts between different branches of government. Number, tenure and recruitment of the judges vary considerably across the six countries, and other constitutional units are either directly or indirectly involved in the process of their appointment.

The differences are even more pronounced with respect to bicameralism, both in terms of the composition and the powers assigned to the upper house (see table 1.3). The German Bundesrat stands out most prominently as a states house, since it explicitly represents the governments of the Länder and has an absolute veto in affairs directly affecting their jurisdiction or requiring their administrative resources. In all other fields, the Bundesrat's veto is suspensive only and may be overruled by a simple majority in the lower house. In contrast, bicameralism in Switzerland and the United States is symmetrical and the representatives of both houses are directly elected. The powers of the Canadian Senate are identical to those of the lower house except for the right to initiate financial legislation. The same applies to the Australian Senate. Senators in Australia are directly elected by proportional representation, while their Canadian counterparts are appointed by the Governor-General on the advice of the Prime Minister. It is clear that bicameralism is strong in those countries where powers are equally distributed between the two chambers. The other extreme is Austria. Here the upper chamber is clearly subordinate to the lower house and only holds a suspensive veto that can be easily overruled by the lower house.[45]

Political units are equally represented in Switzerland (full cantons), Australia (at least as far as the six states are concerned; territories have

---

[43] Duchacek, *Comparative Federalism*, p. 256.
[44] The Eidgenössisches Versicherungsgericht located in Lucerne is the appellate court of last resort in social insurance issues.
[45] Herbert Schambeck, ed., *Bundesstaat und Bundesrat in Österreich* (Wien: Verlag Österreich, 1997); Herbert Obinger, 'Vetospieler und Staatstätigkeit in Österreich. Sozial- und wirtschaftspolitische Reformchancen für die neue ÖVP/FPÖ-Regierung', *Zeitschrift für Parlamentsfragen*, vol. 32 (2001), no. 2, pp. 360–86.

Table 1.3 Second chambers in six federations

	Australia	Austria	Canada	Germany	Switzerland	USA
Name	Senate	Bundesrat	Senate	Bundesrat	Ständerat	Senate
Members	76	62	105	68	46	100
Recruitment	Election PR (STV), since 1949	Election by regional parliaments (PR)	Appointment by the Governor-General on the advice of the Prime Minister	Representatives of the regional governments	Election (MR), canton Jura (PR)	Election (MR), since 1913
Tenure	6 years	4–6 years	Until age 75	4–5 years	4 years	6 years
Representation of constitutional units (number of seats)	6 states: 12 each; 2 territories: 2 each	3–12	4 main regions: 24 each; Newfoundland: 6; 3 territories: 1 each	3–6 *en bloc* votes	20 full cantons: 2 each; 6 half cantons: 1 each	50 states: 2 each
Veto power (ordinary legislation)	Absolute	Suspensive	Absolute (formally)	Absolute and suspensive	Absolute	Absolute
Involvement of constituent units in constitutional amendment procedure	Referendum: $\frac{2}{3}$ of states have to approve	$\frac{2}{3}$ majority in Bundesrat (since 1984)[1]	Suspensive veto (Senate), provincial consent required, with extent of support varying according to issue	$\frac{2}{3}$ majority in Bundesrat	Referendum: A majority of cantons have to approve	$\frac{3}{4}$ of states must support constitutional amendment, $\frac{2}{3}$ majority in Senate
Procedure in case of conflict between the two houses	Navette, threat of double dissolution	Bundesrat can be overruled by a simple majority in the lower house	Navette	Joint Committee (Vermittlungsausschuss)	Joint Committee (Einigungskonferenz)	Conference Committee

Legend: PR = Proportional rule; STV = Single transferable vote; MR = Majority rule.
Notes: [1] A two-thirds majority, though, is only required if the constitutional amendment constrains the legislative and/or administrative powers of the Länder.

lesser representation) and in the United States. In Germany and Austria the number of Länder representatives is weighted in proportion to the population of the constituent units, with smaller Länder having greater weight. This brief overview suggests that the extent to which the constituent units can influence the federal policy-making process varies considerably within our sample.

The different federal institutions sketched here are embedded in and combined with different general governmental structures. Electoral rules, party systems and patterns of democracy are appreciably different in the Anglo-Saxon and the German-speaking clusters. However, there is also substantial variation of federal and governmental institutions within the clusters. The United States is a presidential regime characterized by a strict separation of executive and legislative power. Switzerland shares the same characteristics, although the characteristics of the chief executive role are quite different. The remaining nations are parliamentary democracies.

There are also important differences in executive–legislative relations as between the two clusters. Canada, for instance, may be regarded as the 'first synthesis of Westminster parliamentary institutions with federal principles'.[46] Switzerland is at the other extreme, with the most pronounced horizontal and vertical division of power of all the federal systems.[47] Grand coalitions, that is, governments consisting of the two main political parties, have played a major role not only in post-war Austria, but also in post-war Germany, where inter-cameral partisan differences have been supportive of a compromise-oriented 'grand coalition' state.[48] Hence, different degrees of vertical power division are paralleled by different degrees of horizontal power separation. Consequently, the rules of the political game are either overlapping (negotiation-based in both the partisan arena and the federal arena), as in Switzerland, or conflicting (majoritarian in the partisan arena and negotiation-based in the relationships between the central and the sub-governments) as in Canada. Germany is a special case. Where the partisan complexion of the federal chambers is congruent, there is a potential for overcoming policy stalemate. Where there is incongruence – that is, when the opposition holds the majority in the Bundesrat and the federal government is forced to negotiate with the Länder executives – the scene is set either for compromise between the major party camps or for political gridlock.[49]

---

[46] Elazar, *Federal Systems in the World*, p. 50.   [47] Lijphart, *Patterns of Democracy*.
[48] Manfred G. Schmidt, 'Germany. The Grand Coalition State', in Josep M. Colomer, ed., *Political Institutions in Europe* (London and New York: Routledge, 1996), pp. 62–98.
[49] Gerhard Lehmbruch, *Parteienwettbewerb im Bundesstaat. Regelsysteme und Spannungslagen im Institutionengefüge der Bundesrepublik Deutschland* (Opladen: Westdeutscher Verlag, 1998); Schmidt, 'Germany. The Grand Coalition State', p. 85.

Two of the six federations – Germany and Austria – are members of the European Union. This makes them special cases in our sample. Germany and Austria are embedded in another quasi-federal, multi-tiered system of governance, which is quite complex, veto prone and, nevertheless, influential and successful in its own right, not least in respect of certain aspects of European social policy development.[50] Seen from a *Land* and local government perspective in Austria and Germany, the EU's legal integration activities constitute another super-federal level on top of the existing federal government. The EU restricts these nations' sovereignty mainly by means of negative integration, that is, by displacing national laws or legal clauses, which hinder the unfolding of the Single Market. In Germany and Austria 'negative integration' has already been used to open up national health care systems to European competition, to strike down public monopolies in service provision (e.g. in employment services), and to override restrictions on the provision of German Long Term Care Insurance benefits.

So, Germany and Austria as EU member states confront an extra external 'multi-tier' challenge in addition to the internal ones all federations face. However, legislative impulses from Brussels do not merely provide limitations on and opportunities for national welfare state recalibration. The competencies of Brussels may also be used to bypass national political stalemate or joint decision traps in novel ways. All federations can shift responsibility and blame downwards to the states. Germany and Austria can shift responsibility and blame upwards as well.[51] They can, in other words, play two-level federal games. This is not just an academic matter. Such games are already occurring, most conspicuously in regard to the pressing issue of pension reform, which has been high on the agenda of EU finance ministers' meetings in recent years.

So far we have described the variety of federal institutions and the ways in which these institutions are embedded in the general polity. However, institutions do not determine policies directly, but rather shape actor constellations, their preferences and their strategies for action.[52] Put differently, by defining the rules of the political game, institutions influence the

---

[50] Stephan Leibfried and Paul Pierson, eds., *European Social Policy: Between Fragmentation and Integration* (Washington, DC: Brookings Institution Press, 1995); Fritz W. Scharpf, *Governing in Europe: Effective and Democratic?* (Oxford: Oxford University Press, 1999).

[51] Ute Wachendorfer-Schmidt, 'Der Preis des Föderalismus in Deutschland', *Politische Vierteljahresschrift*, vol. 40 (1999), no. 1, pp. 3–39.

[52] Kathleen Thelen and Sven Steinmo, 'Historical Institutionalism in Comparative Politics', in Sven Steinmo, Kathleen Thelen and Frank Longstreth, eds., *Structuring Politics. Historical Institutionalism in Comparative Analysis* (Cambridge: Cambridge University Press, 1992), pp. 1–32; Pierson, 'Fragmented Welfare States'; Fritz W. Scharpf, *Games Real Actors Play. Actor-Centered Institutionalism in Policy Research* (Boulder, CO: Westview Press, 1997).

Introduction 21

politics of social policy. Distinct institutional settings are likely to create different opportunity structures and incentives for welfare state policy-making. Moreover, institutions influence the relative political strength of traditional welfare state constituencies and the power resources of pro-welfare state groups and of those that oppose them.[53] Nevertheless, social policy is ultimately a matter of political choice and institutions are but one of a range of factors impinging on such choices. Amongst other things, this means that it is always necessary to take account of other middle-range theories of welfare state development, such as the distribution of power inside and outside of parliament and of the ideological orientation of political actors. It also means that other factors impinging on or shaping the context of policy choice must be considered too, including levels of economic development, critical junctures such as the impact of war, and aspects of cultural distinctiveness such as the influence of particular forms of religious belief.

A comparison of the post-war partisan complexion of government in our six cases reveals striking differences (table 1.4). Different electoral systems and different national cleavage structures are mirrored in different party systems and patterns of cabinet formation. Single party government is the norm in Canada, whereas in the United States different parties frequently control Congress and the Presidency. In Australia, centre-right governments are predominantly formed between the (urban) Liberal and the (rural) National (formerly Country) Party – Giovanni Sartori[54] described them as 'a coalescence' rather than a coalition – while all Labour governments have been single party governments. By contrast, in the German-speaking cluster, coalition government is the general rule, although Austria has experienced single party governments for seventeen years, most of them under social-democratic leadership.

Power distributions and ideological orientations of governments also vary substantially amongst these nations (see table 1.4). Christian-democratic parties are non-existent in the Anglo-Saxon countries and the political left (socialist incumbency) is absent in the United States and largely restricted to the provincial level in Canada. In Australia, left and right have always been more balanced – at least, in votes, if not in federal seats – and in the 1980s and 1990s the Australian Labor Party (ALP), along with sister parties in Austria and Spain, was amongst the most dominant leftist parties in the OECD area. In Germany and Austria the party spectrum is dominated by the rivalry between christian democracy and social democracy, leaving relatively little ideological space for

[53] Swank, *Global Capital*.
[54] See Giovanni Sartori, *Parties and Party Systems* (Cambridge: Cambridge University Press, 1976), pp. 187–88.

Table 1.4 *The partisan complexion of central government, interest group pluralism and trade union membership over the post-war period (1945–2001)*

	Australia	Austria	Canada	Germany	Switzerland	USA
Left	37.32	54.59	0.00	24.26	23.21	0.00
Christian Democracy	0.00	37.47	0.00	53.64	29.84	0.00
Liberal and Centre	0.00	1.31	71.93	17.47	32.65	50.00
Conservative	62.67	0.00	28.06	2.71	14.28	50.00
Average number of parties in government	1.61	1.82	1.00	2.03	3.89	1.00–2.00[1]
Index of interest group pluralism	2.66	0.62	3.56	1.38	1.00	3.31
Trade union membership	50.5	60.1	32.6	34.9	30.9	23.3

Notes: [1] Divided government.
Sources: Cabinet share as a percentage of total seats (average 1945–2001). Cabinet shares are calculated on a daily basis. *Basis:* Manfred G. Schmidt, 'Die parteipolitische Zusammensetzung der Regierung in 23 OECD Ländern 1945–2001', unpublished data set (Bremen: Centre for Social Policy Research, University of Bremen).
Index of interest group pluralism (1945–1996). *Basis:* Arend Lijphart, *Patterns of Democracy* (New Haven: Yale University Press, 1999), p. 313. High values indicate pluralist forms of interest mediation.
Trade union membership as a percentage of wage and salary earners (average 1960/1974/early 1990s). *Basis:* Francis G. Castles, *Comparative Public Policy* (Cheltenham: Edward Elgar, 1999), p. 68.

liberal and secular conservative parties. Switzerland, as in so many other respects, falls between these two groupings. The traditional liberal hegemony was incrementally replaced by a balanced distribution of power between social-democratic, liberal, Christian-democratic and conservative forces as the country gradually moved away from majoritarian to consociational practices during the course of the first half of the twentieth century.

Equally, there is huge variation in our sample in respect of systems and forms of interest mediation and industrial relations. In the North American countries, competitive and unco-ordinated forms of interest mediation and adversarial industrial relations are the dominant pattern.[55] Australia is again unique among federal nations in having a system of quasi-judicial wage-fixing, determining in its heyday the remuneration of around 80 per cent of wage-workers and even today around 50 per cent. The German-speaking countries show high degrees of corporatism and hence more co-ordinated and compromise-oriented arrangements for settling industrial conflicts between employers' associations and trade unions. Comparing the power resources of organized labour reveals three pairs of countries. Trade unionism is weak in North America, moderate in Germany and Switzerland and fairly strong in Australia and Austria.

In summary, pro-welfare state parties and their allies outside parliament are weak in the United States and Canada and strong in Austria, Australia and Germany, although the balance between party and trade union strength differs considerably in this latter grouping, while the power resources of pro-welfare and anti-welfare parties in Switzerland fall somewhere between these extremes.

Varieties of welfare states

In addition to variation in institutional forms and power resources, there is also substantial variation in the countries' social policy patterns, their levels of social spending, the timing of welfare state consolidation and the social policy responsibilities of different levels of government.

The timing of welfare state consolidation varies dramatically across the six countries (table 1.5), at least if one focusses on the date of

---

[55] See Alan Siaroff, 'Corporatism in 24 Industrial Democracies: Meaning and Measurement', *European Journal of Political Research*, vol. 36 (1999), no. 2, pp. 175–205; Lijphart, *Patterns of Democracy*, chapter 9. See also Peter Hall and David Soskice, eds., *Varieties of Capitalism. The Institutional Foundations of Comparative Advantage* (Oxford: Oxford University Press, 2001).

Table 1.5 *The introduction of core welfare state programmes at the national level*

	Australia	Austria	Canada	Germany	Switzerland	USA	OECD[1]
Old age	1908	1906	*1927*	1889	*1946*	*1935*	1917
Health	*1948*	1888	*1957*	1883	1912	*1965*	1924
Work injury	1902	1887	*1930*[2]	1884	1918	*1949*[2]	1905
Unemployment	*1944*	1920	*1940*	1927	*1982*	*1935*	1929
Family allowances	1941	*1948*	1944	*1954*	*1952*[3]	–	1944

Legend: Years highlighted in italics indicate that the introduction of a programme lagged behind the OECD average.
Notes: [1] In the OECD column we report the average of 23 OECD countries.
[2] Nation-wide coverage through provincial/state programmes.
[3] Farmers and agricultural employees only.
Source: Manfred G. Schmidt, *Sozialpolitik in Deutschland* (Opladen: Leske & Budrich, 1998), p. 180. The table there has been slightly adjusted by the authors.

adoption of social programmes at the federal level.[56] Germany and Austria were clearly welfare pioneers. Canada, the USA and Switzerland were conspicuous laggards.

The vertical power separation inherent in federal arrangements is mirrored in fragmented welfare states. Table 1.6 reports present jurisdictional arrangements of different tiers of government in these six nations with respect to the core branches of social provision. The table reveals two distinct patterns. The North American welfare states form a group of their own, since exclusive concentration of social policy competencies at one level of government is the exception rather than the rule. Moreover, social policy responsibilities in these countries are more decentralized. Joint jurisdiction and substantial legislative competencies empower all regional governments to influence standards of provision. The remaining four countries clearly concentrate social policy responsibilities at the federal level, the obvious assumption being that, where this is the case, benefit levels and regulatory regimes will be common across the entire federal jurisdiction. A comparison of programme-related jurisdictions shows that old age and unemployment benefits are overwhelmingly federal responsibilities. In contrast, social assistance, that is, the social security net of last resort, is largely a state or provincial responsibility. This obviously

---

[56] Alexander Hicks, Joya Misra and Tang Nah Ng, 'The Emergence of the Social Security State', *American Sociological Review*, vol. 60 (1995), no. 3, pp. 329–49; Manfred G. Schmidt, *Sozialpolitik in Deutschland. Historische Entwicklung und internationaler Vergleich*, 2nd edn (Opladen: Leske & Budrich, 1998).

Table 1.6 *Distribution of legislative authority for social provision as between state and central government*

	Australia	Austria	Canada	Germany	Switzerland	USA	Sum
Old age, survivors and disability	1	1	0.5	1	1	1	5.5
Health	1	1	0.5	1	1	0.5	5
Work injury	0	1	0	1	1	0	3
Unemployment	1	1	1	1	1	0.5	5.5
Family allowances	1	1	0.5	1	1	0.5	5
Social assistance	1	0.5	0	1	0	0.5	3
Sum	**5**	**5.5**	**2.5**	**6**	**5**	**3**	**27**

Legend: 1 = federal jurisdiction, 0 = state or provincial jurisdiction, 0.5 = shared jurisdiction.
Note: See table 8.1 for the historical dynamics in competency development.

suggests a potential for regional heterogeneity in standards of minimum income provision.

A quite different picture emerges if we look back at the distribution of social responsibilities at the beginning of the twentieth century (see below, table 8.1). At around 1900 the established democratic federations all assigned very limited social policy competencies to the central state. Because this was the case, each of these nations experienced major struggles over the appropriate allocation of social policy responsibilities during the course of the next hundred years. This contrasts radically with the situation in monarchical, semi-democratic and semi-federal Germany and Austria. From the very outset the central state was entrusted to regulate most branches of social security.

Aggregate social expenditure levels also appear to be patterned. The most recently available data (see table 1.7) indicate that Austria, Germany and Switzerland all spend between 25 and 30 per cent of GDP for social purposes, while spending in the English-speaking federations is between 15 and 20 per cent. However, if *net* spending is compared, that is if the impact of taxes on benefits and tax expenditures are also taken into account, the range in spending patterns is much narrower.[57] Further evidence of patterning can be found with respect to welfare funding. Social insurance contributions play a significant role in the Germanic welfare states, whereas contributions are non-existent in Australia and moderate in the North American welfare states.

---

[57] For indicative figures for some of these federations, see Willem Adema, 'Net Social Expenditure', OECD, Labour Market and Social Policy Occasional Papers, no. 52 (Paris: OECD, 1999).

We have already noted that the German-speaking federal states correspond broadly with Esping-Andersen's 'conservative' regime type and that the English-speaking countries belong to his 'liberal' regime category. Distinguishing features of the conservative model are the influence of Catholic doctrines – such as the subsidiarity principle, the male breadwinner model and a rejection of class conflict in favour of corporatist consensus – the existence of strong Christian-democratic parties, an authoritarian policy inheritance that is mirrored in occupationally fragmented and mandatory social programmes, and a variety of para-fiscal arrangements providing contribution-based social benefits through agencies wholly independent of the state's budget process.[58] The problem lying at the heart of social policy development in these countries was the *Arbeiterfrage* – the 'worker question' – to which the institutional response was mandatory insurance aimed at status preservation. The philosophical ideas underpinning the 'liberal' model were shaped in the crucible of eighteenth-century British political economy, and emphasize the principle of 'self help' and faith in the superiority of the market.[59] The role of social intervention in such countries is primarily one of poverty alleviation. Hence, social policy is largely residual and means testing is frequently employed to limit benefit entitlement. Private provision and occupational benefits continue to be of considerable significance. This model emerged under political conditions characterized by weak labour movements, a weak Catholic legacy and a strong liberal inheritance.

However, there is a substantial variation within each cluster. For example, the Canadian welfare state represents a mix of models. Its income security programmes, such as old age pensions, unemployment insurance, workers' compensation and social assistance, reflect the liberal approach. However, the core elements of the health care system, including medical and hospital services, reflect a more social-democratic inspiration. Public health insurance is universal, completely eliminating any role for private health insurance for publicly provided services, and charges at the point of service – such as user fees – are prohibited. Australia also exhibits many peculiarities distinguishing it from the welfare state institutions of North America, with Castles and Mitchell labelling the Australian welfare state 'radical' rather than liberal in character.[60] Until quite recently, Australia's

---

[58] Over time, these para-fiscal arrangements have come to systematically envelop the state. Since most public expenditure is for welfare state purposes, and since most expenditure flows via these independent, often overlooked, social insurance agencies, the *para-fiscal* institutional design has become so pervasive today that it is possible to speak of a *para-state* system.

[59] Esping-Andersen, *Social Foundations*, p. 74.

[60] Francis G. Castles and Deborah Mitchell, 'Worlds of Welfare and Families of Nations', in Castles, *Families of Nations*, pp. 93–128.

social protection 'by other means'[61] rested on four pillars designed to protect its economy and living standards from the effects of external competition. First, quasi-judicially regulated wage levels provided a social policy minimum for the vast majority of those dependent on labour market employment. Second, high tariffs protected domestic industries and secured the profits that allowed firms to pay high wages. Third, a selective immigration policy created a tight labour market by keeping out cheap foreign labour.[62] Finally, statist social policy provided a social safety net of last resort. Income support was means tested and residual in order to exclude the well off from benefit entitlement. Only means testing justifies classifying Australia as a member of the 'liberal' regime type, while the other pillars of social protection go hand in hand with a strong regulatory role of the state that is at odds with core liberal principles.

Within the German-speaking cluster, Switzerland stands out. For much of its existence, the Swiss welfare state has had a liberal face. Health insurance and unemployment provision have not been mandatory, while old age insurance was designed as *Volksversicherung* and provided universal flat-rate benefits rather than occupationally fragmented social insurance of the normal Bismarckian type. Private providers and workplace-related benefits have always played a significant role in benefit provision. In recent years, however, there has been a decisive shift towards the 'conservative' pattern and 'conservative' levels of spending.[63] Table 1.7 shows that social expenditure levels in the German-speaking federations are now virtually identical.

Drawing on the data compiled in table 1.7, we have employed cluster analysis to detect welfare state patterns. Figure 1 reveals two clusters that are exactly as might be expected in family-of-nations terms.[64] However, the cluster tree – which measures distances, not time – demonstrates that there is one outlier in each family: while the North American countries on the one hand and Germany and Austria on the other exhibit quite similar spending patterns, Switzerland and Australia are distinct since they merge relatively late with their cousins. This finding

---

[61] Francis G. Castles, 'Social Protection by Other Means: Australia's Strategy of Coping With External Vulnerability', in Francis G. Castles, ed., *The Comparative History of Public Policy* (Cambridge: Polity Press, 1989), pp. 16–55.

[62] For a similar constellation in the US before the New Deal, cf. Elmar Rieger and Stephan Leibfried, *Limits to Globalisation. Welfare States and World Economy* (Cambridge: Polity Press, 2003), chapter 3.

[63] Herbert Obinger, *Politische Institutionen und Sozialpolitik in der Schweiz* (Frankfurt-on-Main: Lang, 1998); Klaus Armingeon, 'Institutionalizing the Swiss Welfare State', in Jan-Erik Lane, ed., *The Swiss Labyrinth. Institutions, Outcomes and Redesign* (London: Frank Cass, 2001), pp. 145–68.

[64] See also Francis G. Castles, 'Developing New Measures of Welfare State Change and Reform', *European Journal of Political Research*, vol. 41 (2002), no. 5, pp. 613–41.

Table 1.7 *Welfare state spending patterns and funding at the turn of the millennium*

	Australia	Austria	Canada	Germany	Switzerland	USA
Total outlays of government as per cent GDP 2000[1]	33.7	48.0	41.8	43.3	34.1	33.9
Total social expenditure as per cent GDP 2001	18.9	26.9	17.8	28.8	27.0	15.2
Public social expenditure and (bracketed) total private mandatory benefits as per cent GDP 2001	18.0 (0.9)	26.0 (0.9)	17.8 (0.0)	27.4 (1.4)	26.4 (0.6)	14.8 (0.4)
Public social expenditure on old age and survivors' benefits as per cent GDP 2001	4.9	13.4	5.2	12.1	13.4	6.1
Public spending on incapacity related benefits as per cent GDP 2001	2.3	2.5	0.8	2.3	3.8	1.1
Family support (cash & services) as per cent GDP 2001	2.8	2.9	0.9	1.9	1.2	0.4
Unemployment benefits (active & passive) as per cent GDP 2001	1.4	1.3	1.2	2.3	0.9	0.5
Public expenditure on health as per cent GDP 2001	6.2	5.2	6.7	8.0	6.4	6.2
Minimum income spending (OECD category 'other contingencies') as per cent GDP 2001	0.1	0.5	2.4	0.5	0.6	0.5
Social security transfers as per cent GDP 2000[1]	9.1	18.8	12.4	18.8	11.9	12.6
Social security contributions as per cent GDP 2001	0.0	14.8	5.1	14.6	7.7	7.0
Social spending of central government as per cent total expenditures of central government[2]	35.5	46.3	44.2	50.0	48.8	28.7
Social spending of state governments as per cent total state government expenditures[2]	4.8	22.8	18.7	17.1	16.9	17.9
Social spending of state governments as per cent social expenditure of central government[2]	9.1	9.9	42.2	13.8	8.8	32.2

Notes: [1] Data for Canada are for 1998, Switzerland for 1999, and USA for 1997.
[2] This line generally refers to expenditures for social security and welfare in 1998, but to 1994 for Austria, 1997 for Canada and 1996 for Germany. Local government expenditures are excluded.
Sources: OECD, Social Expenditure Database, 1980–2001 (Paris: OECD, 2004); OECD, *Historical Statistics, 1970–2000* (Paris: OECD, 2001); OECD, *Revenue Statistics* (Paris: OECD, 2004); IMF, *Government Finance Statistics Yearbook* (Washington, D.C.: IMF, 2000).

Introduction

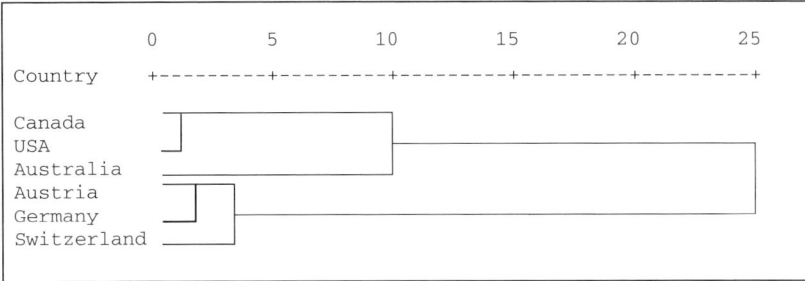

Legend: Hierarchical cluster analysis–dendogramme using Ward method and squared Euclidean distances.
Source: Data are drawn from table 1.7.

Figure 1.1 Clusters of social spending at the turn of the millennium

suggests that the previously noted structural peculiarities of the Australian and Swiss welfare states are also reflected in these countries' spending profiles.

How federalism affects the welfare state: theoretical approaches

What are the theoretical arguments concerning the ways in which federalism might impact on and shape social policy? Quantitative research has traditionally focussed on welfare effort, typically measured by aggregate social expenditure levels. Although econometric research depicts federalism as a stumbling block for welfare state expansion, no common denominator can be distilled from the literature on the precise attributes or mechanisms of federalism which influence the trajectory of social policy development.[65]

Since federalism does not represent a uniform set of institutional arrangements across space and time, it would involve a heroic assumption to argue that it impacts welfare state development similarly across nations. The cross-country diversity of federal institutions, different interfaces and linkages with general governmental institutions, different party systems and systems of interest mediation, as well as different actor constellations with heterogeneous preferences, strategies and interests, constitute a broad range of institutional configurations, making it extremely unlikely that federalism will be associated with uniform patterns of social policy and similar developmental trajectories in all countries.

---

[65] See Castles, 'Decentralisation and the Post-War Political Economy', p. 51.

Not surprisingly, existing (comparative) case studies point to divergent effects crucially depending on institutional settings.[66] A thorough review of this evidence suggests that not only is it possible to question the headline conclusion of the quantitative literature that federalism is a brake on welfare state development, but also that there may be reservations concerning Paul Pierson's hypothesis that 'federalism matters tremendously for the development of social policy', although his main point is that these federalism impacts 'are significantly mediated by other features of a particular political setting'.[67]

It is, therefore, essential to go back to theory in order to obtain a clearer view of the mutual relationship between federalism and social policy. To begin with, we must distinguish various social policy outcomes that may be attributed to federalism. Welfare state development in territorially fragmented states could be different for at least six possible reasons. Federalism might directly or indirectly affect

1. the dynamics of welfare state development;
2. programme generosity;
3. programme uniformity across states or provinces;
4. the extent of vertical redistribution;
5. patterns of social policy intervention;
6. the degree of policy experimentation and innovation.

There is also, however, a determination process that runs in the other direction, closing the feedback loop. Social policy may affect the federal structure by driving changes in

1. jurisdictional arrangements as demands for nation-wide welfare services increase (rising demand for social welfare policies may lead to pressures for common levels of provision as well as centralization; such demands may emanate from fears of a race to the bottom, from provincial demands for fiscal relief or from regional disparities in social standards);
2. inter-governmental and intra-welfare state fiscal arrangements over time.

---

[66] See Robert T. Kurdle and Theodore R. Marmor, 'The Development of Welfare States in North America', in Peter Flora and Arnold J. Heidenheimer, eds., *The Development of Welfare States in Europe and America* (New Brunswick, NJ: Transaction Press, 1987), pp. 81–121; Keith G. Banting, *The Welfare State and Canadian Federalism*, 2nd edn (Montreal: McGill-Queen's University Press, 1987); Pierson, 'Fragmented Welfare States'; Herbert Obinger, 'Föderalismus und wohlfahrtsstaatliche Entwicklung. Österreich und die Schweiz im Vergleich', *Politische Vierteljahresschrift*, vol. 43 (2002), no. 2, pp. 235–71; Ursula Münch, *Föderalismus und Sozialpolitik: Zur Dynamik der Aufgabenverteilung im sozialen Bundesstaat* (Opladen: Leske & Budrich, 1997).
[67] Pierson, 'Fragmented Welfare States', p. 472.

Introduction

It seems reasonable to argue that both of these streams of effects depend on time and on contextual factors including levels of economic performance and fiscal conditions. This is an important reason why the analysis in this volume emphasizes the distinction between the period of welfare state expansion (the 'old politics' of the 'golden age') and the more recent period of welfare constraint and adjustment (the 'new politics' of the 'silver age').

There are two coherent groups of theory from which we can derive hypotheses about the mechanisms by which federalism affects social policy development and the resulting patterns of policy outcomes.

Public choice

The first group of theories is based on economics. One important theoretical strand in the public choice literature argues that federalism is a significant institutional constraint on government growth. The size of government declines as taxes and expenditures are decentralized. Hence, federalism is seen as an institutional device for disciplining the Leviathan. Hayek was the first to suggest that the scope of governmental intrusion is smaller in federal states.[68] Brennan and Buchanan argue that political centralization enhances the growth of the Leviathan by creating a monopoly with unlimited power to extract revenues from society.[69] In contrast, the decentralization of fiscal powers stimulates competition between the constituent units constraining the growth of government. The size of the public sector, therefore, varies inversely with the decentralization of the 'fisc'. This limitation on the expansion of public expenditure also affects the generosity and coverage of social programmes, since social expenditures account for as much as 50 per cent of total government outlays. Federal governments must restrict their social spending, because they are unable to obtain the revenues required for provision on a generous scale. Harold Wilensky is making precisely the same point when he argues that 'political elites who embrace the welfare state in centralized polities can better overcome resistance to the necessary taxes and expenditures than elites in decentralized polities'.[70]

The Leviathan hypothesis rests on two assumptions. One is that opportunistic governments employ public expenditure to assure political

---

[68] Friedrich A. Hayek, 'The Economic Conditions of Interstate Federalism', in *Individualism and Economic Order* (London: Routledge & Kegan Paul, 1976; 1st edn 1939), pp. 255–72.
[69] Geoffrey Brennan and James M. Buchanan, *The Power to Tax: Analytical Foundations of a Fiscal Constitution* (Cambridge: Cambridge University Press, 1980).
[70] Harold L. Wilensky, *The Welfare State and Equality. Structural and Ideological Roots of Public Expenditures* (Berkeley: University of California Press, 1975), p. 52.

support. If spending authority is fragmented territorially, politicians are less free to distribute rents and benefits in exchange for votes and political support because they can only dispose of a specific portion of total public revenues. The other assumption rests on the proliferation of exit options under the circumstances of inter-governmental competition intrinsic to federalism. In Tiebout's model, voting with one's feet leads to an optimal allocation of locally provided public goods.[71] Consumers are seen as opting for the community whose government best satisfies their preferences regarding local public expenditure and revenue patterns.[72] Although most locally provided social benefits may not be regarded as public goods, Tiebout's model reminds us that mobility between communities may be influenced and stimulated by public policy packages. Communities providing more social benefits and services than others may attract new beneficiaries from elsewhere. Were it the case that social beneficiaries were fully mobile and possessed perfect knowledge of local social policy packages, welfare-induced migration would lead to increased spending in such communities unless restrictions, such as residence requirements, were imposed.

Also, in principle, federalism provides an exit option for mobile capital and firms capable of selecting the most business-friendly environment.[73] If there are no inter-state tariffs and no trade barriers to protect local industries from competition, as is the case in every modern federation, new taxes levied by one constituent unit may trigger mobile capital and upper income groups to exit that community. Constituent units maintaining high social standards and tax levels are then exposed to pressures to scale down social standards, since they face a higher demand for social security benefits and are simultaneously confronted with an exodus of taxable capital. In principle, then, horizontal competition between the constituent units lowers the prospects for redistributive social policies and strangles efforts to equalize living standards across the whole country.

Exit options may even constrain the ability of sub-governments to establish social programmes. First and foremost this may be true for programmes that affect the cost of labour, but 'even such legislation as the restriction of child labour or of working hours becomes difficult to carry out for the individual state'.[74] As a result, the absence of inter-state tariffs and the presence of the free movement of persons and capital between political units are seen as having significant consequences for social

---

[71] Charles M. Tiebout, 'A Pure Theory of Local Expenditures', *Journal of Political Economy*, vol. 65 (1956), no. 5, pp. 416–24.
[72] Ibid., p. 418.   [73] Pierson, 'Fragmented Welfare States'.
[74] Hayek, 'Economic Conditions of Interstate Federalism', p. 260.

policy-making. Competitive federalism may propel a downward spiral in social benefit provision, a 'race to[ward] the bottom'.[75]

Yet, much depends on the design of the tax system, the taxing powers conferred on sub-governments and the system of fiscal equalization between the different tiers of government. Such political mechanisms crucially interfere in the revenue patterns of political units and may also dramatically alter the incentives of governmental spending behaviour. These mechanisms help to explain why the empirical evidence in favour of the Leviathan hypothesis is so weak in practice. Oates concluded in 1985 that 'the extent of centralization in the public sector appears to have little effect on the size of government'.[76] In a review article published four years later, he found that the empirical literature 'contains a number of puzzles and inconsistent findings'[77] and his most recent review ends on the same note.[78]

Recently, Jonathan Rodden has attempted to resolve the controversy about whether the decentralization of the fisc curtails the size of the public sector or not.[79] Assuming a simple association between fiscal decentralization and the size of the public sector, he argues, is too easy. What is more important is how local governments fund their expenditure. Different funding arrangements create different incentives for local governments to expand or curtail the public sector. If local governments' budgets are funded by revenue sharing or by inter-governmental grants, they have a strong incentive to 'overfish' common pool resources, since horizontal tax competition is undermined and sub-governments can exploit resources collected at other tiers of government. Hence, decentralization may even stimulate the size of the public sector. Provided that regional governments are sufficiently entrusted with fiscal and policy responsibilities, the incentives for subordinate levels of government change dramatically. However, where sub-governments have to fund public expenditure by local taxes, decentralization is likely to limit the expansion of the

---

[75] Paul E. Peterson and Mark Rom, *Welfare Magnets. A New Call for a National Standard* (Washington, DC: Brookings Institution Press, 1990); Hans Werner Sinn, 'Die Osterweiterung der EU und die Zukunft des Sozialstaates', in Stephan Leibfried and Uwe Wagschal, eds., *Der deutsche Sozialstaat. Bilanzen – Reformen – Perspektiven* (Frankfurt-on-Main: Campus, 2000), pp. 474–89.
[76] Wallace E. Oates, 'Searching for the Leviathan: An Empirical Study', *American Economic Review*, vol. 75 (1985), no. 4, pp. 748–57, p. 754.
[77] Wallace E. Oates, 'Searching for the Leviathan: A Reply and Some Further Reflections', *American Economic Review*, vol. 79 (1989), no. 3, pp. 578–83, p. 582.
[78] Wallace E. Oates, 'An Essay on Fiscal Federalism', *Journal of Economic Literature*, vol. 37 (1999), no. 3, pp. 1120–49, p. 1140.
[79] Jonathan Rodden, 'Reviving Leviathan: Fiscal Federalism and the Growth of Government', *International Organization*, vol. 57 (2003), no. 4, pp. 695–729.

public sector.[80] Because regional governments bear much of the expenditure cost, and because this necessarily enhances tax competition amongst territorial sub-governments, the extent of governmental intervention is likely to be reduced. Rodden's comparative empirical findings support these arguments. Drawing on panel data, he finds that the level of government spending is higher if sub-national expenditures are funded through common pool resources such as inter-governmental grants and tax shares. However, government is smaller in countries in which regional governments are authorized to levy taxes and hence enjoy greater revenue autonomy, with this finding particularly pronounced for federal countries.

As a result, there is no one-to-one relationship between decentralization and the size of the public sector. Given the heterogeneity of financial arrangements in federal states and differing degrees of fiscal decentralization across the six countries, a wide range of expenditure outcomes is possible. Hence, a careful analysis of the financial relations between different tiers of government and of fiscal equalization schemes is required in order to evaluate the incentives faced by sub-governments in public policy-making. In a nutshell, so much depends on idiosyncratic institutional configurations that no a priori generalizations are possible.

Besides disciplining rent-seeking political entrepreneurs, economists emphasize other advantages that arise from a vertical separation of power. It is argued that competition between the constituent units fuels innovation and efficiency in a manner analogous to that of markets. Moreover, decentralization is seen as leading to a better match between local policies and regional preferences. These advantages supposedly outweigh the higher decision-making costs typically prevailing in federal polities. The idea that federalism provides opportunities for territorially based policy experiments and for sub-governments to learn from each other's experiences are arguments that are widely rehearsed in the literature. Like economic competition, federal competition may be seen as a 'discovery mechanism' for new ideas and creative problem-solving. If that were so, competition between constituent units could be seen as a source of innovation and best practice solutions in policies associated with spill-over effects to the federal level. At first glance, the argument appears to conflict with the previous line of economic reasoning that inter-jurisdictional competition may fuel a race to the bottom in social standards. Relaxing the strict assumption of fully mobile factors that underpins this scenario, and allowing for institutional rigidities and distinct regional voter

---

[80] Ibid.; see also Jonathan Rodden and Erik Wibbels, 'Beyond the Fiction of Federalism. Macroeconomic Management in Multitiered Systems', *World Politics*, vol. 54 (2002), no. 3, pp. 494–531.

preferences, makes policy experimentation more probable on public choice premises.

Political institutionalism(s)

The second group of theories is centreed around issues of institutional design. Institutions create opportunity structures for political actors that facilitate or constrain policy authority.[81] Three lines of reasoning can be distinguished.

In the first, the emphasis lies on the indirect and long-term effects of federalism on the political economy and its actors. Federalism indirectly influences welfare states by affecting a broad array of other socioeconomic and political variables which in turn affect trajectories of welfare state development. Federalism is founded on and generates diversity, encouraging the emergence of territorially diverse political economies, each with its own set of deeply rooted political interests and values. Not only does federalism determine how markets and collective actors are organized, but it also dramatically increases the number of actors and institutions involved in policy-making. Institutional division promotes political fragmentation.[82] Swank notes that dispersion of policy-making authority diminishes the size of political interests, undermines their unity and the coherence of their strategies, and reduces the availability of conventional political resources. He argues that 'this is especially true for decentralisation of authority through federalism and its close correlate, strong bicameralism'.[83] Federalism thus modifies the political capacities and power resources of key actors, such as parties, unions and business organizations, undercuts the formation of national policy strategies and makes the formation of powerful welfare state alliances more difficult.[84] This last stipulation, that federalism weakens the bargaining power of pro-welfare state coalitions, is relevant for both the 'old politics' and 'new politics' of the welfare state. Federalism's effect on norms and political values, that is, an inherent drift towards competition and anti-statism, likewise weakens coalitions under both the 'old politics' and the 'new politics'. Swank posits that 'norms of cooperation, reciprocity, and consensus building, potentially conducive to defence of the welfare state

---

[81] R. Kent Weaver and Bert A. Rockman, eds., *Do Institutions Matter? Government Capabilities in the United States and Abroad* (Washington, DC: Brookings Institution Press, 1993).
[82] See Pierson, 'Fragmented Welfare States', p. 453.
[83] Swank, *Global Capital*, p. 48.
[84] Duane H. Swank, 'Political Institutions and Welfare State Restructuring. The Impact of Institutions on Social Policy Change in Developed Democracies', in Pierson, ed., *New Politics of the Welfare State*, pp. 197–237, p. 211.

against substantial and rapid cuts, will be weaker in political systems of dispersed authority than in other polities, [while] the norms of conflict, competition, and anti-statism will be stronger'.[85]

The second line of institutional reasoning maintains that the fragmentation of power between multiple actors and levels of government that is intrinsic to federalism increases the number of institutional veto points,[86] providing additional access points and greater veto opportunities for minorities.[87] Based on this logic, many scholars have argued that a constitutional structure, which disperses political power and offers multiple veto points, is inimical to welfare state expansion.[88]

Theoretically, George Tsebelis' account of veto players provides the link between institutional fragmentation and public policy dynamics. According to Tsebelis,[89] a veto player is a collective or individual actor whose approval is required to alter the status quo. Policy stability increases with the number of veto players, their ideological distance and internal cohesion. The institutional safeguards of federalism including bicameralism, referendum procedures and constitutional courts are essential features of vertical power dispersion.[90] But, by separating powers, federalism proliferates veto players and, hence, is a barrier to policy change. The welfare state, as the most important single subset of modern policy action, is subject to the same logic.

However, as the preceding section has demonstrated, cross-national variation in the character of federal institutions requires a more detailed analysis of the kinds of institutions that are most likely to function as institutional veto players. With regard to bicameralism, it seems clear that the Austrian Bundesrat cannot be classified as a veto player, and, with regard to ordinary legislation, the German Bundesrat can also be overridden. Only if bills are on the agenda requiring Bundesrat assent, and only when majorities in the two houses diverge, should the German Bundesrat be classified as a veto player. The Senate in the United States and Australia, as well as the Ständerat in Switzerland, are, in contrast,

---

[85] Swank, *Global Capital*, p. 50.
[86] Ellen M. Immergut, *Health Politics: Interests and Institutions in Western Europe* (Cambridge: Cambridge University Press, 1992).
[87] Fiona Ross, 'Cutting Public Expenditures in Advanced Industrial Democracies: The Importance of Avoiding Blame', *Governance*, vol. 10 (1997), no. 2, pp. 175–200, p. 178.
[88] Theda Skocpol and Edwin Amenta, 'States and Social Policy', *Annual Review of Sociology*, vol. 12 (1986), no. 1, pp. 131–57; Evelyne Huber, Charles Ragin and John D. Stephens, 'Social Democracy, Christian Democracy, Constitutional Structures, and the Welfare State', *American Journal of Sociology*, vol. 99 (1993), no. 3, pp. 711–49, p. 722; Huber and Stephens, *Development and Crisis*; Swank, *Global Capital*.
[89] George Tsebelis, *Veto Players. How Political Institutions Work* (Princeton: Princeton University Press, 2002).
[90] Lijphart, *Patterns of Democracy*, p. 186.

strong veto players, given the more or less symmetrical allocation of powers between houses and the normally incongruent majorities in the two chambers of the legislature.

Constitutional referenda are frequently used in Switzerland and, to a far lesser extent, in Australia. In the remaining four countries they are either non-existent or of minor importance. Ordinary legislation in Switzerland and in many US states is subject to a referendum provided that there are enough supporters to launch a plebiscite. Vested interests may exploit these opportunities to oppose and/or overturn policy reform.

Constitutional courts are powerful autonomous actors holding considerable veto rights. Switzerland apart, judicial review is strong in all these federations. In Austria and Germany the parliamentary opposition – that is around one-third of all members of parliament – is constitutionally empowered to initiate judicial review of ordinary federal legislation. Sub-governments enjoy the same rights in respect of federal bills. Hence a political conflict over the shape of the welfare state may easily be extended beyond the parliamentary arena and only be resolved by a Constitutional Court decision.

Veto players impose considerable constraints on unrestricted majority rule and may strengthen the negotiations-based logic of decision-making typical of federal countries. In contrast, in Westminster-style unitary democracies the government and the parliamentary majority are much less institutionally constrained in their actions. Since political authority is concentrated in the executive, governments in such centralized polities generally have sufficient power resources to exercise policy leadership. There is usually no need to form coalitions or to enter into protracted negotiations with different branches of government.

Federal systems are necessarily, to some extent, joint decision systems, that is, 'constellations in which parties are either physically or legally unable to reach their purposes through unilateral action and in which joint action depends on the (nearly) unanimous agreement of all parties involved'. Such constellations emerge when functional interdependence is prevalent, so that 'goals of a particular kind or beyond a certain order of magnitude cannot be attained without collaboration'.[91] Thus, from a procedural perspective, public policy in territorially fragmented political systems requires the co-ordination of fragmented resources of action, if competencies and administrative powers are to be shared across different tiers of government. Since federal systems inflate the number of actors involved in the policy-making process,[92] and because sub-governments

---

[91] Both citations are taken from Scharpf, *Games Real Actors Play*, p. 143.
[92] Pierson, 'Fragmented Welfare States', p. 455.

frequently pursue their own strategies in a given policy field, any major policy change requires the co-ordination of multi-layered interests and the approval of a host of actors, who have to bargain until they agree on a joint course of action and – especially important for expensive areas of public policy such as social policy – on the cost sharing associated with this course.

Thus, social policy-making in fragmented and intertwined systems of decision-making is likely to delay decisions or may possibly result in suboptimal policy outcomes and lowest common denominator policies. A joint course of action is difficult to realize if the number of constituent units is high and if large majorities or unanimity is required to alter the status quo. In addition, deep ethnic, political and socio-economic cleavages between states or provinces make consensus on policy change even more unlikely. Such an institutionally induced policy stalemate seems to be relevant for both the 'old politics' and the 'new politics' of the welfare state. However, there are strategies for avoiding protracted decision-making and deadlock. Costs for social programmes may be externalized to actors not involved in the bargaining process and stimulus for policy reform may come from the decisions of institutions, such as courts or supra-national actors, which cannot be overruled by political actors.

Since many veto players restrict policy change, it can be argued that federal institutions create a 'ratchet effect' that also hampers retrenchment efforts. Such a 'downwards' stickiness, that would contribute to a resilience of the welfare state in hard times, might originate from two different sources. First, the secondary institutions of federalism are also veto points that can be exploited by the opposition to avert a rollback of the welfare state in times of austerity.[93] In addition, political minorities and well-organized pressure groups can rely on these veto rights to defend the status quo in social affairs. Second, vertical power separation means more democracy. Federalism goes hand in hand with a higher frequency of elections, which makes retrenchment politically risky. Unpopular policies pursued at the national tier often affect regional electoral outcomes, because voters also express their views about national policies in such elections. Since the new politics account is strongly based on the assumption that politicians are oriented towards gaining office and seeking re-election, the inflation of electoral battles in federal systems should also be a factor contributing to restraining retrenchment initiatives, especially where party systems are vertically integrated and congruent.

---

[93] Pierson, *Dismantling the Welfare State?*; Pierson, 'New Politics of the Welfare State'; Swank, 'Political Institutions and Welfare State Restructuring'.

Introduction 39

While the veto player theory emphasizes the status quo bias of federal institutions, which slow the pace of policy change in respect of both expansion and retrenchment of the welfare state, a case has also been made that federalism might be particularly facilitative of retrenchment efforts. Shared jurisdictions may ease retrenchment policies, because political accountability of political action is not concentrated at central government level alone. Complex and interwoven decision-making and funding arrangements provide opportunities for the central government to embark on a strategy of 'blame avoidance'.[94] By tightening benefit eligibility and cutting inter-governmental transfers, blame may be shifted to lower tiers of government.

The third institutional line of reasoning focusses on the way in which path dependency and policy pre-emption limit the scope for subsequent policy change. Combining this approach with an understanding of the role of veto players may contribute a good deal to explaining the dynamics of the 'old politics' of the welfare state in federal countries. Central to theories of path dependency[95] is the idea that earlier stages in a sequential decision process matter more than do the later stages. Even small decisions taken at an early point in time may have lasting and self-reinforcing effects. Technically, such a process exhibits increasing returns, which denote that the costs of path reversal increase over time. If we take theories of path dependence seriously, then we have to turn back to history and examine forms and patterns of early policy pre-emption. Insofar as our concern is with understanding the genesis of early social policy intervention in federal states, it is not only important to identify when such initiatives occurred, but also which tier of government was first in taking them. The latter is, in turn, influenced by which tier of government was originally constitutionally empowered to initiate policy action. Hence, the initial jurisdictional arrangements of federal states may be seen as having structured the developmental trajectories of their subsequent welfare state development, since distinct patterns of social policy pre-emption and policy initiatives at different levels of government have given rise to distinct trajectories and patterns of social policy-building by the federal government.

To illustrate the importance of policy pre-emption for welfare state consolidation and expansion, that is, of the 'old politics' of the welfare state, consider a federal nation where (almost) all social policy

---

[94] Weaver, 'Politics of Blame Avoidance'.
[95] See Paul Pierson, 'Increasing Returns, Path Dependency, and the Study of Politics', *American Political Science Review*, vol. 94 (2000), no. 2, pp. 251–67; see now his *Politics in Time. History, Institutions, and Social Analysis* (Princeton: Princeton University Press, 2004), pp. 17–53.

responsibilities remain at the local level, as was initially the case in all the democratic federations in our sample. If competitive federalism is weakly developed, policies will be pre-empted locally and welfare state consolidation will take place from the bottom up. Given distinct local policy orientations, different institutional structures across constituent units, pronounced horizontal socio-economic, ethnic and political cleavages and distinct regional voter preferences, decentralized social policy initiatives are likely to lead to a patchwork of heterogeneous social policy programmes and social experiments varying substantially in organization, funding, benefit level and programme design.

As a consequence of local policy pre-emption, the degree of freedom for federal social policy intervention declines. Every attempt of the federal government to impose social policy legislation has to cope with multiple problems. First of all, the central state has to acquire the necessary jurisdictional space to enact federal laws. In the process, social policy often becomes an aspect of competitive state-building, of assuring the mass loyalty that increases prospects of re-election. As a consequence, it is very likely that democratic federations will experience severe struggles over the allocation of social policy jurisdiction. A broad consensus among the constituent units is usually necessary in order to alter the inter-governmental distribution of powers spelled out in the constitution. Rigid procedures for constitutional amendments – like super-majorities or unanimity rules – may turn into joint decision traps that lead to policy stalemate or lowest common denominator policies.

Moreover, the ability of the federal government to act often depends on how the constitutional court interprets the allocation of jurisdictions. The federal governments' social policy initiatives can be blocked if a powerful constitutional court acts as a gatekeeper of the constituent units' powers. If a constitutional court is inclined to a narrow interpretation of the federal constitutional mandate, the prospects for federal social policy initiatives are markedly reduced. On the other hand, court rulings may also enhance the central government's capacity to act if 'implied powers' are acknowledged or if existing federal policy responsibilities are interpreted in a broader way. A well-known example of the latter is the Commerce Clause – Article I, section 8 [par. 3] of the US Constitution – which gives Congress the power to regulate inter-state commerce.[96] Initially, a rigid interpretation of this clause by the Supreme Court thwarted Congress' efforts to regulate child labour. However, a subsequent relaxation of the strict interpretation of the clause was later

---

[96] Vicki Lens, 'The Supreme Court, Federalism, and Social Policy', *Social Service Review*, vol. 75 (2001), no. 2, pp. 318–36.

used to support federal powers to tax and to provide for the general welfare.

If a federation has acquired the powers required for social policy regulation, there may still be a need to overcome additional obstacles. As a consequence of local policy pre-emption, federal legislation may have to reckon with social policy arrangements as they exist at the local level. Since many interests have already crystallized around existing decentralized social programmes, and because local social policies represent sunk costs[97] and are a source of political support and legitimacy, the constituent units and local carriers of these programmes are likely to be reluctant to support federal policy intervention. If the constituent units have a strong influence on the federal policy-making process, and if veto points exist that enable the carriers of locally emergent social security arrangements to influence federal decision-making, then it is rather unlikely that local programmes will be easily superseded by federal policy initiatives. Consequently, the federal government needs to take the design of locally grown social security arrangements into account and adjust federal programmes accordingly. Policy pre-emption and rivalries in competitive state-building[98] may even restrain the federal government from intervening or restrict it to setting minimum standards only, leaving sufficient leeway for local preferences. Early policy pre-emption at the local level is, therefore, an important reason why the nationalization of social policy has tended to proceed relatively slowly in the federations that were democratic long before they were welfare states.

It would be a mistake, however, to only consider the distribution of social policy responsibilities. Of equal importance are the fiscal powers allocated to different levels of governments as well as the administrative capacities of each tier of government. Vertical and horizontal imbalances of fiscal powers are likely to impact on regulatory capacity in the social policy field. If the financial resources of the constituent units are weak, they may simply abstain from local social policy initiatives or press for policy intervention at the federal level, despite themselves having the power to legislate. Conversely, federal social policy may fail or be postponed if the federation has jurisdiction but lacks sufficient revenues to fund federal programmes and therefore is at the mercy of the localities to provide the required funding. Hence, (in)congruence of fiscal and social policy competencies may be vital to an understanding of welfare state dynamics in federal states.

[97] Pierson, 'Fragmented Welfare States'.
[98] See Keith Banting, 'The Welfare State as Statecraft: Territorial Politics and Canadian Social Policy', in Leibfried and Pierson, *European Social Policy*, pp. 269–300, *inter alia* p. 284.

Synthesis

By bringing institutionalist and public choice approaches together, a synoptic approach to potential federalism effects becomes possible. With respect to the 'old politics' of the welfare state, we might expect policy constraining effects to occur as a consequence of the following:

- Policy pre-emption by lower tiers of government where federal social policy jurisdiction is lacking: extensive social policy responsibilities at lower tier levels may hamper the centralization of social policy, give rise to lowest common denominator policies, and may affect the patterns of federal social policy intervention.
- A strong decentralization of the fisc: decentralized spending and taxing authority may contribute to economic competition between constitutional units; exit options for mobile capital may block social policy efforts and motivate states or provinces to refrain from social policy experimentation; in addition, insufficient federal revenues may delay the adoption of generous programmes.
- Policy stalemate as a consequence of strong veto powers of second chambers, constitutional courts and direct democracy: such veto powers give sub-governments a considerable influence on federal policy-making; prospects of political gridlock and policy stalemate are increased by constitutional rigidity, divided governments, a conflicting logic of decision-making between the partisan and the federal arenas, incongruent partisan complexion of different branches of government, ethnic tensions, competitive state-building and socio-economic cleavages among regions.
- A lack of necessary bureaucratic capacities at the federal level and a weak bargaining power of pro-welfare state coalitions caused by territorially fragmented interest organization.

Federalism also may function as a welfare state catalyst or be policy neutral. Sources for an expansionary effect may be as follows:

- Policy experiments undertaken by lower tiers of governments associated with spill-over effects to the federal tier or horizontally to tiers at the same level ('races to the top or the middle ground') and with competitive innovation by different tiers of government.
- Fragmentation of spending and taxing authority across different tiers of government, which allows some tiers of government the luxury of overgrazing the fiscal commons.[99]

---

[99] Rodden, 'Reviving Leviathan'.

Introduction 43

- Sub-national governments, which may call for federal social policy regulation as a consequence of fiscal stress and/or large-scale social problems that they cannot solve on their own.
- Strategies for bypassing the joint decision traps causing political gridlock: for instance, by externalizing costs to third parties not involved in the bargaining game between different branches of government;[100] 'third parties' include para-fiscal social insurance institutions, which are, as explained earlier, independent of the state and have their own fiscal, that is, contribution base.

With respect to the 'new politics', a ratchet effect hampering retrenchment efforts could result from a variety of sources:

- Federalism inflates the number of elections and goes hand in hand with a permanent electoral battle that makes retrenchment politically risky. Since the new politics paradigm is strongly based on the assumption that democratic politicians are office and re-election seeking actors, they will refrain from policy reform that hurts their prospects of achieving these goals.
- Well-organized pro-welfare state groups may use the numerous institutional veto points available in the federal arena to water down unwelcome policies.

However, there are also arguments that federalism may facilitate retrenchment:

- Political accountability for unpopular benefits cuts is harder to pin down and thus – in the aggregate – lower in fragmented political systems. A federal state structure provides opportunities for bringing about 'retrenchment by stealth', since the federal government can offload blame onto subordinate tiers of government; for example, by cutting transfers for social programmes run by the lower-tier units. Responsibilities may also be offloaded to a variety of 'third parties' via the regulatory route of replacing direct with mandatory provision. In general, federalism provides the potential for shifting blame across different levels of government and for obfuscating political accountability.
- Devolution and cutting inter-governmental transfers may be a source of social dumping, which may be further accelerated by

---

[100] See Frank Nullmeier, 'Der Zugriff des Bundes auf die Haushalte der Gemeinden und Parafisci', in Hans-Hermann Hartwich and Göttrik Wewer, eds., *Regieren in der Bundesrepublik* IV (Opladen: Leske & Budrich, 1992), pp. 147–80; Wachendorfer-Schmidt, *Federalism and Political Performance*.

horizontal fiscal competition and by improved exit options for mobile capital.
- Federalism undercuts the bargaining power of pro-welfare coalitions to defend the welfare state.

As this overview makes clear, the potential effects of federalism on welfare state development are multiple. They are in no way singular or unidirectional. Moreover, such effects are not uniform and invariant with time. Like other institutional effects, they are contingent on institutional configurations, actor constellations, actor orientations and on a broad range of contextual parameters. In particular, they may depend on

1. jurisdictional splits and fiscal transfer arrangements
2. veto points, that is, the secondary institutions of federalism
3. characteristics of the welfare clientele, for example whether beneficiaries are viewed as deserving and whether they are well organized and geographically concentrated
4. policy feedbacks, including effects on clientele organization and power resources
5. the government's budgetary situation
6. the partisan complexion of government, the nature of the party system, the power of the interest organizations of labour and capital and the institutionalized interaction between them.

In table 1.8 the ways in which selected contextual factors make the hypothesized effects of federalism on social policy more or less likely to occur are summarized.

Given the complexity identified in table 1.8, the point of departure for this volume is a recognition that federalism and its inter-relationship with policy is likely to differ across both space and time. This has important methodological implications. Measuring federalism with a dummy variable or a simple and time invariant additive index, as is the standard practice in quantitative research, in no way captures all the variants of federal institutions and their changing nature over time. Similarly, the assumption of a time invariant linear and one-directional relationship between federalism and social policy oversimplifies the institutional impacts on public policy outcomes and neglects interaction effects, historical contingencies and critical junctures. Rather, policy configurations and policy development in these nations result from an interplay between specific federal institutions, the general governmental structure and societal conflicts mediated by political parties and interest organizations, and are decided according to the prevailing distribution of power in the relevant policy arenas. A comprehensive analysis of the relationship between

Table 1.8 *Potential federalism effects on social policy contingent upon contextual factors*

Potential federalism effect	Strengthened/made more likely by	Weakened/made less likely by
Stalemate resulting from provincial policy pre-emption	■ Lack of federal jurisdiction ■ Multiple veto points ■ Territorially concentrated ethnic or political minorities (competitive state-building)	■ Dominance of federal jurisdiction ■ Fiscal stress at provincial level ■ Powerful pro-welfare state coalitions
Stalemate resulting from multiple veto points/joint decision traps	■ Consensus or super-majorities required for policy change ■ Conflicting logic underlying partisan competition and inter-governmental relations ■ Heterogeneous partisan complexion of government at different levels of government ■ Incongruence of fiscal and social policy power distribution	■ Clear exclusive federal jurisdiction ■ Strong, well-organized constituency ■ Homogeneous partisan complexion of government at different levels of government ■ Critical junctures (e.g. war)
Stimulation/emulation and diffusion of innovation	■ Beneficiaries are poorly organized but potentially powerful ■ Political heterogeneity across states and provinces	■ High cost of innovation will put province at a competitive disadvantage ■ Fiscal stress
Competitive innovation by federal and state and provincial governments	■ Concurrent or unclear jurisdiction ■ Strong voter support for action	■ Clear, exclusive jurisdiction ■ Voter apathy ■ Strong interest group opposition
Policy inaction or race to the bottom	■ Exclusive sub-state jurisdiction ■ Budget austerity pressures ■ Unpopular constituency ■ Weak pro-welfare state coalitions	■ Exclusive federal jurisdiction ■ Developed fiscal equalization ■ Popular constituency ■ Powerful pro-welfare state coalitions
Policy inaction through 'passing the buck'	■ Unclear jurisdiction ■ Strong organized interest opposition	■ Clear exclusive federal jurisdiction
Muting retrenchment through inflation of elections	■ Vertically integrated and congruent party system	■ Decentralized and incongruent party system
Policy retrenchment through cuts in transfers	■ Shared jurisdiction with fiscal transfers	■ Exclusive national jurisdiction

federalism and social policy therefore requires a historical comparative approach, which allows these complexities to be explored in their historical detail. We believe that such an approach offers the most appropriate methodological strategy for dealing with the complex causal patterns of institutional effects on public policy, including interactions among causal and contextual variables, the impact of time and the presence of reciprocal causalities.

The book at a glance

In the first part of this volume we examine the relationship between federalism and welfare state development in the New World of settler states outside of Europe. Part 2 explores this relationship as it is manifested in the three European, and largely German-speaking, federations. The ordering of the country chapters in each of these families of nations is alphabetical, but, quite coincidentally, corresponds, within each section, with the reverse order in which the countries adopted their federal constitutions.

In the first chapter of part 1, Francis G. Castles and John Uhr provide an account of the Australian experience, a story quite different from that of developments on the North American continent. In North America, democratic federalism preceded the emergence of a modern welfare state. In Australia, they were born simultaneously, and the authors show how the imperatives of collectivism and regulation became intertwined with those of decentralization and the division of powers, explaining why, in so many respects, Australia appears as an aberrant member of the New World family of federalism.

In North America democratic federalism emerged before the development of a modern welfare state. Keith Banting discusses the Canadian experience, pointing to the late emergence of social policy programmes and their subsequent development along different tracks, depending on whether relationships between the central government and the provinces were articulated on 'classical', 'shared-cost' or 'joint decision' lines. His analysis shows that this same diversity of interactions between governments at different levels conditions policy responses in the 'silver age', with programmes governed exclusively by the federal government on the one hand or the provinces on the other much more exposed to the chill winds of welfare retrenchment than programmes subject to inter-governmental decision-making.

The final chapter of part 1 examines the relationship between federalism and the welfare state in the United States, the country in which modern democratic federalism was born. Kenneth Finegold reviews both

Introduction 47

the institutions of this classical instance of inter-state federalism and the slow and still incomplete evolution of US social programmes. His account focusses on the way in which US federalism fosters welfare state experimentation and brings a new perspective to the debate on the development of US social policy by arguing that federal institutions have been, in some instances at least, the means for overcoming policy stalemate.

Our account of the European experience in part 2 starts with a chapter on Austria by Herbert Obinger. In North America federalism came early and the welfare state came much later, but in Austria and Germany the pattern was decidedly different: the welfare state was established much earlier than federalism in Austria, and in Germany the two developed almost simultaneously. Obinger explains why this was so in Austria, pointing to policy pre-emption by the pre-1918 non-democratic regime, the twentieth-century emergence of bipartisan consensus on the welfare state and the absence of strong institutional veto players as the main factors.

The German case is particularly important to our analysis because Germany is widely regarded as the birthplace of the modern social security state. In his chapter, Philip Manow is also concerned to explore the circumstances under which federalism and high levels of social expenditure can co-exist. His answer is that the institutional dynamics of intra-state federalism, and particularly the emergence of a contributions-based para-fiscal state – in the end a para-state – insulated from veto politics, have an inherent expansionary potential, allowing Germany to bypass federal constraints on expenditure development, although sometimes, as at present, at considerable fiscal cost.

Our account of the final Swiss case is a collaboration by four authors: Herbert Obinger, Klaus Armingeon, Giuliano Bonoli and Fabio Bertozzi. The Swiss case is the odd man out in the European family of federalism, with federal institutions making welfare state consolidation a long drawn-out and bottom-up process. The authors draw special attention to the effects of direct democracy, the continuing existence of distinct cantonal 'worlds of welfare' and the belated emergence of Switzerland as a big-spender at a time when other federal nations were entering their 'silver age' of social policy constraint.

The concluding chapter of the volume addresses the questions posed in this introduction in light of what we have learned from these six case studies. Under what circumstances is federal government a constraint on welfare state development and does welfare state development, in turn, have feedback effects on the evolution of federal institutions? Beginning with a country-by-country synthesis of historical and contemporary interaction patterns between federalism and the welfare state, we go on to consider the distinctive features of that interaction under both the 'old politics' and the 'new politics' of the welfare state. Moving on to broader analytical issues, we then consider the role of the welfare state in the federal 'laboratory of democracy' and examine the ways in which the development of the welfare state in these very different nations has reshaped the nature of their federalisms.

PART 1
New World experiences

2 Australia
Federal constraints and institutional innovations

FRANCIS G. CASTLES AND JOHN UHR

Introduction

Considerations of systematic coverage apart, there are a number of reasons why a comparative study of the impact of federalism on the development of the welfare state might wish to dwell on the Australian case. Perhaps the most important is that the Australian case seems to exemplify all of the key hypotheses identified in the theoretical literature linking these phenomena. If the basic hypothesis linking federalism to the 'old politics' of the welfare state is that federal institutions hinder welfare state expansion, Australia appears to fit the bill rather well. With the exception of a decade or so of radical experimentation immediately after federation, the story of the Australian welfare state in the first half of the twentieth century is one of the late adoption of schemes increasingly common elsewhere and, after World War Two, of levels of expenditure that are consistently towards the bottom of international league tables.

Since the early 1980s, however, things appear to have changed. In the 'silver age' of welfare state development, Australia has been hailed as one of the few OECD countries to combine measurable success in economic performance with a significant improvement in welfare provision.[1] On the surface, this seems to fit with the 'new politics' notion of federal institutions exercising a 'ratchet effect' on expenditure development, making it difficult for political forces opposed to statist intervention to obtain the

---

[1] See Herman Schwartz, 'Social Democracy Going Down vs. Social Democracy Down Under?', *Comparative Politics*, vol. 30 (1998), no. 3, pp. 253–72; Fritz W. Scharpf, 'Economic Changes, Vulnerabilities and Institutional Capabilities', in Fritz W. Scharpf and Vivien A. Schmidt, eds., *Welfare and Work in the Open Economy*, vol. I, *From Vulnerability to Competitiveness* (Oxford: Oxford University Press, 2000), pp. 21–124.

leverage required to reverse existing policies. The point, then, is that Australia is an important test case for understanding the impact of federalism on the development of the welfare state. If the apparently contradictory trajectories of Australian welfare state expansion over the past century cannot be sheeted home to the character of the federal compact, at least to some extent, then, these hypotheses derived from theory may have to be discarded or in some way modified.

The Australian case also appears to offer confirmation of the hypothesis that welfare state development can, in turn, modify the functioning of federal institutions. A modern welfare state demands some uniformity of provision, an adequate resource base and a capacity for central direction. At the time of federation, however, the new constitution of the Commonwealth of Australia gave little promise that it contained the mechanisms required to bring such a project to fruition. Over time, however, ways were found of using institutions in new ways to realize the purposes of the welfare state. Above all, the fact that, from early on, almost any positive actions by states or Commonwealth required collaboration between both meant that there was a major stimulus to collaborative federalism in the area of the 'welfare state' as in other fields. It, therefore, seems highly probable that Australian evidence will be immediately relevant to the argument that the relationship between federalism and the welfare state is reciprocal rather than unidirectional in character.

Another reason why the Australian case is particularly illuminating is that the linkage between federal institutions and the welfare state is, in part, spelled out in the Australian Constitution itself, making some aspects of the relationship more transparent than might otherwise be the case. Because the Australian Constitution came into force in 1901, at a time when ideas for modern social reform were first becoming practical politics, the social policy responsibilities of the Australian Commonwealth were explicitly identified in the federal compact. Those responsibilities were initially quite limited. By the 1940s the restricted nature of federal powers in the social policy area was widely recognized and, in 1946, the post-war Labor government secured one of the very few substantive constitutional referendum victories in Australian history, allowing the federal government to legislate in order to provide a much wider range of social service benefits.

Accordingly, a linkage between Australia's late adoption of welfare schemes and the Commonwealth's restricted powers in the area prior to World War Two would seem to be an obvious initial hypothesis. However, after 1946 the federation appeared to possess virtually all the constitutional power required to build an extensive and expensive welfare state. Some post-war expansion of social spending did occur, but the fact that much of the growth was delayed until the 1970s and that, by international standards, it was extremely modest suggests a weaker correspondence between constitutional change and expenditure development than might be expected. Locating the sources and mechanisms of discrepancies between the ostensible powers of the federation and the realities of social policy development provides us with a means of assessing federalism's impact on both the expansion and the contraction of the welfare state and its relative weight versus other causal influences.

Our analysis begins by identifying the institutional context of Australian politics as it emerged in the constitution of 1901. It proceeds with a discussion of the development of the Australian welfare state between 1900 and 1980, which seeks to untangle the wide range of factors impacting on that development. In particular, it attempts to locate reasons why the trajectory of Australian social security expenditure followed a different pattern from that of the 'old politics' of the welfare state as manifested in other western nations. This discussion helps to nuance our account of the correspondence between constitutional prescriptions and trajectories of social policy development and also permits us to consider the question of how far welfare state imperatives have had a reciprocal impact in modifying the institutions and practices of Australian federalism. Our account of the 'new politics' of the welfare state from 1980 onwards is much briefer. It focusses on the ways federal institutions have evolved in such a way as to frustrate pressures for social expenditure retrenchment. Our conclusion is not, however, an optimistic one in the vein of the 'new politics' literature, for we argue that resistance to expenditure retrenchment has been accompanied by the serious attrition of uniquely Australian institutions of social protection.

The federal settlement

The federal Constitution of the Commonwealth of Australia came into effect on 1 January 1901, bringing together the six former British colonies – New South Wales, Queensland, South Australia, Tasmania, Victoria and Western Australia – that had hitherto governed the island continent. These six colonies became Australia's original states and, although constitutional provision was made for creating new states, the only twentieth-century additions have been two territories – the Australian Capital Territory (the seat of federal government) and the Northern Territory, both with present-day populations of less than half a million and somewhat more limited powers of self-government.

The federal compact did not mark the beginning of democratic self-government on the Australian continent. From the 1850s onwards the colonies had evolved political systems based on manhood (and, in South Australia, from 1894, universal) suffrage and representative and responsible government moderated only by the conservative influence of property-franchised or nominated upper houses and the ultimate, but distant, suzerainty of the British Parliament.[2] The imperatives which brought colonial politicians to embrace the federal idea over the decade of the 1890s were threefold: the need to create an independent defence capability, the need to remove the vexation of tariff barriers between the colonies and the need to control immigration to Australia's shores.[3] Unlike most other nations that have come together to create federal political systems, the Australian population at the time of federation was extremely homogeneous,[4] divided neither by religion nor language and sharing a common culture in which strong adherence to the rule of law[5] was conjoined with 'a living tradition of parliamentary self-government, often sharpened and intensified by radical democratic ideas'.[6] The differences which, despite this remarkable homogeneity, made federation rather than unification the most appealing solution to the imperatives of the 1890s were essentially geographical (vast distances separating colonies when transport by sea was, in most instances, the most rapid means of communication), institutional (loyalties and inertia built around established governmental structures and policies) and economic (vested interests related to the established basis of each colony's production, commerce and trade).

Because the Australian Constitution was drawn up when it was, the founding fathers had the opportunity to consider and to borrow from existing federal constitutions. Understandably, the models foremost in their minds were those of the United States and Canada, the two other federations born of former British colonies. With one major exception, the template chosen was American rather than Canadian. However, the exception was hugely significant. Rather than adopt a separation of powers between legislature and executive wholly alien to the British system of

---

[2] See Paul D. Finn, *Law and Government in Colonial Australia* (Melbourne: Melbourne University Press, 1987).
[3] See Helen Irving, *To Constitute a Nation. A Cultural History of Australia's Constitution* (Cambridge: Cambridge University Press, 1999), pp. 79–86.
[4] Bruce W. Hodgkins, John J. Eddy, Shelagh D. Grant and James Struthers, eds., *Federalism in Canada and Australia: Historical Perspectives 1920–1988* (Peterborough: Forest Centre for Canadian Heritage and Development Studies, Trent University, 1989).
[5] See Martin Krygier, 'The Grammar of Colonial Legality: Subjects, Objects and the Australian Rule of Law', in Geoffrey Brennan and Francis G. Castles, eds., *Australia Reshaped: Essays on Two Centuries of Institutional Transformation* (Cambridge: Cambridge University Press, 2002), pp. 220–60.
[6] Lesley F. Crisp, *Australian National Government*, 3rd edn (Melbourne: Longman, 1967), p. 2.

parliamentary government, the architects of Australian federalism enshrined the practices of responsible and representative government with which they were familiar. The federal parliament was to consist of two chambers: a lower house, the House of Representatives, elected on the basis of territorial constituencies of roughly equal population size, and an upper house, the Senate, with an equal number of representatives elected from each state.

In direct conflict with the separation of powers doctrine, ministers were required to be members of one or other chamber of parliament. The constitution did not lay down rules for how the executive government would operate, assuming, no doubt, that the existing colonial and British practice of a government formed with the support of the majority in the lower house and a Prime Minister (a role unmentioned in the constitution) who was leader of the largest party constituting the majority would continue as before. In late nineteenth-century colonial practice, as well as in the early years after federation, parties were often fissiparous and party lines extremely malleable, encouraging considerable independence on the part of legislators. However, with caveats concerning the role of the Senate in recent decades to be discussed later, the main trend of twentieth-century Australian parliamentary practice has been towards a two-party system based on strong party discipline.[7] In consequence, the practice of executive government in Australia has experienced a substantially similar evolution from cabinet government to prime ministerial government as has occurred in the United Kingdom.[8]

Much of the recent debate on the relationship between federalism and the development of social policy has focussed on the impact of federalism in proliferating veto points and veto players in the political system in a manner that diminishes the system's capacity for policy change.[9] The fusion of legislature and executive inherent in parliamentary government clearly means that Australian federalism lacks one of the pivotal veto points of the American system. However, other constitutional features,

---

[7] For a discussion of this development and its consequences, see Ian Marsh, *Beyond the Two Party System* (Cambridge: Cambridge University Press, 1995), pp. 17–44.

[8] For a variety of perspectives on the evolution of the Australian prime ministership, see Patrick Weller, ed., *Menzies to Keating: The Development of the Australian Prime Ministership* (Melbourne: Melbourne University Press, 1998).

[9] This case has been variously elaborated in Ellen Immergut, *The Political Construction of Interests: National Health Insurance Politics in Switzerland, France and Sweden, 1930–1970* (Cambridge: Cambridge University Press, 1992); Evelyne Huber, Charles Ragin and John Stephens, 'Social Democracy, Christian Democracy, Constitutional Structure and the Welfare State', *American Journal of Sociology*, vol. 99 (1993), no. 3, pp. 711–49; George Tsebelis, 'Decision Making in Political Systems: Veto Players in Presidentialism, Parliamentarianism, Multicameralism and Multipartism', *British Journal of Political Science*, vol. 25 (1995), no. 3, pp. 289–325.

which the founding fathers borrowed from the American constitutional model, build in a whole series of veto points that have no counterpart in British parliamentary practice. These include an upper house whose powers nearly rival those of the lower house, a strong power of constitutional review, a method of constitutional amendment extremely difficult to implement and an enumerated set of Commonwealth powers leaving all unstipulated areas in the domain of the states.

The federal Senate can be regarded as being amongst the most powerful upper chambers in the democratic world. Although by convention the Prime Minister must come from the lower house, the only other restrictions on the legislative reach of the upper house are that it cannot introduce money bills or amend them. However, it can refuse and it has refused the government Supply, that is, the budgetary resources to continue the conduct of government. In 1974, by threatening to do so, it forced the Whitlam Labor government (the first Labor government for twenty-three years) to go to the polls for a fresh electoral mandate. In 1975, by refusing to pass the Supply bills required to implement the budget, it precipitated a constitutional crisis and the replacement of the government. More normally, the procedure for settling deadlocks between the houses is for the House of Representatives to pass a bill for a second time and return it to the Senate. If the bill is again defeated, the Governor-General (the monarch's representative in Australia) on the Prime Minister's advice may dissolve both houses, and if, following the resulting election, the Senate again fails to pass the legislation, the matter is settled by a joint meeting of both houses. For many commentators, viewing the practice of Australian government through the prism of the Westminster model, the strong powers of the Senate and its potential to frustrate the will of the lower house on whose majority the government rests is a serious anomaly in Australian parliamentary practice that undermines its claims to constitute a fully responsible system of government.

However, while it is true that the Senate is a key veto player in the Australian system, it is by no means necessarily the case that its role is democratically illegitimate or that it privileges state interests against wider Commonwealth concerns. Early interpretations of the relevant chapter of the constitution saw the Senate as a states house, but a more recent view is that what was intended by the stipulation that Senators should be 'directly chosen by the people of the State' was a duality of state and national citizenship inherent in the federal design.[10] The Labor Party has, in the past, favoured the abolition of the Senate, and its Prime Minister

---

[10] See Brian Galligan, *A Federal Republic: Australia's Constitutional System of Government* (Cambridge: Cambridge University Press, 1995), pp. 67–68.

from 1991 to 1996, Paul Keating, in a charmingly direct Australian way, described Senators as 'unrepresentative swill'. His successor, the Liberal Prime Minister John Howard also canvassed the case for a weakening of the Senate's powers of obstruction.

However, the case that the Senate is unrepresentative can only be made in principle. For fifty years the Senate has been elected by what is effectively a list system of proportional representation and its composition usually reflects the national distribution of votes rather more accurately than does the House of Representatives.[11] As a consequence of party system dominance, the Senate has been a party house rather than a states house for much of its existence, and what has made it a significant veto player on occasion has been that its party composition has differed from that of the House of Representatives. What makes it particularly significant for contemporary Australian politics, and possibly part of the explanation for why Australia has resisted the recent trend in the English-speaking world to welfare down-sizing, is that since 1980 very from governments have commanded an absolute majority in the Senate, giving third parties and independents a real capacity to block government initiatives. This is a topic taken up in the final section of this chapter.

The founding fathers modelled the High Court of Australia on the American Supreme Court, even toying with the idea of confirmation of appointment by the Senate, although in the end settling for the more parliamentary practice of appointment by the Governor-General on the advice of the government of the day. The Judiciary Act of 1903 implemented the constitution's intent by giving the High Court, consisting of a Chief Justice and six puisne or inferior judges, virtually exclusive jurisdiction over the interpretation of the constitution. The Judiciary Act saw one of the court's roles as offering advice to the government on the validity of Commonwealth legislation. However, the court itself rejected this Canadian practice as unconstitutional, satisfying itself with the American procedure of constitutional interpretation arising from the cases coming within its jurisdiction. The High Court is not bound by the precedent of its own previous decisions and views originally receiving only minority support have, on occasions, become those of a majority.

An important case in point for the prospects of an interventionist social policy was the celebrated Engineer's Case of 1920. Prior to that date the leading figures in the court were amongst the most prominent of the founding fathers of the constitution. Their tendency was to interpret the constitution broadly as a contract between the peoples of the several

---

[11] David W. Lovell, Ian McAllister, William Maley and Chandran Kukathas, *The Australian Political System* (Melbourne: Longman, 1995), pp. 47–49.

colonies, interpreting the balance between states and Commonwealth in terms of 'implied prohibitions' limiting the centralizing ambitions of the latter. By the early 1920s, however, a new generation of justices, some of them radicals who, in the 1890s, had pushed for stronger powers for the Commonwealth, had taken over the leadership of the court. They rejected the notion of the constitution as a contract, replacing it with a quasi-literalist reading without consideration of the possible implications for the federal balance. As Galligan notes, '[t]hat favoured the consolidation of national powers because now the Commonwealth's enumerated powers were to be read, with some minimal restrictions, in a full and plenary sense regardless of their impact on the States'.[12]

This trend of interpretation, which, with qualifications, continues to be the court's favoured reading of the constitution, was crucial to Commonwealth fiscal centralization in the first half of the twentieth century and, hence, to the creation of a national welfare state. That does not, however, mean that the High Court has invariably sided with the Commonwealth. In the 1940s it ruled against the Labor government's attempt to create a pharmaceutical benefits scheme and interpreted the Australian Constitution's section 92 insistence on 'absolutely free' trade amongst the states as restricting the Commonwealth's extension of its economic powers. The court has been neither a principled opponent of constitutional change nor a consistent sponsor of increased Commonwealth power. It has, however, played an extremely significant role in Australia's twentieth-century economic and social policy development.

Seemingly a more serious obstacle to change were the constitutional provisions relating to the amendment of the constitution itself. The amendment procedure is, provisions for citizen initiatives apart (which do not exist in Australia), modelled on those of the Swiss Constitution. Initiatives passed by an absolute majority of both houses of parliament (or one house, if passed for a second time) are submitted by the government of the day to a referendum of the electors of the states and territories and become part of the constitution if they receive a majority of votes in the federation as a whole as well as in a majority of states. While the founding fathers do not appear to have considered the constitutional document as finished business, this procedure has produced very few constitutional changes during Australia's first hundred years of federation. Of forty-three constitutional amendments put to the Australian people, only eight have received the requisite majorities and, of the plethora of mostly Labor-inspired proposals to extend the original powers granted

[12] Galligan, *Federal Republic*, p. 174.

to the Commonwealth, only that relating to the extension of the social services has been adopted.

A number of considerations help to explain this relative inability to change the Australian Constitution. The provision that the referendum pass in a majority of states gives a privileged position to those at state level who seek to maintain the status quo, and there is some evidence of patterns of state voting in referenda congruent with divergent perceptions of state interest.[13] More generally, the very fact that some policy initiatives require constitutional amendment invests them 'with a significance that other proposals do not have . . . [and] gives a strong advantage to those who wish to oppose the policies in question'.[14] Perhaps most important of all has been the influence of party and of party ideology. In the context of a two-party system, for the opposition to support a government's referendum proposal means effectively conceding their opponents an own goal. As a result, referendum proposals usually become a matter of party politics. In the case of Labor referendum proposals to extend the economic powers of the Commonwealth, that has been reinforced by the strong ideological antipathy not only of the conservative parties, but also of the economic interests which they represent. In the most recent period, either because of its history of futility in seeking to amend the constitution or because of its own increasing economic moderation, Labor has learned to live with federalism.[15] Its last attempt to extend the economic powers of the Commonwealth was in 1973.

From the point of view of the subsequent development of the welfare state in Australia, arguably the most significant aspect of the constitutional settlement was the division of powers between the states and the Commonwealth. Again, despite some debate in the constitutional conventions, the model adopted was American rather than Canadian practice, with a listing of Commonwealth competencies rather than state powers. The constitution enumerates only a very limited number of exclusive Commonwealth powers. These relate to the seat of government, the control of the Commonwealth public service and the right to impose customs and excise duties. The Commonwealth's control of these latter sources of taxation was, of course, integral to the purposes of federation and, given that such revenues constituted the bulk of colonial taxation, represented

---

[13] Campbell Sharman, 'Patterns of State Voting in the National Referendums', *Politics*, vol. 16 (1981), no. 2, pp. 261–70.
[14] P[ercy] H[erbert] Partridge, 'The Politics of Federalism', in Geoffrey Sawer, ed., *Federalism: An Australian Jubilee Study* (Melbourne: F. W. Cheshire, 1952), p. 190.
[15] See Brian Galligan and David Mardiste, 'Labor's Reconciliation with Federalism', *Australian Journal of Political Science*, vol. 27 (1992), no. 1, pp. 71–86.

an important first step on the road to fiscal centralization. This did not, however, mean that the Commonwealth got to spend the taxes it raised. Under the provisions of section 87, over the first ten years after federation the states were to receive three-quarters of the customs duties collected by the Commonwealth. This compromise was widely seen as the linchpin of the whole constitutional settlement, since it removed what one of the founding fathers described as the 'lion in the path' of federation, how to resolve the tariff question, by simultaneously creating the basis for a free trade area within the area of continental Australia while protecting the expenditure base of the former colonies. What subsequently became known as 'vertical fiscal imbalance' – a systematic disjuncture between the central government's powers to tax and the states' primacy in respect of expenditure – was effectively built into Australia's original constitutional settlement.

Section 51 lists most of the remaining powers of the Commonwealth parliament under thirty-nine headings. The wording of this section states only that the Commonwealth has the power to make laws on these matters, not that the states are proscribed from doing so. In principle, then, the majority of enumerated powers are concurrent, but some are monopolistic by their nature (obvious examples are external affairs, defence, coinage and weights and measures), while in other areas Commonwealth control is guaranteed by the provision of section 109 that '[w]hen a law of a State is inconsistent with a law of the Commonwealth, the latter shall prevail, and the former shall, to the extent of the inconsistency, be invalid'. Taxation other than customs and excise is an area in which the original intention was clearly concurrent, but where the Commonwealth has effectively monopolized the field. While there is no enumeration of state powers in the constitution, their residual powers are protected by section 107, which stipulates that, except in instances where the Commonwealth has exclusive powers, the powers of the states shall continue to be as they were at the establishment of the Commonwealth.[16] This division of powers has guaranteed the states a continuing strong role in service provision, especially in the areas of education, health and housing.[17] It has not, however, always ensured that the Commonwealth has kept out of the states' backyards. Quite the contrary. The combination

---

[16] At the time of federation, this was not seen as a conservative stipulation. See Gordon Greenwood, *The Future of Australian Federalism* (Melbourne: Melbourne University Press, 1946), pp. 47–48. Many on the Labor side saw the Senate as a barrier to change and felt that radical social reform was more likely to be enacted at state level. See Partridge, 'Politics of Federalism', p. 192.

[17] Compared with many other countries, the role of the states is further enhanced by the fact that local government is extremely weakly developed in Australia. See Ronald Mendelsohn, *The Condition of the People* (Sydney: Allen & Unwin, 1979), pp. 33–34.

of fiscal centralization and the seemingly innocent power given to the Commonwealth under section 96 'to grant financial assistance to any State on terms and conditions as the Parliament sees fit' has often given the Commonwealth the necessary leverage to persuade the states to implement national programmes in areas of ostensibly state competence under the constitution.

Commonwealth powers under section 51 include such matters as trade and commerce with other countries, military defence, coinage, weights and measures, naturalization and aliens, marriage and divorce, immigration and emigration, external affairs and relations with the islands of the Pacific. The list contains only three items that can even remotely be regarded as welfare state powers, all of them reflecting contemporary concerns. The only health power was that of quarantine, where the key issue was that of controlling devastating outbreaks of disease, such as bubonic plague, which was rampant in Sydney in the year the constitution was enacted. The only social services power in a modern sense was the power to make laws in respect of invalid and old age pensions. This provision was Germany's only direct contribution to the Australian Constitution. Its inclusion was an expression of the progressive view strongly represented at constitutional conventions that such concerns could no longer be seen as questions of charity appropriate to the domestic (and, hence, state) arena, but rather must be regarded as matters falling within the legitimate ambit of the national (and, hence, federal) regulation of a set of economic relations that now overstepped state boundaries.[18]

Regulation of the economic sphere was even more to the fore in the inclusion of the only remaining welfare power, the power to make laws with respect to '[c]onciliation and arbitration for the prevention and settlement of industrial disputes extending beyond the limits of any one State'. This power had its origins in the experience of serious industrial conflict between unions and employers in the Australasian colonies during the depression of the early 1890s, leading to the enactment of legislation providing for compulsory arbitration of industrial disputes in both South Australia and New Zealand. In 1904 the Commonwealth established a Commonwealth Court (in later times, Commission) of Conciliation and Arbitration, with the power to terminate industrial disputes by compulsory wage-setting. As will be shown later, this unusual power (not conferred by the constitution of any other federation) was to have momentous implications for the shape and subsequent development of the welfare state in Australia.

[18] Irving, *To Constitute a Nation*, pp. 94–96.

Overall, the constitutional settlement could hardly be regarded as promising for future welfare state development. The new constitution only gave extremely limited welfare powers to the Commonwealth, leaving areas such as hospitals, housing, charitable relief and education firmly in the hands of the states. Moreover, as the Labor Party rapidly found out in the early years after federation, there was little possibility of increasing the Commonwealth's economic powers by way of constitutional amendment. Finally, the main interest of the High Court was in preserving the existing federal balance, a stance that had already had deleterious effects on the development of social policy as judgement after judgement of the Arbitration Court was overturned through the process of judicial review. In the next section we seek to explore the main features of the historical evolution of the Australian welfare state from around 1900 to the late 1970s, focussing particularly on the twin questions of how the constitutional features we have described have influenced the emergence of social programmes and the growth of social expenditure, and whether there is evidence to support the reciprocal proposition that the social policy imperative has itself been a major factor in shaping the development and functioning of federal institutions.

Why no 'old politics' in Australia?

The term 'old politics of the welfare state' has been used to designate the political dynamic underlying the mass expansion of social security and social expenditure in the decades following World War Two. In the majority of western nations that dynamic was largely a matter of left and centre-left (and, in Europe, Christian-democratic) parties claiming credit with the electorate for enacting policies offering greater social security to working-class and white-collar constituencies. Australia, however, was not amongst them. With the exception of just a few years in the 1970s, Australian welfare growth lagged well behind that of other western nations, just as it had throughout the inter-war years. In 'old politics' terms, the obvious reason was the virtual absence of reforming governments of the left during these years. The question we address in this section is whether federal arrangements may also have contributed to this outcome.

Social expenditure trends

Australia's unusual course of social policy development can be formally charted using social expenditure data from 1900 onwards. Table 2.1 reports figures for total social welfare spending as percentages of GDP at

Table 2.1 *Australian welfare state spending (1900–1979)*

Year[1]	Total social spending as per cent of GDP	Per cent share of states	Per cent share of Commonwealth	Social security as per cent of GDP	Education as per cent of GDP	Health as per cent of GDP
1900–01	1.7	100	0	0.3	1.0	0.4
1910–11	1.9	69	31	0.7[a]	0.9[a]	0.3[a]
1920–21	4.0	44	56	2.1	1.3	0.5
1930–31	6.9	49	51	4.6	1.7	0.7
1940–41	5.2	50	50	3.5[b]	1.3[b]	0.6[b]
1950–51	7.0	30	70	4.3	1.2	1.5
1960–61	9.4	39	61	4.7[c]	2.0[c]	2.3[c]
1970–71	12.0	42	58	4.3	4.4	3.5
1978–79	19.1	30	70	8.2	6.1	4.8

[1] Australian financial years run from 1 July to 30 June.
[a] 1909–10.
[b] 1939–40.
[c] 1959–60.
Sources: Data to 1970 calculated from figures in a statistical appendix reporting data from relevant state and Commonwealth yearbooks in Ronald Mendelsohn, *The Condition of the People* (Sydney: Allen & Unwin, 1979). Corresponding figures for 1970 onwards from Ronald Mendelsohn, ed., *Australian Social Welfare Finance* (Sydney: Allen & Unwin, 1983), tables 2.1, 2.2 and 2.4.

ten-yearly intervals from 1900 to the late 1970s, together with percentage shares of state and federal spending and percentages of GDP devoted to social security, education and health for the same time points.

These figures tell us many important things about the broad trajectory of welfare spending in Australia. They tell us that, as in most other western nations, there was a massive expansion of aggregate social spending over the course of the twentieth century, although even with the spurt of the 1970s, this was quite insufficient to overtake even the OECD social expenditure rearguard. The figures also make clear that there was a no lesser change in the locus of expenditure control from state to federal auspices, with the most decisive shift occurring in the 1940s. Finally, they tell us that trajectories of growth were quite different for different items of expenditure. Social security expenditures went from almost nothing to just over 4 per cent of GDP during the first thirty years of federation, and went up by almost another four percentage points during the course of the 1970s. In the intervening period of forty years they did not increase at all, despite a major extension of Commonwealth powers in the area of social services provision. This plateau effect is entirely absent in the cases of education and health spending. These latter categories of expenditure grew slowly, if at all, during the first half of the century, but then expanded steadily from 1950–51 onwards. Paradoxically, then, the story of educational and health spending in Australia appears rather as one might expect on the basis of an 'old politics' of the welfare state account of the trajectory of post-war spending, while the growth path of social security expenditure, which that account was primarily designed to illuminate, appears altogether different.

Future portents

Despite the potentially conservative implications of their constitutional engineering, the idea that Australia might, by the second half of the twentieth century, have been regarded as being in the international rearguard of social reform is one that the founding fathers would, almost certainly, have regarded with total astonishment. In the last decade of the nineteenth century and the early years of the twentieth century Australia and New Zealand (a colony that had initially contemplated joining the Australian federation) were widely regarded, both at home and abroad, as being 'social laboratories' of progressive reform in the fields of democratic politics, labour relations and social welfare provision.[19] The colonies had been pioneers in inventing the secret ballot (widely known at the time as the 'Australian ballot'), had been in the vanguard in introducing representative and responsible government, and, in the 1890s, were again pioneers in giving women the vote. The first federal election in 1903 was conducted under a system of universal suffrage and has been seen as qualifying Australia as the world's first fully 'democratic' nation in the modern sense of the word.[20] In the area of labour relations, the battle for the eight-hour day had been won in some trades as early as the 1850s,[21] and was the Australian norm by the turn of the century. Following the great strikes of the early 1890s, all the colonies, together with the federation of Australia, had established judicial or quasi-judicial mechanisms for settling industrial disputes, either through arbitration courts or wages board systems. Nor were the Australian colonies laggards in the area of social security itself. Age pensions became a reality in New South Wales

---

[19] See Francis G. Castles, 'Social Laboratory', in Graeme Davison, John Hirst and Stuart Macintyre, eds., *The Oxford Companion to Australian History* (Oxford: Oxford University Press, 1998), pp. 592–93.
[20] See Göran Therborn, 'The Rule of Capital and the Rise of Democracy', *New Left Review*, vol. 103 (1977), no. 1, pp. 3–41.
[21] See Noel Ebbels, ed., *The Australian Labor Movement 1850–1907* (Sydney: Hale & Iremonger, 1983), pp. 58–72.

in 1900, in Victoria in 1901 and in Queensland in 1908. In 1909 all three schemes were superseded by the Commonwealth age pension using the power explicitly conferred by section 51 (xxiii) of the federal constitution for that purpose. A New South Wales invalidity pension of 1908 was superseded by a 1910 Commonwealth provision for an invalidity benefit for those above the age of 16 who were unable to work on the grounds of disablement or blindness. In 1912, in what, in retrospect, may be considered the last act of the progressive era, a federal Labor government, ignoring the restrictions imposed by the constitution, passed legislation providing lump sum maternity allowances to women on the birth of their children.

Contemporary commentators would also probably have seen the fact that this was the act of a labour government – in fact, the world's first majority labour government – as a portent of a radicalism yet to reveal its full potential. Although much of the colonies' social experimentation was a product of an admixture of 'radical' and 'social-liberalism',[22] Labor was rapidly achieving electoral prominence and, in the process, real policy leverage. Already in 1891 it had won 30 per cent of the lower house seats in New South Wales, declaring its guiding principle to be:

> Support in Return for Concessions. If you give us concessions, then our votes will circulate on the Treasury Benches; if you do not, then we shall withdraw our support. But we have not come to this House to make and unmake Ministries. We have come into this House to make and unmake social conditions.[23]

Although Labor had almost no hand in the constitution-making of the 1890s, in the period after federation it rapidly achieved a position in the Commonwealth parliament analogous to that it had earlier held in New South Wales, using its third-party leverage to good effect both in facilitating revenue arrangements for the federal pension and in extending the coverage of the federal arbitration system.

A probable future in which Labor held federal office in its own right seemed to promise still more in the way of progressive social policy, but this was not to happen in anything like the timeframe that contemporaries might have expected. In part, that was itself an indirect consequence of federalism, since much of federal Labor's radical energies during the next three decades were diverted to fighting losing battles for extending the economic and arbitration powers conferred by the constitution.[24] In part, it was simply a matter of bad luck, which, between 1914 and 1972,

---

[22] See Marian Sawer, *The Ethical State: Social Liberalism in Australia* (Melbourne: Melbourne University Publishing, 2003).
[23] George Black, *Parliamentary Debates* (NSW), vol. LII (1891), p. 126.
[24] See Crisp, *Australian National Government*, pp. 148–51.

ordained that Labor would hold office only during World War One, the Great Depression and World War Two and its immediate aftermath, thus never enjoying a period free of the pressures of external events. For those who subscribe to the 'politics matters' school of explanation, Australia is a crucial test case.[25] More than any other modern state, it manifests a disjunction between the salience of class politics (Labor had a consistently strong electoral showing and strong union support throughout this period) and the extent of democratic-socialist incumbency (Labor was rarely in office at a federal level and never at the right time).[26] For those who see democratic-socialist incumbency as an important determinant of social policy development, federal Labor's difficulties in securing and holding on to political office in the five decades from 1920 to 1970 provide an obvious counter-explanation to the constraining impact of federalism in accounting for the slow pace of Australian social security development.

If the prospects for radical politics turned out badly, two other early portents had a more ambivalent legacy. Australian pensions legislation was pioneering in a variety of ways. Before the 1900 New South Wales legislation, only Denmark (1891) and New Zealand (1898) had introduced schemes offering benefits on a non-contributory basis. Moreover, the New South Wales legislation, unlike that of Denmark, gave no discretion to the authorities as to the form of the pension or its amount in individual cases. Like all early non-contributory benefit schemes, the NSW pension was means tested, but again contrary to practice elsewhere, benefits were payable even when the applicant had some minor income from another source and quite considerable assets in the form of property.[27] The Commonwealth age pensions legislation retained all these features, as have the vast majority of social security schemes enacted in Australia since that day.[28] For those who see social security development in terms of path dependent growth, Australia constitutes what is, perhaps, the best example. The legacy is ambivalent because it left Australia with the most means-tested social security system in the world, but also,

---

[25] See Francis G. Castles, *The Working Class and Welfare* (Sydney: Allen & Unwin, 1985).
[26] This latter was not true in the states. At various times, Queensland, Tasmania and New South Wales have experienced long-term Labor hegemony of almost Scandinavian dimensions.
[27] For details of this and the Commonwealth scheme, see T[homas] H[enry] Kewley, *Social Security in Australia: The Development of Social Security and Health Benefits from 1900 to the Present* (Sydney: Sydney University Press; London: Methuen, 1965), pp. 43–95.
[28] The unusual coherence of Australian social security provision is noted in Helen Bolderson and Deborah Mabbett, 'Mongrels or Thoroughbreds: A Cross-National Look at Social Security Systems', *European Journal of Political Research*, vol. 28 (1995), no. 1, pp. 19–39.

arguably, the means-tested system with the least discretionary and least residual emphasis, offering flat-rate benefits to the vast majority of ordinary Australians and excluding only those with incomes and assets well above community norms. Irrespective of how one evaluates such a system, the fact that it provides only flat-rate payments on a selective basis must help to explain why the trajectory of growth of social security expenditure in Australia over the course of the twentieth century has been less expansive than it has in most other nations.

Giving the Commonwealth the power to legislate on conciliation and arbitration also had important implications for the future of the welfare state in Australia. A Commonwealth Court was established in 1904 and, by 1907, its second President, Mr Justice Higgins, was arguing that the only appropriate standard for a 'fair and reasonable' wage was one providing for 'the normal needs of the average employee, regarded as a human being living in a civilized community'.[29] Using this quite ostensibly social policy criterion, the High Court established the minimum or 'living' wage as one that would support a family of four or five in modest comfort.[30] From the time when this judgement was delivered until well into the 1980s, the Commonwealth arbitration system has been the central focus of wage-fixing in Australia, either through its direct control of outcomes where workers from more than one state were involved or because state tribunals came to adopt its wage-setting standards. The use of Commonwealth powers in the industrial arena has always been extremely controversial and the scope of those powers has been much influenced by successive High Court decisions over many decades, in the early years after federation, restricting the ambit of federal wage-setting[31] but, in the years thereafter, much extending its reach.[32] However, the legacy of federal arbitration was once again an ambivalent one, since, to the extent that the 'living wage' succeeded in raising the wages floor, and, thereby, compressing the overall distribution of incomes, it was doing things that in other climes and later times were to be functions of advanced social security systems. The underlying premise of a wage determination system

---

[29] Henry B[ournes] Higgins, *A New Province for Law and Order: Being a Review, by its Late President for Fourteen Years, of the Australian Court of Conciliation and Arbitration* (London: Dawsons of Pall Mall, 1965), p. 3; originally published in 1922.

[30] Higgins also based his decision of a 42 shillings a week minimum for an unskilled man on a sort of amateur poverty line calculation, arguing that this was the least sum that could provide for 'light, clothes, boots, furniture, utensils, rates, life insurance, savings, accident or benefit societies, loss of employment, union pay, books and newspapers, tram or train fares, sewing machine, mangle, school requisites, amusements and holidays, liquors, tobacco, sickness or death, religion or charity' for a family of this size; ibid., p. 4.

[31] Robin Gollan, *Radical and Working Class Politics* (Melbourne: Melbourne University Press, 1960), pp. 205–06.

[32] Mendelsohn, *Condition of the People*, p. 142.

that was effective in achieving its social policy goals was that, for wage earners at least, it could make the welfare state unnecessary.

Marking time

There is widespread consensus among domestic commentators that, between the world wars, the Australian welfare state was marking time. Typical are accounts in terms of a shift in emphasis from the encouragement of 'social experimentation' to the promotion of 'material development',[33] of an era of 'disappointment, loss of vision and loss of national will'[34] and of a time in which 'Australia was left behind and exposed . . . by its incapacity to cope with mass unemployment'.[35] Arguably, the picture is a little more mixed than these judgements imply. Certainly it is true that, with the exception of the establishment of a system of repatriation benefits for returned servicemen after 1918,[36] the Commonwealth failed to move into any major new fields of social provision. No less certainly, the lack of a concerted strategy to ameliorate the poverty caused by unemployment was a disaster in the early 1930s, when almost one in three Australian men were out of work. Relief for the unemployed remained throughout a state responsibility, with most states relying on a mixture of food relief and public works activity of a non-productive kind. This was an area where Australia was quite unequivocally behind most other nations of the time.[37] Nor were the deficiencies of the inter-war welfare state simply a question of sins of omission. In the early 1930s pension rates for the aged, for invalids and even for returned servicemen were reduced and maternity allowances became subject to means testing. While these cutbacks occurred in the context of mass unemployment and compulsory wage reductions across the board, they were clearly attacks on those who were already vulnerable.

On the other hand, there were also some positive developments. A number of states introduced their own social security schemes covering a limited range of eventualities. Queensland established a contributory

[33] Gordon Greenwood, *Australia: A Social and Political History* (Sydney: Angus & Robertson, 1978), p. 298.
[34] Mendelsohn, *Condition of the People*, p. 44.
[35] Jill Roe, 'Social Policy and the Permanent Poor', in E[dward] L[awrence] Wheelwright and Ken Buckley, eds., *Essays in the Political Economy of Australian Capitalism*, vol. I (Sydney: Australia and New Zealand Book Company, 1975), pp. 130–52, p. 141.
[36] This was no minor exception in expenditure terms. Between the financial years 1918/19 and 1925/26 expenditure on repatriation benefits was as great as or greater than the sum of age and invalidity pension expenditure. After World War Two repatriation was once again a substantial component of the welfare budget. See Mendelsohn, *Condition of the People*, p. 142.
[37] See Stuart Macintyre, *Winners and Losers* (Sydney: Allen & Unwin, 1985), p. 63.

system of unemployment insurance in 1923 and New South Wales introduced exchequer-funded widows' pensions in 1926 and child endowment in 1927. In terms of its ultimate significance, even more important was the further extension of the Commonwealth arbitration power permitted by the High Court's abandonment of 'implied prohibitions', with cost-of-living indexation of the 'living' wage and the inclusion of paid sick leave in employment contracts[38] being major advances occurring in the early 1920s. Finally, one must note that domestic commentators have tended to judge Australia's inter-war stagnation against the benchmark of its radical past. However, in terms of cross-national relativities, there were areas in which Australia was doing reasonably well. Since the provision of paid sick leave quickly became a feature of both federal and state wage awards, this conclusion almost certainly applies in the case of compulsory sickness coverage, even though Australia as yet had no formal social security scheme in this area. Despite the benefits cuts of the early 1930s, it is also the case in respect of age pensions, which, in the years immediately preceding World War Two, had coverage and replacement rates that were appreciably higher than in the majority of comparable overseas nations.[39] Since very few of these countries had introduced invalidity benefits, and since the invalidity pension rate was the same as the age pension rate, a similar conclusion would appear to be appropriate in this area also.

The absence of new Commonwealth programmes during this period cannot be attributed to a lack of parliamentary interest in social security matters or even to an absence of legislative endeavour. In the 1920s there was serious discussion of the introduction of a Commonwealth child endowment or family allowances, which was only abandoned as infeasible on the majority recommendation of a Royal Commission set up to consider the scheme. A Commonwealth unemployment scheme was also discussed, although it was taken no further. In 1929 and 1938 bills were introduced into parliament with the aim of establishing contributory social insurance schemes largely modelled on the British National Insurance Acts of 1911 and 1925, although in the Australian case unemployment insurance was excluded from the proposed legislation. Both of these bills were sponsored by conservative coalition governments, the first

[38] See Francis G. Castles, 'On Sickness Days and Social Policy', *Australian and New Zealand Journal of Sociology*, vol. 28 (1992), no. 1, pp. 29–44.
[39] In 1939 the average proportion of the population over 65 receiving pensions in fourteen European and New World countries was 40 per cent. In Australia, it was 54 per cent. The average figure for the after tax replacement rate pensions as a percentage of net wages was 15.5 per cent. In Australia it was 19 per cent. For these figures, see Gøsta Esping-Andersen, *The Three Worlds of Welfare Capitalism* (Cambridge: Polity Press; Princeton: Princeton University Press, 1990), p. 99.

lapsing because of an imminent general election, the second actually passing both houses of parliament before being indefinitely postponed because of the impending threat of war.

It might easily have seemed to contemporaries that contributory social insurance was an idea likely to come into its own in the inter-war period. Opinion in the first decade of the twentieth century had decreed that contribution was unlikely to work in Australia because of the large number of itinerant workers. However, quite soon the non-Labor parties were beginning to be concerned about the impact of exchequer funding in reducing thrift and, by 1913, a national insurance scheme had already become part of the electoral programme of the Liberal Party. The lineal descendents of the Liberal Party, first the National Party and then the United Australia Party, were in office for all but two years of the two decades following the First World War. Moreover, questions of cost were becoming as salient as those of thrift and moral virtue. How to fund the increasing exchequer cost of pensions became a matter of concern to politicians of all persuasions and a major preoccupation of the Royal Commission on National Insurance, on whose recommendations the 1929 proposed legislation was based. In that year pensions took up 13.1 per cent of total budget expenditure, an amount almost precisely equivalent to total Commonwealth income tax receipts for the year. By 1938, when there was a second attempt to legislate, pensions expenditure was in excess of 18 per cent.[40]

Without question, the major difficulty of investigating the expenditure-constraining effects of federalism is that it requires establishing why events did not take place. However, in the case of the abortive welfare initiatives of the inter-war period in Australia, we are assisted by the extensive discussions and debates these initiatives inspired. On this basis we can distinguish a variety of factors which combine to account for the welfare state passivity of the period. One, clearly, was the federal division of powers. In the case of child endowment, the issue was straightforwardly whether the Commonwealth had the necessary powers. When the Royal Commission reported in 1928, it was only two years since a referendum to give the Commonwealth full industrial powers had failed decisively,[41] and the Commission believed that such powers were essential to the adequate functioning of a system of family allowances.[42] In

---

[40] These figures come from Kewley, *Social Security in Australia*, p. 134.
[41] Interestingly, in light of the general tendency to see the Labor Party as the initiator of attempts to centralise the Australian Constitution, this was a referendum sponsored by a non-Labor government.
[42] The problem was that the 'living wage' was designed to provide for a husband, wife and two or three children. However, the only way in which child allowances could be

general, however, the issue was less one of divided powers than of anxieties and implicit demarcation lines born of those powers, with the Commonwealth seeking to avoid taking on new responsibilities and, in particular, new expenditures, and the states viewing with suspicion proposals initiated at a federal level.[43] This is not to say that the states and Commonwealth did not discuss such questions. In fact, all the proposals for welfare reform were raised and thoroughly debated at Conferences of Commonwealth and State Ministers held at regular intervals. It is just that here, as on many other matters, views were substantially conditioned by the way participants interpreted their own and others' institutionally defined concerns.

For 'politics matters' theorists, another seemingly obvious part of the explanation for welfare passivity has to be that Labor was out of federal office for all but two years of the inter-war period, with the potential impact of the incumbency factor further underlined by the fact that all the state initiatives in the social security field that did take place in these years occurred where Labor held the reins of office. A more idiosyncratically Australian factor delaying progress towards social insurance along European lines was opposition to the contributory principle on the grounds that employee contributions effectively meant a tax on the 'living wage'. Since a no lesser body than the Commonwealth Court of Conciliation and Arbitration had defined the 'living wage' as the minimum required for 'civilized existence', it was hardly likely that reductions in take-home pay would be acceptable to trade unions seeking to protect wage-earner interests. Moreover, given the peculiar logic of the arbitration system, this was an opposition shared with some employers, who were concerned that employee insurance contributions would be seen by the wage-fixing authorities as a reason for increasing award wages by an equivalent amount. Finally, there were other interests opposed to particular schemes, with friendly societies particularly prominent in criticizing the 1920s variant of national insurance and medical pressure groups the 1930s variant. However, the 1938 Act demonstrates that, by itself, an interest group account is not enough. The proposed legislation brought together trade unions, employers and doctors in opposition,

---

introduced without prohibitive expense would have been for state and Commonwealth wage awards to be modified so that they no longer made automatic provision for the needs of children. Clearly, such a move would have been strongly contested by the trade unions at both state and federal level. This episode is an illustration of the way in which policy pre-emption can limit the scope for subsequent federal social policy intervention, although, in this instance, the prior occupant of the relevant policy space was not another level of government, but rather the quasi-judicial authority of the Court of Arbitration.

[43] See Kewley, *Social Security in Australia*, pp. 165–69, for a full discussion of this point.

and it alienated other important sectional interests, whose constituencies were excluded from coverage (small farmers and the self-employed),[44] but party discipline ensured that the legislation duly passed in both houses of parliament. Although proving negatives is again a problem, it would seem that all that saved Australia from a national insurance along British lines was the advent of war.

Federal departures

Although the years prior to World War Two were a lean time for the Australian welfare state, there were institutional departures in this period that were to be important in underpinning a more interventionist Commonwealth role in the years thereafter. By a Financial Agreement between the states and the Commonwealth in 1927, ratified by referendum in the following year, the Australian Loan Council was established. This gave the Commonwealth exclusive power to raise governmental loans in return for taking over existing state debts and agreeing to pay a stipulated sum towards their servicing, with the states paying the remainder. The centralizing impact of this agreement was rapidly demonstrated when, during the Great Depression, the High Court ruled that the Commonwealth had first call on a state's revenues should it default on its interest payments. A second institutional innovation was the Commonwealth Grants Commission, established in 1933. This was a further attempt to adjust the revenue basis of the federation, made transparently fragile by the economic realities of the time. The smaller states had always needed Commonwealth assistance to provide services on anything like the same scale as the more populous states, but their predicament was now much exacerbated by the need to fund unemployment relief on a massive scale. The role of the Commission was to recommend additional funding under circumstances where a state could not discharge its functions as a member of the federation, with the degree of assistance being 'determined by the amount of help found necessary to make it possible for the State by reasonable effort to function at a standard not appreciably below that of other States'.[45] This principle of federal distribution to the states in proportion to 'fiscal need' was ultimately to become a doctrine of 'fiscal equalization', making Australia, arguably, 'the most equalizing federalist system in the world'.[46]

---

[44] See Michael Anthony Jones, *The Australian Welfare State: Growth, Crisis and Change* (Sydney: Allen & Unwin, 1983), pp. 42–44.
[45] Commonwealth Grants Commission, *Third Report* (Canberra: AGPS, 1936), p. 75.
[46] The quotation is from Edward M. Gramlich, '"A Fair Go": Fiscal Federalism Arrangements', in Richard E. Caves and Lawrence B. Krause, eds., *The Australian Economy: A View from the North* (Washington, DC: Brookings Institution Press, 1984),

The decisive step towards complete Commonwealth fiscal domination was a wartime development. The constitution had initially granted the Commonwealth a monopoly of excise duties, the major revenue source of early twentieth-century Australia. Now, in 1942, a new wartime Labor administration gave the Commonwealth what amounted to a monopoly of income taxation by levying uniform income taxes throughout the Commonwealth and reimbursing to the states a sum equivalent to their former revenues on the condition that they vacated this area of taxation. Although this action was challenged by the states on a number of occasions both during and after the war, the High Court consistently ruled that the Commonwealth's actions fell within the scope of its concurrent taxing powers under section 53 and its power to attach conditions to grants to the states made in accordance with section 96. Moreover, the court was quite explicit in concluding that, by attaching conditions to grants, the Commonwealth would always succeed in getting its own way, with the only remedy 'to be found in the political arena and not in the courts'.[47] From the point of view of understanding the subsequent development of the Australian welfare state, this development is hugely significant. It explains why the combination of fiscal centralization and the section 96 power was ultimately to become so important in extending the social service functions of the states once Labor again belatedly achieved Commonwealth office in the 1970s and 1980s. At the same time, it suggests that the almost glacial pace of social security expenditure development in the intervening years cannot readily be attributed to any fundamental lack of constitutional authority on the part of the federal government.

This latter explanation is further reinforced by the fact that war was not merely the occasion for further fiscal centralization, but also for an extension of Commonwealth social services and Commonwealth social services powers. This process began in 1941, when a conservative coalition government introduced a child endowment scheme, funded by a payroll tax, which, by excluding the first child, helped overcome at least some of the differences with the states that had frustrated earlier attempts. Also in 1941, the coalition appointed a Joint Parliamentary Committee on Social Security, which, in a long series of largely unanimous reports, recommended a very substantial extension of Commonwealth social service

---

pp. 231–74, p. 231, who sees fiscal redistribution on this scale as a major source of economic inefficiency. A much more positive view is to be found in Russell Matthews, 'Fiscal Equalisation: Political, Economic and Social Linchpin of Federation', Inaugural Russell Matthews Lecture (Canberra: ANU, Federalism Research Centre, May 1994).

[47] *South Australia v. Commonwealth* (First Uniform Tax Case) (1942) 65 CLR (Commonwealth Law Reports) 373, p. 429.

provision. Many of these measures were implemented by the Coalition's Labor successor, which took office in the following year and governed for the next eight years. Widows' pensions were introduced in 1942, partly as a trade-off to the states for their reduction in taxing powers. In 1943 a funeral benefits scheme was introduced as the next instalment of what the Labor government now described as a 'national welfare scheme' to be funded from a National Welfare Fund established from the Commonwealth's newly acquired tax resources. In 1944 legislation was passed establishing unemployment, sickness and pharmaceutical benefits schemes. With the exception of the child endowment scheme, the coverage of which was universal, all other benefits introduced in the wartime period were flat rate and means tested in the by now accustomed Australian fashion.

The outer limits of the new welfare consensus stopped at issues of health and freedom of medical practice. The pharmaceutical benefits scheme was strongly opposed by the non-Labor parties and by the medical profession, which regarded it as the thin end of the wedge of a nationalized health service. In 1945 the High Court declared the legislation to be invalid in terms suggesting that a challenge to other existing social services schemes might also be successful. Labor's response was to initiate a successful referendum campaign aimed at extending the social services powers of the Commonwealth to cover all the new wartime welfare measures as well as 'dental and medical services (but not so as to authorize any form of civil conscription)'.[48] Although the constitutional amendment of 1946 secured the status of existing social services, it did not protect further pharmaceutical benefits legislation passed by Labor in 1947, which, after further amendment designed to force a still resistant medical profession to comply with its provisions, was adjudged by the High Court in 1949 to constitute a form of civilian conscription and, hence, to be unconstitutional. Further legislation in 1948 to establish a National Health Service was no less militantly opposed by the non-Labor parties and by the Australian Medical Association and lapsed with the electoral defeat of the Labor government in December 1949.

The implications of this episode are ambiguous. On the one hand, it constitutes a clear example of a major Australian interest organization successfully manipulating constitutional veto points in order to limit the scope of welfare state reform. On the other hand it offers, perhaps, the only really good example we have of successful activity of this kind in Australia and one that contrasts sharply with the failure of a wider array of interests to stop the enactment of the 1938 social insurance

---

[48] The Commonwealth of Australia Constitution Act, section 51 (xxiiiA).

legislation. It therefore leaves open the issue of whether this particular episode reveals the visible tip of the iceberg of a mechanism through which federalism has limited the development of the welfare state in Australia or whether it is the exception that proves the rule. Indeed, the ambiguity is further compounded. Possibly underlining the exceptional character of such activity in an Australian context is the fact that the interest group in question is one with a long-established and internationally proven track record of using federal institutional arrangements to limit the scope of public intervention in the area of their practice.[49] However, accounting for the Australian exception in this way simply creates another mystery, with the question being why federal institutions in so many countries have proved so vulnerable to pressure from this source.

There is also some ambiguity in what the federal departures of this era tell us about the role of the welfare state in modifying and reshaping federal arrangements. A simplistic account might see the close coincidence of the Commonwealth's acquisition of enhanced taxing powers and the introduction of a whole raft of social services schemes bringing Australia up to speed with social policy practice in other western nations as evidence that popular pressures for the expansion of the welfare state had at last been victorious over the strictures of a conservative constitution. However, such an interpretation ignores the context of total war within which both developments occurred. In terms of the intentions of real historical actors, a more convincing account is of the Commonwealth seeking greater fiscal control in order to finance the war effort, and of using a rhetoric of social policy reform to justify a substantially increased tax burden falling mainly on ordinary wage earners hitherto untouched by income taxation.[50]

But this account also misses something. The very fact that wartime governments focussed their rhetoric around the theme of increased income security was an acknowledgement of the potency of that appeal. Comparative research has shown how the fiscal demands of total war prepare the way for post-war, public expenditure growth[51] and how wartime solidarity translates into more expansive social solidarity thereafter.[52] Similar forces were at work in Australia. Creating a 'national welfare scheme'

---

[49] See on this topic Immergut, *Political Construction of Interests*.
[50] For this argument see Robb Watts, *The Foundations of the National Welfare State* (Sydney: Allen & Unwin, 1987). See also Kewley, *Social Security in Australia*, p. 244.
[51] See Alan Peacock and Jack Wiseman, *The Growth of Public Expenditure in the United Kingdom*, 2nd edn (London: Allen & Unwin, 1967).
[52] Robert Goodin and John Dryzek, 'Risk Sharing and Social Justice: The Motivational Foundations of the Post-War Welfare State', *British Journal of Political Science*, vol. 16 (1986), no. 1, pp. 1–34.

when welfare need was at an all-time low may have been cynical, and establishing a National Welfare Fund from tax revenues rather than from contributions may have been disingenuous, but after the war there was no turning back. The Commonwealth, despite occasional promises to the contrary, had no intention of returning income tax powers to the states and, more than ever, needed the justification that it was providing essential services in return for its fiscal hegemony.[53] By the same token, repeal of the new social services provisions would have been electoral suicide. In this sense, it is probably fair to conclude that, while war was the immediate occasion for the departures under consideration here, it was popular sentiment favouring welfare reform that underpinned these changes and made them, effectively, irreversible.

A balance of probabilities

We finally arrive at the period of the 'old politics' proper, the post-war era in which in most western nations social expenditure began to expand extremely rapidly. As table 2.1 shows, this was not the case in Australia. The expenditure gradient for social expenditure in the two decades 1950–51 to 1970–71 only appears steep – the five percentage points change being equivalent to a 71 per cent increase in overall spending – because spending levels were so very low to start with. During these decades there was absolutely no change in the proportion of national product going to social security programmes, health expenditure increased only modestly as the conservative government in power sought to build a health system based largely on subsidizing private insurance and only educational spending kept up with trends overseas. During the course of the 1970s, however, there was a more than 50 per cent increase in total social expenditure measured as a percentage of GDP, a doubling of social security effort from 4.3 per cent to 8.2 per cent of GDP and not inconsiderable increases in both health and education spending. Understandably, then, from a domestic perspective, Australian commentators have tended to regard the 1970s, and, in particular, the years of the Whitlam Labor government from 1972 to 1975, as a period of welfare state catch-up after a long era of public expenditure stagnation presided over by a conservative Liberal–Country Party coalition.

---

[53] Because of the activities of the Commonwealth Grants Commission, this was an argument with a surprisingly strong appeal to the smaller states. See Julie Smith, 'Financing the Federation: From the Federation Debates to 1970', in Jim Hancock and Julie Smith, eds., *Financing the Federation* (Adelaide: South Australian Centre for Economic Studies, 2001), pp. 5–43 (see http://www.adelaide.edu.au/saces/publications/other/Financingthe Federation.pdf).

In fact, apart from education, the extent of catch-up with the world outside was relatively modest. The OECD uses the term 'social protection' to denote the combined total of social security and health spending. In 1970, in a grouping of nineteen OECD countries, only Japan spent less than Australia on social protection as a proportion of GDP.[54] At the high point of Australian spending later in the decade, the only other country Australia had managed to overtake was Greece. In 1970 only three of the nineteen nations spent a lower proportion of GDP on public health than Australia. Eight years on, the tally was four, with Australia spending 89 per cent of the OECD mean as compared to 79 per cent previously. Social security catch-up was marginally more impressive in terms of movement towards the mean, although from a much lower base. In 1970 the only OECD country spending less on social security than Australia was Japan. By the end of the period, Australia had increased spending as a proportion of GDP from 42 to 58 per cent of the OECD average, but had only succeeded in putting one more country between itself and the bottom of the OECD expenditure league table. In contrast, the change in Australia's comparative standing in education was genuinely impressive. Although educational spending had increased faster than other categories of expenditure in the immediate post-war decades, the Australian figure remained well below the mean for this group of countries in 1970. Eight years on, with 6.3 per cent of GDP devoted to education, Australia was amongst the West's biggest spenders in this area of provision, only just missing out a place in the top quartile.[55]

A comprehensive comparative analysis would be required to establish the factors responsible for Australia's trajectory of welfare state development in this period. In its absence, the historical case-study approach employed here can only identify candidate variables, which, on the basis of an analysis of the sequencing of events and/or the immanent logic of social policy development, can be seen as contributing to an understanding of the phenomenon in question. As between these candidate variables, the further question of which contributed to the greatest degree and which more slightly can, at best, be established as a balance of probabilities, always open to further interpretation in the light of a closer reading of the historical record. Here we suggest that there are four strong candidates for explaining Australian welfare performance in the decades following World War Two and seek to identify their respective roles in shaping

---

[54] All OECD data on social protection, health and social security spending cited in this paragraph are from or calculated from OECD, *New Orientations for Social Policy*, Social Policy Studies no.12 (Paris: OECD, 1994), pp. 57–58.

[55] The educational spending data on which these calculations are based are from UNESCO, *Unesco Statistical Yearbook* (Paris: UNESCO, 1972 and 1981).

post-war developments. Since, ultimately, we believe that all four variables have at least some bearing on observed outcomes, we do not discuss them as rival accounts, but rather as a series of components needed to construct a reasonably complete account of what happened to the Australian welfare state in these years.

Federalism was an important factor, but one that should, for the most part, be regarded as an antecedent condition rather than an immediate cause of much that occurred in the post-war period. Clearly, the absence of Commonwealth social services powers prior to the 1940s, and the federal–state anxieties and demarcation lines to which that gave rise, are parts of the explanation for the late start for most social security schemes, which, in turn, helps to account for the initially low levels of spending of most of these schemes at the beginning of the post-war era. Catch-up is all the harder when one starts out so far behind the eight ball. Arguably too, in areas such as health and education, where the states were the major providers, the Commonwealth's quasi-monopoly of taxation was a potentially important background condition for appraising proposals for the extension of services, since the states could only expand provision by pressuring the Commonwealth to tax more or, at least, to direct more tax revenues to the states. Finally, federal arrangements played an extremely significant part in the medical profession's successful attack on Labor schemes for 'socialized medicine' in the second half of the 1940s, and this prepared the way for a coalition health policy in the 1950s and 1960s built around subsidizing private health insurance and providing hospital treatment on a means-tested basis. In the early 1970s medical pressure groups again used all available constitutional levers in seeking – ultimately unsuccessfully – to frustrate Labor's next attempt to introduce a publicly funded national health service.[56]

Federal arrangements cannot, on the other hand, easily account for the absence of expenditure growth in the early post-war decades, because, already by the late 1940s, the Commonwealth possessed all the fiscal and spending powers that were later to be used by the Whitlam government to expand expenditure so rapidly. This, in particular, applies to the combined use of the Commonwealth's monopoly over income taxation and its reliance on the section 96 power to require the states to comply with federally imposed conditions in order to obtain Commonwealth grants. In the 1960s Whitlam had been a vociferous opponent of federalism in the old Labor tradition; by 1972 he was preaching a 'new federalism', which was to use special purpose grants as a means of funding reforms in

---

[56] The legislation was twice rejected by the Senate before becoming one of a number of defeated bills used by the government to justify a double dissolution of parliament in 1974.

health, education and in urban and regional planning.[57] It is clear that it was not constitutional obstacles that prevented Whitlam's Liberal predecessors from employing such methods to expand social policy spending, since the Liberals had no hesitation in using them to expand university funding and to extend state aid to independent schools. Using the same powers in the health and community services arenas, as Whitlam was to do in the 1970s, was simply not on the Liberal policy agenda in the 1950s and 1960s.

The question is why not, and the obvious answer is because the Liberals and their coalition partner, the Country Party, were conservative parties that were ideologically opposed to the extension of public spending. While the impact of federalism contributes to our understanding of why expenditure levels were so low in the early post-war period, a 'politics matters' account appears to offer the most convincing account of the post-war trajectory of Commonwealth social spending. Between 1950–51 and 1970–71 there was no increase in social security spending and the trend of health spending was rather modest in comparison with other OECD countries. Between 1949 and 1972 a Liberal–Country Party government was continuously in office, the longest period of uninterrupted majority rule by a right-wing government in a democratic western nation in the post-war era. Labor was elected in 1972 and, during the next three years, all categories of social expenditure increased substantially. After 1975, with the Liberals back in office, expenditure growth slowed markedly, peaking in 1977, and did not resume its upward trend, albeit then more slowly, until the election of the Hawke Labor government in 1983 (see table 2.2 below). Overall, the coincidence of party control and social expenditure trajectory is as close as in any country in the OECD during the post-war decades, and extending the series backwards to cover the inter-war period appears to strengthen the association further.

Finally, we turn to what is perhaps the greatest anomaly of all: why Australia experienced no expansion in social expenditure as a percentage of GDP in precisely the years when it was growing fastest elsewhere. Party incumbency alone seems insufficient to explain this impact, which is so much more pronounced than in most other countries experiencing substantial periods of right-wing hegemony. Indeed, the only country with a comparable social security record in this period was non-federal, but decidedly right-wing New Zealand,[58] which shares two further characteristics with Australia: namely, a highly selective social policy

---

[57] See Peter Groenewegen, 'Federalism', in Allan Patience and Brian Head, eds., *From Whitlam to Fraser* (Oxford: Oxford University Press, 1979), pp. 50–69, pp. 56–57.

[58] New Zealand was the only OECD country in which social security spending as a percentage of GDP actually declined markedly in the 1960s. OECD, *New Orientations for Social Policy*, p. 57.

resting exclusively on flat rate and means-tested benefits and a wages system based on arbitrated wage minima. A strongly selective social policy provided a logic of expenditure growth, which, under the circumstances of ultra full employment prevailing in the 1950s and 1960s, was most unlikely to lead to increased spending as a percentage of GDP. For expenditure effort measured in this way to increase, benefits rates had either to be increasing faster than the rate of real GDP growth or benefit eligibility had to be increasing markedly. The first was within the control of the government, the second was minimized by the conjunction of large-scale immigration, full employment and high economic growth that characterized Australia at the time. Indeed, taking these factors into account, there was actually some room for the Liberal governments of the 1950s and 1960s to liberalize means tests in response to demands from the conservative parties' own middle-class constituencies.[59]

By itself, however, selectivity is probably not a sufficient explanation of social security inaction. There are a number of nations with a strong selectivity bias, but, other than in Australia and New Zealand, this did not wholly prevent social security growth during this period. What seems to have made the vital difference in Australia and New Zealand was that the wages system produced a logic of collective action that substantially reduced the probability of organized working-class protest against the structure and generosity of the welfare system.[60] High minimum wages meant that these countries had relatively few 'working poor' and that what poverty there was occurred largely amongst benefit recipients with no access to other income.[61] Within the working class itself, the functioning of the wages system made for a considerable equality of condition, with the majority of wage earners and their families going up the incomes ladder in lockstep with the expansion of the economy. Combined with full employment and an extremely high level of private home ownership, Australia could and did see itself in the early post-war decades as a 'lucky country',[62] in which the condition of those who remained poor would also improve as the economy continued to prosper. This optimism evaporated with the adverse economic changes heralded by the First Oil Shock. By a twist of fate that extended Labor's unfortunate run of never being in office at the right time, this occurred rather less than twelve months after

---

[59] See Jones, *Australian Welfare State*, p. 59.
[60] This case is argued in Castles, *Working Class and Welfare*, pp. 74–109.
[61] See Ronald F. Henderson, 'Social Welfare Expenditure', in R. B. Scotton and Helen Ferber, *Public Expenditures and Social Policy in Australia*, vol. I, *The Whitlam Years* (Melbourne: Longman, 1978), pp. 160–78, pp. 167–69.
[62] See Donald Horne, *The Lucky Country: Australia in the Sixties* (Ringwood, Vic.: Penguin, 1964).

the Whitlam government took office. In Australia, the 'old politics' of the welfare state in the European sense of big spending and big taxing programmes ended almost before it had begun.

A dialectic of old and new?

The 'old politics' of the welfare state was a matter of mobilizing support for the expansion of a wide range of services and income support measures demanded by democratic citizens. The supposed emergence of a 'new politics' of the welfare state is about governments finding ways of avoiding blame for expenditure cutbacks made necessary by changing economic conditions and, in particular, by pressures emanating from the global economy.[63] In the period since 1970 Australia has experienced efforts by both major political parties to control public expenditure growth and an important part of this effort has been successive attempts to recalibrate the relationship between federal and state governments, with governments of all political complexions seeking to rationalize the process of inter-governmental relations. Accompanying these changes has been a further process of political evolution whereby the roles of existing federal institutions have been considerably modified, with consequences, at least in some respects, favourable to the entrenchment of welfare rights.

However, alongside these seemingly 'new politics' trends have gone a number of attacks on the fundamentals of the Australian welfare state as it has developed over the past century, and against these attacks federal institutions have been largely powerless. Our verdict, then, is of a continuing dialectic between the 'old politics' and the 'new politics' of the welfare state, with federal institutions playing an important role, but one which, in the long run, is unlikely to be decisive. In what is necessarily an extremely summary treatment, we now focus on recent social expenditure trends, innovations and renovations of federal institutions protective of existing and sometimes even expanded social spending, and changes relating to the structure of welfare benefits and the arbitration system, which have undermined other aspects of Australia's welfare state.

Recent social expenditure trends

The course of Australia's social expenditure development since 1980 is charted in table 2.2. This data comes from the OECD and is

[63] For successive elaborations of this argument, see Paul Pierson, 'The New Politics of the Welfare State', *World Politics*, vol. 48 (1996), no. 2, pp. 143–79 and contributions to Paul Pierson, ed., *The New Politics of the Welfare State* (Oxford: Oxford University Press, 2001).

Table 2.2 *Australian social expenditure levels and changes as a percentage of GDP (1980–2001)*

	Age pensions	Health	Spending on unemployment	Other social spending	Total social expenditure
1980	3.3	4.4	0.7	2.9	11.3
1985	3.0	5.3	1.7	3.5	13.5
1990	2.9	5.2	1.4	4.7	14.2
1995	4.3	5.5	2.0	6.0	17.8
1999	4.0	6.0	1.4	6.1	17.5
2000	4.3	6.2	1.5	6.6	18.6
2001	4.0	6.2	1.4	6.4	18.0
1980–2001[3]	0.7	1.8	0.7	3.5	6.7

Notes:[1] Spending on unemployment comprises unemployment benefit expenditure plus expenditure on active labour market policy.
[2] Major expenditures under the other heading include disability, sickness and family cash benefits as well as services to the elderly and to families.
[3] Row 7 minus row 1.
Sources: All data from or calculated from OECD, *Social Expenditure Database 1980–2001*, CD-Rom (Paris: OECD, 2004).

categorized in a somewhat different manner from that appearing in table 2.1. This means that comparisons pre-1980 and post-1980 can only be very approximate. On the other hand, the fact that the data appearing in table 2.2 comes from an extensive international database means that comparisons are possible with other federal nations and with the OECD as a whole.

This data suggests two conclusions. The first is that Australia's social spending levels have remained relatively low compared to the generality of OECD countries and even compared with the other federal countries featured in this study. In the case of pensions, Australia continued to be a spectacular laggard. In 1980, of long-term OECD members, only Canada and Japan spent less than Australia on age pensions and, by the turn of the millennium, only Ireland spent less. In the area of health, Australia did somewhat better. In 1980 only Portugal, Greece and the US were lower spenders, but by the end of the period Australian spending levels were close to the OECD median and higher than those of other federal countries, such as Austria and the US. However, despite increased expenditure on health and the doubling of expenditure on other programmes, by the end of the period Australia was still almost at the bottom of the overall expenditure distribution in the late 1990s, with only Ireland, Japan and the US spending comparably low levels of its GDP on public welfare.

The second conclusion is rather different. Although Australia did not markedly improve its relative standing during this period, it cannot be considered an expenditure growth laggard. Between 1980 and 2001 total social expenditure in Australia grew by 6.7 per cent of GDP, well above the average figure for the OECD as a whole. Nor can this increase be dismissed as a consequence of the growth of unemployment that occurred in these years, since this category of spending increased by only just above half a percentage point of GDP between 1980 and 2001, while total expenditure increased by around ten times that amount. Table 2.2 shows that pensions expenditure rose by 0.7 per cent of GDP and health by 1.8 per cent. More detailed figures from the OECD show that services to the old increased by 0.6 per cent and spending on cash benefits to families more than doubled – from 0.9 to 2.4 per cent of GDP.[64] The story told by these figures is that Australia's federal institutions had ceased to function as a strong brake on social spending precisely when that brake was beginning to be applied more forcefully elsewhere.

Innovations and renovations

A major reason for a diminished braking effect on expenditure is that federal institutions began to function in new ways. Earlier we discussed the process whereby constitutional limitations on the federal government's capacity to legislate in the area of social services were removed, demonstrating that federal institutions should never be regarded as permanent barriers to change. In recent decades the gradual transformation of the Senate and the High Court[65] into institutions defending existing social rights have been no less significant. Traditional scholarship has long noted that neither of these institutions used 'states' rights' to justify their contribution to national governance. What has attracted less attention, however, is that both institutions displayed at a very early stage their potential to use 'the Constitution' to justify their role in expanding the scope of national governance. That is, those in positions of power in both institutions appreciated that 'federalism' did not simply mean 'divided sovereignty' and 'limited government'. Federal institutions such as the High Court and the Senate could contribute effectively by *multiplying* sovereignty instead of dividing it, and by *developing* government instead of limiting it.[66]

---

[64] This data is from the OECD's *Social Expenditure Database 1980–2001*, CD-Rom (Paris: OECD, 2004).
[65] A key role of the High Court has been in the area of aboriginal affairs (another sort of social policy), where its rulings on indigenous land rights have played a significant part in a shift towards indigenous self-determination.
[66] See also Galligan, *Federal Republic*, chapters 3 (Senate) and 7 (High Court).

Recent Australian experience also demonstrates the positive potential of systems of shared sovereignty to strengthen national capacities through inter-governmental partnerships, with the social policy responsibilities of modern government serving as a major incentive to co-operation and joint action. A recent example is the development of COAG, the Council of Australian Governments, which brings together national state and territory governments to authorize and implement many shared public policies. COAG arose in the early 1990s out of inter-governmental struggles over the national government's virtual monopoly of direct taxation revenues, and over the associated policy leverage seized by national governments of all persuasions. Established as an inter-governmental agreement in 1992, the development of COAG reflects in no small part the determination of state governments to lock the national government into a new federal framework: one involving a new balance between the national government's traditionally large taxation revenue and a national agenda of expenditure priorities increasingly reflecting substantial state government input.

This new-found state contribution meant that the states were prepared to accept federal government calls for greater programme responsibilities over efficiencies of policy implementation, conditional on a greater say by states over national policy and expenditure priorities. COAG has developed a broad range of cross-jurisdictional ministerial councils, which have brought together many of the strands of inter-governmental decision-making in a new structure of federalism. This new rendition of Australian federalism works in two directions. It not only allows the federal government to bring greater fiscal discipline to the states, but it also strengthens the capacity of the states to lock the federal government into a sustained funding of many national social policies. Separately, each of the states might be very much weaker than the federal government, but collectively they can arrange terms of a policy partnership to strengthen their capacity as designers as well as deliverers of welfare services.[67]

If COAG is an example of federal innovation, the Senate can be considered an example of federal renovation. Although the High Court has emerged as an important promoter of a rights orientation in Australian government, the Senate has demonstrated the power of traditional federal political institutions to take on new political roles, particularly

---

[67] Ibid., pp. 211–13; see also Dugald Munro, 'The Role of Performance Measures in a Federal-State Context: Examples of Housing and Disability Services', *Australian Journal of Public Administration*, vol. 62 (2003), no. 1 (March), pp. 70–79; Andrew Parkin, 'The States, Federalism and Political Science: A Fifty Year Appraisal', *Australian Journal of Public Administration*, vol. 62 (2003), no. 2 (June), pp. 101–12.

in protecting social rights against neo-liberal reformist governments. Importantly, the Senate's electoral system since 1949 has been one of proportional representation, which has allowed Australian voters to elect to the Senate an increasing number of minor party and independent senators, so much so that these minor players have come to exercise the Senate balance of power since the early 1980s.[68] Although Australia has had nothing resembling minority governments at the national level, this development of minority players holding the Senate balance of power has meant that pressure groups have targeted the minor parties in the federal chamber, when interests have been threatened by changing government priorities.

In withstanding pressures for the retrenchment of welfare expenditure, it is the Senate that has played the key role, becoming the foremost veto point against attempts to pare back existing welfare entitlements. Originally, the 'federal' contribution of the Upper House was expressed in its promotion of negative rather than positive rights. However, since 1980 the Senate has effectively been dominated by parties of the left, with much of the policy pace being set by minor parties, which are fully aware that they will never face the budgetary responsibilities of parties in government. Parliamentary reforms under the Hawke Labor government made it even harder for either of the major parties to control the Senate. But the larger story is that the major parties can command an effective majority only by taking seriously the preferences of those minor parties holding the balance of power. Given the remarkable legislative power of the Senate to veto any government bill, it should come as no surprise to find Senate majorities clustering around the agenda of positive rights, promoting and expanding access and eligibility rights by individuals and groups to government services. In an era when governments of all complexions have become increasingly persuaded that a shift to new priorities was urgently required, the Senate has often stood four-square as an institutionalized bulwark of an older approach to the politics of the welfare state.

The most widely examined instance of Senate modification of a government's budget and expenditure priorities is the fate of the Keating Labor government's 1993 budget after its re-election earlier that year.[69] The situation was typical in that neither the governing party nor the official opposition had a majority in the Senate. The balance of power was

---

[68] John Uhr, 'Explicating the Senate', *Journal of Legislative Studies*, vol. 8 (2002), no. 3 (autumn), pp. 3–26. As a result of the October 2004 election, the government for the first time in twenty-three years has an absolute majority in both House and Senate.

[69] See Liz Young, 'Minor Parties and the Legislative Process in the Australian Senate', *Australian Journal of Political Science*, vol. 34 (1999), no.1, pp. 7–27.

in the hands of various minor parties (Australian Democrats, Greens and an Independent), no one of which alone had the numbers to secure a victory for the government. In this instance, formal modification of the government's budget was arranged through private negotiations between the government and the minor parties rather than through public debate on the floor of the Senate. But the minor parties used the threat of their formal voting power to bring the government to the negotiating table to redress the equity implications of the budget: the Australian Democrats were successful in getting the budget redrafted to increase levels of tax rebates to low income earners, to retain government health cover for eye tests, and to drop retrospective provisions for some new taxes; and the Greens were successful in obtaining compensation packages for low income earners adversely affected by new taxes. The effect in all cases was to increase public expenditure over the government's preferred levels.

The Howard Liberal government, which took office in 1996, was also forced to learn to govern without a Senate majority. Recent budgetary politics provides good examples. In 2002 the non-government parties in the Senate voted down a proposal to increase user charges for pharmaceutical benefits and also caused the government to withdraw another budget bill designed to tighten eligibility criteria for disability pensions. In both cases, Senate action effectively prevented proposed government cutbacks to welfare expenditure. The 2003 budget saw the Senate go even further, with the non-government party groupings holding the balance of power actively negotiating budget-related legislation after extracting government commitments to very considerable expenditure increases in such areas as health and tertiary education. All this is oddly reminiscent of the traditional Labor strategy of providing 'support in return for concessions'. In both cases, newly elected progressive parties were in a position to use their balance-of-power opportunities to sidestep the antagonistic practices of the formal opposition and to offer their support for the governing party, so long as the governing party incorporated the policies being advanced by the new party.

The end of the Australian model?

These examples of Senate obstruction to proposed social expenditure reductions seem like perfect instances of a federal ratchet effect in operation, but that is, in our view, too upbeat a way to conclude the story of the long interaction of Australia's federal system and its welfare state. The problem is that the ratchet effect does not appear to work in all welfare-relevant areas of policy. As noted previously, two of the key institutions of Australia's welfare state – its systems of non-discretionary means-tested benefits and of conciliation and arbitration of industrial disputes – have not been about big-ticket social expenditure at all. They were, however, the institutions that gave the Australian system of social protection an egalitarian and distinctive cast. Over the past quarter-century, despite successes in holding back the forces of expenditure retrenchment, both of these institutions have been substantially undermined, much reducing the distinctiveness of the Australian system of provision and producing a victory for the conservative variant of the 'old politics' by the back door.

The non-discretionary character of the benefits system and its capacity to serve as an adequate social safety net have been threatened by an ever increasing conditionality of provision. Benefits are still available, but only where other resources are demonstrably exhausted, and where the good faith of recipients is demonstrated by compliance with stringent activity tests.[70] Increasing conditionality began under Labor administrations in the 1980s and 1990s and has been much intensified under Liberal governments from 1996 onwards. There has also been a major scaling back of the wage awards system, which has been justified by the argument that wage rigidities lead to economic inefficiency.[71] Beginning in the 1980s, labour-market decentralization emerged as a policy priority shared by Labor and Coalition governments. The Coalition government's workplace relations reforms have gone much further than earlier Labor changes in shifting the locus of wage bargaining from the national level to the enterprise level. Awards used to protect around 80 per cent of Australian workers. By 1999 the figure was nearer 50 per cent.[72] Greater conditionality and workplace reform have both been introduced under the banner of improved labour market efficiency, an area of policy in which the Senate balance of power is quite ineffective because of what amounts to a long-term consensus between Labor and the Coalition on the need for greater 'rationalism' in the functioning of the economy. In Australia politics continues to matter, even in the era of the 'new politics of the welfare state', because the ratchet effect of federal institutions can only operate where the major parties are

---

[70] See Francis G. Castles, 'A Farewell to Australia's Welfare State', *International Journal of Health Services*, vol. 31 (2002), no. 3, pp. 537–44.

[71] See Francis G. Castles, 'Australia's Institutions and Australia's Welfare', in Geoffrey Brennan and Francis G. Castles, eds., *Australia Reshaped: 200 Years of Institutional Transformation* (Cambridge: Cambridge University Press, 2002), pp. 47–49.

[72] Sue Richardson, 'Regulation of the Labour Market', in Sue Richardson, ed., *Reshaping the Labour Market: Regulation, Efficiency and Equality in Australia* (Cambridge: Cambridge University Press, 1999).

in disagreement. For over more than a century the flexibility of federal institutions has been readily compatible with the expansion and, more recently, the preservation of Australian levels of social spending. Over the past quarter of a century, however, federal institutions have proved powerless to prevent the attrition of Australia's once distinctive system of social protection.

3 Canada
Nation-building in a federal welfare state

KEITH BANTING

Introduction

Canadians developed their version of the welfare state in the context of a vibrant federal state, with strong governments at both the federal and provincial level. Their experience highlights in fascinating ways the reciprocal interplay between federalism and social policy. In comparative context, the Canadian case underscores the need for more nuanced analysis than is found in much of the comparative literature of the welfare state, which is summarized in the introduction to this book. Attention normally focusses on simple dichotomies: federal versus non-federal, centralized versus decentralized, concentrated power versus multiple veto points. It is widely argued that federal, decentralized and/or fragmented decision-making inhibited the expansion of the welfare state in the twentieth century, but has slowed the processes of restructuring in the contemporary period. Such propositions do find echoes in Canada. For example, decentralization helped to slow the pace of development in the first half of the twentieth century.

The primary lessons to be drawn from the Canadian experience, however, emerge from the modern social programmes put in place in the second half of the twentieth century. Canada did not develop a single, integrated public philosophy of federalism in this period, and federal–provincial relations in social policy incorporated three distinct models, each with its own decision rules. At any point in time, governments were shaping or reshaping different programmes according to different rules and processes. Canada therefore constitutes a natural laboratory in which to analyze the implications of different models of federalism. As we shall see, the different sets of incentives and constraints inherent in different models help to explain a number of puzzles about the Canadian welfare state, especially the striking contrast between the liberal nature of the country's income security programmes and the more social-democratic character of its health care, and the highly uneven impact of retrenchment in recent years. The wider lessons are that different models of federalism have distinctive implications for social policy, and that different models of federalism can co-exist within an individual federal state.

The Canadian experience also highlights the reciprocal influence of the welfare state on the federal state. At the most obvious level, the arrival of the welfare state helped to centralize the federation during the middle decades of the twentieth century. But at a deeper level national social programmes have also played a role in defining the nature of the political communities on which the federal state rests. Political identities are highly contested in Canada, and social programmes have emerged as instruments of nation-building. For the central government, social policy has been seen as an instrument of territorial integration, part of the social glue holding together a vast country subject to powerful centrifugal tendencies. National social programmes create a network of relations between citizens and the central government throughout the country, helping to define the boundaries of the national political community and enhancing the legitimacy of the federal state. However, provincial governments, especially the Quebec government, have also seen social policy as an instrument for building a distinctive community at the regional level, one reflecting the linguistic and cultural dynamics of Québécois society. For both levels of government, therefore, social policy has been an instrument not only of social justice but also of statecraft, to be deployed in the competitive processes of nation-building.

This chapter develops these themes in five sections. The first section sets the context by describing the territorial dimensions of Canadian politics and its federal institutions. The second section examines the impact of federalism on the expansion of the welfare state, and the third section examines the impact on the politics of restructuring during the last quarter of the twentieth century. The fourth section reverses the perspective, exploring the impact of the welfare state on Canadian federalism, and the final section concludes by pulling together the threads of the argument.

Territorial politics and Canadian federalism

In some ways, the political economy of social policy in Canada follows the patterns found in many other western democracies. Social programmes have been shaped by political struggles and coalitions among a familiar cast of characters, including political parties, business interests, organized labour, social welfare groups, the women's movement and others. More than in many countries, however, Canadian politics are also territorial politics, rooted in linguistic and regional divisions. To borrow Livingstone's language, Canada is not only a federal state but also a federal society.[1] The division between English-speaking and French-speaking communities has been an elemental feature of politics in northern North America since the defeat of the French by the British in 1763, and the formation of the federation in 1867 was seen by many French-Canadian leaders as a compact between two peoples. Although there are small francophone communities in several provinces, the primary linguistic divide is now between Quebec and the rest of Canada. The French-speaking people of Quebec have come to see themselves as a distinct society, with their own history, culture and political identity. A nationalist ethos pervades the entire political spectrum within the province, and a strong separatist movement has on occasion threatened the survival of a single Canadian state.

Wider conflicts among the regions of the country are also as old as the federation. Regional divisions take root in the geography of a country much larger than all of Europe. Although modern communication and transportation have diminished the salience of geography, they have not eliminated the political distance between the centre and the peripheries. This natural inheritance has been reinforced by economic and cultural development. Much of the economic history of the country can be written in terms of regionally uneven development and enduring tensions among the industrial heartland of central Canada, the resource economy of the west, and the weaker economies of Atlantic Canada. Social differences overlay economic ones, as different patterns of settlement and immigration bestowed distinctive ethnic blends and cultures on the regions.

Territorial politics matter for Canadian social policy. Most importantly, the salience of territorial politics helps to explain the historic failure of national political life to polarize along class lines. Territorial divisions have cross-cut class-based politics, and the politics of equality have always centred as much on regional inequalities as on class inequalities. As a result, the agenda of national integration, with its constant need to balance linguistic and regional interests, has tended to diffuse efforts to focus debate on a left–right basis. Historically, the dominant political parties have represented coalitions of regional as well as class interests, and have tended to govern from the middle of the political spectrum. The centrist Liberal Party has been particularly adept in the art of brokerage politics,

---

[1] William S. Livingstone, *Federalism and Constitutional Change* (Oxford: Clarendon Press, 1956).

accommodating regional interests and bending to the left or right as political currents shift. The party dominated federal politics for most of the twentieth century, yielding only occasionally to its historic adversary, the Conservatives. Challenges to these traditional parties have come from parties of regional protest, which have emerged suddenly to play important – although often temporary – roles on the national stage. The party system was realigned by such populist surges in the 1920s, the 1960s and the 1990s.

In this context, the political left has had problems establishing itself as a national force. Regional divisions have long been a barrier to the growth of a truly national labour movement, and contemporary social movements representing women and other activists have been similarly fragmented.[2] In English Canada, the Cooperative Commonwealth Federation (CCF) was founded in the 1930s by a coalition of farmer organizations, labour unions and socialist intellectuals, and was restructured in the early 1960s as the New Democratic Party (NDP), a more conventional social-democratic party with organic links to organized labour. However, the CCF/NDP has never governed nationally, and has held power in only four of the ten provinces. Although the party played a decisive role at several historical junctures in the politics of social policy, its overall role has always been a secondary one. Within Quebec, the social-democratic part of the spectrum has been occupied by nationalist and increasingly sovereignist parties. As a result, the national question has complicated social-democratic alliances across the linguistic divide, although informal coalitions of the Quebec government and NDP provincial governments have been important at times.

These territorial politics have been reflected and amplified by the structure of Canadian federalism. Authority over social policy is divided between the federal government, ten provincial governments and three northern territories in ways that make Canada one of the most decentralized federations in the world. From the outset, the Constitution Act of 1867 gave the provinces a central role in social policy, with specific sections granting them authority over education, hospitals and related charitable institutions. In addition, the courts extended the provincial role by subsuming social policy under provincial powers over 'property

---

[2] Tom McIntosh, 'Organized Labour in a Federal Society: Solidarity, Coalition Building and Canadian Unions', in Harvey Lazar and Tom McIntosh, eds., *How Canadians Connect: Canada: The State of the Federation 1998/99* (Montreal: McGill-Queen's University Press, 1999), pp. 147–78, p. 149; Jill Vickers, 'Why Should Women Care About Federalism?', in Douglas M. Brown and Janet Hiebert, eds., *Canada: The State of the Federation 1994* (Kingston, Ont.: Institute of Inter-governmental Relations, Queen's University, 1994), pp. 135–51.

and civil rights' and 'matters of a local or private nature'. In a key decision in 1937, the courts struck down a federal social insurance programme as intruding on these provincial powers.

Despite the centrality of provincial jurisdiction, the federal government also has a significant presence in social policy. Amendments to the constitution in the middle of the twentieth century gave federal authorities full jurisdiction over unemployment insurance and substantial jurisdiction over contributory pensions. Federal tax powers also constitute a powerful instrument in redistributive policies, especially with the development of refundable tax credits in recent decades. However, the cornerstone of the federal role has been implicit rather than explicit in the constitution. According to Canadian constitutional doctrine, 'the federal Parliament may spend or lend its funds to any government or institution or individual it chooses, for any purpose it chooses; and it may attach to any grant or loan any conditions it chooses, including conditions it could not directly legislate'.[3] This convention, known as the doctrine of the spending power, has been challenged both politically and judicially. In the mid-1950s, for example, a Quebec royal commission asked: 'What would be the use of a careful description of legislative powers if one of the governments could get around it and, to some extent, annul it by its taxation methods and its fashion of spending?'[4] Nevertheless, court decisions repeatedly sustained the federal position, and the spending power became the constitutional footing for a number of central pillars of the welfare state. It has helped to sustain federal benefits paid directly to citizens, such as family allowances; it provides constitutional legitimacy to shared-cost programmes through which the federal government supports provincial social programmes; and at the outset it provided authority for equalization grants, which are federal transfers to the poorer provinces designed to enable them to provide average levels of public services without having to resort to above average levels of taxation.[5]

With federal and provincial governments both engaged in social policy, much depends on the mechanisms through which they manage their interdependence. Canada was the first country to fuse federal institutions with the Westminster system of parliamentary government, which concentrates power in the hands of executives at both the federal and provincial levels. The Prime Minister and Premiers, their

---

[3] Peter Hogg, *Constitutional Law in Canada* (Toronto: Carswell, 2001), pp. 6–15 (section 6.8a).

[4] Royal Commission of Inquiry on Constitutional Problems in the Province of Quebec, *Report of the Royal Commission of Inquiry* . . . [The Tremblay Report] (Quebec: Province of Quebec, 1956), 5 vols., vol. II, p. 217.

[5] Since the adoption of Section 36 of the Constitution in 1982, equalization grants have specific constitutional footing and no longer depend on the federal spending power.

cabinets and senior officials dominate the policy process in their respective governments; and it is these executives who manage federal–provincial relations through elaborate diplomacy and federal–provincial agreements which can rival international treaties in their complexity. Compared to some federations, however, these inter-governmental processes tend to be relatively informal and unstructured, with few formal venues, no firm decision rules, and no effective mechanisms for resolving disputes and roadblocks.

There are few counter-balances to executive dominance of inter-governmental relations. Unlike the German or US systems, there is little space for the mediation of territorial disputes through legislatures. Members of the parliamentary caucus of the governing party play a role, but MPs from a province do not speak for their provincial government. Indeed, they may be political opponents. Moreover, the governing party is often weak in certain regions, depriving those parts of the country of champions around the cabinet table and in the party caucus. Furthermore, the upper chamber of Parliament, the Senate, remains an unelected body without the political legitimacy to serve as a forum for the resolution of regional or inter-governmental disputes. Nor does the party system integrate levels of government. Parties at the two levels are highly autonomous: federal and provincial parties bearing the same name are separate organizations, both in law and in political reality. Their leaders have separate career paths; their finances are unrelated; and their electoral bases are distinct. In several provinces, completely different parties operate in the federal and provincial arenas. Consequently, there are few, if any, vertical party mechanisms through which inter-governmental disputes can be managed.

As a result, many of the country's social programmes are forged in the crucible of federal–provincial negotiations. Such a decision-making process tends to be particularly responsive to the political and bureaucratic interests of the governments at the table, and to social and economic issues that can be defined in regional terms. Such issues are readily championed by provincial governments. In contrast, other social interests – organized labour, women's groups, welfare rights organizations – have long complained of their relative exclusion.[6]

As emphasized at the outset, however, federal–provincial relations differ sharply from one social programme to another. Indeed, three distinct models of federal–provincial relations are embedded in the welfare state, each with its own decision rules.

---

[6] The classic reference is Richard Simeon, *Federal–Provincial Diplomacy: The Making of Recent Policy in Canada* (Toronto: University of Toronto Press, 1972).

- Classical federalism. Some programmes are delivered by the federal or provincial governments acting independently within their own jurisdiction: unemployment insurance, child benefits, non-contributory old age pensions at the federal level; workers' compensation at the provincial level. This model involves unilateral decisions by both levels of government, with minimal efforts at co-ordination even when decisions at one level have implications for the other.
- Shared-cost federalism. Under this model the federal government offers financial support to provincial governments on specific terms. In practice, the substance of such programmes tends to be hammered out in bargaining between the two levels. In formal terms, however, the model involves each government making separate decisions. The federal government decides when, what and how to support provincial programmes; and provincial governments decide whether to accept the money and the terms. As a result, this model contains the potential for unilateralism, as became clear when the federal government began to cut its financial commitments to provincial programmes from the mid-1970s onwards.
- Joint decision federalism. In this model, the formal agreement of both levels of government is required before any action is possible. Unilateralism is not an option here. The major Canadian example is the Canada Pension Plan. This joint decision-making is analogous to the German federation. The institutions differ, since the provincial governments are not represented in the upper chamber of the national legislature, but the central dynamic is similar. Nothing happens unless formal approval is given by both levels of government.

As will be seen, each of these models of inter-governmentalism has had remarkably different implications for the expansion and the restructuring of the welfare state.

Federalism and the expansion of the welfare state

In analyzing the impact of federalism on the expansion of social programmes, it is useful to contrast two historical periods: the decentralized era that lasted until 1939, which was characterized by a slow start to social policy development; and the expansionist phase from 1940 until the mid-1970s, when income security programmes and health care developed rapidly but also moved along separate pathways.

96 Federalism and the Welfare State

Source: Compiled from data in: Statistics Canada, *Historical Statistics of Canada* (Ottawa: Canadian Govt. Publ. Center, second edition 1980); Statistics Canada, CANSIM II; and Statistics Canada, Labour Force Survey.

Figure 3.1 Union density: unionized workers as a percentage of the non-agricultural labour force (1921–2002)

Decentralized welfare and a slow start

In terms of comparative social policy, Canada had a slow start. Welfare provision in the first decades of the twentieth century was still largely based on 'relief' organized at the local level by municipalities, private charities and religious institutions.[7] The introduction of modern social programmes came much later than the German initiatives of the 1880s, the Australian innovations in 1901–12, and even the US New Deal of the 1930s. The first stages in the construction of the Canadian welfare state, which emerged in the inter-war years, were halting and incomplete; and major programmes for the population as a whole had to wait until the Second World War and the decades that followed.

A number of factors contributed to the slow start. The country was only beginning the transition from a predominantly agricultural economy, and national politics were dominated by conservative interests, parties and ideas. As a result, the social basis for a large coalition in favour of welfare was still missing. As figure 3.1 indicates, as late as 1930 only 14 per cent of the non-agricultural labour force was unionized, and organized labour remained regionally diverse and ideologically splintered. Moreover,

---

[7] Gerard Boychuk, *Patchworks of Purpose: The Development of Provincial Social Assistance Regimes in Canada* (Montreal: McGill-Queen's University Press, 1998); Dennis Guest, *The Emergence of Social Security in Canada*, 3rd edn (Vancouver: University of British Columbia Press, 1997).

relations between unions, farmers and social reformers were uneasy, narrowing the scope for a powerful cross-class alliance based on labour and agricultural organizations.[8] Women's groups, veterans' organizations and church groups were pioneers in campaigning for social reform, but they influenced politics from the margin, not the centre.

Decentralization, however, also constrained the response to social needs. Provincial governments were certainly not paralyzed in this period, and several welfare initiatives did emerge through innovation and diffusion at that level. In 1914 workers' compensation was introduced in Ontario, the most industrialized province, providing benefits to injured workers based on contributions from employers. Diffusion across the country was slow, but by 1940 workers' compensation modelled on the Ontario programme existed in every province except Prince Edward Island. The inter-war years also saw the diffusion of provincial minimum wage laws and Mothers' Allowances, a categorical means-tested benefit for widowed mothers with dependent children. Mothers' Allowances were introduced in response to regional campaigns led by women's groups in Manitoba in 1916, Saskatchewan in 1917, Alberta in 1919 and Ontario in 1920.[9]

Despite these early successes, provincial authorities clearly felt constrained by decentralized institutions. First, they were plagued by fiscal imbalances. Two of the three provincial welfare initiatives of this era, workers' compensation and minimum wage laws, did not require public financing at all. Only Mothers' Allowances were financed from provincial and municipal revenues, and the costs greatly exceeded initial estimates. Poorer provinces were especially vulnerable. Two of them – New Brunswick and Prince Edward Island – still had not introduced Mothers' Allowances by the outbreak of the Second World War and, as table 3.1 indicates, sharp regional differences in benefits levels quickly developed among the existing plans. The fiscal constraints were made even clearer by the mass unemployment of the Depression years. In the worst year, 1933, nearly one-quarter of the country's labour force was unemployed, and an estimated 15 per cent of the population was on some form of relief. The burden swamped existing relief mechanisms. The problems were undoubtedly exacerbated by the tradition of municipal responsibility for relief, but the financial burdens would have been distorted even if provincial governments had taken over completely. As

---

[8] Ann Orloff, *The Politics of Pensions; A Comparative Analysis of Britain, Canada, and the United States, 1880–1940* (Madison: University of Wisconsin Press, 1993).

[9] Veronica Strong-Boag, 'Wages for Housework: Mothers' Allowances and the Beginnings of Social Security in Canada', *Journal of Canadian Studies*, vol. 14 (1979), no. 1, pp. 24–34; Margaret Little, *'No Car, No Radio, No Liquor Permit'. The Moral Regulation of Single Mothers in Ontario, 1920–1997* (Oxford: Oxford University Press, 1998).

Table 3.1 *Average monthly provincial benefit levels (1942, 1949)*

Province	Mothers' allowances, 1942 (in Can. $)	Old age pensions, 1949 (in Can. $)
Prince Edward Island	–	34.46
Nova Scotia	28.55	35.33
New Brunswick	–	36.01
Quebec	26.64	37.63
Ontario	28.91	38.05
Manitoba	35.79	38.36
Saskatchewan	13.77	37.29
Alberta	22.96	37.87
British Columbia	39.19	37.26

Source: Keith Banting, *The Welfare State and Canadian Federalism*, 2nd edn (Montreal: McGill-Queen's University Press, 1987), table 20.

a royal commission reported in 1940, 'the costs of relief varied inversely with the ability to meet them. In Western Canada where incomes fell most rapidly, relief costs were relatively the highest. The weight of the burden in Saskatchewan, the province most severely affected, was about five times as great as in the Maritimes and Ontario, the provinces least affected.'[10] The country lacked a mechanism for spreading risk across the country as a whole.

Secondly, inter-war provincial leaders were concerned about the mobility of labour and capital in a federal state. In 1924 the Saskatchewan government emphasized the problem in recommending federal leadership on pensions to a House of Commons committee. In 1927 the Premier of Manitoba complained to the Prime Minister that 'If any City or Province singly adopted plans to solve unemployment, that City or Province would become the Mecca to which the unemployed in other cities or provinces would drift.'[11] Federal officials tended to agree. In 1931 the Prime Minister told the House of Commons that 'insurance against unemployment, sickness and invalidity can never be successful if each province has a different system or if one province has a system and another does not'.[12] Warnings about regional economic competitiveness were sounded by commissions of inquiry at both the provincial

[10] Royal Commission on Dominion–Provincial Relations [Rowell-Sirois Commission], *Report* (Ottawa, Ont.: King's Printer, 1940), book I, *Canada*, pp. 163–64.
[11] Quoted in Keith Banting, *The Welfare State and Canadian Federalism*, 2nd edn (Montreal: McGill-Queen's University Press, 1987), p. 64. See also Leslie Pal, *State, Class, and Bureaucracy: Canadian Unemployment Insurance and Public Policy* (Montreal: McGill-Queen's University Press, 1988), chapter 6.
[12] R. B. Bennett, House of Commons Debates, Session 1931, vol. 1, pp. 1099–100.

and federal levels. In 1933 a Quebec commission argued that the introduction of family allowances 'would perhaps place our manufacturers in a disadvantageous position with reference to other provinces', and that 'ordinary prudence suggests that unemployment insurance should be federal in character'.[13] A few years later, the federal Royal Commission on Dominion–Provincial Relations also recommended federal jurisdiction because of the danger of placing employers in one province 'in a position of competitive disadvantage in comparison with employers in provinces where there are not contributory social services'.[14] Alain Noël has argued that these perceptions are not necessarily evidence of a real, systematic constraint, since perceptions 'could just be erroneous'.[15] Perhaps. But perceptions matter in politics.

Not surprisingly, pressure built for federal action. Initially, federal politicians tried to avoid responsibility. Except for the introduction of veterans' pensions after the First World War, they referred demands for old age pensions and unemployment protection back to the provinces for as long as possible. In the case of unemployment in the 1930s for example, the mayors of major cities, who were on the front line of relief efforts, were shunted back and forth between provincial and federal offices. In 1930 a delegation of western mayors was rebuffed by the Prime Minister, who sent them home to lobby their provincial governments; and when in 1935 the Dominion Conference of Mayors demanded 'Relief from Relief' through complete federal responsibility for the unemployed, they were met with the same response. In the words of one analyst, 'it was Ottawa that jealously defended provincial rights while the premiers were centralist'.[16]

This game of jurisdictional hide-and-seek was not politically sustainable in the long term. Federal action on old age pensions was forced in 1926–27, when the Liberal government was in a parliamentary minority and depended for its survival on two labour MPs, who extracted action on pensions as the price for their support. The Old Age Pension Programme provided a means-tested pension of $20 per month for those aged 70

---

[13] Quebec Social Insurance Commission [Monpetit Commission], *Third Report* (Quebec: Publié par ordre de L'Honorable Ministre Du Travail, 1933), p. 108; *Sixth Report* (Quebec: Publié par ordre de l'Honorable Ministre Du Travail, 1933), p. 203.
[14] Canada, Royal Commission on Dominion–Provincial Relations, *Report* (Ottawa, Ont.: King's Printer, 1940), book II, *Recommendations*, p. 36.
[15] Alain Noël, 'Is Decentralization Conservative?', in Robert Young, ed., *Stretching the Federation* (Kingston, Ont.: Institute of Intergovernmental Relations, Queen's University, 1999), pp. 195–219, p. 199.
[16] James Struthers, *No Fault of their Own: Unemployment and the Canadian Welfare State 1914–1941* (Toronto: University of Toronto Press, 1983), p. 209. See also John Taylor, '"Relief from Relief": The Cities' Answer to Depression Dependency', *Journal of Canadian Studies*, vol. 14 (1979), no. 1, pp. 17–23.

and older. However, the federal government insisted on shared federal–provincial responsibility: Ottawa would pay 50 per cent of the costs of provincial pensions that met its conditions. Provincial adoption was slow, taking nine years to produce country-wide coverage, with many poorer provinces joining only after 1931 when Ottawa raised its contribution to 75 per cent of the costs.[17] In the case of Quebec, the longest hold-out, the concerns were cultural and jurisdictional. The provincial government insisted that such matters were best left to religious institutions and private charity, and that the plan infringed provincial jurisdiction. However, the pensions were popular with the Quebec electorate, and the government succumbed just before a provincial election in 1936.[18] By the late 1930s, therefore, a national system was in place. As table 3.1 confirms, in contrast with the incomplete coverage and wide variations in the exclusively provincial Mothers' Allowances, the federal–provincial pension provided comparable benefits across the country as a whole.

Federal inaction on unemployment benefits was also politically untenable. In 1930 the Liberal Prime Minister, Mackenzie King, lashed out at provincial demands for money for 'alleged unemployment purposes' and declared that he 'would not give . . . a five-cent piece' to provinces governed by the Conservatives.[19] Not surprisingly perhaps, the Liberals lost the federal election later that year. Their Conservative successors provided grants-in-aid for provincial relief, following a precedent set in the years immediately after World War One. At the outset, federal support was officially temporary, established each year for one year, and always prefaced with a legislative preamble reasserting that relief was primarily a municipal and provincial responsibility. In the end, however, federal grants were substantial, and had to be supplemented by loans to the western provinces, some of which were effectively bankrupt. Federal contributions amounted to almost half of total relief expenditures and over 70 per cent of expenditures in the western provinces.

In 1935 it looked as if electoral pressures had finally produced a more formal programme. The Conservative government, itself facing imminent electoral defeat, passed an Employment and Social Insurance Act. Desultory inter-governmental consultations on constitutional reform to formalize federal jurisdiction in the area had gone nowhere, and Prime Minister Bennett simply asserted that the federal government already

---

[17] Orloff, *Politics of Pensions*; Kenneth Bryden, *Old Age Pensions and Policy-Making in Canada* (Montreal: McGill-Queen's University Press, 1974).
[18] Bernard L. Vigod, 'The Quebec Government and Social Legislation During the 1930s: A Study in Political Self-Destruction', *Journal of Canadian Studies*, vol. 14 (1979), no. 1, pp. 59–69.
[19] House of Commons Debates, Sessions 1930, vol. 2, pp. 1225–28.

possessed the necessary authority. He was wrong, however, both politically and legally. Death-bed repentance did not save the government, and the Liberals were returned to power. They delayed implementation of the Act, referring it to the courts, and in 1937 the courts struck it down as intruding on provincial jurisdiction. The Liberals started another round of discussions over constitutional reform, but failed to secure sufficient provincial consent before the war.

Thus, despite manifest hardships, the 1930s did not witness a watershed in Canadian social politics, and no innovations on the scale of the New Deal in the United States took place. Decentralization was not the only, or even the most important factor at work, and some analysts question whether federalism was significant at all.[20] Obviously, it is impossible to prove definitively that Canada would have had a more robust response had the constitutional constraint not existed. But in the judicious assessment of Les Pal, 'federalism weighed on the side of the set of forces that together acted to delay implementation', and Canada would likely 'have had UI sooner had constitutional complications not stood in the way'.[21] Certainly, the 1937 decision of the courts convinced an entire generation of social planners, labour leaders and social reformers, at least in English-speaking Canada, that decentralization was a roadblock on the way to social justice.

Semi-centralized welfare and diverging trajectories

In the post-war era changes in the political economy of Canada strengthened the forces of reform. By the 1940s a clear majority of Canadians lived in urban centres. As figure 3.1 indicates, a third of the non-agricultural labour force was unionized by the 1950s, a proportion that was to rise further in the 1960s. At the same time, the labour movement became more institutionally and ideologically unified. In addition, the post-war decades were characterized by strong economic growth and buoyant tax revenues, and Canadian policy elites become active adherents to Keynesian economics, reflecting a faith in the capacity of state action to solve important economic and social problems.

Developments in the party system strengthened reformist orientations. The political left was finding its feet. In 1942 the CCF won several federal by-elections; in 1943 the party became the official opposition in Ontario; and in 1944 it took power in Saskatchewan and basked in the warmth of national polls suggesting the party was competitive with the

---

[20] Struthers, *No Fault of their Own*, p. 209; Noël, 'Is Decentralization Conservative?'
[21] Pal, *State, Class, and Bureaucracy*, pp. 152, 167.

governing Liberals. The euphoria proved transitory, and the party settled into minority status at the national level after the 1945 election. But potential strength on the left had a significant impact on the Liberals. The long-term Liberal Prime Minister, Mackenzie King, was haunted by the prospect of a British-style polarization between left and right, squeezing out the centrist liberal party. At moments of left strength, the Liberals therefore refashioned themselves as a party of social reform. This proved critical during the Second World War, when the Liberals introduced several major programmes. A similar pattern played out in the mid-1960s. The transformation of the CCF into the NDP in 1962, with its much closer alliance with organized labour, produced a renewed Liberal determination to fight for the support of working-class voters, and a new generation of reformist Liberals came to power within the party. These dynamics were reinforced by the balance in Parliament. During the critical years between 1963 and 1968 the Liberals formed a succession of minority governments, dependent on small parties such as the NDP, a pattern that was repeated in 1972–74.[22]

Political change was amplified by institutional change. The 1940s ushered in a period of unparalleled political dominance by the federal government. The war centralized power dramatically, bequeathing federal authorities a highly professional bureaucracy and – most importantly – dominance of the primary tax fields. When a federal–provincial conference failed to agree on a new system of revenue sharing in early 1941, the federal government simply pre-empted the provinces, announcing dramatic increases in all tax fields, including fields previously occupied exclusively by the provinces. Ottawa offered sustaining payments to provinces that eliminated their personal and corporate incomes taxes. Given the pressures of war, this was an offer that the provinces could not refuse. As a result, the federal government entered the postwar era in a powerful position. During the subsequent decades Ottawa was anxious to retain enough of the tax fields to expand conditional grant programmes and equalization payments to the poorer provinces. Provincial governments, however, fought to recapture tax room in order to finance their education, health and social services on their own terms. In effect, it was a struggle for control over the Canadian welfare state: 'the federal government wanted to use income taxes to establish national standards of public services, whereas the provinces wanted them in order to tailor public expenditures to suit their own priorities.'[23] Federal dominance was

---

[22] See Penny E. Bryden, *Planners and Politicians: Liberal Politics and Social Policy 1957–1968* (Montreal: McGill-Queen's University Press, 1997).

[23] David Perry, *Financing the Canadian Federation: 1867 to 1995* (Toronto: Canadian Tax Foundation, 1997).

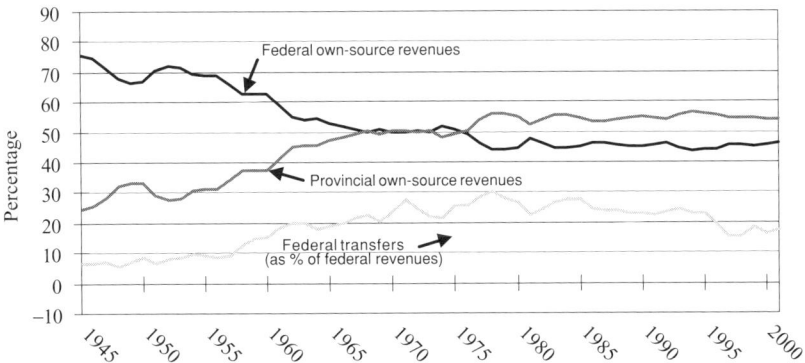

Source: Harvey Lazar, France St-Hilaire and Jean-François Tremblay, 'Vertical Fiscal Imbalance: Myth or Reality?', in Harvey Lazar and France St-Hilaire, eds., *Money, Politics and Health Care: Reconstructing the Federal–Provincial Partnership* (Montreal: Institute for Research on Public Policy, 2004), pp. 135–87, p. 171.

Figure 3.2 Federal and provincial/local governments' share of total public revenues according to the National Accounts

to erode over time, as figure 3.2 indicates. But in the early days Ottawa controlled the purse strings.

In addition, linguistic and regional tensions, while never absent, were at a historic low tide in the 1940s and 1950s. The federal government was able to build a pan-Canadian agenda centred on the development of social programmes, which did not pit region against region.[24] The provinces accepted constitutional amendments to strengthen federal jurisdiction, and many English-speaking provinces lobbied for broader federal engagement. In the early post-war years only Quebec complained about federal pre-emption of social policy terrain, but it was not in a strong position to resist. Dominated by a conservative, clerical tradition, the province was not committed to building its own social programmes. As in the case of old age pensions in 1936, the Quebec government was vulnerable to federal initiatives that proved popular with the Quebec electorate.[25]

The federal government capitalized on its position, introducing several social programmes during the war years and announcing a sweeping package of proposals for social policy reform as part of post-war reconstruction in a series of 'Green Books' before the 1945 election. The package collapsed at a federal–provincial conference held later that year, when the two largest provinces rejected the associated proposals on inter-governmental

[24] Richard Simeon and Ian Robinson, *State, Society and the Development of Canadian Federalism* (Toronto: University of Toronto Press, 1990).
[25] Yves Vaillancourt, *L'Évolution des politiques sociales au Québec, 1940–1960* (Montreal: Presses de l'Université de Montréal, 1988).

finances. Nevertheless, the Green Book proposals represented a coherent agenda that the federal government was to pursue on an incremental basis over the next two decades.

The high tide of federal dominance turned out to be short-lived. By the 1960s provincial resistance was beginning to grow. Most important was the resurgence of Quebec nationalism and the *révolution tranquille*, a modernization drive that transformed the role of government in the province. Beginning with the election of a reinvigorated *Parti libéral* in 1960, Quebec was increasingly determined to build a *provincial* welfare state, one reflecting a Québécois sensibility. The province declared an end to new jurisdictional concessions, and launched a protracted campaign to recapture the ground lost in earlier decades. In 1965 Quebec won the right to 'opt out' of a number of national shared-cost programmes, receiving additional tax room from the federal government so that it could operate the programmes on its own. The victory was partly symbolic, since the province agreed to meet existing conditions associated with the programmes. Nevertheless, symbolic asymmetry signalled that the era of easy centralization was over. In time, other provinces also came to resent the detailed controls and financial tensions implicit in traditional shared-cost programmes, and by the 1970s provinces generally began to push back. As we shall see, new federal social programmes faithfully reflected this evolving inter-governmental balance. Programmes enacted in the 1940s and 1950s tended to give Ottawa the dominant role, whereas those introduced in the 1960s gave more scope to provincial governments.

The semi-centralized welfare state that emerged in this era overcame the constraints that slowed progress in the inter-war years. However, federal institutions continued to leave their imprint on new social programmes in more subtle ways. Much depended on the model of inter-governmental relations and the related decision rules that governed new programmes, and it is useful to examine three clusters of programmes: classical federalism; joint decision federalism; and shared-cost federalism.

Classical federalism and exclusively federal programmes
The federal government mounted several income security programmes that deliver payments directly to citizens. There is no formal provincial role in these programmes, and provincial governments are simply one of many lobbyists that seek to shape federal decisions. As a result, these programmes are defined by the shifting currents of national politics, much as they would be in a unitary state. Although federal officials still have to cope with the territorial features of Canadian politics, they are unconstrained by provincial vetoes.

This exclusively federal process reduces the range of political perspectives that have to be accommodated in decision-making. In comparison with the need for consensus among governments of different political ideologies that characterizes an inter-governmental process, decisions about exclusively federal programmes reflect the ideological orientation of the governing party. Since the Liberals formed the government continuously from 1935 until the end of the 1970s, with the exception of a short interregnum from 1957 to 1963, the programmes were shaped by the 'liberal' orientation of a centrist party. The social-democratic perspective of the CCF/NDP was articulated by the party's representatives in Parliament, but theirs was only one voice in the political cacophony of the day. The NDP did have more influence when the Liberals were in a minority in Parliament in 1963–68 and 1972–74, but even then, the party's influence was indirect, affecting choices made within the Liberal cabinet. Once legislation was introduced, the NDP was in a tight spot. It could attempt to amend legislation of liberal inspiration, but it was seldom in a position to insist, since defeating the government risked losing the bill. The choice between liberal legislation and no legislation was no choice for the CCF/NDP.

These dynamics proved critical in the field of income security, which – in comparison with health care – assumed a decidedly liberal cast. The first step came in 1940 when, following the defeat of the nationalist Duplessis government in Quebec, all the provinces agreed to a constitutional amendment giving the federal government full authority over unemployment insurance. The Unemployment Insurance (UI) programme, which followed quickly, was the first major social insurance programme in the country, the first to establish benefits as a right, complete with appeals machinery for claimants who felt unfairly treated. By comparative standards, however, the Liberals' plan was modest in design. While it covered most of the urban, industrial workforce, it excluded workers in agriculture, fishing and private domestic service, as well as public employees and high income earners. Moreover, the benefit replacement rate was only 50 per cent of wages, with a modest supplement of 15 per cent for married claimants.

Family Allowances came next. In 1944 the federal government introduced a universal, flat-rate benefit funded from general tax revenues. Unlike the Australian Child Endowment Scheme established a few years earlier, benefits were payable for the first child and increased with the child's age; but the benefits were modest, providing an average monthly payment of $14.18 per family.[26] There was little federal–provincial

[26] Guest, *Emergence of Social Security in Canada*, p. 132. See also Bridgette Kitchen, 'The Introduction of Family Allowances', in Allan Moscovitsch and Jim Albert, eds., *The Benevolent State* (Toronto: Garamond Press, 1987).

conflict over the programme. Quebec did object, and passed a short bill authorizing a provincial plan if the federal government would withdraw. However, the province's opposition 'was launched too late and soon decreased as the political danger of fighting such a popular measure became clear'.[27] This is not to say that the debate was free of linguistic tension. Higher birthrates in Quebec than elsewhere led to criticisms, including by the Conservative parliamentary opposition, that Family Allowances represented a bribe to the Quebec electorate. To defuse the possibility of the debate dividing along ethnic lines, the programme provided smaller payments for fifth and subsequent children, but the provision was dropped without much debate in 1949.

Pensions represented the final step. In 1951 another constitutional amendment gave the federal government authority to provide old age pensions directly to citizens, as opposed to the 1927 model of supporting provincial programmes. At the time the Quebec government was not interested in launching its own programme, but it did preserve its options for the future, insisting that the constitutional amendment retain provincial paramountcy by stipulating that no federal pension plan should affect the operation of any future provincial legislation.[28] The Old Age Security (OAS) was a universal, flat-rate pension of $40 per month for elderly citizens funded through general tax revenues. In 1966 the benefit was extended by the Guaranteed Income Supplement (GIS), an income-tested supplement that is added to the OAS payment for elderly citizens with middle and low incomes. The GIS payment is reduced by 50 cents for every dollar in other income, in effect, providing a guaranteed income for the elderly. In 1975 a similar Spouses Allowance was added for younger spouses of pensioners.

These exclusively federal programmes, unencumbered as they are by inter-governmental constraints, remained responsive to the centrist currents of federal politics. During the post-war decades, these currents were largely expansionist, and parties entered election campaigns armed with promises to raise benefits. In 1957, for example, Conservative attacks on the paltry nature of an OAS increase helped topple the long-entrenched Liberal government. After 1966 these electoral dynamics increasingly focussed on the GIS, which cost less to increase. The supplement was initially introduced as a small, temporary measure that would fade away with the maturation of the contributory pensions introduced at the same time. However, the GIS was repeatedly enriched in real terms, usually

---

[27] Dominique Jean, 'Family Allowances and Family Autonomy', in Bettina Bradbury, ed., *Canadian Family History* (Toronto: Copp Clark Pitman, 1992), pp. 401–41, p. 403.
[28] Vaillancourt criticizes the Quebec position as incoherent and a sign of provincial immobilism (*Evolution des politiques sociales au Québec*, pp. 430, 486).

just before or after an election, steadily transforming its role. By the mid-1980s the maximum GIS was worth more than the OAS and the supplement provided full or partial support to almost half of the elderly population, significantly delaying the day at which it would fade as an important component of the retirement income system.

Similarly, the federal government was free to expand UI and Family Allowances on its own terms. In 1971 legislation broadened the UI programme to include all employees, increased the replacement ratio to 66 per cent of wages, introduced extended benefits in regions with high levels of unemployment, and covered unemployment resulting from sickness and temporary disability. All of this came with remarkably little consultation with the provincial governments; even the regional features of the plan represented 'the federal government's own policy priorities in regional development', and 'were not pressed upon Ottawa by the provinces'.[29] Notably, the 1971 legislation also introduced maternity benefits. As Ann Porter points out, tying maternity benefits to UI had the effect of excluding women who were not in the labour force, who were self-employed, or who were unable to find the stable kinds of jobs needed to qualify for an insurance-based benefit.[30] Yet at no point was a separate maternity programme seriously considered. A separate programme would have fallen into provincial jurisdiction. Unemployment Insurance was a federal instrument, and unemployment insurance it was.

With Family Allowances, Liberal governments zigzagged with abandon. In 1970 they proposed to transform the universal benefit into an income-tested Family Income Supplement, analogous to the GIS, in order to target resources on low income families. However, Liberal MPs encountered resistance to the idea of taking the Family Allowance away from middle-income families during the 1972 election. Reduced to a minority position in Parliament and dependent for their survival on the NDP, the Liberals promptly changed direction. They maintained the universal programme and tripled the payment overnight, thereby restoring most of its original purchasing power. In 1978, however, the Liberals returned to income testing in an incremental way, introducing a refundable Child Tax Credit, financed in part through a reduction in the universal Family Allowance. Over the next decade, a tortuous set of changes integrated the two programmes into a single, income-tested Child Benefit. All of these shifts had major implications for provincial social assistance programmes, but the provinces had no role in the decisions.

[29] Pal, *State, Class, and Bureaucracy*, p. 161.
[30] Ann Porter, *Gendered States: Women, Unemployment Insurance, and the Political Economy of the Welfare State in Canada, 1945–1997* (Toronto: University of Toronto Press, 2003), p. 91.

Joint decision federalism
In comparison, the introduction of contributory pensions in 1965 and their subsequent evolution were governed by a complex process of joint decision, which diversified the ideological perspectives brought to bear on programme design and slowed change.

The legal origins of joint decision-making lay in the provincial paramountcy embedded in the 1951 constitutional amendment on pensions. When the issue of a contributory pension plan came to the fore in the mid-1960s, Quebec announced that it would operate its own plan. As a consequence, the Quebec Pension Plan (QPP) operates in that province, and the Canada Pension Plan (CPP) operates throughout the other provinces and the territories. In addition, although the other provinces were content with a federally delivered plan, they wanted to preserve significant control over it, and the limitations of the 1951 amendment gave them leverage. A new constitutional amendment was required to include survivor and disability benefits in the plan, and the provinces insisted on joint decision-making in return for agreeing to the amendment. As a result, changes in the CPP require the consent of the federal government and two-thirds of the provinces representing two-thirds of the population of the country, a requirement more demanding than the amending formula for most parts of the Canadian Constitution.

Asymmetry and joint decision-making create complex veto points. First, to avoid the administrative and political headaches that would emerge if the two plans diverged sharply, pension planners in Ottawa and Quebec City accept that the Canada and Quebec plans should remain broadly parallel, with neither side making significant changes alone. Second, the formula for provincial consent to changes in the CPP means that Ontario alone, or a variety of possible combinations of other provinces, can block changes approved by the federal parliament. In effect, then, the CPP rules and the pressure for parallelism between CPP and QPP create a system of multiple vetoes: Ottawa, Ontario, Quebec or several combinations of the other provinces can all stop change. Under such decision rules, policy change requires a high level of federal–provincial consensus and depends on elaborate inter-governmental negotiations.

The introduction of the plans illustrates the dynamics well. Federal leadership was critical to catapulting contributory pensions to the top of the national agenda in the 1960s. In his analysis of federal–provincial diplomacy in that period, Richard Simeon concludes that if contributory pensions had remained an exclusively provincial jurisdiction, 'it is most unlikely that a plan comparable to CPP would have been enacted'.[31]

---

[31] Simeon, *Federal–Provincial Diplomacy*, p. 270; see also Bryden, *Old Age Pensions*, and Bryden, *Planners and Politicians*.

Contributory pensions were not a provincial priority, and many provinces would likely have followed Ontario's plan to rely on the private sector, with employers above a certain size required to provide occupational pensions. Ontario was governed by the Conservatives, and its ideological orientation was reinforced by the insurance industry, which is largely headquartered in the province. Industry representatives were deeply involved in Ontario's planning and included in its delegations to federal–provincial conferences. The province recognized that the federal proposal was popular with the public, and accepted that contributory pensions of some sort were inevitable. But it held out for a limited plan that left ample scope for private pensions and minimized redistribution by relating individual contributions and benefits closely.

Initially, federal officials assumed Ontario was the major obstacle, and trimmed their sails accordingly, for example, reducing the proposed benefits from a replacement rate of 30 per cent to 20 per cent of average wages. But during a 1963 federal–provincial conference, the Quebec government created a sensation by outlining its plan, which included more generous benefits levels and a more redistributive funding formula. Moreover, in contrast to the federal preference for a pay-as-you-go model, Quebec called for a partially funded plan, with the accumulated fund purchasing provincial government bonds, effectively loaning the capital to the provincial government on favourable terms. This idea was attractive to other provinces as well. At that point, the federal proposal was dead. A final round of secret negotiations between Ontario and Quebec City produced a compromise plan: Ottawa accepted partial funding; Quebec accepted an earlier phase-in of benefits; the replacement rate was set at 25 per cent of average monthly earnings, lower than Ottawa's initial preference but higher than its Ontario-focussed version; and the plan had broader benefits and a more redistributive structure than Ottawa had originally anticipated. The Ontario government and the insurance industry were not happy and felt that Ottawa 'had used Quebec to turn the tables on them'.[32] But Ontario too was attracted by the funding model, and in the end accepted the need for parallelism with Quebec.

In subsequent decades, multiple vetoes slowed the pace of expansion and helped deflect electoral pressures away from the CPP/QPP towards the exclusively federal GIS. However, expansion of an income-tested supplement, even one reaching close to half of retired Canadians, is a much more limited instrument than a broadly-based contributory pension. The 1970s did witness one major effort to expand the CPP/QPP. In 1975 the Canadian Labour Congress and social groups launched a 'Great

---

[32] Tom Kent, *A Public Purpose: An Experience of Liberal Opposition and Canadian Government* (Montreal: McGill-Queen's University Press, 1988), p. 286.

Pension Debate', urging a doubling of CPP benefits. The federal Liberals were initially sympathetic to some expansion, and an advisory commission in Quebec was also supportive. Wider provincial support, however, was lacking. As the CPP Advisory Committee noted in 1975, 'the CPP has become the backbone of provincial debt financing', contributing more than 30 per cent of total provincial borrowing and even more in periods of stress in capital markets.[33] In this situation, provinces had a vested interest in opposing any liberalization of benefits that would erode the size of the fund. The campaign's momentum was slowed, and the historic moment passed. By the time an inter-governmental consensus emerged ten years later, economic recession and an increasingly conservative political climate had shifted the centrist currents of Canadian politics: all governments opposed expansion of the CPP/QPP, and focussed instead on encouraging occupational pensions and private retirement savings in tax-sheltered accounts. The 1985 changes in the contributory plans were limited to division of credits on divorce and remarriage, and a schedule of increases in the contribution rates.[34]

These institutional dynamics help to explain the relatively 'liberal' nature of Canadian pensions. In combination, the OAS and the maximum CPP/QPP benefit replace approximately 40 per cent of earnings for the average wage earner, a modest amount by European and even US standards. The average Canadian retiree receives a larger portion of his or her income from private occupational pensions, personal retirement accounts and other forms of savings than in most other western countries.[35] Consistent with this liberal ethos, the strength of the Canadian system is at the bottom of the income distribution. The size and reach of the Guaranteed Income Supplement ensures that the replacement rate is much higher for low income workers. As a result, despite lower

---

[33] Canada Pension Plan Advisory Committee, *The Rate of Return on the Investment Fund of the Canada Pension Plan* (Ottawa, Ont.: Minister of Supply and Services, Canada, 1975), pp. 7–8 and appendix 4.

[34] Keith Banting, 'Institutional Conservatism: Federalism and Pension Reform', in Jacqueline Ismael, ed., *Canadian Social Welfare Policy: Federal and Provincial Dimensions* (Montreal: McGill-Queen's University Press, 1985); Marc Desjardins, 'Les Gouvernements provinciaux et les instruments de l'intervention gouvernementale', in Jean Crête, Louis-Marie Imbeau and Guy Lachapelle, eds., *Politiques Provinciales Comparées* (Sainte-Foy, Quebec: Sainte-Foy Presses de l'Université Laval, 1994). Bruno Théret argues correctly that ideological shifts explain the changes in 1985, but gives too little credit to joint decision in slowing the momentum of the advocates of expansion in the 1970s; see his *Protection sociale et fédéralisme: L'Europe dans le miroir de l'Amérique du Nord* (Brussels and Montreal: P. I. E.-Lang S. A. and Presses de l'Université de Montréal, 2003), chapter 8.

[35] Daniel Béland and John Myles, 'Stasis Amidst Change: Canadian Pension Reform in an Age of Retrenchment', SEDAP [Social and Economic Dimensions of an Aging Population] research paper no. 111 (Hamilton, Ont.: McMaster University, 2003).

expenditures, the combined programmes have a stronger redistributive structure and a more dramatic impact on poverty among the elderly than does social security in the United States, the benefits of which are more strictly proportional to income.[36]

Shared-cost federalism
The third model, shared-cost federalism, structured federal–provincial relations in the fields of health care and social assistance. In contrast to exclusively federal programmes, the shared-cost model broadens the range of governments and ideologies influencing policies, but in contrast to the joint decision rules, this model does not give a veto to any particular province. These differences in decision rules altered the participants in the process and redistributed power among them, with significant implications for the ideological balances struck in the emerging policies.

Health care Provincial control over health care was firmly entrenched in the constitution, and there were no constitutional amendments expanding federal jurisdiction. There is thus no Canadian equivalent of Medicare in the United States or medical and pharmaceutical benefits in Australia, which are delivered directly to citizens by the central government. In Canada, the federal role flows through shared-cost mechanisms.

In the early days federalism slowed progress towards public health insurance. As was shown earlier, the courts invalidated the federal government's social insurance legislation in 1937 and the provinces rejected the Green Book proposals in 1945, both of which included health insurance. Initially, federal action was limited to grants to the provinces for hospital construction and public health initiatives introduced in 1948. This hiatus was to have lasting consequences. During the 1930s and 1940s Canadian thinking on health care was strongly influenced by British ideas. As Carolyn Tuohy has observed, 'if a window of opportunity for policy change had opened in Canada in the 1940s, the resulting scheme would undoubtedly have borne a closer resemblance to the NHS (though undoubtedly without the Labour-inspired nationalization of the hospitals) than did the Canadian plan that developed twenty years later. But no such window opened in wartime or the immediate post-war period, given the state of federal-provincial relations.'[37]

Nevertheless, federalism did create opportunities for innovation at the provincial level, which the political left used to establish a universal system

---

[36] Robert Brown and Jeffry Ip, 'Social Security – Adequacy, Equity and Progressiveness: A Review of Criteria Based on Experience in Canada and the United States', *North American Actuarial Journal*, vol. 4 (2000), no. 1, pp. 1–19.
[37] Carolyn Tuohy, *Accidental Logics: The Dynamics of Change in the Health Care Arena in the United States, Britain, and Canada* (Oxford: Oxford University Press, 1999), p. 44.

as the leading option for the country as a whole. In 1947 the CCF government of Saskatchewan implemented universal hospital insurance, the first jurisdiction in North America to do so. Two other western provinces – British Columbia and Alberta – followed in quick succession. At that point the spread across the country stalled, and the provinces increasingly looked to the federal government to build a national approach. The Prime Minister, Louis St Laurent, vacillated, insisting that his government would support provincial health insurance programmes only when a majority of the provinces representing a majority of the population was ready to join a national scheme. By the mid-1950s, however, this condition was met when Ontario and Newfoundland joined the list of provinces demanding federal action. In 1957 the federal government introduced a universal hospital insurance programme, which shared the costs of provincial programmes, and within four years all of the provinces had joined. Quebec was the last in, joining after the election of the Liberal Party in 1960.

A similar cycle extended health insurance to physicians' services. In 1962 the NDP government of Saskatchewan again took the lead, introducing a Medicare plan, despite a bitter three-week doctors' strike, the first organized withdrawal of services by medical professionals in North America. Key elements in the settlement that ended the strike – universal and comprehensive coverage, the right of patients to choose their own doctors, and the preservation of a fee-for-service payment for physicians – became the starting point for national debate. The Saskatchewan experience demonstrated that the social-democratic approach was feasible in administrative and political terms. Doctors no longer had to provide uncompensated care, and their incomes actually rose in the early years of the programme, easing the danger of militant opposition elsewhere. This early success gave ammunition to reformist forces in national politics, and their opportunity came in 1963 with the return to power of the federal Liberal Party. The Liberals were committed to a national Medicare programme of some sort, a move 'aimed at co-opting the CCF-NDP's health reform agenda'.[38] Moreover, the new government was in a minority in Parliament and depended on the support of the minor parties, including the NDP.

Conservative political forces mounted a fierce resistance to the universal model. The Canadian Medical Association and the insurance industry were opposed, and ideological conflict coursed through intergovernmental channels. Conservative governments in Ontario, Alberta

---

[38] Antonia Maioni, *Parting at the Crossroads: The Emergence of Health Insurance in the United States and Canada* (Princeton: Princeton University Press, 1998), p. 128.

and British Columbia were committed to private coverage for the majority of the population, with public programmes limited to the 'hard to insure', such as the elderly and the poor. Without federal action, this position would undoubtedly have prevailed in large parts of the country, and health insurance in Canada would have more closely resembled the system emerging at the same time in the US. However, after a royal commission recommended a universal programme, the federal government came down on that side of the debate. This policy was a difficult ideological pill for conservative provincial governments to swallow, but they were caught in a familiar vice. The federal programme was popular with their electorates, and if they refused to join, their residents would still have to pay federal taxes to support the programme in other provinces. The long-serving health minister in Alberta resigned in protest. The Premier of Ontario denounced Medicare as 'one of the greatest frauds that has ever been perpetrated on the people of this country'.[39] Unlike in the case of contributory pensions, however, Ontario lacked the leverage of a veto. By 1971 all the provinces had Medicare programmes in place.

The degree of conditionality in these programmes reflected the intergovernmental politics of the day. The 1957 legislation incorporated relatively demanding conditions and accounting requirements. The Medical Care Act of 1966, however, had few detailed controls and simply specified broad principles. To qualify for support, provincial plans had to provide universal coverage to all provincial residents, cover all medically necessary services, ensure public administration of medical plans, and guarantee the portability of benefits outside the province. Within those parameters, however, provinces retained full responsibility for health care. They regulate hospitals, clinics, nursing homes and other health institutions; they regulate the medical professions and shape medical education; they negotiate fee schedules with doctors and other professions, set global budgets for hospitals, and have the final responsibility for the costs of health care. Although federal legislation requires provinces to cover all 'medically necessary' procedures, the definition of medical necessity is left to the provinces and coverage does vary at the margins.

Federalism thus played a distinctive role in the politics of health insurance. Although jurisdictional issues delayed action in the early years, federalism also created room for a reformist province to implement health insurance on social-democratic principles. In the end, federal action was required to transform this regional initiative into a national programme. But federal–provincial interaction launched health insurance on a

---

[39] Quoted in Malcolm Taylor, *Health Insurance and Public Policy in Canada*, 2nd edn (Montreal: McGill-Queen's University Press, 1987), p. 375.

social-democratic trajectory that contrasts sharply with the contributory pensions being developed at the same time by the same governments. While the pension reforms carefully left substantial room for occupational pensions and private savings, health insurance displaced the private insurance industry completely from core hospital and medical services. Decision rules were not the only difference between the sectors. But they were critical.

Social assistance and social services The same dynamics did not shape social assistance. The federal government assumed social assistance would shrink to a residual role after the new income security system matured, and it never sought to establish a powerful national framework for provincial welfare programmes. The result was to deprive the CCF/NDP provinces of the sort of leverage they were able to exert in health care.

The 1945 Green Book proposals envisioned full federal responsibility for all unemployed people, including those not covered by unemployment insurance, and a number of provincial governments pressed Ottawa to honour its proposals. In the end the federal government agreed to a shared-cost programme, partly as a way, in the words of a cabinet document, to 'bury the Green Book proposals once and for all'.[40] In introducing the 1956 Unemployment Assistance Act (UAA), the minister of National Health and Welfare proclaimed that it would 'write finis to the deadlock which has existed in this country for a decade or more . . . [as] each jurisdiction has argued that responsibility belonged to another level of government'.[41] In 1965 the Canada Assistance Plan (CAP) consolidated existing shared-cost programmes in the field and extended support to Mothers' Allowances for the first time.

Despite the funding, the federal policy role in social assistance was tepid. Eligibility requirements and benefit levels were left to the provinces. Under the CAP, provinces were required to support all persons 'in need', to establish a formal appeal machinery and to abolish provincial residency requirements for social assistance. Otherwise, they had complete control. Despite some pressure from social policy groups, no serious thought was given to national benefit standards, and even a proposal to require provinces to report annually on their policies was quashed within the federal government by the Department of Finance.[42]

---

[40] Quoted in James Struthers, 'Shadows from the Thirties: The Federal Government and Unemployment Assistance, 1941–1956', in Jacqueline Ismael, ed., *The Canadian Welfare State: Evolution and Transition* (Edmonton: University of Alberta Press, 1987), p. 24.
[41] Quoted in Banting, *Welfare State and Canadian Federalism*, p. 69.
[42] Rodney Haddow, *Poverty Reform in Canada 1958–1978: State and Class Influences on Policy-Making* (Montreal: McGill-Queen's University Press, 1993); Rand Dyck, 'The Canada Assistance Plan: The Ultimate in Cooperative Federalism', *Canadian Public Administration*, vol. 19 (1976), no. 4, pp. 587–602.

Federal financial support did trigger 'a major restructuring of social assistance across Canada on a scale unseen since the Depression'.[43] Spending on social assistance and services rose strongly as a percentage of total provincial expenditures from the mid-1950s until the mid-1970s. The increase was not simply a reflection of rising caseloads, since benefit levels also rose in real terms, especially in the ten years after the introduction of CAP. Although it is impossible to know how much provincial spending would have risen in the absence of federal transfers, the increase was larger in programmes eligible for cost sharing than in non-shareable services; and federal and provincial officials certainly believed the federal transfers were critical, especially in poorer provinces. Within this overall pattern, however, federal programmes left room for provincial programmes to evolve along distinctive trajectories. There was some convergence in benefit levels across provinces in the decade after the introduction of CAP, but the effects were transitory and benefits have gone through cycles of convergence and divergence over the years. CAP also supported the expansion of social services, especially child care, triggering a flurry of provincial initiatives in the late 1960s. Federal regulations tipped this emerging service in the same broad direction, targeting public provision on low income families and favouring non-profit agencies over commercial operators. As in the case of social assistance, however, the provinces retained considerable discretion and provision varied considerably across the country, both in coverage and form.[44]

Summary
The expansion of the federal role in social policy during the middle decades of the twentieth century largely overcame the constraints inherent in decentralization during the inter-war years. Ottawa quickly implemented major income security programmes of its own in the 1940s and early 1950s, and led the nation-wide development of provincial programmes in the 1950s and 1960s. However, new and more subtle relationships were emerging in the post-war era. Different models of federalism altered the mix of officials at the table and redistributed power among those that got there by requiring different levels of consensus for action. The result was a differing interaction between institutions and policy in each case. Exclusively federal programmes were shaped by centrist politics

---

[43] James Struthers, *Limits of Affluence: Welfare in Ontario, 1920–1970* (Toronto: University of Toronto Press, 1994), p. 190.
[44] This paragraph is based on Boychuk, *Patchworks of Purpose*; Health and Welfare Canada, Program Audit and Review Directorate, *Evaluation of the Canada Assistance Plan* (Ottawa, Ont.: Health and Welfare Canada, 1991); and Jane Jenson and Sherry Thompson, *Comparative Family Policy: Six Provincial Stories* (Ottawa, Ont.: Canadian Policy Research Networks, 2000).

and launched on largely liberal premises, joint decision-making provided institutional buffering against political pressures for expansion in contributory pensions in the years after their introduction, and the shared-cost model gave opportunities to social-democratic forces in health care, but not in social assistance where the federal government did not try to define a national approach.

Federalism and the politics of restructuring

Major turning points in history rarely announce themselves as such. In retrospect, however, it is clear that the mid-1970s represented the high-water mark of the post-war welfare state. A new politics came to dominate during the last quarter of the twentieth century, as governments focussed on retrenchment and restructuring. The politics of restructuring in Canada were driven by the same economic changes that were reshaping the welfare state in OECD countries generally: the slowing of economic growth and higher levels of unemployment, the acceleration of technological innovation, and the globalization of international trade. In the Canadian case, globalization essentially meant deeper integration with the American economy, which absorbed well over 80 per cent of Canadian exports by the 1990s. Although the 1988 Canada–US Free Trade Agreement and the 1994 North American Free Trade Agreement did not create a political union comparable to the European Union, intense controversy centred on whether deeper economic integration would require Canada to harmonize its social programmes with US standards. There is little evidence that the Canadian and US welfare states have, in fact, converged.[45] However, conservative political voices in Canada constantly emphasize the importance of economic competitiveness in the American marketplace.

In domestic politics, the centre of gravity moved from the centre/centre-left to centre/centre-right. The Conservatives won two successive majority governments at the federal level for the first time since the First World War, governing from 1984 until 1993, and the Liberals were pulled to the right when they held power, especially in the mid-1990s. As in many countries, historical champions of the welfare state such as organized labour were on the defensive and old alliances splintered. Tensions

---

[45] Keith Banting, 'The Social Policy Divide: The Welfare State in Canada and the United States', in Keith Banting, George Hoberg and Richard Simeon, eds., *Degrees of Freedom: Canada and the United Sates in a Changing World* (Montreal: McGill-Queen's University Press, 1997); Gerard Boychuk and Keith Banting, 'The Paradox of Convergence', in Richard Harris, ed., *North American Linkages: Opportunities and Challenges for Canada* (Calgary: University of Calgary Press, 2003).

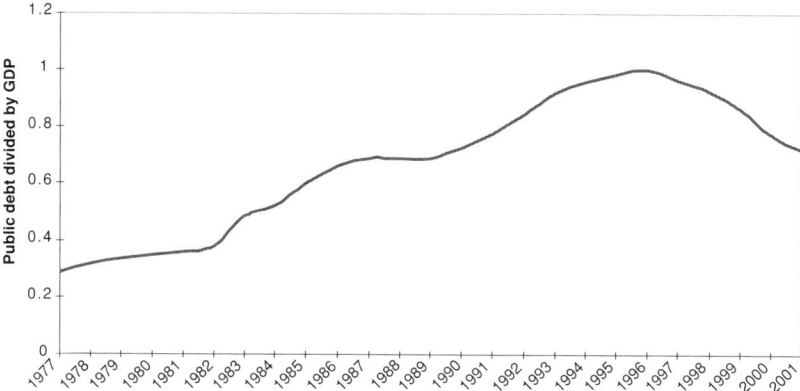

Note: Proportion determined by dividing debt data by GDP data and rounding to the nearest hundredth.
Source: GDP Data: Statistics Canada. Canadian Economics Observer cat. no. 11-210; Consolidated Debt Data: Statistics Canada/CANSIM II. Table no. 385-0017.

Figure 3.3 Consolidated public debt as a percentage of GDP, all levels of government (1977–2001)

grew between the public sector and the private sector unions and between organized labour and NDP provincial governments, which were forced into retrenchment mode. Other champions stepped forward, including the women's movement, welfare rights groups and the providers of social services. Nevertheless, supporters of the welfare state faced a tough climate. By international standards, the fiscal problems of the Canadian state were particularly acute. As figure 3.3 indicates, the ratio of public debt to GDP rose steadily from the late 1970s until the mid-1990s, by which time Canada rivalled Italy as the most indebted of G7 nations. At the worst point, approximately 35 per cent of all federal revenues was pre-empted by interest payments on federal debt, and several provinces faced problems placing their bonds in financial markets. In this context, public opinion stiffened. Universal programmes such as health care and pensions retained strong support, but opinion polls recorded more resistance to unemployment and social assistance benefits and greater support for tax cuts, a pattern that peaked in the mid-1990s.

The new politics of social policy was compounded by an intensification of territorial politics, which increasingly challenged the social role of the federal government. In 1976 the Parti québécois won power in the province of Quebec, confirming its status as a major political force. In 1980 and 1995 the country was to live through emotionally wrenching referenda on the separation of Quebec, with the separatist option losing in 1995 by less than 1 per cent of the vote. Regional economic conflicts also deepened, with the energy crisis of the 1970s and free trade in the 1980s pitting region against region. These conflicts plunged the country into protracted federal–provincial negotiations over constitutional reform, which consumed enormous political energy for thirty years.[46] Throughout this constitutional odyssey Quebec, supported in varying degrees by other provinces, pressed for restrictions on the federal spending power. In the end the country failed to coalesce around a new constitutional model, and the spending power was not formally limited. But the social role of the federal government was constantly on the defensive.

Eventually, territorial conflict and the failure of constitutional reform fragmented the party system at the federal level. In the 1993 election the Conservative Party, which had been dominant for almost a decade, was decimated, retaining only two seats in Parliament. New regional parties suddenly emerged. The separatist Bloc québécois, a sister party to the provincial Parti québécois, became the official opposition in Parliament, and the Reform Party, a populist neo-conservative party, sprang up in the west to become the third largest party. The NDP barely survived as an officially recognized party. The Liberals, the only party with support across the country, returned to government, but they faced a massive deficit and two opposition parties – the Bloc and Reform – that were strongly committed to decentralizing the federation.

The 'new politics' of social policy and the politics of territory thus reinforced each other. The result was an era of social policy restructuring and retrenchment. The impact, however, varied enormously from one programme to another. Some programmes were better insulated than others from the chill winds of the day, and federalism was part of the buffering process, constraining retrenchment in the same way it had constrained expansion in earlier days. Once again, however, much depended on the model of inter-governmental decision-making in play.

Classical federalism and exclusively federal programmes

Federal decision-makers were unconstrained by federalism in restructuring programmes in their own jurisdiction. But they were also fully exposed to their own electorate, without the protection offered elsewhere by jurisdictional confusion. As a result, the outcomes faithfully reflected the power of different client groups, with a stark difference in the fate of pensioners and the unemployed. In the case of OAS–GIS, governments tried a variety of cutbacks, but regularly retreated in the face of angry

---

[46] Peter Russell, *Constitutional Odyssey: Can Canadians be a Sovereign People?*, 3rd edn (Toronto: University of Toronto Press, 2004).

Canada: nation-building in a federal welfare state 119

elderly voters. In 1985 the Conservatives proposed partial de-indexation of OAS, but backed down quickly. A decade later the Liberal government proposed to replace the OAS and GIS with an integrated income-tested Seniors' Benefit, but abandoned the idea in the face of attacks on the left from women's groups and the NDP and on the right from investment brokers worried about eroding the incentive to save for retirement. The only change that actually survived was a more stealthy measure to 'claw back' OAS from high income seniors through the tax system. However, the measure affects barely 5 per cent of seniors.[47]

In comparison, UI was under intense pressure. The programme was central to new policy perspectives that questioned 'passive' income transfers and celebrated 'active' employment programming, and the unemployed enjoyed much less electoral protection than the elderly.[48] The result was large cuts. The process proceeded slice by slice, beginning in the late 1970s and culminating in the mid-1990s. The replacement rate was reduced from the peak of 66 per cent established in 1971 to 60 per cent in 1978, 57 per cent in 1993, 55 per cent for some workers in 1994, and 50 per cent for repeat beneficiaries in 1996 (although offset for some recipients by an increased family supplement). Thus by 1996 the replacement rate resembled that in 1940. In addition, increasingly restrictive eligibility requirements contributed to a sharp erosion in the proportion of beneficiaries actually receiving benefit, as figure 3.4 indicates.[49] Despite a dramatic decline in payments, cuts in contribution rates were negligible, producing an immense surplus in the UI account, a surplus that was available to the federal treasury in a way that the CPP fund is not.

The primary constraint on federal discretion over this programme was the politics of regionalism. In many countries proposals to reduce unemployment benefits pitted politicians against organized labour; in Canada, the most effective opponents of cutbacks are politicians from poor regions.[50] A ritualized political dance was repeated many times: governments proposed reductions; backbench MPs and provincial governments

---

[47] Ken Battle, 'Relentless Incrementalism: Deconstructing and Reconstructing Canadian Income Security', in Keith Banting, Andrew Sharpe and France St-Hilaire, eds., *Review of Economic Performance and Social Progress. The Longest Decade: Canada in the 1990s* (Montreal: Institute for Research on Public Policy, 2001), pp. 183–229.

[48] Stephen McBride, *Not Working: State, Unemployment, and Neo-Conservatism in Canada* (Toronto: University of Toronto Press, 1992).

[49] The decline in the proportion of unemployed receiving benefits also reflected changes in forms of employment, which decrease eligibility for the programme. See Human Resources Development Canada, *An Analysis of Employment Insurance Benefit Coverage* (Ottawa, Ont.: Applied Research Branch, HRDC, 1998).

[50] Pal, *State, Class, and Bureaucracy*, pp. 165–68; Porter, *Gendered States*, pp. 166–72, 195–210, 215–24.

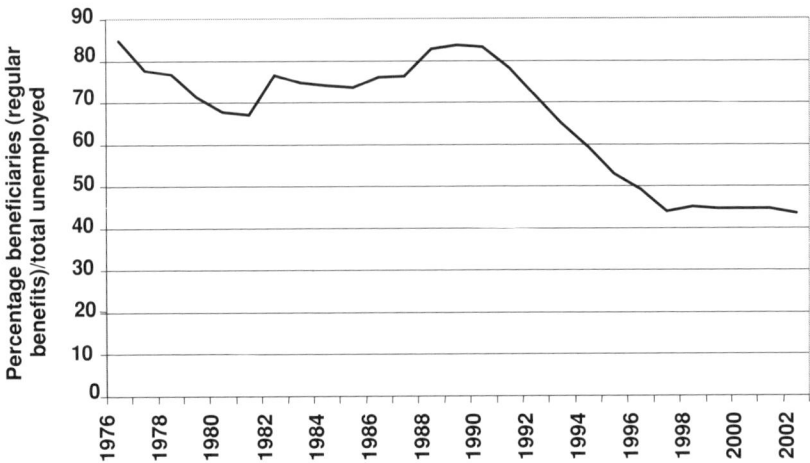

Source: Gerard Boychuk, 'A History of the Canadian Social Architecture' (Ottawa: Canadian Policy Research Networks, 2004).

Figure 3.4 Ratio of UI beneficiaries to total unemployed (1976–2002)

from Atlantic Canada and Quebec mounted fierce resistance; the government compromised in ways that softened the impact in poor areas. This dance, performed by both Liberals and Conservative governments in the late 1970s and 1980s, resulted in growing regional variations in both qualification requirements and benefit duration. At the height of the fiscal crisis in the 1990s, the Liberals returned to the file, introducing more dramatic cuts. But after Liberal losses in Atlantic Canada at the next election, the impact in poorer regions was softened once more. The unemployed in more affluent provinces such as Ontario and British Columbia received no such protection.

Joint decision federalism

In contrast, the consensus-driven, incremental logic inherent in joint decision-making helped protect the CPP/QPP. During the 1990s actuarial reports raised questions about the long-term financial status of the contributory pensions, triggering extensive rhetoric about unsustainability. Yet the final adjustments largely served to stabilize the programme. Joint decision-making was not the only factor at work. The electoral sensitivity of pensions, evident in the OAS case, was undoubtedly important here as well. Yet contributory pensions create rich opportunities for subtle adjustments that are largely invisible to the electorate in the short term but which have major effects in the long term. The fact that these opportunities were exploited primarily to reinforce rather than to weaken the programme is due in part to the need for inter-governmental consensus.

An inter-governmental review was launched in 1996, with the release of a joint discussion paper on reform options.[51] From the outset, however, negotiations focussed on a narrow range of options, and radical changes were never considered seriously. The province of Quebec announced that it would not consider significant reductions in benefits, a position supported by NDP governments in Saskatchewan and British Columbia. Advocates of privatization also found little resonance for their ideas. Such proposals faced a large double-payment problem inherent in moving from a largely pay–go system, an issue that confronts such proposals in all countries.[52] In Canada, such proposals confront distinctive issues. Privatization would weaken the role that the CPP/QPP funds play in provincial finances, and undermine the Caisse du dépôt et de placement, the Quebec government agency that invests the QPP fund. As we shall see, the Caisse has come to play a symbolic role in nationalist politics in the province. In the end, the federal and provincial governments agreed to accelerate increases in contribution rates from 5.5 per cent to 9.9 per cent of earnings over a ten-year period. There was a modest trimming of some benefits, and the two NDP governments refused to sign the final agreement. But governments did not even try for more dramatic retrenchment, such as an increase in the retirement age, and the final changes largely stabilized the role of contributory pensions in the retirement income system.[53]

Shared-cost federalism

The most intense federal–provincial politics in this era centred on shared-cost programmes, which provided ample opportunity for offloading, blame avoidance and mutual recrimination. The stage for these conflicts was actually set as far back as 1977, when bloc funding was introduced in response to frustrations with the traditional form of cost sharing. The federal Department of Finance became concerned that the commitment to pay half of the cost of expensive provincial programmes reduced its control over the federal budget. Provincial governments were irritated

---

[51] *An Information Paper for Consultations on the Canada Pension Plan Released by the Federal, Provincial and Territorial Governments* (Ottawa, Ont.: Department of Finance, 1996).
[52] John Myles and Paul Pierson, 'The Comparative Political Economy of Pension Reform', in Paul Pierson, ed., *The New Politics of the Welfare State* (Cambridge: Cambridge University Press, 2001), pp. 305–33.
[53] Béland and Myles, 'Stasis Amidst Change'.

by shared-cost programmes, which they complained distorted provincial priorities and locked them into endless arguments about whether specific projects qualified for federal support. After extensive inter-governmental negotiations, the two levels agreed to shift to a bloc grant for health and post-secondary education. The federal government gained greater control over its finances, and provincial governments gained greater freedom. Although the conditions attached to the federal health programmes remained in place, provinces were able to allocate federal funding as they saw fit. Indeed, there was no explicit requirement that the funding actually be devoted to health and post-secondary education.

Over time, however, the provinces were to pay a high price for the additional flexibility, as the federal government was no longer committed to paying half of the costs of provincial programmes. At the outset, increases in federal support were tied to the rate of growth in the economy as a whole. But as federal deficits grew, Ottawa repeatedly made unilateral cuts: in 1986 indexation of the transfer was limited to the increase in GDP less two percentage points; in 1990 the transfer was frozen in absolute terms for four years; and the budget of 1995 introduced a broader bloc fund, the Canada Health and Social Transfer (CHST), and cut the cash payment to the provinces dramatically. These changes, which were conceived in secrecy and imposed without warning, provoked a bitter reaction among the provinces, and seriously eroded the legitimacy of the federal role in provincial eyes. The impact of this process, however, varied from programme to programme, depending on the extent to which the federal government tried to sustain a national policy framework, as the contrast between health care and social assistance once again illustrates.

Health insurance   In the case of health care, federalism helped to buffer the universal model from fundamental change but facilitated tough expenditure restraint within the model. In other words, federalism facilitated retrenchment but inhibited restructuring.

The federal government, especially when the Liberals were in power, defined itself as the guarantor of the universal model of health care against efforts by conservative provincial governments to introduce user fees or to increase the role of the private sector in heath care. Poll after poll showed that Canadians strongly supported the existing model, and the federal Liberals could mobilize that opinion in conflicts with the provinces. However, the ability of federal health ministers to play Sir Galahad also reflected the dry realities of inter-governmental finances. Under the bloc-grant system, the federal treasury was not directly affected by changes in provincial health expenditures, and therefore did not bear the costs associated with the defence of universal health care. As a result, federal health ministers were freer to defend the principles of universality and equality of access. Indeed, they did so even as their colleague, the Minister of Finance, was reducing transfers to the provinces. In effect, health care during the 1980s and 1990s displayed many characteristics of unfunded mandates in the United States.

This dynamic unfolded in stages. Just before the 1984 election the federal Liberals nailed their colours to the mast with the passage of the Canada Health Act (CHA). During the early 1980s a growing number of doctors began charging patients a supplementary fee in addition to the payment they received from the provincial medical plan, a practice known as 'extra-billing'. At the same time, a number of provinces began to flirt with the idea of hospital fees for patients. The federal Liberals opposed both practices as inhibiting equal access to health care, and the new CHA prohibited user fees and all charges at the point of service. To facilitate enforcement, the legislation also determined that such charges would lead to dollar-for-dollar deductions in the federal transfer.

The CHA was opposed by all provincial governments. But it was immensely popular with the electorate, and passed unanimously in the House of Commons. Despite an unprecedented appearance by provincial health ministers before the Senate, approval in that chamber was also unanimous. The federal government proceeded with penalties, withholding a total of $247 million from those provinces that allowed charges. The financial penalties were not large enough to have induced provincial compliance on their own. The real sanctions were political. Provincial electorates supported the principles of the CHA, and were upset when their provincial government was declared to be in violation of its terms. One by one, provinces moved to comply. In doing so, they had to face difficult negotiations with the medical profession, which demanded compensation for the banning of extra-billing. Ontario faced a 25-day strike by a majority of doctors, and Saskatchewan doctors held rotating one-day strikes. The doctors made important financial gains in a number of provinces, costs that the provinces alone had to absorb. But within a few years all the provinces were in compliance.[54]

In contrast to its forceful policy role, the federal financial role declined steadily in the 1980s and 1990s. The extent of the erosion depends on how one defines the 'real' federal contribution.[55] At the time of the introduction of bloc funding in 1977, the federal transfer was split into an annual

---

[54] Tuohy, *Accidental Logics*; Carolyn Tuohy, 'Health Policy and Fiscal Federalism', in Keith Banting, Douglas Brown and Thomas Courchene, eds., *The Future of Fiscal Federalism* (Kingston: Queen's University, School of Policy Studies, 1994), pp. 189–212.

[55] Harvey Lazar and France St-Hilaire, eds., *Money, Politics and Health Care: Reconstructing the Federal–Provincial Partnership* (Montreal: Institute for Research on Public Policy, 2004).

Table 3.2 *Federal transfers for health care as a percentage of provincial health expenditures (1975–2000)*

Year	Cash	Tax	Total
1975	41.3	–	41.3
1977	25.2	17.1	42.3
1980	25.3	17.7	43.7
1985	23.8	15.6	39.7
1990	17.9	16.0	33.9
1995	16.4	15.8	32.1
2000	12.8	16.5	29.3

Source: Data from Keith Banting and Robin Boadway, 'Defining the Sharing Community: The Federal Role in Health Care', in Harvey Lazar and France St-Hilaire, eds., *Money, Politics and Health Care: Reconstructing the Federal–Provincial Partnership* (Montreal: Institute for Research on Public Policy, 2004), table 4.

cash payment and a transfer of tax points (which involved the federal government lowering its taxes and the provinces raising their taxes by the same amount). The result was a bitter dispute over the size of the federal share. Ottawa insists that its contribution includes both the cash payment and the current value of the tax points transferred in 1977. Provinces reply that the tax points are now simply part of the provincial tax base, and the federal contribution is limited to the cash. Table 3.2 demonstrates the difference: provinces look only at the first column; Ottawa focusses on the final column. Clearly, the difference is dramatic. On either accounting, however, the federal share of health spending declined in the 1980s and 1990s.

The imbalance between the policy role and the financial role of the federal government sparked bitter federal–provincial conflicts. The 1990s saw the emergence of private clinics providing specialized medical services such as cataract surgery, and charging a 'facility fee', which in some cases was substantial. The federal Liberal government challenged the fees in 1995, the same year in which it cut transfers to the provinces dramatically. CHA penalties were calculated for four provinces, including Alberta where government support for private clinics was strongest. In the end, the provinces largely moved to compliance by banning facility fees.[56] But the coincidence of federal cuts and its campaign against fees deepened inter-governmental tension, and the issue has re-emerged with

---

[56] Joan Price Boase, 'Federalism and the Health Facility Fees Challenge', in Duane Adams, ed., *Federalism, Democracy and Health Policy in Canada* (Montreal: McGill-Queen's University Press, 2001), pp. 179–206.

the opening of several private clinics offering Magnetic Resonance Imaging (MRI) diagnostic services in Quebec.[57]

Federal–provincial dynamics thus helped to buffer the basic model of health care. Indeed, its overall stability is striking. The conditions of the CHA, while certainly strained at the edges, remain intact, and health services are still provided primarily by non-profit and community hospitals on one side and doctors working on a fee-for-service basis on the other. There has been some de-insuring of marginal procedures and new reproductive technologies. But there has been nothing like the revolution wrought south of the border by Health Maintenance Organisations (HMOs) and for-profit hospital chains, or by experiments with internal markets in the UK.

While federalism helped to buffer the model, it also facilitated cost containment within the model. Provincial governments have formidable powers over health expenditure. Because Ottawa does not pay health providers directly, and there is no private insurance for core hospital and medical services, the provinces are the only payer for these services. They therefore have the capacity to cap budgets for hospitals and physicians' services, and to restructure or close hospitals altogether. During the 1990s the provinces used these powers aggressively, reducing per capita expenditures in real terms each year between 1993 and 1996, a deeper retrenchment than that found in other western countries, which struggled simply to slow the rate of growth.[58] Such pressure was difficult to sustain for long. Beginning in the late 1990s, newspaper reports increasingly described a system in decline: the closing of hospital wards; the slow acquisition of new technologies; declining staffing levels; controversy about waiting times for non-emergency surgical procedures; crowded emergency departments. Moreover, polls suggested that Canadians' faith in their health care had fallen more rapidly than in other western nations.[59] The limits of retrenchment had been reached, and governments began to reinvest in health care in the late 1990s. But the limits on retrenchment were electoral, not federal in nature.

Social assistance In contrast with health care, social assistance saw a much more straightforward decentralization. The CAP was not included in bloc funding in 1977, but full cost sharing fell victim in the early 1990s to the battle against the federal deficit and a struggle between the federal

[57] Brian Laghi, 'Stop clinics from billing their patients, Quebec told', *Globe and Mail*, 10 February 2004, p. A4.
[58] Katherine Fierlbeck, 'Cost Containment in Health Care: The Federalism Context', in Adams, ed., *Federalism, Democracy and Health Policy*, pp. 131–78, table 1, p. 136.
[59] Cathy Schoen, Robert Blendon, Catherine DesRoches and Robin Osborn, *Comparison of Health Care System Views and Experiences in Five Nations, 2001* (New York: Commonwealth Fund, May 2002).

Conservative government and the NDP, which was governing Ontario for the first time. Social assistance benefits in the province had increased dramatically under successive governments, and the federal Conservatives were determined not to pay half of the increased costs. In 1990 they unilaterally imposed a 'cap on CAP' for the three richest provinces, limiting growth in the federal contribution to 5 per cent a year. With the onset of a serious recession shortly afterwards, the federal share of welfare costs in these provinces fell sharply; within a few years the Ontario government reported that Ottawa was contributing only 28 per cent of its welfare costs.[60]

The final step came in 1995, when the federal Liberal government abolished the CAP altogether, incorporating social assistance in the new bloc fund, the CHST. This change significantly increased provincial discretion, as the federal funding no longer had to be devoted to social assistance. Ottawa also took the opportunity to eliminate the requirements that provincial programmes respond to all persons in need and maintain appeals procedures. Only the prohibition on provincial residency requirements remained. However, even this modest provision was difficult to enforce. British Columbia, complaining about an alleged inflow of welfare recipients from Alberta, promptly imposed a three-month residency requirement on migrants from other provinces. In contrast to health care, this act of defiance was popular with the British Columbia electorate, and the province was under little pressure to retreat. After lengthy negotiations, the province eliminated the requirement in return for an increase in federal funding for another programme. But Ottawa had been put on notice that enforcing even the vestigial conditionality associated with social assistance would be difficult.

Many social policy advocates predicted that decentralization would trigger a race to the bottom. Although CAP had never set national benefit rates, they argued that cost sharing had dampened the effects of interprovincial competition, since provincial treasurers would reap only half of any savings generated by cuts. They also argued that the CAP requirement that provincial programmes assist all persons 'in need' precluded the more draconian forms of workfare and term limits that had emerged in the US. In fact, benefits did decline. In Ontario, for example, benefits were cut by 20 per cent in 1996. Figures 3.5a and 3.5b provide a national view. Average benefits declined in real terms, especially for single employables but to a lesser extent for others as well. As always, it is hard

---

[60] Thomas Courchene with Colin Telmer, *From Heartland to North American Region State: The Social, Fiscal and Federal Evolution of Ontario* (Toronto: Faculty of Management, University of Toronto, 1998).

Canada: nation-building in a federal welfare state 127

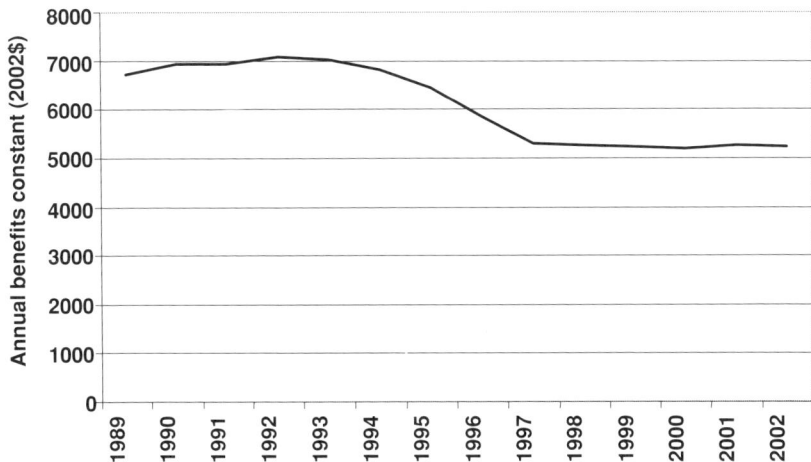

Source: Gerard Boychuk, 'A History of the Canadian Social Architecture' (Ottawa: Canadian Policy Research Networks, 2004).

Figure 3.5a Provincial average Social Assistance benefits, single employable (1989–2002)

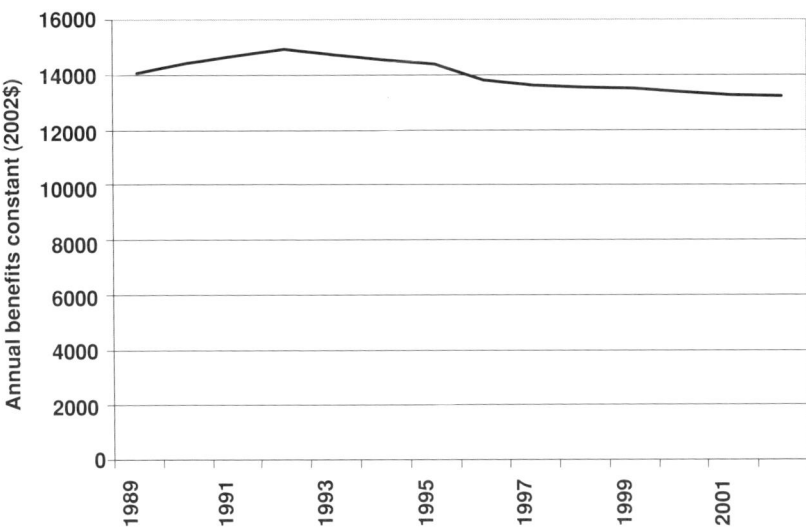

Source: Gerard Boychuk, 'A History of the Canadian Social Architecture' (Ottawa: Canadian Policy Research Networks, 2004).

Figure 3.5b Provincial average Social Assistance benefits, total income, single parent, one child (1989–2002)

to isolate the impact of decentralization. The downward trend in benefits began in 1992, before CAP's elimination, and stabilized again in the late 1990s. Moreover, there is little evidence of convergence in the benefit rates of neighbouring provinces, suggesting that inter-provincial migration of recipients was not driving the process. A careful study of these trends concludes that provinces were 'slouching', not racing, towards a bottom.[61] And clearly the process did not reach any absolute bottom. The consequences for eligibility are clearer, however. Beneficiaries were under increasing compulsion to participate in employability programmes, and liens on home equity were introduced in Ontario.[62] The most draconian step came in 2002, however, when British Columbia introduced time limits, restricting employable people without children to two years of support in any five-year period. Subsequent revisions reduced the numbers affected significantly.[63] But such provisions would have been fully precluded by CAP.

With the abolition of CAP, its regulations shaping provincial child care programmes also disappeared. Most provinces retained CAP's targeted approach, and several took the opportunity to expand the role of commercial operators in delivering the service. Quebec, however, struck out in a different direction. In 1997 the province committed itself to universal access to regulated child care for a flat fee of $5 per day. The programme has been hugely popular, and the province has had difficulty in keeping up with demand for spaces, leading to substantial waiting lists across the region. Nevertheless, decentralization has clearly led to greater divergence in child care across provinces.[64]

Summary

As in the past, the new politics of social policy had to flow through the three distinctive institutional filters created by federal institutions. The differences in the filters help to explain the uneven impact of retrenchment on different social programmes. Exclusively federal programmes

---

[61] Gerard Boychuk, 'Slouching Toward the Bottom? Provincial Social Assistance in Canada, 1980–2000', unpublished ms (Waterloo, Ont.: University of Waterloo, 2003), to be published in Kathryn Harrison, ed., *Races to the Bottom?* (Vancouver: University of British Columbia Press).

[62] National Council of Welfare, *Welfare Incomes 2002* (Ottawa, Ont.: Minister of Public Works and Government Services [vol. 119], 2003); Sylvia Bashevkin, *Welfare Hot Buttons: Women, Work, and Social Policy Reform* (Toronto: University of Toronto Press and University of Pittsburgh Press, 2002); Little, *No Car, No Radio*, pp. 185–86.

[63] British Columbia, Ministry of Human Resources, 'Time Limit Policy to Protect People in Need', 6 February 2004.

[64] Jane Jenson, 'Against the Current: Childcare and Family Policy in Quebec', in Sonya Michel and Rianne Mahon, eds., *Childcare Policy at the Crossroads: Gender and Entitlements at the Crossroads* (New York and London: Routledge, 2002), pp. 309–32.

were fully exposed to the shifting currents of centrist politics, while joint decision helped to protect contributory pensions. Shared-cost federalism helped to buffer the basic model of the health care system, but the mild protection afforded by social assistance collapsed, exposing recipients more fully to provincial politics. Interestingly, the cumulative impact of these changes was to deepen a disjunction at the heart of Canadian social policy. Income security shifted more firmly into the liberal mould, as unemployment insurance and social assistance were weakened and universal benefits such as Family Allowances and to a lesser extent Old Age Security were shifted towards income testing. In contrast, the universal model of health care was protected, at least in hospital, physicians' and diagnostic services. The two worlds of Canadian welfare moved further apart.

The mid-1990s represented the high point of federal retrenchment and the low point in federal–provincial relations. Since then, governments have sought to repair some of the damage in two ways. First, with the return of federal fiscal health in the late 1990s, Ottawa began to reinvest in social programmes, increasing both its child benefits and its transfers to provinces for health care. Second, the federal government and all of the provinces except Quebec adopted a Social Union Framework Agreement designed to nurture more co-operative inter-governmental decision-making. Despite these developments, however, the rupture of the mid-1990s has not fully healed, and the federal government has had difficulty in reasserting a leadership role. It had some success in leading a federal–provincial reform of child benefits and social assistance programmes in the late 1990s.[65] But health care has been much tougher. Although Ottawa significantly increased its funding again in 1999, 2000, 2002 and 2004, efforts to attach conditions to the new money or to give priority to specific reforms have been frustrated by provincial resistance to federal direction. The prospects for new national social policy initiatives remain limited.

The impact of the welfare state on federalism

Federalism has clearly shaped Canadian social programmes, in ways both pervasive and subtle. But, as noted at the outset, the relationship is reciprocal. The welfare state also reshaped the federal state. During the

---

[65] This reform represents the Canadian version of a wider trend in 'liberal' welfare states. See John Myles and Paul Pierson, 'Friedman's Revenge: The Reform of "Liberal" Welfare States in Canada and the United States', *Politics and Society*, vol. 25 (1997), no. 4 (Sept.), pp. 443–72; Ken Battle and Michael Mendelson, 'Benefits for Children: Canada', in Ken Battle and Michael Mendelson, eds., *Benefits for Children: A Four Country Study* (Ottawa, Ont.: Caledon Institute of Social Policy, 2001), pp. 93–188.

middle decades of the twentieth century responsibility for social policy gravitated to the federal government because of its greater economic and political strength. But as federal programmes matured, they in turn reinforced the presence of the central government in the federation and in the daily lives of Canadians, and the weakening of the same programmes in recent years has raised questions about the strength of the pan-Canadian political community.[66]

At the most obvious level, the post-war welfare state was a centralizing force in the Canadian federation. Social policy sustained the fiscal power of the federal government in the decades after World War Two; rising social expenditures offset declining defence commitments, and legitimated federal dominance of the tax fields. Control over financial flows of this magnitude enabled the federal government to harmonize the tax regime for the country as a whole, and gave credibility to its commitment to Keynesian economic management in the post-war period.[67] As we have seen, post-war federal fiscal dominance did decline over the years. Deprived of the political legitimacy inherent in national social programmes, however, federal fiscal power would have faded faster and further.

At a deeper level, social programmes also played a role in defining the nature of the Canadian communities on which the federation rests. Ever since the introduction of social insurance by Bismarck in the 1880s, the welfare state has been recognized as an instrument of social integration in divided societies. In most countries, attention focusses on the role of social policy in mediating class divisions. In Canada, however, social programmes are seen primarily as an instrument of territorial integration. National social programmes create spheres of shared experience in a country otherwise marked by territorial diversities, and strengthen the links between the central government and individuals across the country. While economic and cultural policies tend to pit the interests of one region against the other, the federal government can fashion appeals on social issues that cut across territorial divisions. In the 1960s, for example, federal Liberals saw social programmes as 'part of a strategy to strengthen the presence of the federal government and encourage "nation"-building in Canada'.[68] The strategy worked. Many Canadians, especially in English Canada, have come to see Medicare and other national social programmes as part of the Canadian identity, something that distinguishes them from

---

[66] This section builds on Keith Banting, 'The Welfare State as Statecraft: Territorial Politics and Canadian Social Policy', in Stephan Leibfried and Paul Pierson, eds., *European Social Policy: Between Fragmentation and Integration* (Washington, DC: Brookings Institution Press, 1995), pp. 269–300.

[67] Perry, *Financing the Canadian Federation*.   [68] Maioni, *Parting at the Crossroads*, p. 132.

their powerful neighbours to the south, and part of the social glue holding their vast country together.

The politics of territorial integration can be seen in the responses of two regions of the country to the post-war expansion of federal social programmes: Atlantic Canada and Quebec. For the poorer provinces of Atlantic Canada, federal social programmes were welcome instruments of inter-regional equality. Debates about inter-regional redistribution normally focus on the equalization grants, which are designed to reduce the immense gap in the fiscal capacity of rich and poor provinces. Equally important, however, are the inter-regional transfers implicit in national social programmes. The populations of poor regions have larger proportions of needy people who benefit from social programmes, whereas tax-payers in those same regions provide a smaller proportion of the taxes that support them. Table 3.3 illustrates these dynamics in health care. Although the supply of health professionals varies across provinces, poorer regions are not systematically disadvantaged in terms of doctors and nurses, whereas they are in dentistry, which falls outside of the CHA. Moreover, poor provinces' very high spending as a portion of provincial GDP would be insupportable without powerful instruments of interregional redistribution. Given these patterns, it is hardly surprising that politicians from Atlantic Canada were leading proponents of a strong central government. During the recurring negotiations over constitutional reform and the division of taxing authority from the 1950s to the 1980s, the Atlantic premiers repeatedly opposed proposals that would weaken the federal government. Indeed, they often advocated a stronger federal government than did federal officials themselves.[69] The federal government could normally walk into a federal–provincial conference confident of the support of at least half of the voices at the table.

In the 1980s and 1990s, however, the fading of the federal role in social policy has weakened these dynamics. Poorer provinces no longer have the same faith in the federal government as a champion of regional economic development and inter-regional redistribution. The repeated battles over unemployment insurance shook communities in eastern Canada, and the decline in federal transfers for programmes such as health care have angered poor provinces as much as rich ones. As a result, the federal government can no longer count on the quasi-automatic support of poorer provinces in battles over social policy, and increasingly faces a united phalanx of angry provinces when issues surrounding the social role of the federal government emerge.

[69] Simeon, *Federal–Provincial Diplomacy*.

Table 3.3 *Health services and expenditures by province (2001)*

Province	Health professionals per 100,000			Health expenditures[1]	
	Nurses	Doctors	Dentists	Per capita	% GDP
Newfoundland	1,020	177	31	3,129	12.2
Prince Edward Island	912	136	44	2,865	11.7
Nova Scotia	906	200	49	2,972	11.6
New Brunswick	978	156	35	2,944	11.1
Quebec	787	213	54	2,870	9.5
Ontario	674	180	61	3,312	8.9
Manitoba	894	182	49	3,500	12.0
Saskatchewan	808	153	35	3,056	9.3
Alberta	743	167	55	3,163	6.6
British Columbia	664	197	65	3,260	10.2

[1] Expenditures are for 2000.
Source: Canadian Institute for Health Information, *Health Indicators 2003* (Ottawa: CIHI, 2003).

The integrative potential of national social programmes was much more contested from the start in Quebec, in part because Quebec nationalists also saw social policy as an instrument of nation-building. For Quebec nationalists, social policy was a means of enhancing the linguistic and cultural distinctiveness of québécois society. In 1956 the Tremblay Commission described federal social programmes as a form of cultural imperialism that would erode the province's distinctive character: 'As far as the assimilation of French Canada is concerned, thirty years of social history will thus have had more effect than a century and a half of political history.'[70] After the 1960s Quebec governments came to see social policy as central to the preservation and enhancement of a distinctive French-speaking community in North America. For Denis Saint-Martin, 'there is a clear historical link between the development of the welfare state and the building of an identity for Quebeckers distinct from that of "French-Canadians" or simply "Canadians"'.[71] Nationalists also appreciated the economic power inherent in social policy, as the QPP illustrates. The partially funded plan created a pool of public capital that was invested in the economic development of the province. The government agency that manages the QPP fund, the Caisse du Dépôt et de Placement du Québec, emerged as the owner of the largest portfolio of common stocks in Canada and a critical purchaser of the bonds of public

---

[70] Royal Commission of Inquiry on Constitutional Problems, *Report*, p. 130.
[71] Denis Saint-Martin, 'Why so much Opposition to Social Policy Change in Quebec?' (Ottawa, Ont.: Canadian Policy Research Networks, 6 January 2004).

corporations engaged in major developments in the province, especially Hydro Québec. For Quebec nationalists, the Caisse symbolized a growing québécois presence in the world of public finance, a training ground for French-speaking financial executives, and a key instrument of provincial industrial strategy.[72]

Competitive nation-building agendas helped fuel jurisdictional battles between the federal and Quebec governments during the 1960s and 1970s. As has been seen, Quebec struggled to recapture jurisdiction lost to the federal government during the decades of quiescence, opted out of a number of established programmes, insisted on Quebec control over new programmes and continuously advocated formal limits to the federal spending power. However, federal authorities, especially during the long reign of Prime Minister Trudeau, were convinced that the federal government needed to remain relevant in the daily lives of Quebeckers and resisted a significant transfer of power to the provinces.[73] The intensity of conflict in this period can only be understood by appreciating the extent to which the two governments were competing to retain the loyalty of Quebeckers, and enhance the political identity from which they draw institutional power, the pan-Canadian identity for the federal government and the Québécois identity for the Quebec government.

There is considerable debate about whether national social programmes can, in fact, strengthen the Canadian identity in Quebec. Federal programmes play a much less central role in defining political identities there than in English-speaking Canada. However, attitudinal studies show that most Quebeckers retain a sense of attachment to Canada, which has both emotional and instrumental dimensions. At the emotional level, francophone Quebeckers take pride in the Canadian system of health care and other social programmes, a historical accomplishment, which French-speaking and English-speaking Canadians built together. At the instrumental level, the question of whether social programmes are more effectively protected inside or outside of Canada remains important, especially for less nationalist voters. The political importance of these linkages was etched out sharply during the 1980 referendum on Quebec sovereignty. During the campaign federal ministers campaigned vigorously on the implications for social programmes, charging that independence would threaten the standard of living of voters and that an independent Quebec would not be able to sustain the social programmes that they enjoyed as citizens of Canada. Monique Bégin, the federal minister

---

[72] Stephen Brooks and Brian Tanguay, 'Quebec's Caisse de Dépôt et de Placement: Tool of Nationalism?', *Canadian Public Administration*, vol. 28 (1985), no. 1, pp. 99–119.

[73] See, for example, the federal government's 1969 proposals for constitutional reform, which were presented in Pierre E. Trudeau, *Income Security and Social Services* (Ottawa, Ont.: Information Canada, 1969).

of National Health and Welfare, repeatedly pointed to the inter-regional transfer implicit in federal social programmes, and warned elderly voters that their GIS would probably disappear. The Parti Québécois protested these tactics vehemently, but were on the defensive. On voting day the referendum proposal was defeated by a decisive margin.

Retrenchment weakened the integrative potential of social policy, as the 1995 referenda on Quebec secession revealed. The 1995 vote came after a decade of incremental federal cuts, and a mere six months after the draconian cuts imposed by the 1995 federal budget. Federal ministers could no longer pose as defenders of social benefits, and the separatist forces took the offensive. During the first weeks of the campaign the Parti Québécois charged that only sovereignty could save pensions and other benefits, and this time the federalist forces were on the defensive, explaining why Quebeckers should stay in a federation that cut their benefits. This referendum proved to be a near-death experience for federalist forces: the referendum was defeated by less than 1 per cent of the vote. Obviously, the shift from a decisive federalist win in 1980 to a near loss in 1995 cannot be attributed solely or even primarily to the weakening of the federal presence in social policy. Fundamental issues of political identity and attachment were at the centre of the debate. Nevertheless, the two battles highlighted the strategic role that politicians attribute to social policy in the life and death of states.

The slow decline of the federal role in social policy during the last decade has triggered a search for other elements of Canadian life that can act as the social glue holding Canada together. Some analysts take comfort in the belief that newer instruments such as the Charter of Rights and Freedoms are capable of breathing life into the sense of a pan-Canadian community, defining those elements that Canadians hold in common by virtue of their common citizenship. But others worry that the Charter does not define a strong social policy dimension to citizenship, and that it creates its own tensions within Quebec nationalist circles. From this perspective, the federation confronts the future with a weaker set of bonds that tie.[74]

Conclusions

The story of the Canadian welfare state is, in part, a story about federalism. The structures of the federal state left their imprint on social

---

[74] Interestingly, efforts by the Quebec government to reduce its own social commitments in 2003–04 triggered a similar concern among Quebec nationalists: 'dismantling the (Quebec) welfare state is seen, rightly or wrongly, as an attack on Quebeckers' collective identity'. Saint-Martin, 'Why so much Opposition'.

programmes, and help explain a number of puzzles about Canadian social policy: the slow start; the different ideological trajectories of income security and health care; and the uneven impact of restructuring in recent decades. These dynamics became enmeshed with the wider set of political and economic interests at work, and it is difficult to isolate the independent influence of political institutions. At a minimum, however, it is possible to identify the set of incentives and constraints embedded in the different models of federal–provincial relations, and to determine the direction of their influence.

Canadian experience adds confirmation to traditional interpretations of federalism and the welfare state. As in many countries, decentralization slowed the early development of the welfare state. Provincial politicians in the inter-war period felt constrained by the institutional framework in which they operated, and major breakthroughs had to wait for the expansion of the federal role after 1940. Undoubtedly, centralization was not the only possible route forward, and it is interesting to perform a thought experiment by asking what would have happened if the federal–provincial balance had not shifted decisively during the Second World War. Provincial initiatives would undoubtedly have brought some progress in the post-war era, and pockets of radicalism might have survived. But the diffusion of major innovations across the country would have been deeply constrained by the mobility of capital and labour, the ideological diversity of provincial governments, and the inequality in fiscal capacity of rich and poor provinces. The expansion of the federal role facilitated a common tax and benefit regime, forged ideological compromises among key provinces, and substantially equalized the fiscal capacity of provinces. Without federal action, key landmarks of the Canadian welfare state would not exist on a country-wide basis. As was seen, it is most unlikely that Medicare would have spread across the country, and health care in large parts of the country would have resembled the US model. Nor is it likely that contributory pensions would have emerged nation-wide. A decentralized Canada would have been a more unequal Canada.

The distinctive lessons from the Canadian story, however, are the ways in which it extends existing theories of the relationship between federalism and the welfare state. The traditional dichotomy between federal and non-federal states misses the very divergent impacts of different models of federalism at work in different countries. It also misses the extent to which different social programmes within an individual federation can be governed by different models of federalism. The Canadian federation embraces three distinct models of federalism: classical federalism, shared-cost federalism and joint decision federalism. Each model generates its own decision rules, altering the range of governments and ideologies at the table, redistributing power among the governments that get there, and requiring different levels of inter-governmental consensus for action. Under the classical model, governments operate independently in their own jurisdiction, behaving in their own domain much as unitary governments would do. The shared-cost model places greater emphasis on inter-governmental negotiation and agreement, but retains the potential for unilateral action. Joint decision federalism formally requires the agreement of both levels of government, precluding unilateral action and setting the bar high in terms of inter-governmental consensus. In Canada these models of federalism created different interactions between institutions and policy. At any point in time, during both the years of expansion and the years of retrenchment, the same federal and provincial governments were shaping or reshaping different programmes according to different rules, and with different outcomes.

Clearly, progress requires typologies of types of federalism and further analysis of the separate policy implications of the different types. But it is also important to understand that individual federations may fall into different categories of federalism, depending on the policy at stake. The consequences are potentially powerful, as Canadian pension programmes illustrate. In the case of the OAS–GIS programmes, federalism is largely irrelevant, and policy-makers behave much as they would do if the country were governed through a unitary state. In the case of the CPP/QPP, federalism is central. A complex system of joint decision increases the range of participants, diversifies the ideological voices at the table, bestows vetoes on particular participants, increases the level of consensus required, and locks this tier of the retirement income system into an evolutionary path. It is time for our theories to recognize that all forms of institutional fragmentation are not born equal.

The other lesson from the Canadian experience is the impact of the welfare state on federalism. The expansion of social policy was a centralizing force in Canadian political life, increasing the economic and political power of the central government, especially in the middle decades of the twentieth century. But social policy also played a deeper role in the definition of community and the nurturing of political identities, a process highlighted by the competitive nation-building agendas of the federal and Quebec governments during the 1960s and 1970s, and by the anxieties triggered by the fading of the federal role in the last twenty years.

Contested identities radically increase the significance of the often mundane world of inter-governmental relations. In Canada the co-existence of multiple political identities transforms the debate about the division of powers from a discourse about effectiveness into a discourse about community and national unity. Social programmes become cultural instruments, and controversies over jurisdiction take on a political symbolism that has made their resolution more difficult. These debates continue today. Advocates of decentralization of social programmes see greater provincial jurisdiction as a means of accommodating the diversity of the country and of eliminating a lingering source of tension between Canada and Quebec. Defenders of the federal role counter that the decentralization of social programmes diminishes the role of the central government in the daily lives of Canadians, and that it erodes the underlying sense that, at some level, all citizens are part of a common political community with shared commitments to each other.

4 The United States
Federalism and its counter-factuals

KENNETH FINEGOLD*

Evaluating the effects of federalism

The development of American social policy appears peculiar when compared with a stylized, Eurocentric model of the welfare state. As many scholars have noted, the United States lagged behind other industrialized states in the development of social policy.[1] The US safety net remains incomplete, most notably in the absence of universal health coverage. Benefits provided publicly elsewhere are provided privately, through employers, albeit with public regulation and subsidies.[2] Even the language of social policy is distinctive in the US, where 'welfare' and 'social security' are used to refer to specific programmes rather than to invoke broader concepts and values.

The United States is a federal system, and it has been one longer than any of the other nations discussed in this volume. Is it federalism, then,

---

* With thanks to Frank Castles, Martha Derthick, Jacob Hacker, Stephan Leibfried and Herbert Obinger for their comments on earlier versions of this chapter. The views expressed in it are my own and do not necessarily reflect those of the Urban Institute, its board or its sponsors.
[1] For examples from diverse research approaches, see Harold L. Wilensky, *The Welfare State and Equality: Structural and Ideological Roots of Public Expenditures* (Berkeley: University of California Press, 1975); Seymour Martin Lipset, *American Exceptionalism: A Double-Edged Sword* (New York: Norton, 1996); Arnold J. Heidenheimer, Hugh Heclo and Carolyn Teich Adams, *Comparative Public Policy: The Politics of Social Choice in Europe and America*, 2nd edn (New York, St Martin's Press, 1983); poverty focused, going beyond economics, Alberto Alesina and Edward L. Glaser, *Fighting Poverty in the US and Europe* (Oxford: Oxford University Press, 2004); Joel F. Handler, *Social Citizenship and Workfare in the United States and Western Europe: The Paradox of Inclusion* (Cambridge: Cambridge University Press, 2004).
[2] Jacob S. Hacker, *The Divided Welfare State: The Battle over Public and Private Social Benefits in the United States* (Cambridge: Cambridge University Press, 2002).

that has prevented the development of a more extensive welfare state? For Nathan Glazer, the answer is yes: 'Federalism', he says, inevitably meant 'that there were going to be far fewer national policies in the sphere of social protection in the USA'.[3] Yet many scholars have invoked other factors to explain the limits of American social policy. These include the weakness of the labour movement; the absence of a socialist party; winner-take-all plurality elections, which inhibited the rise of new parties that might have proposed more extensive social policies than the Democrats or Republicans; the occupational and geographic mobility of the working class; the resistance of the South to policies that might disturb its paternalistic labour system; and ethnic and racial divisions among the potential beneficiaries of an American welfare state. Finally, Theda Skocpol emphasizes the negative influence of the Civil War pension system, which elites came to see as corrupt.[4]

All these factors are plausibly interrelated. Theodore J. Lowi, for example, suggests that federalism provides the best answer to Werner Sombart's 1906 question, 'Why is there no socialism in the United States?'[5] In this chapter I do not try to sort everything out and provide a comprehensive explanation for the development of US social policy. Instead, I identify five ways that federalism has affected that development.

Federalism, first of all, has fostered policy variation. This may seem obvious, but it is worth reiterating, because it provides the basis for the other effects. Second, the dynamics of an inter-state 'race to the bottom', in which policy-makers compete to attract business and high income taxpayers by reducing spending on social programmes, have discouraged the expansion of social policy at the state level. Constitutional limits, third, have in some periods precluded action by the national government. Fourth, the capacity of a federal system for policy experimentation has at key moments contributed to the dissemination of policies deemed successful at the sub-national level. And fifth, a federal system expands the range of possible outcomes for conflicts over social policies, so that a deadlock over national policies can sometimes be resolved by agreement to delegate decision-making to the states.

The race to the bottom and constitutional restrictions have limited social policies, but the capacity of a federal system for experimentation

---

[3] Nathan Glazer, 'The American Welfare State: Exceptional no Longer?', in Henry Cavanna, ed., *Challenges to the Welfare State: Internal and External Dynamics for Change* (Cheltenham: Edward Elgar, 1998), pp. 7–20, p. 10.
[4] Theda Skocpol, *Protecting Soldiers and Mothers: The Political Origins of Social Policy in the United States* (Cambridge, MA: Harvard University Press, 1992).
[5] Theodore J. Lowi, 'Why is There No Socialism in the United States? A Federal Analysis', in Robert T. Golembiewski and Aaron Wildavsky, eds., *The Costs of Federalism* (New Brunswick, NJ: Transaction Books, 1984), pp. 37–53.

and for compromises based on policy variation have helped to overcome existing constraints. American federalism, therefore, has facilitated as well as retarded the expansion of social policies.

This argument builds on other recent studies that emphasize the conditional effects of federalism.[6] It departs from them, however, in stressing a factor that has hitherto been relatively unexplored – how the possibility, in a federal system, of policies that vary from jurisdiction to jurisdiction can sometimes resolve national political stalemates. The impact of federalism on US social policy appears more positive when this aspect of federalism is taken into account.

I expand upon the mechanisms by which federalism can affect social policy below. I then review the salient characteristics of the US federal system and provide an overview of the diverse patterns of national–state relations in contemporary social policy. The bulk of the chapter is a sketch of the historical development of US social policy. As part of this sketch, I compare the actual development of US social policy, in the context of a federal system, with a counter-factual: what might have occurred in the 1930s and the 1990s if the US had had a unitary system instead. Federalism, I conclude, has operated at some times to make social policy more extensive than it would have been in a unitary system, and at other times to make social policy less extensive than it would have been in a unitary system.

Policy variation

One way that federalism affects social policy is by creating the likelihood of policy variation across sub-national units. As Aaron Wildavsky has said, 'Uniformity is antithetical to federalism. The existence of states free to disagree with one another and with the central government inevitably leads to differentiation.'[7] Some of the most important national programmes are really sets of fifty state programmes – and even more when the District of Columbia and the territories are included in the count. This variation would not exist, or at least would not be as extensive, if the US was governed as a unitary system.

---

[6] Examples include Keith Banting's chapter in this volume; Paul Pierson, 'Fragmented Welfare States: Federal Institutions and the Development of Social Policy', *Governance*, vol. 8 (1995), no. 4 (Oct.), pp. 449–78; Jacob S. Hacker, 'Reform Without Change, Change Without Reform: Comparative Politics and Policymaking at the New Century', paper presented at Gordon Public Policy Center, Brandeis University, November 2002.

[7] Aaron Wildavsky, 'Federalism Means Inequality: Political Geometry, Political Sociology, and Political Culture', in Golembiewski and Wildavsky, eds., *Costs of Federalism*, pp. 55–69, p. 57.

Policy variation, in turn, produces violations of the principle of horizontal equity, for families with similar incomes will be treated differently according to their state or province of residence.[8] Purely national policies are more likely to be uniform. For example, the formula for calculating Social Security, Old Age, Survivors and Disability Insurance benefits and the rate of the associated payroll tax are the same throughout the US, despite the state-to-state differences in wage rates, cost of living and age structure.

A corollary to the likelihood of policy variation is the possibility of regional differentiation. Throughout American history the most salient regional distinction has been between the South and the rest of the US.[9] Demand for slave labour to raise cotton, tobacco and rice brought blacks into the South, where those crops grew best. Slavery was abolished in 1865, but the paternalistic labour system of sharecropping and tenancy that replaced it provided a similar base for the Southern plantation economy.[10] A complementary political order was based on mass disfranchisement and institutionalized violence. It was in this context that the interests of the South were identified with the needs of white plantation owners, and that their social and economic dominance was protected when the New Deal Democrats, led by Franklin Roosevelt, enacted the central programmes of US social policy.

Table 4.1 suggests the extent of variation in federal social policies by showing the state-level variation in cash assistance for a single parent, not working and working, under what is now the means-tested 'welfare' programme, Temporary Assistance for Needy Families (TANF). States have great flexibility in determining TANF eligibility and benefit levels. Variation in Food Stamp benefits, which for this purpose can be considered virtually equivalent to cash, partially compensates for the variation in TANF because the benefit levels and eligibility standards of the Food Stamp programme are uniform across the states except for adjustments to reflect the much higher cost of living in Alaska and Hawaii, and TANF income is included in Food Stamp benefit calculations.

---

[8] Robin Boadway, 'The Imperative of Fiscal Sharing Transfers', *International Social Science Journal*, vol. 53 (March 2001), no. 167, pp. 103–10, p. 107.
[9] Throughout this chapter I follow V. O. Key in defining 'the South' as the eleven states that seceded from the Union during the Civil War: Alabama, Arkansas, Florida, Georgia, Louisiana, Mississippi, North Carolina, South Carolina, Tennessee, Texas and Virginia. See V[aldimer] O[rlando] Key, Jr, *Southern Politics in State and Nation* (New York: Knopf, 1949; reprinted, Knoxville: University of Tennessee Press, 1977), pp. 10–11.
[10] See Lee J. Alston and Joseph P. Ferrie, *Southern Paternalism and the American Welfare State: Economics, Politics, and Institutions in the South, 1865–1965* (Cambridge: Cambridge University Press, 1999).

Table 4.1 *State variation in social programme benefits (1999)*

	No earnings			Works 40 hours/week at federal minimum wage ($ 5.15/hour)		
	Total income $	TANF* $	Food stamps $	Total income¹ $	TANF $	Food stamps $
*Mean*²	705	389	316	1.383	73	174
*Minimum*²	499	164	239	1.308	0	0
*Maximum*²	892	628	335	1.764	628	257
*Standard deviation*²	111	133	27	89	133	52
*Coefficient of variation*²	15,7	34,1	8,5	6,4	182,2	30,0
*Mean South*³	558**	223**	335**	1.360	61	163
*Mean Non-South*²	748	438	311	1.389	76	177

* TANF = Temporary Assistance for Needy Families.
** Differences in means significant at the .01 level.
¹ For all states, includes $886 in earnings, $68 in federal payroll taxes, and $318 in federal Earned Income Tax Credit (EITC). Figures do not include state EITCs.
² Excludes Alaska and Hawaii.
³ Alabama, Arkansas, Florida, Georgia, Louisiana, Mississippi, North Carolina, South Carolina, Tennessee, Texas and Virginia.
Sources: Urban Institute, 1999 State TANF Income Calculator, http://www.urban.org/Content/Research/NewFederalism/Data/ANFData.htm

Table 4.1 also suggests that social policies in the South remain distinctive, long after the mechanization of southern agriculture and the enforcement of civil rights laws transformed the political economy of the region. For non-working parents, TANF benefits and total income are lower in the South than in the rest of the nation. TANF benefits for non-working parents are, on average, nearly twice as high outside the South.

Race to the bottom

Federalism can work against the expansion of social policies by creating an inter-state 'race to the bottom'. State and local governments, Paul Peterson argues, will lower taxes and benefits to make themselves more attractive to businesses and affluent families, and less attractive to poor people who cost more than they pay in taxes.[11] David Brian Robertson

---

[11] Paul E. Peterson, *The Price of Federalism* (Washington, DC: Brookings Institution Press, 1995).

emphasizes this dynamic in explaining why the US did not enact modern social policies before the New Deal.[12] Building on Robertson's interpretation, Jacob S. Hacker and Paul Pierson suggest that American federalism retarded the development of US social policy by accentuating the structural power of business, the influence it exercises through the threat of disinvestment.[13] The race to the bottom hypothesis has become ever more plausible as capital mobility has increased. Contemporary governors and state legislators travel to Tokyo as well as to New York to attract investment, and they worry about losing jobs to Mexico or China as well as to other states.

Evidence that poor people actually move in pursuit of larger welfare benefits is mixed: proximity to jobs and relatives appear to be bigger factors.[14] Similarly, access to labour and markets is more important to business location decisions than state taxes or economic development incentives.[15] Even if unfounded, however, the fear of becoming a 'welfare magnet' can still influence the decisions of state policy-makers.[16] Policy-makers may keep taxes and benefits low because they believe that doing otherwise will make their states uncompetitive, regardless of the empirical evidence.

Constitutional limits

The concept of a race to the bottom is most useful in explaining social policy inaction at the state and local levels. We still need to understand why the national government, more insulated from competitive pressures than sub-national units, did not do more on its own.

The answer, sometimes, is that the national government did not have the constitutional authority to act, and it is this impediment to reform which commentators generally have in mind when they suggest that federalism in the United States delayed the adoption of nation-wide programmes as compared with other countries without such institutional obstacles. Prominent in this respect has been the role of the Supreme

---

[12] David Brian Robertson, 'The Bias of American Federalism: The Limits of Welfare-State Development in the Progressive Era', *Journal of Policy History*, vol. 1 (1989), no. 3, pp. 261–91.
[13] Jacob S. Hacker and Paul Pierson, 'Business Power and Social Policy: Employers and the Formation of the American Welfare State', *Politics and Society*, vol. 30 (2002), no. 2 (June), pp. 277–325.
[14] Jan K. Brueckner, *Welfare Reform and Interstate Welfare Competition: Theory and Evidence*, Assessing the New Federalism occasional paper no. 21 (Washington, DC: Urban Institute, 1998), pp. 13–17.
[15] John D. Donahue, *Disunited States* (New York: Basic Books, 1997), appendix.
[16] Brueckner, *Welfare Reform and Interstate Competition*, pp. 19–23.

Court, which has in certain periods held that the American Constitution places severe constraints on the legislative powers of Congress. As Robertson notes, early twentieth-century courts ruled that on some matters, such as child labour and working hours, neither the national government nor the states could legislate.[17]

However, since 1937, when the Supreme Court upheld the constitutionality of the Social Security Act, the constitutional barriers to national social policy have been much looser.[18] Even before that date, as I point out below, the court upheld the constitutionality of federal grants to the states. Arguably, it is a lasting legacy of the pre-1937 constitutional limits on national authority that so much of contemporary social policy takes the form of grants to state and local governments, as opposed to direct assistance from the national government to individuals.

Policy experimentation

If federalism works against social policies by proscribing direct national action and fostering sub-national races to the bottom, it also creates the potential for policy experiments that promote social policy expansion or reform. The classic expression of this potential is Justice Louis D. Brandeis' statement, in a 1932 dissent: 'It is one of the happy incidents of the federal system that a single courageous state may, if its citizens choose, serve as a laboratory; and try novel social and economic experiments without risk to the rest of the country.'[19]

Such policy experiments rarely follow scientific standards and the results are not always as happy as the Brandeis quote suggests. State policy innovation and the diffusion of innovation among the states have been important to the development of US social policy nonetheless. The capacity of a federal system for policy experimentation has, at key moments, contributed to the dissemination of policies deemed successful at the sub-national level. Wisconsin served as a locus of innovation in the 1930s, with unemployment insurance, and again in the 1990s, with welfare reform. Each time, the state's policies helped to make a national breakthrough possible. The ill-fated Clinton health care proposals in 1993–94, in contrast, could not be framed as applying successful state-level policies at the national level, which made them vulnerable to the most extreme claims of affected interest groups and political opponents.

---

[17] Robertson, 'Bias of American Federalism', pp. 277–79.
[18] The Social Security Act cases are *Carmichael v. Southern Coal & Coke Co.*, 301 *US 495* (1937); *Chas. C. Steward Mach. Co. v. Davis*, 301 *US 548* (1937); and *Helvering v. Davis*, 301 *US 619* (1937).
[19] *New State Ice Co. v. Liebmann*, 285 *US* 262 (1932).

Expanded alternatives

A federal system also expands the range of possible outcomes for conflicts over social policies, so that a deadlock over national policies can sometimes be resolved by agreement to delegate decision-making to the states. This, I argue, is what happened in the 1930s, when Congress approved federal solutions to the problems of old age assistance, aid to dependent children, and unemployment insurance, and in the 1990s, when a Congress that had rejected Clinton's national health care proposals funded state-level efforts to expand insurance coverage among low income children.

At these two key junctures in the development of US social policy, I suggest, the federal structure created alternatives to the expansion or contraction of social policy that would not have been available in a unitary system. In a unitary system the multiplicity of veto points at the national level would have worked to preserve the status quo, whatever it was at the time, against efforts to either expand or contract social provision.

The American federal system

The US Constitution, which was ratified in 1789, established a national government with multiple veto points. This national government is linked to the states in several different ways.

Congress is divided into two chambers of different size, with roughly equal, but differentiated, powers, serving terms of different length, and representing the voters at different levels of aggregation (see table 4.2). The state basis of representation is obvious for the Senate, where each state, regardless of population, is guaranteed two seats, and members are chosen in state-wide elections. Senators were originally selected by state legislatures; ratification of the Seventeenth Amendment (1913) severed this formal connection between the state and national governments by establishing the direct election of all Senators. Senate rules often require super-majorities. Through the mechanism of the filibuster, for example, 41 of 100 Senators can often block actions supported by the majority.

The House of Representatives is also based on the states: representation is proportional to the population of each state, with each state guaranteed at least one seat, and no legislative district can cross state lines. Minority parties typically do not have as much influence on the legislative process in the House as in the Senate.

Malapportioned districts, both for the US House and for state legislatures, gave rural voters more influence than urban ones until a series of Supreme Court decisions in the 1960s established the principle of one

Table 4.2 *Structural features of the House of Representatives and the Senate*

	House of Representatives	Senate
Number of members	435	100
Frequency of elections	all seats up every two years	6-year term, staggered (one-third of seats up every two years)
Special powers	originates revenue bills	confirms appointments, ratifies treaties
Electoral unit	state and district	state
Apportionment	proportional to population (1 to 52 per state)	equal (two per state)

person, one vote. The Senate, where one small-state voter counts more than one voter from a large state, continues to be a constitutional exception to this principle, and will remain so because no state can be deprived of equal representation without its consent. In practice, this system is particularly favourable to the states of the inland west, which are typically large on the map but small in population.

The presidency The President is elected separately from Congress, but in a manner that also refers back to the states. The voters do not directly elect a President; instead, they choose, state-by-state, among electors who then choose the President. The early development of political parties guaranteed that electors would function as members of party slates, not as independent decision-makers. Besides creating the possibility that the candidate with the most popular votes will not be elected, as occurred in 2000, the electoral college establishes the state as the basic unit of presidential politics. The candidate who wins the most votes state-wide receives all of a state's electoral votes in 48 of the 50 states and the District of Columbia.[20] Each state has as many electoral votes as it has seats in both houses of Congress, so the over-representation of small states applies to presidential elections as well. Winner-take-all rules, however, also expand the influence of large, electorally competitive states: New York, for much of the nineteenth century, California in the 1980s and 1990s, or Florida today.

Presidents since the early twentieth century have actively and visibly set the legislative agenda, and enjoy even greater latitude in war-making and international affairs. The President is also a veto player in the most

---

[20] In Maine and Nebraska two electors are chosen on a state-wide, winner-take-all basis, and the rest are chosen by congressional district.

literal sense. Bill Clinton, for example, vetoed two Republican welfare reform bills in 1995 and 1996 before signing a third version. Congress can only override a presidential veto with two-third majorities in each chamber. This has been a difficult standard to meet: the Republicans, who controlled both houses for six of Clinton's eight years as president, and demonstrated their attitude towards him by initiating the first presidential impeachment since 1867, were only able to override him twice. A credible veto threat can give the President influence over the legislative process, so that an unacceptable bill never reaches the President's desk.

The Supreme Court Interpretation of the constitution is the province of the Supreme Court, whose justices are nominated by the President and confirmed by the Senate. The Supreme Court is a less state-based institution than the presidency, Senate or House. Regional balance, however, has often been a factor in selection decisions, and one way that cases reach the Supreme Court is on appeal from the highest court of a state's judicial system. The lower federal courts, from which cases can also be appealed to the Supreme Court, are organized by state. Federal district courts serve states or geographical subdivisions within them. The Courts of Appeal, at a level between the district courts and the Supreme Court, are organized by circuit, with each circuit covering several states in the same region. In a few types of cases defined in the constitution, such as disputes between two states, the Supreme Court is the first and only court to hear a case, but most cases reach it by appeal from the state courts or the lower federal courts.

National law is supreme in a conflict with state law, and the Supreme Court can overturn the decisions of the top state courts as well as those of lesser lower federal courts. It can also declare acts of Congress unconstitutional and can strike down state laws, and even state constitutions, it finds to be in conflict with either the US Constitution or federal statutes.

The Supreme Court's interpretation of particular constitutional provisions has set the boundaries of state and national authority. The national laws that govern labour organization, agricultural policy and civil rights all rest on the broad understanding of the Commerce Clause (the power of Congress to 'regulate Commerce ... among the several states') that the Supreme Court adopted after 1937. The Tenth Amendment – in its entirety, 'The powers not delegated to the United States by the Constitution, nor prohibited by it to the States, are reserved to the States respectively, or to the people' – has set strict limits on the powers of the national government in some periods, and been more or less ignored in others.

Constitutional amendment Congress can respond to Supreme Court decisions it dislikes by initiating the process of constitutional amendment.

An example of particular importance for federalism and social policy is the Sixteenth Amendment, which was ratified in 1913 and which gave Congress the power to levy an income tax. It had the effect of reversing an 1895 Supreme Court decision that the income tax was unconstitutional.[21] Proposals are occasionally advanced to revise the Tenth Amendment to give it more teeth.

Amending the US Constitution, however, is difficult, requiring two-thirds approval by each house of Congress and then legislative ratification in three-quarters of the states. The first ten amendments, known as the Bill of Rights, grew out of the constitutional ratification process and were enacted soon after the new government was established. Only sixteen other amendments have been approved by Congress and ratified by the state legislatures since 1791.

The only alternative procedures are also state-based. Congress can be bypassed if two-thirds of the states call for a national convention, but this has never occurred. Ratification can be by popularly elected state conventions rather than by the state legislatures: this has happened once, with the amendment repealing the prohibition of alcoholic beverages. There is no mechanism for a national initiative or referendum.

Political parties Extra-constitutional political parties could potentially overcome the fragmentation inherent in this system, but do so only to a limited degree. In recent years party organizations have been weak, and divided government has been the norm (see table 4.3). Even during the recent periods of one-party control (1993–95, for the Democrats, and early 2001 and 2003–05, for the Republicans), the minority party has typically had enough votes to impede legislative action if it remains unified. Proposals favoured by the majority can still become law, but, particularly in the Senate, often require at least some support from minority members. This was the case, for example, with the Republican-sponsored Medicare legislation enacted in 2003.

Though virtually all Republicans and many Democrats would disown the term, both major parties are 'liberal' in the classical sense. A nascent Socialist Party was undone by World War One and the Bolshevik Revolution. And the predominantly Protestant US has never had the Catholic parties that have been associated with the expansion of some European welfare social policies.[22]

State and local governments The fifty states vary tremendously in population and in area. California has sixty-nine times as many people as

---

[21] *Pollock v. Farmers' Loan & Trust Co.*, 157 *US 429* (1895), 158 *US 601* (1895).

[22] On the importance of Catholic parties, see Harold L. Wilensky, *Rich Democracies: Political Economy, Public Policy, and Performance* (Berkeley: University of California Press, 2002), pp. 116–19, 234–36.

Table 4.3 *Party control and social policy in the United States (1933–2003)*

Years	President*	House	Senate	Key events in social policy
1933–35	**FDR**			
1935–37	**FDR**			Social Security Act
1937–39	**FDR**			
1939–41	**FDR**			
1941–43	**FDR**			
1943–45	**FDR**			
1945–47	**FDR/HST**			
1947–49	**HST**			
1949–51	**HST**			
1951–53	**HST**			
1953–55	**DDE**			
1955–57	**DDE**			
1957–59	**DDE**			
1959–61	**DDE**			
1961–63	**JFK**			Food Stamps Program begins
1963–65	**JFK/LBJ**			Food Stamp Act of 1964, Civil Rights Act of 1964
1965–67	**LBJ**			Medicare Act, Voting Rights Act
1967–69	**LBJ**			
1969–71	**RMN**			
1971–73	**RMN**			General Revenue Sharing, SSI[1]
1973–75	**RMN/GRF**			
1975–77	**GRF**			
1977–79	**JC**			
1979–81	**JC**			General Revenue Sharing for states ended
1981–83	**RR**			Omnibus Budget Reconciliation Act, swap proposal
1983–85	**RR**			
1985–87	**RR**			General Revenue Sharing for local governments ended
1987–89	**RR**			Low Income Opportunity Advisory Board created
1989–91	**GB**			
1991–93	**GB**			
1993–95	**BC**			EITC expansion, Clinton health plan withdrawn
1995–97	**BC**			PRWORA[2], SCHIP[3]

(*cont.*)

Table 4.3 (cont.)

Years	President*	House	Senate	Key events in social policy
1997–99	**BC**			
1999–2001	**BC**			
2001–03[4]	**GWB**			
2003–05	**GWB**			

Colours: ▨ Democratic
☐ Republican

* Presidents: FDR = Franklin D. Roosevelt; HST = Harry S. Truman; DDE = Dwight D. Eisenhower; JFK = John F. Kennedy; LBJ = Lyndon B. Johnson; RMN = Richard M. Nixon; GRF = Gerald R. Ford; JC = Jimmy Carter; RR = Ronald Reagan; GB = George H. W. Bush; BC = Bill Clinton; GWB = George W. Bush
[1] Supplemental Security Income.
[2] Personal Responsibility and Work Opportunity Reconciliation Act.
[3] State Children's Health Insurance Program.
[4] Senate divided 50–50 after 2000 election. Vice-President Richard Cheney voted to give Republicans control, which they held until 6/5/2001, when Senator James Jeffords (Vermont) switched from Republican to Independent and voted to give Democrats control.
Sources: Presidential and congressional data from Roger H. Davidson and Walter J. Oleszek, *Congress and its Members*, 9th edn (Washington, DC: CQ Press, 2004), pp. 466–67.

Wyoming, and Alaska is 547 times as large as Rhode Island, though more people live in the latter state. These differences notwithstanding, state governments, like the national government, all have written constitutions, independently chosen governors and (except in unicameral Nebraska) bicameral legislatures. Twenty-seven states, disproportionately located in the west, depart from the national model by permitting referenda and/or initiatives. Local governments have no constitutional status: the Supreme Court has declared that they are legally 'creatures of the state'.[23] Some states, however, have granted extensive home rule to their cities or counties. No state's boundaries may be altered without its consent.

Taxation and spending Neither the national government nor the states may tax exports; only the national government may levy a tax on imports, an important source of revenue in the nineteenth century but a minor one today. Otherwise, both levels of government enjoy broad powers of taxation. The single largest source of federal revenue is the progressive

---
[23] *Atkin v. State of Kansas*, 191 US 207 (1903).

income tax, which was established in 1913. Originally, only the wealthiest had to pay any income tax. During World War Two, however, the introduction of a new rate structure and the withholding of taxes from workers' regular pay cheques gave the income tax the broader base it has today. Regressive payroll taxes finance the Social Security and Medicare programmes. Federal excise taxes cover specific goods such as gasoline, alcoholic beverages and tobacco products, but there is no general sales tax or VAT at the federal level. The largest sources of state revenue are income taxes, which are nearly always less progressive than the federal tax, and sales taxes. Property (that is, real estate) taxes are the main source of local revenue.

Every state except Vermont operates under a balanced budget requirement of some kind. These vary in stringency, but private bond rating agencies enforce fiscal discipline in all states, including Vermont, by the threat of lowering a state's bond rating and thereby increasing its debt service costs, or even, in extreme cases, excluding it from borrowing at all. Neither the constitution nor the bond markets, in contrast, prevent the national government from engaging in deficit spending. Many state constitutions, moreover, include limits on spending and/or revenues, which cannot be found in the US Constitution.

Figure 4.1 shows the shares of government spending by the federal government and by state and local governments since 1929. The federal government, the lesser presence before the Great Depression, spent more during the 1930s and dominated the fisc during World War Two and the Korean War. Its share of government spending has been declining slightly since then, but remains larger than the state and local share. Grants-in-aid from the national government to state and local governments transferred 15 per cent of total government spending in 1934 and 1935, when the Roosevelt administration sponsored huge public works programmes. They reached a post-war high of 10.3 per cent in 1978 and have been approaching that level again. While these grants expand state and local financial capacity, they do little overall to redistribute income from richer to poorer states.

Because the national totals in figure 4.1 include military spending, they may provide a misleading picture of the balance between the nation and the state, particularly in wartime. Figure 4.2 presents estimates of the federal proportion of domestic governmental expenditures by William H. Alexander, Jr.[24] The two big jumps in the series coincide with the Civil War and the New Deal.

---

[24] William Paul Alexander, Jr, 'The Measurement of American Federalism', in William H. Riker, ed., *The Development of American Federalism* (Boston, MA: Kluwer, 1987), p. 103.

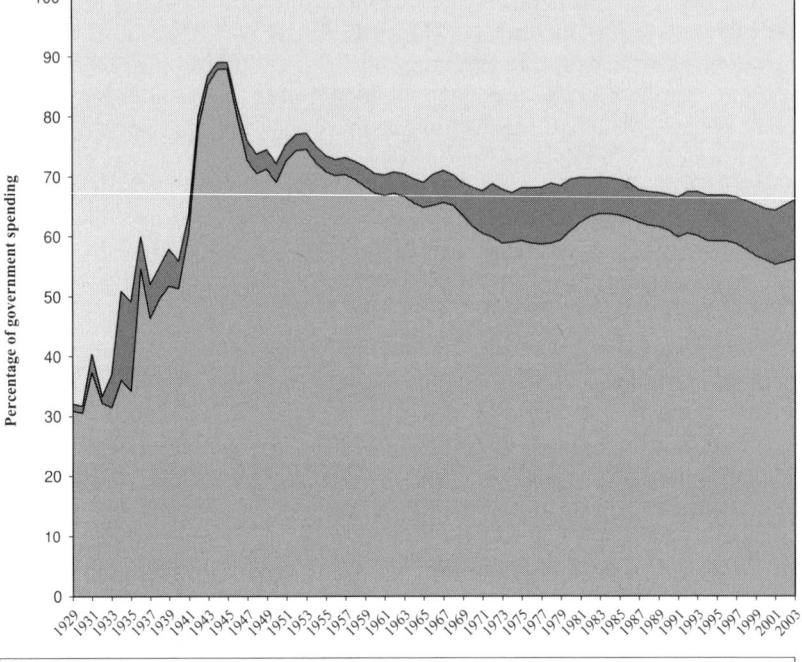

| ■ Federal expenditures (excluding grants-in-aid)   ■ Grants-in-aid   □ state and local expenditures (excluding grants-in-aid) |

Source: US Department of Commerce, Bureau of Economic Analysis, National Income and Product Accounts, tables 3.2 and 3.3.
http://www.bea.gov/bea/dn/nipaweb/GetCSV.asp?GetWhat=SS_Data/Section3All_xls.xls&Section=4
Accessed 2 March 2004.

Figure 4.1   Federal, state and local spending (1929–2003).

An overview of US social policies

Social policy relationships between the national government and the states take a wide variety of forms. Table 4.4 lists the most important components of US social policies, in approximate order from most national to most state-based, with their current level of national funding. Between the extremes of purely national Social Security and purely state General Assistance, we find state administration of federally financed benefits, federal matching of state expenditures, state supplementation of federal benefits, state-financed assistance to immigrants who are ineligible for federal benefits, and block grants, under which state or local governments enjoy substantial discretion in spending federal aid for broadly defined

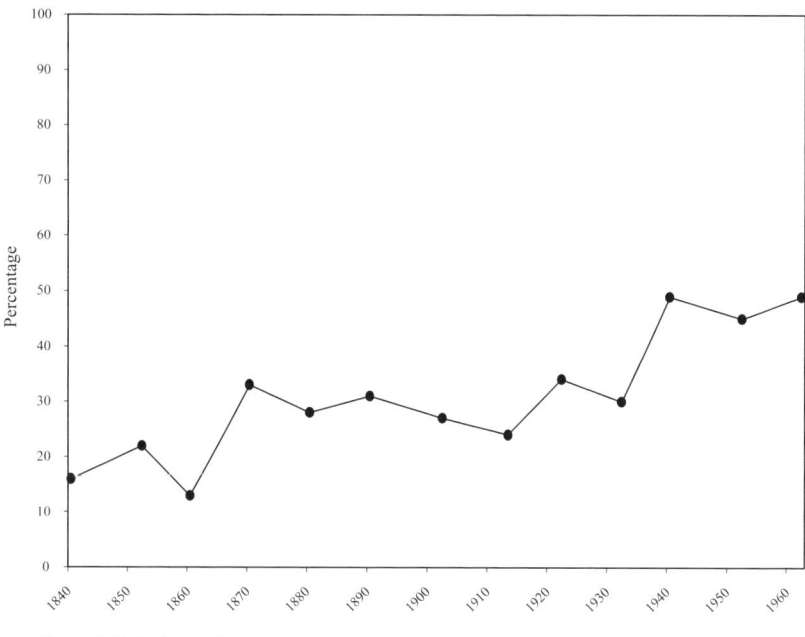

Note: —●— Federal proportion

Source: William Alexander, Jr, 'The Measurement of American Federalism', in William H. Riker, ed., *The Development of American Federalism* (Boston, MA: Kluwer, 1987), p. 103.

Figure 4.2 Federal percentage share of domestic expenditures (1840–1962).

purposes such as community development or temporary assistance to needy families.

This diversity raises questions about the notion that federalism has been an impediment to the growth of a full welfare state in the US. Federalism has not prevented the national government from extending new types of benefits to new groups of recipients. Instead, differences among the states, and the electoral interests of state officials, have been accommodated with programme designs that reflect political alliances, particularly those in effect when the programmes were created, and the particular constituencies involved in the programmes, as recipients, providers or intermediaries. At critical junctures, federalism may have actually facilitated the expansion of social policy by offering vehicles for compromise that would not have been available in a unitary system.

Social Security, as the term is used in the US, refers to Old Age, Survivors and Disability Insurance (OASDI), and not to the broad range of policies the term might encompass in some of the other countries discussed in this volume, or even to the other programmes that were also part of the landmark Social Security Act of 1935. An individual worker who establishes a minimal work history receives a benefit related to average lifetime earnings. Benefits are paid in cash to the retired or disabled earner, or to a surviving spouse or children. The programme is financed by payroll taxes on current workers.

The Social Security system has always been wholly national: the states play no role in financing or administering the programme. It is worth noting that devolution to the states is not discussed in the on-going debate about radical changes to the programme, which revolves instead around privatization.

Medicare, the uniform national contributory programme of partial health insurance for the elderly and disabled, was created in 1965. (Confusingly enough, the same legislation created Medicaid, the separate, means-tested, state-based programme of medical assistance for the poor that I discuss below.) Medicare is a national programme funded by a combination of a payroll tax on current workers, a monthly premium paid by programme participants and general revenues. Medicare covers participants' hospital care and physicians' services, without regard to current work status.

As with Social Security, debates over the future of Medicare have focussed on the possibility of privatization rather than on devolution to the states. I list Medicare below Social Security in table 4.4 because of the overlap issues regarding 'dual eligibles' who qualify for Medicare on the basis of age or disability and for Medicaid (discussed below) on the basis of income. State Medicaid programmes pay these individuals' Medicare premiums, deductibles and co-insurance while providing them with the long-term care and pharmaceutical coverage that Medicare does not offer.[25] With the ageing of the American population and contemporary medicine's increasing reliance on new, expensive and heavily advertised prescription drugs, dual eligibles have become a significant burden on the states.

Supplemental Security Insurance (SSI) provides cash assistance to poor people who are also aged, blind or disabled. SSI is a national programme, but about half the states supplement the national benefit. These state supplements are a vestige of the state-based programmes for the aged, blind and disabled poor that SSI replaced in 1972. Some state programmes are administered by the federal Social Security Administration, whereas

---

[25] Barents Group, *A Profile of QMB-Eligible and SLMB-Eligible Medicare Beneficiaries* (Baltimore, MD: Health Care Finance Administration, 1999).

Table 4.4 *Federalism and United States social policy (2003)*

More national authority		Estimated FY 2004 Federal Spending (in $ millions)
↑	Social Security	494,696
	Medicare	297,035
	Supplemental Security Income (SSI)	31,208
	Earned Income Tax Credit (EITC)	33,551
	Food Stamps	29,044
	Medicaid	177,282
	Temporary Assistance for Needy Families (TANF)	18,866
	State Children's Health Insurance Program (SCHIP)	5,232
	Unemployment Insurance (UI)	46,169
↓	General Assistance (GA)	–
More state authority		

Sources: Spending data from *Budget of the United States Government, Fiscal Year 2005, Historical Tables* (Washington, DC: US Government Printing Office, 2004), pp. 218, 270.

other states run the supplemental programmes themselves. Benefits, even with the state supplements, are meagre. In 1999 an elderly couple was eligible for a benefit of $751 per month; the median supplement, in those states that provided one, was $28.[26]

The *Earned Income Tax Credit* (EITC) redistributes income through tax expenditures, which more frequently benefit upper income tax-payers or business firms. The EITC, which is now a larger source of income support than Food Stamps, Supplemental Security Insurance or Temporary Assistance for Needy Families, is a refundable credit against federal income taxes. That is, federal income tax liability is reduced by the amount of the credit; if the credit exceeds tax liability, the additional amount is paid out as a cash transfer. The EITC has a unique design, which is meant to encourage work and offset the disincentive effects of other low income programmes. Only people with earnings can receive the credit, and in the lowest income brackets its value increases as earnings go up. Benefits are much larger for families with children than for childless adults.

[26] US Congress, House Committee on Ways and Means, *2000 Green Book: Background Material and Data on Major Programs Within the Jurisdiction of the Committee on Ways and Means* (Washington, DC: USGPO, 2000), pp. 229, 239.

Participation in the EITC has been higher than for other low income programmes, in part because commercial tax preparation firms, which profit from high interest loans to clients expecting refunds, have the incentive and knowledge to prepare returns that claim the credit. Because it promotes work, the EITC has been more popular than other transfer programmes among conservatives. It was expanded as part of the tax reforms of 1986, with support from the Reagan White House and the Republican-controlled Senate, and further expansion, championed by the Clinton administration, aroused little opposition in 1993.[27] The Bush administration, however, has announced new pre-certification requirements for some EITC recipients, with the stated purpose of reducing erroneous payments. The new rules are expected to reduce claims among eligible as well as ineligible families.[28]

Fifteen states – none of them in the South – and the District of Columbia offer their own EITCs, usually in the form of an added percentage of the federal credit.[29] Like SSI, then, the EITC demonstrates state supplementation of federal benefits as a pattern of inter-governmental relations. States may use funds from the Temporary Assistance for Needy Families block grant (described below) to finance the refundable portion of their credits. As at the federal level, states administer the credit through their income tax systems. The nine states that do not have a broad-based income tax, however, would incur larger administrative costs if they offered an EITC, and none of them do.

The *Food Stamps Program* provides recipients with benefits that can be used in place of cash for the purchase of food items only. Benefits were originally provided in coupon form, but almost all participants now receive and use food stamps electronically, through transactions over machines installed at supermarket checkout counters. The maximum benefit level is based on the price of a low cost diet that meets basic nutritional standards. Because this amount is recalculated annually, food stamps have maintained their value over time. Most of the other means-tested benefits do not have a mechanism for automatic adjustment to inflation, and so tend to lag behind the cost of living.

Basic eligibility standards and benefit levels for the Food Stamps Program are set nationally, but the states are responsible for its administration. The national government pays the full cost of benefits and splits

---

[27] Christopher Howard, *The Hidden Welfare State: Tax Expenditures and Social Policy in the United States* (Princeton: Princeton University Press, 1997), pp. 145–49, 156–60.

[28] Robert Greenstein, *The New Procedures for the Earned Income Tax Credit* (Washington, DC: Center on Budget and Policy Priorities, 2003).

[29] Nicholas Johnson, *A Hand Up: How State Earned Income Tax Credits Help Working Families Escape Poverty in 2001* (Washington, DC: Center on Budget and Policy Priorities, 2001), p. 7.

administrative costs with the states. The central measure of national welfare reform, the 1996 Personal Responsibility and Work Opportunity Reconciliation Act (PRWORA), increased the range of state policy options in the Food Stamps Program. States now decide whether to exempt able-bodied adults without dependents from Food Stamps time limits and whether to fund state-only programmes for benefits to people ineligible under PRWORA's restrictions on aid to non-citizen immigrants. States can also use various options or waivers to adapt the programme to the needs of the working poor. For example, the states can now exclude the entire value of automobiles (which may be needed to get to work) in determining whether an applicant's assets are above the programme's limits.

Medicaid, the programme of medical assistance for the poor, was created by the same 1965 legislation that created Medicare. Maximum income levels are generally higher for children than for parents, and higher for parents than for childless adults, whom some states do not cover no matter how poor they are. Covered services include prescription drugs, long-term care, hospitalization and doctor visits. Participants either choose among private providers or receive care through a private managed care plan. Children and parents make up about two-thirds of Medicaid participants, but they are relatively cheap to cover. About one-third of participants are elderly, blind or disabled; these groups, which include participants who are also eligible for Medicare, account for about two-thirds of Medicaid spending.

Unlike Medicare, Medicaid has always been a state-based programme. More precisely, it is an individual entitlement administered by the states under extensive federal rules. States determine eligibility and benefits within a framework of national regulations that identifies certain groups and services as mandatory and other groups and services as optional. The matching rate, known as the Federal Medicaid Assistance Percentage, varies inversely with state per capita income: the national government picks up over 75 per cent of the costs for the poor states of Mississippi and West Virginia, while paying the minimum 50 per cent for relatively rich states such as New York and Colorado. About one-fifth of state expenditures are for Medicaid, and increases in Medicaid costs contributed to the fiscal problems that nearly all the states have experienced in recent years.

'Welfare', like 'Social Security', has a narrower meaning for Americans than for citizens in some of the other federal systems discussed in this volume. The term now refers to the *Temporary Assistance for Needy Families* (TANF) block grant, which gives states fairly broad discretion in spending funds allocated among them by statutory formula. TANF participants receive cash assistance along with work-related services such as child care or job training. Participants are subject to work requirements and can lose eligibility for various infractions. PRWORA, which created the programme, explicitly says that there is no individual entitlement to assistance, although the courts have yet to determine exactly what this means.

TANF programmes in every state emphasize work. Some states seek only to move participants into a job as quickly as possible; others also offer post-employment services or programmes to remove barriers to work among groups that are particularly hard to employ, such as mothers with mental health problems or a limited ability to speak English. Whether they work or not, TANF participants are subject to a lifetime limit of five years of federally funded cash assistance.

The newest programme in tables 4.3 and 4.4, the *State Children's Health Insurance Program* (SCHIP) was created in 1997 to cover children whose family incomes are above Medicaid limits. Compared with Medicaid, SCHIP offers states more flexibility and a somewhat more generous federal matching rate. A few states use SCHIP funds to cover parents as well as children.

The current system of *Unemployment Insurance* (UI) was established under the same Social Security Act of 1935 as the much more centralized Old Age, Survivors and Disability Insurance. States administer the programme and make decisions about the size of benefits, who can qualify for them and how long they will last. Only a minority of the unemployed actually receive UI benefits. Unemployed workers do not receive UI if they have not worked enough to meet minimum standards, were fired for cause, voluntarily quit their last job or have exhausted their time-limited benefits.[30]

The UI system is financed by state and federal taxes on employers. State tax rates, which provide most of the funding, are adjusted so that employers with higher turnover pay more. The federal tax shows how a relatively small amount of federal funding can be used to induce higher state spending while avoiding outright compulsion. The federal tax is nominally higher than the state tax, but employers can claim a credit against most of the federal tax as long as their state UI system meets federal standards. This mechanism strongly encourages states to set their taxes at least as high as the level of the federal credit. The remainder of the federal tax covers state and federal administrative expenses and half the cost of extending benefit periods during economic downturns.

---

[30] US Congress, *2000 Green Book*, pp. 280–96.

Last, and indeed least, *General Assistance* (GA) programmes are administered and financed by state or local governments, with no national government involvement. These programmes provide benefits to childless adults, who do not qualify for TANF, and to families with children who are ineligible, or awaiting determination of eligibility, for SSI and TANF. As of 1998, ten states, seven of them in the South, had no GA programmes at either the state or county level. A majority of the states that do provide GA reduced eligibility between 1989 and 1998, and virtually all have allowed inflation to erode benefit levels that were already very low.[31]

Summary
A few points emerge from this ranking. First, the programmes based on age are more national and better funded than the policies based on income. Second, among the means-tested programmes, funding for medical assistance dwarfs funding for income transfers. Third, the elderly, the disabled and children are treated as deserving even if they do not work. Parents can also receive support, but most of it is conditional in some way upon work, for which some parents are better equipped than others, and which may be hard to find when unemployment is high. Able-bodied, non-elderly, childless adults receive the least support.[32] They are ineligible for Temporary Assistance for Needy Families, the only population subject to Food Stamps time limits, and the least likely to receive public medical coverage. They may be eligible for Unemployment Insurance or General Assistance, but both programmes are notoriously inadequate.

Finally, most of the programmes shown in table 4.4 have stayed about where they started on the national–state continuum. The replacement of existing programmes has produced greater changes in the overall division of responsibility between the national government and the states than the evolution of continuing programmes. The creation of SSI, in 1972, represented centralization: the new national programme replaced disparate state programmes for the aged, blind and disabled that were closer to the ideal type of pure state authority. The 1996 replacement of Aid to Families with Dependent Children (AFDC) by Temporary Assistance

---

[31] L. Jerome Gallagher, *A Shrinking Portion of the Safety Net: General Assistance from 1989 to 1998*, Assessing the New Federalism Policy Brief A-36 (Washington, DC: Urban Institute Press, 1999); L. Jerome Gallagher, Cori E. Uccello, Alicia B. Pierce and Erin B. Reidy, *State General Assistance Programs, 1998*, Assessing the New Federalism Discussion Paper 99-01 (Washington, DC: Urban Institute Press, 1999).

[32] Stephen H. Bell and L. Jerome Gallagher, *Prime-Age Adults Without Children or Disabilities: The 'Least Deserving of the Poor' – or Are They?*, Assessing the New Federalism, Policy Brief B-26 (Washington, DC: Urban Institute Press, 2001).

for Needy Families (TANF) represented decentralization, as states gained more flexibility in spending federal welfare money. At the same time, however, they became subject to new restrictions such as time limits or prohibitions against assistance to non-citizen immigrants. Under AFDC, moreover, they had always been able to set income standards and benefit levels, as they are under TANF, so in this respect welfare reform did not bring significant change.

The trajectory of US social policies

Before the New Deal

The first 140 years of the republic (1789–1929) produced important legal precedents, but few enduring social policies at either the national or the state level. As Morton Grodzins and Daniel Elazar showed, pragmatic co-operation across levels of government has been part of the American federal system from the start.[33] In Grodzins' metaphor, the federal system has been a marble cake, not a layer cake. Joint stock companies mixed local, state and national governments with private enterprise in ways that would be unthinkable today but that made it possible to build the canals and railroads that expanded the country beyond the eastern seaboard. Under the Morrill Act of 1862, land grants from the national government to the states built a network of agricultural colleges. After the Sixteenth Amendment (1913) authorized a federal income tax, cash grants became the characteristic vehicle for federal–state co-operation. Only the form, and not the fact, of co-operation changed.

Little of this pre-New Deal co-operation involved anything we today would recognize as social policy. Two important exceptions were the Civil War pension system, established (for Union veterans only) in 1862 and expanded after the war, and the maternal and infant health programme created under the Sheppard-Towner Act of 1921.[34] The Civil War pensions eventually died out with the veterans and their widows and children, whereas funding for the Sheppard-Towner Program, which had aroused the fierce opposition of ideological conservatives and the American Medical Association, ended in 1929.

A Supreme Court decision dismissing challenges to Sheppard-Towner, however, provided the legal basis for future programmes of grants-in-aid. In *Commonwealth of Massachusetts* v. *Mellon* (1923), the Supreme Court

---

[33] Morton Grodzins, *The American System* (Chicago: Rand McNally, 1966); Daniel J. Elazar, 'Federal–State Collaborations in the Nineteenth-Century United States', *Political Science Quarterly*, vol. 79 (1964), no. 2, pp. 248–81.
[34] Skocpol, *Protecting Soldiers and Mothers*.

rejected Massachusetts' claim that Congress, in enacting the maternal and infant health grants, had exercised powers reserved to the states under the Tenth Amendment.[35] The court did not directly address the Tenth Amendment arguments, ruling instead that Massachusetts, because it remained free to reject the grants and the conditions attached to them, could not demonstrate that it had been harmed by the Act. Nor could an individual tax-payer demonstrate that the Act harmed her by using her taxes for improper purposes, for her taxes had been combined with those of many others to finance the grants. As neither states nor individuals had legal standing to challenge the Act in court, the issues surrounding the law were 'political questions', to be decided by the legislative rather than the judicial branch.

The *Massachusetts v. Mellon* decision came at a time when the Supreme Court was striking down other kinds of laws, such as the prohibition on child labour, as violations of the Tenth Amendment and other constitutional provisions. By placing federal grants to the states beyond judicial scrutiny, it made possible the transfer of resources displayed in figure 4.1, and allowed Congress to strongly influence state actions through the conditions it attaches to its grants. Volumes of regulations stipulating what states must do to receive Medicaid matching funds demonstrate how extensive these conditions can be. Later decisions upholding the authority of Congress to use highway funding to get states to raise their drinking ages and lower their speed limits demonstrate that grant conditions can be tangential to the main purposes of the programmes to which they are attached.[36]

The New Deal

The central measure of New Deal social policies, the Social Security Act of 1935, included the key programmes of Old Age Insurance, later expanded into the present Old Age, Survivors and Disability Insurance; Old Age Assistance and Aid to the Blind, both later absorbed into Supplemental Security Income; Unemployment Insurance (UI); and Aid to Dependent Children, later renamed Aid to Families with Dependent Children (AFDC).[37] The Old Age Insurance Program was

---

[35] *Commonwealth of Massachusetts v. Mellon*, 447 US 262 (1923).
[36] *South Dakota v. Dole*, 483 US 203 (1987); Lynn A. Baker, 'Constitutional Federal Spending and States' Rights', *Annals of the American Academy of Political and Social Science*, vol. 574 (March 2001), pp. 104–18.
[37] This section draws on Jill Quadagno, *The Color of Welfare: How Racism Undermined the War on Poverty* (Oxford: Oxford University Press, 1994); Robert C. Lieberman and John S. Lapinski, 'American Federalism, Race and the Administration of Welfare', *British Journal*

established as a contributory programme administered directly by the national government. UI, in contrast, was administered by the states and financed mostly by state taxes on employers. Wisconsin had become the first state to offer unemployment insurance in 1932, and a desire to protect that state's approach contributed to the decision to create a devolved federal programme. The non-contributory, means-tested programmes for dependent children, the aged and the blind combined state administration with partial federal financing in the form of matching funds.

The South was at this time almost completely Democratic. Southern Democrats were an important component of the New Deal Democratic coalition and controlled most congressional committees under the seniority system. Most southern politicians represented plantation owners rather than their mostly disfranchised labour force.

None of the major programmes of the Social Security Act challenged the paternalistic labour system of the South, and some reinforced it. Although payroll taxes, eligibility and benefits under the Old Age Insurance Program were uniform across the states, agricultural and domestic workers were originally not covered. These groups, which in the 1930s included most black workers, would instead depend on separate, state-administered Old Age Assistance programmes.

Congressional committees chaired by Southerners removed a provision in the Roosevelt administration's bill that would have required states receiving federal public assistance grants to provide 'a reasonable subsistence compatible with decency and health'. The result was that grants for Old Age Assistance, Unemployment Insurance and Aid to Dependent Children were lower in the South than in the rest of the country, and administered to give higher benefits to whites than to blacks. Fifty years after the Social Security Act, Wilbur Cohen, who had been a research assistant to the executive committee that developed the administration proposal, described the deletion of the reasonable subsistence provision as 'the bill's most significant loss', and blamed it on Virginia Senator Harry F. Byrd.[38] Paul H. Douglas, writing in 1936, attributed the change primarily to

---

of Political Science, vol. 31 (2001), no. 2, pp. 303–29; Ann Shola Orloff, 'The Political Origins of America's Belated Welfare State', in Margaret Weir, Ann Shola Orloff and Theda Skocpol, eds., *The Politics of Social Policy in the United States* (Princeton: Princeton University Press, 1988), pp. 37–80; Kenneth Finegold, 'Agriculture and the Politics of US Social Provision: Social Insurance and Food Stamps', in Weir, Orloff and Skocpol, eds., *Politics of Social Policy*, pp. 199–234.

[38] Wilbur Cohen, 'The Social Security Act of 1935: Reflections Fifty Years Later', in Alan Pifer and Forrest Chisman, eds., *The Report of the Committee on Economic Security, 1935* (Washington, DC: National Conference on Social Welfare, 1985), pp. 3–14, p. 9.

the fear on the part of many Southern Senators and Representatives that the earlier provision might be used by authorities in Washington to compel the southern states to pay higher pensions to aged Negroes than the dominant white groups believed to be desirable . . . In fairness to the South, it should be added that there were Congressmen from other sections of the country where there were unpopular racial or cultural minorities who wanted to have their states left more or less free to treat them as they wished. The desire of some states not to expend much money for this purpose was also a strong factor.[39]

This is where a counter-factual analysis can be illuminating. What would have happened in the 1930s if everything else was the same, but the US had a unitary system of government? This, to be sure, is a dangerous question to ask. Fortunately, however, Philip E. Tetlock and Aaron Belkin suggest some principles to ensure that counter-factuals, though by definition different from the real world, bear enough resemblance to it that conclusions from counter-factual analysis can be accepted as valid and generalized to other situations.[40] Table 4.5 lists their six rules and how the counter-factual analysis of the 1930s and 1990s in this chapter is consistent with each.

Well-specified antecedents and consequents are desirable in any analysis, whether it involves counter-factuals or not. Here, the antecedent is the US as it was in all respects except that national and regional governments are connected by a unitary system rather than a federal one. The consequent for the 1930s is a US in which social policy is not expanded, and therefore a US in which basic social policies were enacted even later, or not at all.

The principle that links the antecedent to the New Deal consequent is the effective Southern veto from the 1930s to the 1960s, based on the combination of a Democratic Congress (which put Southerners in the majority), the seniority system (which gave them control of key committees), and the filibuster rule (which empowered obstructionists to block the bills to which they most objected). Each of these is imaginable without a federal system, and thus co-tenable with the assumption that the US did not have one.

The notion that co-tenability requires that antecedent and consequent be fairly close together suggests that a counter-factual analysis of the

---

[39] Paul H. Douglas, *Social Security in the United States: An Analysis and Appraisal of the Federal Social Security Act* (New York: Whittlesey House, 1936), pp. 100–01, 110–11.

[40] Philip E. Tetlock and Aaron Belkin, 'Counterfactual Thought Experiments in World Politics: Logical, Methodological, and Psychological Perspectives', in Philip E. Tetlock and Aaron Belkin, eds., *Counterfactual Thought Experiments in World Politics: Logical, Methodological, and Psychological Perspectives* (Princeton: Princeton University Press, 1996), pp. 1–38.

Table 4.5 *Application of Tetlock and Belkin's criteria for counter-factuals to a unitary United States*

Rule	How rule applies to 1930s	How rule applies to 1990s
Well-specified antecedents and consequents	If US unitary system, then no expansion of social policy	If US unitary system, no welfare reform and no expansion of insurance coverage for children under Medicaid and SCHIP
Cotenability: logical consistency of connecting principles	Effective southern veto in Congress	Absence of natural sites for policy experimentation in unitary system
Consistency with well-established historical facts	Mother country (Great Britain) is unitary system; Alexander Hamilton supported near unitary system at Constitutional Convention	
Consistency with well-established theoretical laws	Disfranchised lack political influence	Federalism increases potential for experimentation
Consistency with well-established statistical generalizations	Voting behaviour of Southern Democrats	Democratic resistance to welfare reform; failure of pre-Clinton efforts to enact national health care
Projectability	Impact of federalism on social policy depends on institutional configurations at critical junctures	

Sources: Based on analysis in Philip E. Tetlock and Aaron Belkin, 'Counterfactual Thought Experiments in World Politics', in Philip E. Tetlock and Aaron Belkin, eds., *Counterfactual Thought Experiments in World Politics* (Princeton: Princeton University Press, 1996), pp. 1–38.

1930s or 1960s should not be based on the assumption that the US had had a unitary system since 1789. Too many other things would conceivably have been different; the Civil War, for example, might never have occurred. We can get around this problem by assuming for analysis of the New Deal era that the US became a unitary system in the progressive era, the 1920s, or even the early New Deal.

A counter-factual cannot be perfectly consistent with historical facts; if it was, it would describe reality rather than an imagined alternative. Tetlock and Belkin suggest, however, that well-established facts should establish the plausibility of counter-factual conditions. One fact that suggests the plausibility of a non-federal US is that the source for American (and Australian and Canadian) law and language, and even for much of

American federal theory, is, like most of the industrialized democracies in the OECD, a unitary system.[41] The mother country, after all, is now officially known as the United Kingdom (singular), while its former colonies became the United States (plural).

Another fact that suggests the plausibility of a unitary US is that Alexander Hamilton, co-author of the *Federalist Papers* and architect of the American financial system, supported a near unitary system before and during the Constitutional Convention. In Hamilton's ideal, the states would be limited to roads and law enforcement, and perhaps would wither away.[42] Harold Laski expressed similar views in the New Deal era.[43]

The consequences of a unitary United States are consistent with the theoretical law that the disfranchised (Southern blacks in the 1930s) lack political influence. They are also consistent with statistical generalizations about the voting behaviour of Southern Democrats in Congress during the 1930s.[44] The results of the analysis are projectible in that they argue against covering laws such as 'federalism retards the expansion of social policy', suggesting instead that, as the editors emphasize in both their introductory and concluding comments, the impact of federalism on social policy is highly contingent.

In a unitary United States, Southern Democrats might have used their controlling positions in Congress to block any expansion of social policy. An infusion of federal funds into what had been the poorest region of the nation since the end of the Civil War was welcomed. Yet without the option of delegating policy-making and implementation for unemployment insurance, old age assistance and aid to dependent children to the states, white Southern elites could not have been confident that these policies would not be used against them. A unitary national government could have decentralized implementation of these programmes, but this approach would not have been as reassuring, and eligibility and benefit levels would likely have been uniform.

This analysis does not require a choice between the competing racial and economic interpretations of the motives of Southern elites.[45] It is also

---

[41] Samuel H. Beer, *To Make a Nation: The Rediscovery of American Federalism* (Cambridge, MA: Belknap Press of Harvard University Press, 1993) traces the mostly British roots of American federal theory.

[42] John C. Miller, *Alexander Hamilton and the Growth of the New Nation* (New York: Harper & Row, 1959), pp. 155–63.

[43] Donahue, *Disunited States*, p. 26.

[44] On Southern Democrats in Congress, see Key, *Southern Politics*, chapters 16–17; Alston and Ferrie, *Southern Paternalism*, chapters 3–4; Ira Katznelson, Kim Geiger and Daniel Kryder, 'Limiting Liberalism: The Southern Veto in Congress, 1933–1950', *Political Science Quarterly*, vol. 108 (1993), no. 2 (summer), pp. 283–306.

[45] See, respectively, Lieberman and Lapinski, 'American Federalism, Race and the Administration of Welfare' and Alston and Ferrie, *Southern Paternalism*.

compatible with the arguments by Gareth Davies and Martha Derthick that concerns about the administrative difficulties of Old Age Insurance coverage for agricultural and domestic workers, and about the budgetary problems the impoverished Southern states would have meeting decency and health standards, had factual bases, and therefore should not be dismissed as rationalizations for racial exclusion.[46]

Southern Democrats in Congress, Ira Katznelson, Kim Geiger and Daniel Kryder have shown, voted with Northern Democrats on legislation concerning fiscal policy, planning, regulation and welfare; with Republicans on labour issues; and against both Northern Democrats and Republicans on civil rights issues.[47] The Social Security Act was at once a welfare, labour and civil rights measure, or rather it would have been in a unitary system. A federal system made it possible for benefit levels to differ by state, so they would not raise the low wages of Southern workers, and for programmes to be administered so that they reinforced the South's racial order. In a federal system, then, Southern Democrats could support the Social Security Act and the other welfare measures of the era, which would bring federal money into the impoverished region, even as they used their effective veto to block other measures that directly affected labour laws or civil rights. At a juncture that was unusually favourable to the expansion of social policy because of the continuing depression and Democratic super-majorities in Congress, then, the federal system made this expansion more likely, even as it guaranteed that there would be variation in the social safety net by state and by race.

The war on poverty

United States social policy remained fairly stable for almost thirty years after the Social Security Act. President Harry Truman's post-war attempts to enact national health insurance failed, and the Taft-Hartley Act of 1947 weakened labour unions, which had supported both the Democratic Party and more extensive social policies. The 1952 election produced a unified Republican government for the first time since the New Deal (table 4.3), but President Dwight Eisenhower ratified Democratic social policies by declining to undo them. The skills of experts in the Social Security administration, and the popularity of their insurance analogy, helped them to win expansion of the programme beyond its original base and to fend off efforts to develop the rival Old Age Assistance

---

[46] Gareth Davies and Martha Derthick, 'Race and Social Welfare Policy: The Social Security Act of 1935', *Political Science Quarterly*, vol. 112 (1997), no. 2, pp. 217–35.
[47] Katznelson, Geiger and Kryder, 'Limiting Liberalism'.

programme into a more uniform and adequate non-contributory system of social provision for the elderly.[48]

The changes of the 1960s, a period of unified Democratic control (table 4.3), were more substantial. It is hard to separate these changes from the concomitant struggles over civil rights. The Congress that passed the landmark Civil Rights Act of 1964 also passed the Food Stamp Act. In 1965 Congress approved the Voting Rights Act, which ultimately ended the disfranchisement of most Southern blacks; in the same year, it passed the statute creating both Medicare and Medicaid. All these measures reflected the leadership of President Lyndon Johnson, who went so far as to declare a national 'War on Poverty'.

The voucher-based Food Stamps programme was introduced by administrative action in 1961. It revived an approach that had been used in the late 1930s to absorb farming surpluses, then dropped when wartime mobilization provided a different solution to the farming problem. Passage of the Food Stamp Act of 1964, which gave the programme statutory authorization, was a product of bargaining between the urban Democrats, who championed Food Stamps, and the rural legislators, who needed votes for expensive commodity support programmes. This set a recurring pattern, most recently displayed when the Food Stamp programme was reauthorized as part of the 2002 Farm Bill.

The Medicare Act of 1965 expanded governmental involvement in health care in accord with the two-pronged approach of the Social Security Act: a uniform national contributory programme (Medicare) for the elderly, and a means-tested, state-based programme (Medicaid) for the poor. Doctors, organized in the American Medical Association and other professional associations, had been able to kill earlier proposals along these lines by charging that they were 'socialized medicine'. After the election of 1964, however, the passage of health care legislation was seen as a certainty: the Democrats won their largest congressional majorities since the New Deal, giving them enough votes to pass a Medicare bill, and President Lyndon Johnson won a landslide victory over Barry Goldwater in an election in which health care for the elderly was a major issue.[49] Even with subsequent expansions, neither Medicaid nor Medicare cover the bulk of the American population, those who are neither elderly nor

---

[48] Martha Derthick, *Policymaking for Social Security* (Washington, DC: Brookings Institution Press, 1979); Jerry Cates, *Insuring Inequality: Administrative Leadership in Social Security* (Ann Arbor: University of Michigan Press, 1983); Finegold, 'Agriculture and the Politics of US Social Provision'.

[49] Marilyn Moon, *Medicare Now and in the Future*, 2nd edn (Washington, DC: Urban Institute Press, 1996); Robert Stevens and Rosemary Stevens, *Welfare Medicine in America: A Case Study of Medicaid* (New York: Free Press, 1974); Theodore R. Marmor, *The Politics of Medicare* (Chicago: Aldine, 1973).

poor. Tax subsidies encourage employers to provide access to private insurance, but do not require them to do so. As of 2002, an estimated 10 per cent of children and 17 per cent of adults below 65 years of age were uninsured.[50]

President Johnson's declared 'War on Poverty' included a range of grant programmes in addition to the Food Stamps, Medicaid and Medicare entitlements. Some of these were aimed at rural poverty, in regions such as Appalachia and the Mississippi Delta. Urban programmes were more controversial, especially when they bypassed unsympathetic state governments to give direct federal aid to cities, or bypassed state and local governments to give the money to community groups. Without major legislative changes, finally, welfare caseloads, under the Aid to Families with Dependent Children programme, tripled between 1960 and 1972. Application of civil rights protest tactics to Northern welfare offices, urban rioting and court decisions invalidating paternalistic welfare practices such as night-time searches for a 'man in the house' all contributed to this growth – and to the backlash against it.

Nixon and Reagan[51]

Since the election of Richard Nixon in 1968, Republicans have made a series of efforts to roll back the changes of the 1960s. The congressional Republicans who took power in 1995, joined in 2001 by President George W. Bush, have been more successful in achieving this goal than their predecessors, and have reached beyond it to challenge the policy legacies of the New Deal.

The South, by this period, had become very different from what it had been in the 1930s. Mechanization brought the end of the paternalistic labour system that was the basis of the plantation economy. Federal intervention brought the end of segregation and enforcement of the right to vote. And, in response, the once solidly Democratic South became Republican. Southern politics and national racial tensions both affected federal–state relations in US social policy.

Nixon, in some ways, continued or even expanded the social policies of the 'War on Poverty'. He proposed a negative income tax and employer

---

[50] Genevieve Kenney, Jennifer Haley and Alexandra Tebay, 'Children's Insurance Coverage and Service Use Improve', *Snapshots of America's Families III*, no. 1 (Washington, DC: Urban Institute Press, 2003); Stephen Zuckerman, 'Gains in Public Health Insurance Offset Reductions in Employer Coverage among Adults', *Snapshots of America's Families III*, no. 8 (Washington, DC: Urban Institute Press, 2003).

[51] This section draws heavily on Timothy J. Conlan, *From New Federalism to Devolution: Twenty-Five Years of Intergovernmental Reform* (Washington, DC: Brookings Institution Press, 1998).

mandates to provide health insurance, and made no attempt to get rid of Medicare or Medicaid, let alone Social Security. If Nixon was, in retrospect, closer to Kennedy and Johnson than to Reagan or either Bush in the content of his social policies, his ambitious proposals to reshape the federal system went directly against the thrust of the 'War on Poverty', which had forged alliances between an activist national government and the beleaguered cities. Nixon, in contrast, proposed to reduce federal control and strengthen the ties between the national government and the states through revenue sharing and block grants.

Nixon's success in winning adoption of his 'New Federalism' was limited by Democratic control of Congress throughout his administration (table 4.3) and ultimately by the repercussions of the Watergate scandal. General Revenue Sharing, enacted in 1972, transferred money from the national government to state and local governments with virtually no strings attached. Nixon's proposal to replace many categorical grants with more flexible block grants also pointed away from the Johnson administration's targeted interventions on behalf of the urban poor. Only two of the proposed block grants, for community development and for employment training, became law.

Nixon also oversaw the 1972 enactment of Supplemental Security Insurance (SSI), for the aged, blind and disabled. Nixon's proposed Family Assistance Plan, a negative income tax, failed in Congress, but led to the replacement of the state-based Old Age Assistance and Aid to the Blind programmes established by the Social Security Act and the similar programme for the disabled, added to the Act in 1950, with nationally administered, means-tested support for these 'deserving' groups. The creation of SSI represented the biggest movement on the national–state continuum of any programme listed in table 4.4. It also shifted some of the burden of supporting the elderly poor from OASDI, financed by regressive payroll taxes. SSI, in contrast, was and is funded from general revenues, financed primarily by the progressive income tax.[52]

Ronald Reagan's greatest impact on federalism in US social policy came early in his presidency with the passage of the Omnibus Budget Reconciliation Act of 1981. This act altered national spending in accord with Reagan's priorities: defence spending went up and social spending went down. The act also consolidated 77 categorical grants into 9 block grants. Nixon's block grants were accompanied with funding increases, so that communities whose proportional share fell were not necessarily worse off in absolute terms. Reagan's block grants, accompanied

---

[52] Vincent J. Burke and Vee Burke, *Nixon's Good Deed: Welfare Reform* (New York: Columbia University Press, 1974), chapter 9.

with funding reductions, had double impact on the localities losing out.

The funding shifts of 1981, combined with the big tax cut of that year, have had lasting effects on American public policy. In contrast, the grand reallocation of social policy responsibilities announced in 1982 fizzled out. Reagan used that year's State of the Union address to propose a 'swap' that would end the sharing of fiscal responsibility for major social programmes. Under the swap plan, the federal government would assume the state share of Medicaid, and the states would take over Food Stamps and the federal portion of the AFDC welfare programme. The states would also receive revenues from a new trust fund to finance other federal–state programmes, for which they would be expected to assume full responsibility. Inter-governmental organizations such as the National Governors Association and the National Conference of State Legislatures wanted the federal government to do something about rising Medicaid costs, but expressed suspicion of the proposal and contributed to its demise.

The era of revenue sharing, so central to Nixon's new federalism, ended during Reagan's presidency. Originally, one-third of General Revenue Sharing funds had gone to the states and two-thirds had gone to local governments. The state portion ended in 1980 as President Jimmy Carter revised his budget to cope with the combination of high unemployment and high inflation. Members of Congress were also unhappy that many states had voted to initiate a constitutional amendment requiring a balanced national budget. President Reagan, citing the federal deficit and the (temporary) fiscal health of most state and local governments, targeted the local portion of revenue sharing for elimination in February 1985. With a Republican Senate unlikely to override a possible veto, Congress allowed the programme to expire at the end of Financial Year 1986.[53]

The importance of the Reagan administration's use of waivers, finally, is more apparent in retrospect than it was at the time. As mentioned earlier, waivers are provisions that allow states to request exemptions from some of the rules that would otherwise apply to federal programmes. From 1962 through 1987, waivers had been a benign if under-utilized feature of AFDC, Medicaid and Food Stamps. The Reagan administration, however, discovered that the executive branch, in alliance with like-minded governors, could use waivers to implement policy changes that Congress

---

[53] Bruce A. Wallin, *From Revenue Sharing to Deficit Sharing: General Revenue Sharing and Cities* (Washington, DC: Georgetown University Press, 1998), chapter 4; Robert W. Rafuse, Jr, 'Fiscal Federalism in 1986: The Spotlight Continues to Swing Toward the States and Local Governments', *Publius: The Journal of Federalism*, vol. 17 (1987), no. 3 (summer), pp. 35–41.

would never approve. The Interagency Low Income Opportunity Advisory Board was established in 1987 to encourage state experimentation within a well-defined set of federal procedures for waiver approval and norms for demonstration evaluation.[54] Although the board soon disappeared, Presidents Bush and Clinton would make similar use of waivers as the vehicles for policy changes, particularly welfare reforms that had been or would have been rejected by the Democratic majority in Congress.

Clinton and Gingrich

The US retrenchment of the 1980s parallels events in other advanced industrial democracies and appears, at first glance, to reflect the changing economic climate of the times. Ronald Reagan and Margaret Thatcher, for example, both displaced moderates within their own parties, defeated incumbents of the rival parties to their left, came to power in economic slumps, cut social programmes, smashed unions, waged small wars, won re-election by large margins, and handed office to successors who could win one election but not two.

The failure of President Clinton's 1993 health care proposals might be consistent with the concept of social policy retrenchment, but the legislative success of welfare reform does not fit the changing economic performance model so well. The Republican Congress that gained control in the election of 1994, with Speaker of the House Newt Gingrich as its leader, approved the most fundamental transformation of welfare policy since the 1930s as well as related changes in Food Stamps, child care and other programmes. These changes, which Richard Nathan describes as a 'devolution revolution',[55] occurred in a period of economic expansion, were not primarily driven by concerns about budget deficits or international competitiveness, and have increased spending on social programmes. The welfare policies they altered were unpopular, and politicians sought to claim credit, rather than avoid blame, for reforming them.

President Clinton's Health Security proposal was released in the fall of 1993, following deliberations by a task force headed by the First Lady, Hillary Clinton.[56] The complex proposal was designed to simultaneously

---

[54] US Domestic Policy Council Low Income Opportunity Working Group, *Up from Dependency: A New National Public Assistance Strategy* (Washington, DC: US Government Printing Office, 1986).

[55] Richard P. Nathan, 'The "Devolution Revolution" – An Overview', *Rockefeller Institute Bulletin* (1996), pp. 5–13.

[56] My discussion of the Clinton health plan draws on US Department of Commerce, National Technical Information Service, *The President's Health Security Plan: Comprehensive Overview* (Springfield, VA: US Department of Commerce, National Technical Information Service, 1993); US Department of Commerce, National Technical

provide universal health coverage and reduce the rapidly increasing costs of public and private medical care. It was based on the principle of managed competition among private health plans, an approach that was thought to require less government intervention than a Canadian-style single payer system or a British-style national health service. Health alliances, established by states or corporations, would negotiate with the plans, within a framework of state and national regulation. Every American would receive a Health Security Card guaranteeing access, and every American would be responsible for paying part of the cost of health care coverage.

At the time the plan was introduced, it was widely believed to be the proposal that would finally make health care coverage universal in the US. The Democrats had control of both Congress and the presidency for the first time in twelve years, and health care had been one of the issues that Clinton had used successfully against the first President Bush. Yet Democrats divided over their President's proposal, and Republicans made a bold decision to adopt a stance of uncompromising opposition to it. Small insurance companies, who believed with some reason that they would be squeezed out, ran an effective campaign to convince people who already had health insurance that the Clinton proposal would, among other terrible things, rob them of their ability to choose their own doctors.

Within a year, the administration conceded defeat and withdrew the plan from consideration by Congress. In the 1994 elections, Republicans were able to build on their achievement to mobilize voters against big government and against Bill Clinton. They won control of the House of Representatives for the first time in forty years, and attained a Senate majority as well (table 4.3).

Partisan calculations and miscalculations, the personalities of key participants and international distractions all contributed to the outcome as Bill Clinton, like Harry Truman, proved unable to translate electoral success and a unified Congress into the passage of universal health care. In terms of federalism, as in many other respects, opportunities were missed. The Clinton health care plan included a role for the states, which would have responsibility for overseeing the health alliances, certifying health plans and choosing whether to organize their system on the basis

Information Service, *The President's Health Security Plan: Preliminary Summary* (Springfield, VA: US Department of Commerce, National Technical Information Service, 1993); Jacob S. Hacker, *The Road to Nowhere: The Genesis of President Clinton's Plan for Health Security* (Princeton: Princeton University Press, 1997); Jacob S. Hacker, 'Learning from Defeat? Political Analysis and the Failure of Health Care Reform in the United States', *British Journal of Political Science*, vol. 31 (2001), no. 1, pp. 61–94; Theda Skocpol, *Boomerang: Clinton's Health Security Effort and the Turn Against Government in US Politics* (New York: Norton, 1996).

The United States: federalism and its counter-factuals   173

of managed care, single payer or other alternatives. But the plan proposed a system that did not take advantage of the federal potential for policy experimentation because it had no basis in any state health care plan that had already been implemented. President Clinton could not respond to the critics by saying he was only trying to do nationally what he had already done as governor of Arkansas, or what others were doing in some other states. The debate might not have gone quite so disastrously if there had been some reassuring model for the new health alliances or if the voters had been able to see that people were still able to choose their own doctors in, say, Oregon, Minnesota or Tennessee.

The contrast is to welfare reform, which culminated in 1996 with passage of the Personal Responsibility and Work Opportunity Reconciliation Act (PRWORA). PRWORA abolished Aid to Families with Dependent Children (AFDC) and replaced it with Temporary Assistance for Needy Families, a block grant. State policy choices that had required waivers or been prohibited under AFDC became state options or even federal requirements.

More than anything else, these changes emphasized work.[57] Cash assistance recipients were required to work, and states were required to meet goals for the proportion of recipients working or else lose programme funding. Even working recipients were made subject to the five-year time limit on welfare, which states could make even tougher. The block grant can be used for child care, work training, teenage pregnancy prevention and many other purposes besides cash assistance. As cash assistance caseloads declined in most states due to the combination of welfare reform and a strong economy, states were able to devote more of the money to these other uses.

PRWORA also included important changes in other social policies. Food Stamps benefits were trimmed, and a new time limit restricted able-bodied adults without dependants to benefits in three out of thirty-six months if they did not meet work requirements. PRWORA consolidated four separate child care programmes into the Child Care and Development Fund (CCDF) block grant, and continued a trend towards stricter state enforcement of child support that was already underway. For the first time in American history, non-citizen immigrants legally residing in the US became ineligible for most benefit programmes.[58] Medicaid was revised in a partially successful effort to delink that programme from cash

[57] Alan Weil and Kenneth Finegold, 'Introduction', in Alan Weil and Kenneth Finegold, eds., *Welfare Reform: The Next Act* (Washington, DC: Urban Institute Press, 2002), pp. xi–xxi; see also Handler, *Social Citizenship and Workfare*.
[58] Michael Fix and Jeffrey S. Passel, 'Assessing Welfare Reform's Immigrant Provisions', in Weil and Finegold, eds., *Welfare Reform*, pp. 179–202.

assistance.[59] The State Children's Health Insurance Program (SCHIP), a block grant created in 1997, went further by providing coverage to children in families with incomes above Medicaid eligibility levels.

PRWORA thus altered social policies by its insistence on work and its combination of fiscal flexibility, new policy choices at the state level and new federal requirements on the states. Two things made the passage of PRWORA possible. One was the election of a Republican Congress. The Democratic majority in place before then had defused earlier attempts to remake the welfare system, most recently in 1988.

Second, the path to PRWORA was eased by waivers.[60] Bush and Clinton continued the Reagan administration's practice of granting waivers to the states for welfare reforms, including time limits, family caps (no additional aid to welfare recipients who had more children), and disregards that allowed recipients with earnings to remain on the rolls. Although much of the evidence from waivers was not available until after PRWORA had become law, the willingness of federal officials to approve waiver requests, and the absence of obvious social disasters resulting from their implementation, helped to make national work-based welfare reform seem feasible. Republican governors who had used waivers to implement welfare reform, such as Tommy Thompson (Wisconsin) and John Engler (Michigan), moreover, were able to act as proponents of change at the national level.

Federal systems have options for experimentation that unitary systems lack (see table 4.5). Waivers were central to the welfare reforms of the 1990s. In the counter-factual unitary system, waivers would not have been available and any geographically limited effort to experiment with alternative policies might have violated the Fourteenth Amendment's guarantee of equal protection (see table 4.5). Without waivers, moreover, Presidents Reagan, Bush and Clinton would not have been able to go around a Democratic Congress that had repeatedly demonstrated its unwillingness to make drastic changes to AFDC. Congressional Democrats might have continued to block or greatly weaken efforts by Reagan, Bush and Clinton to increase work requirements or put time limits on cash assistance. Clinton might not have believed, in 1996, that he had to sign PRWORA to win re-election, or congressional Democrats might have been able to persuade him to veto it as he had two previous versions. Federalism, then, helped make possible the restructuring of welfare that had seemed impossible a few years before.

---

[59] Alan Weil and John F. Holahan, 'Health Insurance, Welfare, and Work', in Weil and Finegold, eds., *Welfare Reform*, pp. 143–61.

[60] Steven M. Teles, *Whose Welfare? AFDC and Elite Politics* (Lawrence, KS: University Press of Kansas, 1998), chapter 7; R. Kent Weaver, *Ending Welfare as We Know It* (Washington, DC: Brookings Institution Press, 2000), chapter 5.

Federalism also made it possible to expand public health coverage at the state level, despite the collapse of the Clinton plan. In a unitary system the failure of the national health care plan might have doomed any subsequent effort to insure the uninsured. In a federal system the states could implement less ambitious, less threatening programmes, subsidized by Medicaid and by the new State Children's Health Insurance Program (SCHIP).

Conclusion: the relationship between federalism and social policy in the US

Social policy and federalism

The relationship of social policy and federalism operates in both directions. The expansion of social provision in the US from the New Deal to the present has increased the capacity of, and popular confidence in, the states as units of government. Some of the most important social programmes are wholly national. But others are based on the states, or at least give them significant responsibilities. Participation in joint social programmes, and similar arrangements in other policy areas such as transportation, education and criminal justice, give the states money that can be used to hire better trained personnel and to improve technology. As conditions of federal funding, moreover, states must undergo audits, a requirement that has pushed them to adopt higher standards of accounting and management.

Participation in federal programmes, then, has contributed to the modernization of the states, which were once seen as the backwaters of American government. Governors have been transformed from figureheads to chief executives with opportunities for further promotion: four of the last five presidents (Carter, Reagan, Clinton and the current President Bush) have been former governors.[61] State legislatures have become full-time bodies with highly trained staffs, and state bureaucracies and judiciaries have become more professionalized.[62] These changes, in turn, have contributed to increased trust in state and local governments, at the expense of their national counterparts.[63]

The cost, for the states, has been increased vulnerability to fiscal stress. State revenues have always been vulnerable to macro-economic

---

[61] Larry Sabato, *Goodbye to Good-Time Charlie: The American Governorship Transformed*, 2nd edn (Washington, DC: CQ Press, 1983).
[62] Ann O'M. Bowman and Richard C. Kearney, *The Resurgence of the States* (Englewood Cliffs, NJ: Prentice-Hall, 1986).
[63] Richard L. Cole and John Kincaid, 'Public Opinion and American Federalism: Perspectives on Taxes, Spending, and Trust – An ACIR Update', *Publius: The Journal of Federalism*, vol. 30 (2000), nos. 1–2 (winter/spring), pp. 189–201.

fluctuations that the states can do even less than the national government to control. But on the spending side, states have had to cope with rapidly growing Medicaid costs, which might have been alleviated had either Reagan's proposal to swap Medicaid for welfare or Clinton's health care plan become law. In this context of expenditure pressures and inadequate and unstable revenues, each of the last three recessions has produced state and local fiscal crises that lingered after the overall economy had begun to recover.[64]

The US may differ from some of the other federal systems in that expanded social policies have not resulted in changes to the constitutional basis of federalism. In this respect, as in others, the constitution is what the Supreme Court says it is. The justices, appointed for life and bound to some extent by the rule of precedent, have acted autonomously in their interpretations of the boundaries of state and federal authority. Republican victories in 1952, 1968 or 1994, for example, have yet to undo the court's historic shift, in the 1930s, to interpretations of the Tenth Amendment and the Commerce Clause that allowed Congress to regulate labour–management relations, wages and hours, or agricultural production.

Future federalisms and future social policies

Major changes in US social policies have been associated with the ascendancy of one party or the other, in contrast to the more frequent scenario of divided government. In 1995 and 1996 the Republicans proposed converting Medicaid into a block 'Medigrant' and offering states the option to replace Food Stamps with a food assistance block grant, but Clinton vetoed the two pre-PRWORA welfare reform bills that contained these provisions. At the beginning of 2001 Republicans controlled the presidency and both branches of Congress for the first time since Eisenhower, but to their surprise lost the Senate when James Jeffords (Vermont) defected, at a time when the administration had not yet focussed on TANF or other low income programmes.

The Republicans regained control of the Senate and kept control of the House in the 2002 congressional elections. Current administration proposals include 'super-waivers' across programme lines; a five-state

---

[64] Harold Wolman and George Peterson, 'State and Local Government Strategies for Responding to Fiscal Pressure', *Tulane Law Review*, vol. 55 (1981), no. 3 (April), pp. 773–819; Steven D. Gold, ed., *The Fiscal Crisis of the States: Lessons for the Future* (Washington, DC: Georgetown University Press, 1995); Kenneth Finegold, Stephanie Schardin and Rebecca Steinbach, 'How are States Responding to Fiscal Stress?', Assessing the New Federalism, Policy Brief A-58 (Washington, DC: Urban Institute Press, 2003).

experiment replacing Food Stamps with a block grant; conversion of the housing voucher programme into a block grant; and the introduction of block grant features into several other programmes.[65] Most significant, in terms of the amount of money involved, is a proposal to allow states to receive block grant funding in lieu of Medicaid. States would still be required to provide benefits to certain categories of programme participants, but would have greater flexibility to deny coverage to others, reduce the range of covered services or require participants to share the costs of treatment.[66] Whether or not these provisions win congressional approval, they suggest renewed Republican interest in reorganizing the division of responsibility between state and nation for social programmes.

The other possible source of major changes in the relationship of federalism and social policy is the Supreme Court. Recent Supreme Court decisions on federalism issues have revived some interpretations that had been dormant since the New Deal. Thus far, this sequence of federalism decisions has not called into question the constitutional foundations of the core social policies discussed in this chapter, but they could, particularly if future appointments push the court further to the right. Any rethinking of *Massachusetts* v. *Mellon* and cases following from it, for example, might limit the ability of the national government to influence state policies by attaching conditions to federal grants. A revival of the Tenth Amendment would have even broader effects. The Supreme Court might also address a statutory issue it has so far avoided: whether Medicaid creates an individual entitlement, enforceable in court, or only a guarantee of federal funding to the states. Lower courts have issued conflicting decisions on this question.[67]

---

[65] Robert Greenstein, Shawn Fremstad and Sharon Parrott, '"Superwaiver" Would Grant Executive Branch and Governors Sweeping Authority to Override Federal Laws', Washington, DC: Center on Budget and Policy Priorities, 11 June 2002 (http://www.cbpp.org/5-13-02tanf.pdf); Pietro S. Nivola, Jennifer L. Noyes and Isabel V. Sawhill, 'Waive of the Future? Federalism and the Next Phase of Welfare Reform', Washington, DC: Brookings Institution, March 2004 (http://www.brookings.edu/es/research/projects/wrb/publications/pb/pb29.htm); Kenneth Finegold, Laura Wherry and Stephanie Schardin, 'Block Grants: Details of the Bush Proposals', Assessing the New Federalism, Policy Brief A-64, April 2004 (http:// www.urban.org/url.cfm?ID = 310990).

[66] Cindy Mann, 'The Bush Administration's Medicaid and State Children's Health Insurance Program Proposal' (Washington, DC: Georgetown University Institute for Health Care Research and Policy, 2003); John Holahan and Alan Weil, 'Block Grants are the Wrong Prescription for Medicaid', *Health Policy Online*, no. 6, May 2003 (http://www.urban.org/url.cfm?ID = 900624).

[67] Michael S. Greve, 'The Supreme Court Term That Was and the One That Will Be', *Federalist Outlook*, no. 13, July/August 2002 (http://www.aei.org/publications/pubID.15849/pub_detail.asp).

The American federal system, I have suggested, has not consistently contributed to either the expansion or the contraction of US social policy. Federalism has consistently been important to social policy, but just how it has been important has depended upon specific and sometimes short-lived circumstances, particularly patterns of party control of Congress and the presidency. Social policy has been important to federalism too, but within limits set by the constitution, as interpreted by the Supreme Court.

PART 2
European experiences

5 Austria
Strong parties in a weak federal polity

HERBERT OBINGER*

Introduction

In the course of the twentieth century few western nations have experienced political upheaval on the scale of that in Austria. The country's political transformation – involving phases of democratic (1918–33/34), pre-fascist (1934–38) and national-socialist rule (1938–45) – from an economically backward, multi-ethnic superpower to a small democracy at the centre of Europe has corresponded in economic terms with its rise to a position as one of the world's richest nations. While the fate of federalism lay at these political crossroads, the welfare state established under the Habsburg monarchy survived these periods of political upheaval relatively unscathed.

The example of Austria is of particular interest for a comparative analysis of the relationship between federalism and the welfare state because, alongside Germany, it is recognized as being a pioneer of state social policy. This, along with its high government spending and public social expenditure as a percentage of GDP, seems at first glance to flout the hypothesis advanced by Brennan and Buchanan that the Leviathan is bridled by a federal state structure.[1] However, this is only an apparent contradiction, since Austria only adopted a federal political structure in 1920, when social insurance programmes launched in the context of an authoritarian but decentralized unitary state had already been in

---

* I am grateful to Frank Castles, Arthur Benz and Fritz W. Scharpf for their valuable suggestions.
[1] Geoffrey Brennan and James M. Buchanan, *The Power to Tax: Analytical Foundations of a Fiscal Constitution* (Cambridge: Cambridge University Press, 1980).

existence for some time. Indeed, I will show that there is little evidence that federalism has substantially influenced the developmental dynamics of the Austrian welfare state and that this conclusion applies both to the growth phase of the welfare state and to recent attempts to dismantle it.

Why, then, was it that the federalist dog failed to bark in an Austrian context? The reason, I argue, is that in Austria early social policy emerged under non-democratic and non-federal auspices. When the country became a democratic federation after 1920, the welfare state as well as the political parties were already firmly established at the national level. Federalism, therefore, had no leverage for hindering the adoption of programmes, and the developmental trajectory of the welfare state thereafter was crucially shaped by the partisan complexion of government. As regards feedback effects of the welfare state on federalism, there is some evidence to suggest that the triumph of the welfare state served as an engine of centralization and contributed to a hollowing out of federalism.

The birth of the welfare state: the Habsburg monarchy

Founded in 1918 as one of the successor states to the Habsburg monarchy, the German-Austrian Republic (as of 1920, the Republic of Austria) had no federal tradition to fall back on. Until its demise, the Habsburg Empire remained a decentralized unitary state, although similarities with federal state-type structures did exist.[2]

Constitutional framework

Austria's decline following a military defeat by Prussia in 1866 led to compromise (*Ausgleich*) with Hungary and paved the way for the constitutionalism subsequently elaborated in the December Constitution of 1867. From then onwards the Habsburg multi-nation state consisted of two halves of an empire (*Reichshälften*), which were jointly governed by Franz-Josef I and bound together by joint foreign affairs and defence policies. Expenditures were financed by means of a joint budget to which the two halves of the empire contributed in accordance with a quota system. Under the compromise agreements, which were renegotiated every ten years, the Cisleithanian[3] (Austrian) and the Hungarian parts

---

[2] Felix Ermacora, *Österreichischer Föderalismus. Vom patrimonalen zum kooperativen Bundesstaat* (Vienna: Braumüller, 1976), p. 39; Hans Peter Hye, *Das politische System in der Habsburgermonarchie. Konstitutionalismus, Parlamentarismus und politische Partizipation* (Prague: Karolinum, 1998).
[3] The Cisleithanian half of the empire covered the territories of what is today Austria, Italy, the Czech Republic, Poland, Slovenia and the Ukraine.

of the empire formed a single customs and currency area. Alongside this trade and customs union, there was a treaty-based co-ordination of transportation, the postal system and indirect taxation.[4] All other policy sectors – including social policy – were handled separately by the Austrian and the Hungarian halves of the empire. Despite the dominance of their German-speaking and Hungarian-speaking peoples, both halves of the empire were themselves multi-nation states and there was no joint citizenship.[5] Constitutionalism under the December Constitution underpinned processes of industrialization and was accompanied by urbanization, population growth and social pauperization. Economic development, however, occurred in spurts, with alternating phases of stagnation and growth.[6] It is worth noting that the Austrian part of the monarchy was more economically developed than it was in Hungary and its subordinate Länder,[7] although within Cisleithania there were marked economic disparities between the industrial centres on the one hand and the agriculture-based Alpine regions and Galicia on the other.

The December Constitution of 1867 divided legislative authority in the Cisleithanian territory between the *Reichsrat* (Imperial Council or parliament) and the Emperor, guaranteeing liberal civil rights by means of constitutional law. The resulting freedoms of association and assembly were a significant prerequisite for the organization of political parties and trade unions.[8] The government was responsible only to the Emperor and his ministers, who were responsible for the running of the highly developed central administration. The Emperor had an impressive range of powers. All laws required his sanction, he could dissolve the Reichsrat and the *Landtage* (provincial diets or assemblies), he was Commander-in-Chief of the armed forces and had emergency executive powers. The Reichsrat consisted of two equal chambers – the lower house (*Abgeordnetenhaus*) and the upper house (*Herrenhaus*). While the lower house had been directly elected since 1873,[9] the curial and census voting system denied large economically underprivileged groups of the population the right to vote. This was mirrored by a massive overrepresentation of conservative, feudal and liberal forces both in the Reichsrat and the Landtage. It was only in 1907 that universal manhood suffrage was introduced.[10] The

---

[4] József Galántai, *Der österreichisch-ungarische Dualismus 1867–1918* (Vienna: Österreichischer Bundesverlag, 1985), pp. 56–63.
[5] Ibid., p. 70.
[6] Ernst Bruckmüller, *Sozialgeschichte Österreichs* (Vienna: Verlag für Geschichte und Politik, 2001), p. 24.
[7] Transylvania, Croatia and Fiume.
[8] The Social Democratic Party was founded in 1889 and the Christian Social Party in 1890.
[9] Prior to that it was comprised of Landtag deputies.
[10] This did not apply at Länder and municipality level.

upper house recruited from hereditary aristocrats, the clerical elite and public figures personally appointed by the Emperor.

The Austrian part of the Reich consisted of seventeen Crown Länder (*Kronländer*),[11] the historical roots of which could, in part, be traced back to the Middle Ages. Sections 11 and 12 of the December Constitution of 1867 (RGBl 141/1867) prescribed a division of jurisdiction between the Reichsrat and the Landtage that remained valid until 1925. Any responsibilities not explicitly defined as those of the Reichsrat were assigned to the Landtage under section 12. This distribution of responsibilities was a compromise between leftist liberals and right-wing federalists, with conflict between centralism and federalism becoming increasingly overshadowed by nationality conflicts. The liberals, the German majority population and particularly the German-dominated central bureaucracy were largely centralist in orientation, while the Poles and Czechs, along with numerous minority nationalities, favoured federal solutions. The Hungarians were advocates of dualism.

Social policy from the 'top down'

In 1879 Prime Minister Graf von Taaffe took over as the head of a government that relied on a coalition between conservatives and Czech and Polish federalists, and which initiated the first steps in the creation of the welfare state. Taaffe's social reforms took place against the institutional backdrop of a decentralized unitary state with a firmly structured bureaucracy and under semi-democratic conditions. In comparative terms, welfare state consolidation took place at a time of relatively weak economic development of the country as a whole.[12] Social policy from the 'top down'[13] was embedded in a political culture rooted in enlightened absolutism.[14] These social reforms were initiated by a conservative elite that was strongly influenced by Catholic social teaching.[15] The motives inspiring the reforms were multi-layered: legitimization issues were just as prominent as attempts to take the wind out of the sails of the emerging

---

[11] Listed from highest to lowest in population size: Galicia, Bohemia, Lower Austria, Moravia, Styria, Tyrol, Upper Austria, Silesia, Krajina, Bukovina, Dalmatia, Carinthia, Istria, Gorizia and Gradisca, Salzburg, Trieste, and Vorarlberg.
[12] Manfred G. Schmidt, *Sozialpolitik in Deutschland. Historische Entwicklung und internationaler Vergleich* (Opladen: Leske & Budrich, 1998), p. 180.
[13] Jens Alber, *Vom Armenhaus zum Wohlfahrtsstaat. Zur Entstehung der Sozialversicherung in Westeuropa* (Frankfurt-on-Main: Campus, 1982).
[14] Josef Weidenholzer, *Der sorgende Staat. Zur Entwicklung der Sozialpolitik von Joseph II. bis Ferdinand Hanusch* (Vienna and Munich: Europaverlag, 1985).
[15] Emmerich Tálos, *Staatliche Sozialpolitik in Österreich* (Vienna: Verlag für Gesellschaftskritik, 1981).

workers' movement and to protect small business and craftsmen. There was, moreover, an intention to use social policy as a tool to contain the centrifugal forces of the multi-nation state: 'it was clear to every member of the Taaffe government that in dealing with the "social issue" (*soziale Frage*), joint action by means of far-reaching social policy legislation was the only way to provide the adhesive necessary to keep the monarchy together'.[16]

In contrast to Bismarck's social reforms, which were implemented at much the same time, Austrian social policy was backward-looking rather than future-focussed and was aimed at preserving the old economic and social order.[17] By its very nature, the policy stance was anti-capitalist, anti-liberal and anti-industrial in nature.[18] Impetus for reform also came from the municipalities, which, historically, had been responsible for welfare relief for the poor.[19] With the introduction of accident insurance (1887), health insurance (1888), the *Bruderladengesetz* (1889) – which prescribed health and dependants' benefits for miners – and old age pensions for white-collar workers (1906), the central state had assumed major social policy responsibilities. Austria's social insurance system leaned heavily on the German model, while the factory workers' and miners' health and safety acts, which were also introduced in the 1880s, were based not only on home-grown solutions but also on the Swiss experience,[20] and went, in part, beyond the German regulations.[21] Innovations included the introduction of an eleven-hour working day, the prohibition of child labour, Sunday and public holidays as rest days, and the prohibition of night work for women. Social policy legislation in Hungary and its subordinate Länder followed slightly later, with the introduction of health insurance (1892), but was less far-reaching than in the more industrialized Austrian part of the monarchy.[22]

---

[16] Herbert Hofmeister, 'Landesbericht Österreich', in Peter A. Köhler and Hans F. Zacher, eds., *Ein Jahrhundert Sozialversicherung* (Berlin: Duncker & Humblot, 1981), pp. 445–730, p. 517 (my translation).
[17] Hans Rosenberg, *Große Depression und Bismarckzeit* (Munich: Ullstein, 1976).
[18] Tálos, *Staatliche Sozialpolitik*, pp. 43–45.
[19] The legal basis for the provision of alms included the *Reichsgemeindegesetz* (1862) and the *Reichsheimatgesetz* (1863).
[20] Kurt Ebert, *Die Anfänge der modernen Sozialpolitik in Österreich. Die Taaffesche Sozialgesetzgebung für die Arbeiter im Rahmen der Gewerbeordnungsreform (1879–1885)* (Vienna: ÖAW-Verlag, 1975).
[21] Hofmeister, 'Landesbericht Österreich', pp. 524–25; Gerhard Ritter, *Der Sozialstaat. Entstehung und Entwicklung im internationalen Vergleich* (Munich: Oldenbourg, 1991), pp. 61–62.
[22] Eberhard Eichenhofer, 'Deutsche und österreichische Einflüsse auf die Sozialgesetzgebung in Ost- und Südosteuropa', *Sozialer Fortschritt*, vol. 44 (1995), nos. 8/9, pp. 189–93.

Considerable differences between the two Reichshälften were also evident in poverty assistance regulations enacted by the municipalities and Länder.[23] Social assistance was the responsibility of the municipalities. Based on the 1863 Reichsheimatgesetz, the place of birth principle prevailed, giving people the right to claim assistance from the municipality from whence they came. This law authorized the Länder to implement parallel and supplementary measures, which they made use of from the 1870s onwards. Local jurisdiction led to considerable regional disparities across the Cisleithanian Länder with respect to organization, funding and benefit provision.[24]

Judged by its structural make-up, the Austrian social insurance system was initially an obligatory insurance for specific groups of workers, which focussed largely on industrial workers and thus retained a high degree of selectivity. While the health and accident insurance schemes for factory workers were an attempt to bolster the legitimacy of the (authoritarian) state, it was no coincidence that the 1906 old age pension for white-collar workers was introduced almost simultaneously with general voting rights for men in 1907.[25] Agricultural and forestry workers, a group that was large in number, remained without social insurance, as did farmers and the self-employed. The exclusion of agricultural workers was not least a casualty of the strong federalist and agrarian feudal interests that prevailed within the Reichsrat.[26] After a gruelling debate in the lower house, the federalists were successful in their efforts to prevent these groups of workers being removed from the sphere of Länder authority. An attempt to create an imperial framework Act harmonizing legislation in the various Länder was unsuccessful.[27] It was not until 1921 that a further attempt was made to integrate agricultural workers into the state health insurance scheme. However, this was, as I will show later, vetoed by the Constitutional Court.

From an organizational standpoint, the different branches of social insurance were self-administered, semi-public bodies under state

---

[23] Gerhard Melinz and Susan Zimmermann, *Über die Grenzen der Armenhilfe. Kommunale und staatliche Sozialpolitik in Wien und Budapest in der Doppelmonarchie* (Vienna and Munich: Europaverlag, 1991).
[24] Georg Schmitz, 'Organe und Arbeitsweise, Strukturen und Leistungen der Landesvertretungen', in Österreichische Akademie der Wissenschaften, ed., *Die Habsburgermonarchie 1848–1918*, vol. vii/2, *Die regionalen Repräsentativkörperschaften* (Vienna: ÖAW-Verlag, 2000), pp. 1353–544, pp. 1446–58.
[25] Tálos, *Staatliche Sozialpolitik*, p. 177.   [26] Ibid., p. 67.
[27] Without which the Länder also remained inactive, Hofmeister, 'Landesbericht Österreich', pp. 568–69, 572, 614.

supervision.[28] Contrary to the German practice, the administration of accident insurance was initially largely based on the territorial principle and thus possessed federal characteristics. Accident insurance institutes were established in seven Länder,[29] with tripartite executive boards comprising employer and employee representatives and civil servants. Health insurance carriers consisted of six (seven after 1892) different types of insurance funds, which were also organized as self-administrative bodies under state supervision.

Social insurance was fully funded from employers' and employees' contributions. Accident insurance was predominantly funded from employers' contributions, whereas the contribution ratio between workers and employers in health insurance was initially two-thirds to one-third. State subsidies were not provided. The Reichsrat's Commerce and Trade Committee saw this as a 'communist standard'.[30] The occupationally fragmented organization of social insurance and its contributory-based mode of funding survives to the present day, giving the Austrian welfare state the particularist characteristics of a 'conservative' welfare state regime as described by Gøsta Esping-Andersen.[31]

Various plans for reform aimed at extending and codifying workers' social insurance either failed or were sidelined during the early years of the twentieth century.[32] Along with the outbreak of war in 1914, increased ethnic tensions and the resulting politics of obstruction in the Reichsrat played an important role in frustrating progress. Contrary to the Taaffe government's expectations, the welfare state was not an effective means of cementing the legitimacy of the monarchy or of attenuating nationalist divisions. The selective nature of the social insurance system (evident from the low degree of coverage) and differing social standards in the two halves of the empire undermined such aspirations. Instead, what integration there was became the province of the Emperor, the bureaucracy and the army.[33] These were the forces providing institutional backing for Austria-Hungary's entry into the First World War, which finally led to the breakdown of the Habsburg monarchy in 1918.

---

[28] Max Layer, [Internationaler Arbeiterversicherungs-Kongress 7. Tagung. Wien 17.–23. September 1905] *Geschichte der österreichischen Arbeiterversicherung seit dem Jahre 1889 mit besonderer Berücksichtigung des neuen Gesetzesentwurfes* (Vienna: Engel, 1905), p. 10.
[29] Vienna, Salzburg, Prague, Brünn/Brno, Graz, Trieste and Lemberg.
[30] Hofmeister, 'Landesbericht Österreich', p. 547.
[31] Gøsta Esping-Andersen, *The Three Worlds of Welfare Capitalism* (Cambridge: Polity Press; Princeton: Princeton University Press, 1990).
[32] Layer, *Geschichte der österreichischen Arbeiterversicherung*; Ludwig Brügel, *Soziale Gesetzgebung in Österreich von 1848 bis 1918* (Vienna and Leipzig: Deuticke, 1919).
[33] Bruckmüller, *Sozialgeschichte Österreichs*, p. 283.

The German-Austrian Republic (1918–1919) and the First Republic (1920–1933/34)

Constitutional framework

A manifesto proclaimed by Emperor Karl in October 1918 in an attempt to restructure the monarchy into a federal state was not enough to prevent the collapse of the Habsburg multi-nation state along nationality-bound faultlines. The founding of the unitary but decentralized German-Austrian Republic (1918–19) just a few weeks later took place in revolutionary style with the elimination of the imperial prerogative and the implementation of participatory rule. The Paris peace treaties prohibited the idea of union with the Weimar Republic, not least as expressed in the German-Austrian state title until October 1919. With the passing of the Federal Constitutional Law on 1 October 1920, Austria became a federal state.

The new federal constitution together with the federal state it underpinned expressed a political compromise between the federalist ideologies of the Christian Social Party and the more centralist alternatives of the Social Democratic Workers' Party (SDAP). In terms of the federal state, the compromise came about because, while Federal Constitutional Law created a truly federal system, it had from the outset shown strong leanings towards the central state. These strong centralist characteristics can be identified in five features. The purely provisional delegation of powers between the federal state and the Länder was linked to the delegation in the December Constitution of 1867 and gave the central state a clear upper hand in legislation. Further, the 1922 Fiscal Constitution (*Finanzverfassungsgesetz*) was also strongly centralist.[34] Thirdly, and somewhat atypically for a federal state, the judicial function was solely a matter for the federation. Fourthly, and likewise unique in international comparison, an indirect federal administration (*mittelbare Bundesverwaltung*) was established within whose scope federal laws were to be enforced by Länder administrations acting as federal administrative bodies. Finally, although, in common with all other western federations, a two-chamber legislature was established, there was a considerable asymmetry of powers in favour of the National Council (*Nationalrat*). The Federal Council (*Bundesrat*) represents the Länder by means of something that is halfway between the senate principle and proportional representation, and was equipped with a veto, which could suspend legislation, not defeat it.

---

[34] Richard Pfaundler, *Der Finanzausgleich in Österreich. Das System, seine Begründung und Durchführung* (Vienna: Julius Springer, 1931).

One major innovation of the Federal Constitutional Law was a separate Constitutional Court, which, while having affinities to the monarchy's Imperial Court (*Reichsgericht*), had extended responsibilities. The court is composed of a president, vice-president, twelve judges and six alternates. It decides autonomously or on application by the courts whether a federal or state law is constitutional or otherwise. In addition, it pronounces on application by the federal government whether Länder laws are unconstitutional and likewise on application by a Länder government or by one-third of members of the National or Federal Council whether federal laws are unconstitutional.[35]

The newly established system of parliamentary government made for a marked increase in party discipline, while the strong powers of the central state almost automatically made the federal tier of government into the central arena for political conflict between the well-organized Christian-Social/Pan-German and the Social Democratic camps. From the outset, federal–provincial relations were dominated by Austria's highly centralized party system. Party-political activity, in turn, gave further impetus to centralization. Amendments to the Federal Constitutional Law in 1925 and 1929 ratified these developments. The 1929 amendment led to an increase in the Federal President's powers and introduced a quasi-presidential component into the Austrian system of government.

The Federal President is the head of state and is directly elected for a term of six years. Re-election is possible for a second term of office. The President is Commander-in-Chief of the armed forces and holds emergency executive powers. In addition, he is empowered to dissolve parliament – a power never used, even to the present day. In respect of most of his powers the President lacks real power since the majority of his official acts require the counter-signature of the Federal Chancellor or of the competent Federal Minister. The President is not involved in policy-making. His only power in law-making is to confirm by his signature that federal laws were enacted in accordance with the constitution. No President has ever refused to sign a federal law.

Social policy in the First Republic

In terms of social policy, the social laws of the monarchy were transferred to the republic. In the immediate aftermath of the war, between 1918 and 1920, appalling economic conditions led to a grand coalition government of Social Democrats and Christian Socials that initiated a range of new

---

[35] Since 1975 the court also pronounces on whether laws are unconstitutional when an application alleges direct infringement of personal rights.

social programmes. These included the introduction of the eight-hour working day, the introduction of workers' holidays, the Works Councils Act (*Betriebsrätegesetz*), a health insurance scheme for civil servants and the creation of unemployment insurance in 1920. This meant that the basic building blocks of the welfare state were already in place by the time the country became a federal state with the enactment of the new Federal Constitutional Law in 1920.

What is not so widely known is that almost the entire complex of the monarchy's social legislation was unconstitutional: section 11 of the December Constitution 1867 did not delegate the necessary powers to the Reichsrat, so that (according to section 12) it was the Länder that retained the proper authority for such policy-making. This is doubly relevant, because the distribution of jurisdictions under the monarchy was carried over by the republic, and remained in force on a provisional basis until 1925. Thus, early republican social legislation was unconstitutional too,[36] both in respect of social insurance and employment law. However, prior to the establishment of the Constitutional Court in 1920, there existed no instance of judicial review that could intervene and correct. It is, thus, hardly surprising that the Constitutional Court in 1924, while scrutinizing the seventh amendment to the 1921 Health Insurance Act, which prescribed expansion of the health insurance scheme to include agricultural workers, ruled that the law, and indeed *all* other social insurance laws enacted by the monarchy, had been passed without the necessary constitutional authority.[37]

The entry into force of the new 1925 distribution of powers under the 1920 Federal Constitutional Law closed this loophole in the assignment of constitutional jurisdiction: under section 10 the entire social insurance system and, with the exception of agricultural and forestry workers, the entire enactment and enforcement of employment law was assigned to the federal government. For the most part, the same applied to the health sector and to war victims' relief schemes. Under section 12 the responsibilities of the federal government included the right to pass federal skeleton legislation (*Grundsatzgesetzgebung*) on certain social policy issues. These included general welfare, maternity, infants' and children's welfare, hospitals and clinics and welfare for blue-collar and white-collar workers in agriculture and forestry. Thus, by 1925 the federal government

[36] Josef Werndl, *Die Kompetenzverteilung zwischen Bund und Ländern: ihre Ausgangslage, Entwicklung und Bedeutungsverschiebung auf der Grundlage des Bundes-Verfassungsgesetzes von 1920* (Vienna: Braumüller, 1984) expressly cites the law for the establishment of conciliation boards and on collectively agreed employment contracts (1920), the Federal Law on the trades inspectorate, the law on the establishment of works' councils (1919) and that on the establishment of chambers of labour (1920).
[37] See *Sammlung der Erkenntnisse des Verfassungsgerichtshofes* no. 328, new series, 1924, no. 4 (Vienna, 1925), pp. 91–96.

had assumed responsibility for legislation and enforcement in almost all sectors of social security.

From a comparative perspective, this dominance of the federal government in social policy is remarkable, and raises the question of whether in respect of the welfare state, Austria was genuinely federal in any real sense. We would argue that it was, since the federal government was not responsible for the provision of social assistance. Although the National Council in 1929 discussed a skeleton law on welfare for the poor, this never came to fruition.[38] Thus, social assistance remained a responsibility of the nine Länder, which re-enacted the poor relief regulations of the monarchy during the time of the First Republic.

The federal government's virtual monopoly of social policy responsibilities was mirrored in the public finance sector with the 1922 Fiscal Constitution, which, given a background of war-related political and economic crises, gave the federal government enormous leverage over taxation that was never to be rescinded.[39] By the early 1920s, therefore, the federal government was in command of virtually all the necessary powers to command fiscal and social policy. War exigencies apart, this concentration of federal powers was largely a product of partisan competition between the Christian Democrats and the Social Democrats.

The party politics of that era is also largely responsible for the trajectory of social policy that developed thereafter. Following the exit of the Social Democrats from government in 1920, expansion of state social policy continued albeit more slowly than previously. The characteristics of the social policy of the exclusively right-wing bourgeois cabinets that followed included a clientalist approach in terms of privileging those groups of society that supported these parties, the imposition of Catholic social doctrines and the ever-increasing trend towards subordination of social policy to general economic conditions. The first of these characteristics was clearly manifest in the decision of 1921 to expand the health service to include agricultural workers, which was initially revoked by the Constitutional Court, but then finally enacted in 1928 under the new distribution of powers.[40] Clientalist traits were also evident in the White-Collar

---

[38] Gerhard Melinz, 'Das "zweite soziale Netz" – Kehrseite staatlicher Sozialpolitik', in Emmerich Tálos, Herbert Dachs, Ernst Hanisch and Anton Staudinger, eds., *Handbuch des politischen Systems Österreichs. Erste Republik 1918–1933* (Vienna: Manz, 1995), pp. 587–601, pp. 589–90.

[39] Peter Pernthaler, *Österreichische Finanzverfassung. Theorie-Praxis-Reform* (Vienna: Braumüller, 1984), pp. 112–14.

[40] The organization had federalist traits because insurance institutes for agricultural workers were established in Vienna, Linz, Graz, Klagenfurt and Innsbruck. Cf. Friedrich Steinbach, *Die gesetzliche Unfallversicherung in Österreich. Eine Rückschau anläßlich ihres neunzigjährigen Bestandes* (Vienna: Forschungsinstitut für Soziale Sicherheit beim Hauptverband der Österreichischen Sozialversicherungsträger, 1980), p. 119.

Workers' Insurance Act of 1926, which brought considerable improvements to the old age pension scheme for white-collar workers. Of particular importance was an expansion of coverage to include family members in cases of sickness or death.[41] Ideologically, this harmonized with Catholic social doctrines, since it paved the way for a family-oriented model of social security typically providing spouses and dependent children with access to benefits on the basis of their relationship to a male breadwinner.

The increasing importance of general economic conditions manifested itself in two measures. Against the backdrop of post-war inflation and currency reform in the early 1920s, the funding system of social insurance was replaced by the less inflation-sensitive pay-as-you-go system.[42] In addition, the promised introduction of old age pensions for blue-collar workers was linked to the fulfilment of certain macro-economic conditions. But the global economic crisis dashed these hopes and led to a strengthening of social assistance rather than social insurance. Old age pensions for blue-collar workers were replaced by a means-tested old age benefit, while unemployment benefits were slashed.

In terms of financing the welfare state, the social policy of the First Republic was significant, since unemployment insurance and emergency benefit for the long-term unemployed in 1922 marked the first occasion on which the state stepped in to finance social security benefits.[43] This sparked off a phased increase in interdependence between social insurance budgets and public budgets in the form of inter-governmental grants, as was evident in the financing model for the 1922 'productive unemployment system' (*produktive Arbeitslosenfürsorge*). Länder and municipalities received federal grants if they achieved savings on unemployment benefits by placing the unemployed in local employment schemes. Conversely, the Länder and municipalities were obliged to co-finance federal social security schemes such as the 1927 needs-based old age pension system.[44]

Apart from early social policy pre-emption by the federal government, other developments in social policy in the First Republic provide an interesting example of policy innovation within federal systems. Between 1920 and the demise of democracy in 1933–34, the politically short-lived

---

[41] In 1890 some 7 per cent of the population had health insurance. By 1930 this had risen to 60 per cent; see Emmerich Tálos and Karl Wörister, *Soziale Sicherung im Sozialstaat Österreich* (Baden-Baden: Nomos, 1994), p. 24. The Social Democrats also supported the principle of family insurance; see Hofmeister, 'Landesbericht Österreich', p. 630.
[42] Steinbach, *Gesetzliche Unfallversicherung*, p. 111.
[43] Tálos, *Staatliche Sozialpolitik in Österreich*, p. 161.
[44] Melinz, 'Das "Zweite soziale Netz"', p. 592.

federal governments were made up of representatives of the Christian Social Party and the Pan-Germans. Faced with a right-wing federal government, the opposing Social Democrats attempted to use their Vienna bastion to establish a social policy counter-model based on Austro-Marxism.

Federalism as a laboratory of social policy: Red Vienna

Vienna was one of the first of the major cities of Europe in which a leftist party with an absolute majority was able to realize its municipal political ideas.[45] The Social Democrats were in opposition at the federal level from 1920 onwards, but they used their strength[46] in Vienna to conduct a fifteen-year long experiment in social policy leading to the creation of a proletarian counter-culture.[47] Between 1919 and the banning of the party in 1934, the Social Democratic Party (SDAP) governed Vienna with an absolute majority. Bourgeois parties controlled the remaining Länder governments. In them, the SDAP's influence was restricted to local strongholds.[48]

Given the constitutional distribution of powers outlined above, social assistance remained a jurisdiction of the Länder. They also had social-policy-related powers in housing and elementary and secondary education, and it was in these areas that the Social Democrats were able to enact reforms that attracted international acclaim outside Austria. Vienna had been a *Bundesland* in its own right since 1922. This gave the Social Democrats access to taxation policy and the ability to use it for their social policy reform projects. Reforms introduced under the leadership of City Councillor Hugo Breitner used Länder powers to tax and impose excise duties,[49] penalizing the well off (e.g. taxes on household servants, automobiles and luxury goods). Not surprisingly, the bourgeois parties branded this tax policy as 'Bolshevist-style taxation' and Breitner himself

---

[45] Felix Czeike, 'Wien', in Erika Weinzierl and Kurt Skalnik, eds., *Österreich 1918–1938. Geschichte der Ersten Republik 1918–1938*, vol. II (Graz, Vienna and Cologne: Styria, 1983), pp. 1043–78, p. 1045.
[46] In 1929 the SDAP had 418,000 members in Vienna. This amounted to 58 per cent of its total party membership in Austria; see Helmut Gruber, *Red Vienna. Experiments in Working-Class Culture 1919–1934* (Oxford: Oxford University Press, 1991), p. 20.
[47] Anson Rabinbach, ed., *The Austrian Socialist Experiment. Social Democracy and Austro-marxism, 1918–1934* (Boulder, CO: Westview Press, 1985), pp. 60–63; Gruber, *Red Vienna*.
[48] Charlie Jeffery, *Social Democracy in the Austrian Provinces, 1918–1934: Beyond Red Vienna* (Leicester: Leicester University Press, 1995).
[49] Pernthaler, *Österreichische Finanzverfassung*, pp. 113–14.

was dubbed a 'tax vampire' and 'tax sadist'.[50] In 1923 a socially progressive housing tax was introduced to finance municipal housing. Breitner's tax reforms provided a basis for the SDAP's social policy initiatives: 'By shifting the forms of taxes from indirect to direct, from necessities to luxuries, and by introducing a graduated scale that favoured wage earners, the socialists created a source of revenue for public projects truly unique at that time.'[51] These initiatives rested on four closely related pillars – housing, welfare, education and culture. The central idea underpinning social policy in Red Vienna was not only the provision of a decent standard of living for the workers, but also at the same time the re-education of the working class, that is, the creation of a new, proletarian human being.

Drawing on revenues from the housing tax, the City of Vienna created public housing with rents that were affordable to workers. Between 1919 and 1934 the city built about 64,000 new homes, most of them in public apartment dwellings (*Gemeindebauten*). To improve hygiene, and to prevent diseases and epidemics including the then rampant tuberculosis, the new apartments had access to fresh water, electricity and gas and were provided with separate toilets. The city fathers viewed them as 'proletarian oases in which sun and light, space and colour set the tone of a new form of decent and dignified living'.[52] In addition, many *Gemeindebauten* had a well-developed social infrastructure, including kindergartens, day nurseries, sports areas and gardens, welfare centres, bath houses, laundries and libraries.

Public welfare focussed especially on children and young people. The central idea was prevention both with respect to public health and to deviant behaviour. The City Councillor for Welfare, Julius Tandler, was convinced that building 'palaces' for children breaks down prison walls. Nevertheless, public welfare also exhibited elements of social control and surveillance by the social assistance authorities.

An integral part of Austro-Marxism was education. Special emphasis was put on schooling in order to provide equal opportunities to working-class children. School books and material were distributed free of charge, curricula were reorganized, physical punishment was abolished, the training of teachers was improved and whole-day schools as well as kindergartens were established. Adult education played a prominent role in the SDAP's attempt to raise the workers to a higher cultural level and to create a proletarian counter-culture.[53] Examples of the party's cultural

---

[50] Melinz, 'Das "Zweite soziale Netz"', p. 591; Helmut Weihsmann, *Das rote Wien. Sozialdemokratische Architektur und Kommunalpolitik 1919–1934* (Vienna: Edition Spuren, 2002), p. 32.
[51] Gruber, *Red Vienna*, p. 22.   [52] Ibid., p. 58.   [53] Ibid., p. 87.

and educational efforts were public libraries, a wide variety of partisan newspapers and periodicals, subsidized tickets for theatre and opera performances and workers' colleges. In order to reach the broad mass of workers, a dense network of associations was created, covering a wide field of interests including sports, animals and chess.

These policies were extremely popular and secured the Viennese Social Democrats a permanent absolute majority until 1934. However, this island of socialism became more and more isolated, and tensions with the federal government increased steadily. The bourgeois federal government's strong distrust of Red Vienna was strategically and ideologically motivated. As the former imperial capital, with almost 2 million inhabitants, the city formed the most populous *Land*. Almost one-third of the Austrian population lived in Vienna, making it a strategically important location in terms of the electorate. In passing constitutional amendments, the bourgeois federal government required the consent of the SDAP and, prior to the demise of the Republic, was unsuccessful in reducing the Social Democrats' vote below the vital one-third level. This made for increased antagonism between Red Vienna and the bourgeois right-wing federal government. As a consequence, the two major parties revised their attitudes towards federalism: the Christian Socials embraced centralism in an attempt to limit the authority of Red Vienna, while the Social Democrats took, at least in part, to defending federalism.[54] One strategy used to undermine the Viennese position was the curbing of fiscal transfers, with the Constitutional Court being called upon to review unpopular municipal taxes.[55] Ultimately, however, the destruction of Viennese political autonomy was only achieved by unconstitutional means.[56]

Austro-fascism and National-Socialist rule (1934–1945)

The final blow to democracy itself came in the years 1933 and 1934. The establishment of an authoritarian Austro-fascist regime in the aftermath of a short civil war in 1934 led to a further weakening of federalism, before union (*Anschluss*) with National-Socialist Germany in March 1938 extinguished not only federalism but also independent Austrian statehood. Against the backdrop of global economic crisis and an increase in unemployment to 25 per cent, the extent of social expenditure retrenchment under Austro-fascism was unprecedented. Moreover, welfare measures of

---

[54] Irmgard Kathrein, *Der Bundesrat in der Ersten Republik. Studie über die Entstehung und die Tätigkeit des Bundesrates der Republik Österreich* (Vienna: Braumüller, 1983), pp. 50–51.
[55] Czeike, 'Wien', p. 1061.
[56] See Wolfgang Maderthaner and Michaela Maier, eds., *'Der Führer bin ich selbst'. Engelbert Dollfuß – Benito Mussolini, Briefwechsel* (Vienna: Löcker, 2004), p. 33.

a repressive nature became increasingly important.[57] With the Anschluss, the German Reich's social policies, together with the highly centralized German fiscal constitution, were gradually transferred to Austria. The changes that took place in labour law were far more comprehensive than those in social insurance. National-Socialist policy was 'top-down social policy' par excellence.[58] This manifested itself in the replacement of self-administration in social insurance and industrial democracy by the 'leader principle', in a racist approach with respect to eligibility rules and in a restructuring of the social welfare sector. Racist and war-motivated restrictions on welfare benefits were put in place, but there was also a selective enhancement of benefits (e.g. an expansion of old age pensions to include blue-collar workers). In terms of its more lasting legacy, National Socialist rule made for a further centralization of both social and fiscal policy that was only partly reversed with the coming of the Second Republic in the aftermath of World War Two.

The Second Republic (1945 onwards)

Constitutional framework

In April 1945 the provisional government issued a decree nullifying the Anschluss and re-establishing the Republic of Austria under the 1920 Federal Constitutional Law as amended in 1929. Nevertheless, Austria was controlled by the Allied Forces until the State Treaty of Vienna ended foreign occupation and restored full sovereignty in 1955. Federalism was re-established in the form of a multi-level state comprising nine Länder and some 2,400 municipalities. Political organization of the Länder and the municipalities is narrowly specified by the Federal Constitutional Law. The municipalities have an autonomous and delegated sphere of responsibility, that is, they act either independently or as the administrative agents of federal or Länder government.[59] The provincial diets (*Landtage*) are directly elected and in turn elect Land governments each headed by a provincial governor (*Landeshauptmann*), with the governments responsible to the provincial diets. With the exceptions of Vienna and Vorarlberg, for much of the post-war period the Länder governments have been broad coalitions composed of all major parties represented in

---

[57] Tálos and Wörister, *Soziale Sicherung im Sozialstaat Österreich*, pp. 29–30.
[58] Emmerich Tálos, 'Sozialpolitik in der "Ostmark"', in Emmerich Tálos, Ernst Hanisch, Wolfgang Neugebauer and Reinhard Sieder, eds., *NS-Herrschaft in Österreich* (Vienna: ÖBV, 2000), pp. 376–408, p. 400.
[59] Anton Pelinka, *Austria. Out of the Shadow of the Past* (Boulder, CO: Westview Press, 1998), p. 70.

the provincial diets. Since the 1990s, however, this kind of consociational democracy at Länder level has been in decline.

The Länder are under-represented in the federal decision-making arena and have no effective veto powers in the Federal Council that would allow them sustained influence over the federal policy-making process. Until 1984 the Länder had no right to participate in constitutional amendments involving the distribution of (social policy) jurisdictions. In terms of ordinary legislation, the Federal Council veto can only suspend legislation and can be easily overridden by a simple majority in the lower house. In the important fields of fiscal policy, such as the federal budget and federal debt management, the Federal Council has no veto power of any kind.

Despite their weak formal powers, the Länder have more effective access to federal policy-making through informal channels. First, federal bills are subject to an informal pre-parliamentary review process in which the Länder are invited to participate if their interests are affected by the proposed legislation. Second, inter-governmental relations between the federation and the Länder are highly informal. Governors' conferences (*Landeshauptmännerkonferenzen*) and other conferences of Länder executives (*Landesamtdirektoren-* and *Landesreferentenkonferenzen*) are a natural response to the weakness of federal institutions.[60] Representatives of the federal government are regularly invited to these semi-annual conferences. Hence, despite the weak role of the Länder in the legislative process, there is a real co-operative federalism, which is largely based upon informal negotiations and political co-ordination between the executives of different tiers of government. The conferences work without a legal mandate and their decisions are arrived at behind closed doors and based on the unanimity principle. While this imposes a need to compromise and favours lowest common denominator solutions, at the same time it means that decisions are broadly legitimized[61] and represent politically powerful manifestations of Länder interests. The most important agenda items include fiscal equalization issues and the allocation of jurisdictions.[62] And although it is extremely difficult for the federal government to implement a measure against unanimous decisions of the governors' conference, what

[60] Karl Weber, 'Macht im Schatten? Landeshauptmänner-, Landesamtsdirektoren- und andere Landesreferentenkonferenzen', *Österreichische Zeitschrift für Politikwissenschaft*, vol. 21 (1992), no. 4, pp. 405–18.
[61] Weber, 'Macht im Schatten?', p. 414; Kurt Richard Luther, 'Bund-Länder-Beziehungen: Formal- und Realverfassung', in Herbert Dachs, Peter Gerlich, Herbert Gottweis, Franz Horner, Helmut Kramer, Volkmar Lauber, Wolfgang C. Müller and Emmerich Tálos, eds., *Handbuch des politischen Systems Österreichs* (Vienna: Manz, 1997), pp. 907–19, p. 917.
[62] Luther, 'Bund-Länder-Beziehungen', p. 916.

occasionally works in the federal government's favour is that the provincial governors are frequently bound to the intentions of their party headquarters, so that party-political loyalties may overshadow Länder interests.[63] The conferences have been quite effective over the last two decades in defending the Länder interests, and in strengthening their influence on affairs relating to European integration. But since these conferences were not fully developed before the mid-1960s, it is reasonable to conclude that the above informal arrangements did not exert a substantial influence on the 'old politics' of the welfare state.

With the reinstatement of the Federal Constitutional Law in 1945, the distribution of responsibilities of 1925 was re-established. This means that the federal government is responsible for social insurance and labour law, whereas social assistance is the continuing responsibility of the nine Länder. Until 1955 the federal government also had extraordinary powers in economic affairs to overcome war-related damage and to co-ordinate reconstruction. The already strong fiscal powers of the federal government were further strengthened during World War Two and retained under the 1948 Fiscal Constitutional Law that codified many regulations of the German Reich's strongly centralized fiscal system.[64]

Länder powers relating to taxation and excise duties were subject to further restriction over time, so that today revenue policy is largely a matter for the federal government. The Fiscal Constitutional Law of 1948 enumerates five categories of taxation, including exclusively federal taxes, taxes shared between the federal government and the Länder (and municipalities) and exclusively Länder taxes. Under the Fiscal Equalisation Act, taxes are classified into one of these five categories and revenue is distributed accordingly. Revenues from income tax, for instance, are shared between the different tiers of government, whereas tobacco tax and tariffs are exclusively federal revenues. Examples of Länder taxes are real property tax, dog tax or non-income charges related to tourism. Amazingly enough, the Fiscal Equalisation Act is not a constitutional law, so that no super-majorities are required to alter the distribution of fiscal powers.

The Austrian Constitution provides numerous instruments of direct democracy, although only three are relevant in practice.

- A mandatory referendum is required if the constitution is to be subject to a total revision. Accession to the European Union was interpreted as a substantial constitutional revision and therefore subject to a mandatory referendum in 1994.

[63] Karl Weber, 'Die Entwicklung des österreichischen Bundesstaates', in Herbert Schambeck, ed., *Bundesstaat und Bundesrat in Österreich* (Vienna: Verlag Österreich, 1997), pp. 37–64, p. 60.
[64] Pernthaler, *Österreichische Finanzverfassung*, p. 116.

- The lower house can delegate the decision on a bill to the people (optional referendum). Historically, the only referendum of this kind occurred when the people were consulted about commissioning a nuclear power plant in 1978.
- The people's initiative makes it possible to initiate a bill from the bottom up. Irrelevant in practice in the First Republic, this instrument has been frequently employed during the course of the Second Republic. Today, about 8,000 signatures are required to launch an initiative. Provided that 100,000 voters (or a sixth of the electorate in each of three Länder) support the initiative, parliament is obliged to deliberate on the proposition. In no way, however, is the outcome of such an initiative binding on parliament. The popular initiative is an instrument that is frequently utilized by the parliamentary opposition, since it offers a means of agenda-setting and is strategically useful in attracting votes in upcoming elections.[65]

Apart from the mandatory referendum (which naturally is unlikely to occur), the political elite has little reason to fear the exercise of direct democracy. The decision whether to initiate an optional referendum is made by the National Council, while the federal government has complete discretion in how it responds to a people's initiative, since its outcome is not binding for the representative institutions.

Given this constitutional framework, neither direct democracy nor the Federal Council and the Federal President (cf. section 1) can be classified as veto players. This leaves the Constitutional Court as the only institution with the potential to restrict the parliamentary majority's freedom of action.[66] Yet, with a two-thirds majority, the Constitutional Court's veto power can be neutralized, since constitutional law is not subject to judicial review. Unpalatable judgements – given the political will – can thus be prevented (by pre-emption, that is, by passing a bill as a constitutional provision with a two-thirds majority) or cleaned up retroactively (by amendment). From the outset, the court's potential as a veto player was limited by the early expansion of federal powers. Moreover, until the late 1970s the Constitutional Court avoided conflicts with the legislature.[67] This self-restraint came to a head with the resignation in 1977 of the President of the Constitutional

---

[65] Wolfgang C. Müller, 'Party Competition and Plebiscitary Politics in Austria', *Electoral Studies*, vol. 17 (1998), no. 1, pp. 21–43.

[66] Herbert Obinger, 'Vetospieler und Staatstätigkeit in Österreich. Sozial- und wirtschaftspolitische Reformchancen für die neue ÖVP/FPÖ-Regierung', *Zeitschrift für Parlamentsfragen*, vol. 32 (2001), no. 2, pp. 360–86.

[67] Martin Hiesel, *Verfassungsgesetzgeber und Verfassungsgerichtshof* (Vienna: Manz, 1995).

Court, who then criticized the court for having become an arm of the government.[68]

Party politics

From the outset, the party system has been highly centralized, vertically integrated as well as congruent across different levels of government. Politically, post-war Austria was dominated by the Social Democratic Party (SPÖ) and the Austrian People's Party (ÖVP), which together, on average, controlled more than 80 per cent of the parliamentary seats of all three tiers of government until the 1980s.[69] In six of the nine Länder, the *Landeshauptmann* has been a fiefdom of the ÖVP since 1945, while Vienna has remained a Social Democratic stronghold throughout. In programmatic terms, both party camps became more moderate after 1945 and endorsed and often practised co-operation with each other. The ÖVP, the former Christian Socials, advanced a programme emphasizing freedom and social welfare and downplayed the party's confessional legacy by abandoning organizational ties with the Roman Catholic Church. The Social Democrats bade farewell to Austro-Marxism and began gradually to bridge the gulf between the Marxist and Catholic social doctrines. Hence, in contrast to the First Republic, the dominant pattern in the post-war period was one of co-operation between the two major party camps, leading, at a parliamentary level, to coalition governments and oversized cabinets. In the post-war period, since the Christian Democrats have been programmatically committed to state-run social policy, Austria has been ruled by two pro-welfare state parties whose ideological differences have dwindled markedly compared to the past.

Co-operation has also become the dominant pattern of conflict resolution in industrial relations, with the emergence of a system of 'social partnership' in the late 1950s. The peak associations of labour and capital, both functionally and personally allied with the two major political parties, were incorporated into policy-making and strengthened their control in the self-administration of the institutions of social insurance. In 1966 the Grand Coalition between the ÖVP and SPÖ broke down and was replaced by a single party government controlled by the ÖVP, which lasted until 1970. In that year the long period of SPÖ single governments

[68] Karl Wenger, *Gedanken zur österreichischen Verfassungsgerichtsbarkeit* (St Pölten: Verlag Niederösterreichisches Pressehaus, 1978), p. 5.
[69] Herbert Dachs, Franz Fallend and Elisabeth Wolfgruber, *Länderpolitik. Politische Strukturen und Entscheidungsprozesse in den österreichischen Bundesländern* (Vienna: Signum, 1997).

under Chancellor Bruno Kreisky began, which was to last for thirteen years. In 1986 the Grand Coalition was re-established, finally collapsing in 2000 in the wake of the 1999 general election.

The party system's centre of gravity clearly lies at federal level. This is evident not only in the vast powers assigned to the federal government, but also in the high degree of party discipline resulting from the system of parliamentary government. Moreover, the Grand Coalition – the dominant form of government in the Second Republic – has been replicated in seven of the nine Länder in the form of all-party governments (*Proporzregierungen*) constituted along proportional representation lines. Since a negotiation-based mode of policy-making has prevailed at both levels of government, frictions in the rationale underpinning the federal and partisan arena are less likely to occur than in Germany.[70]

Social policy in the 'golden age'

A duopoly of pro-welfare state parties, consociationalism and corporatism, a consequent lack of institutional veto points to reform, together with favourable economic conditions from the 1950s onwards constituted an environment that was highly conducive to welfare state expansion. However, Austria had already entered the post-war period as one of the world's biggest social security spenders. According to International Labour Organisation (ILO) criteria, in 1950 Austria was second only to Germany with respect to its social expenditure–GNP ratio. From a comparative perspective, this leading position is largely a result of the early adoption of social security schemes and income support for war victims, which absorbed about 40 per cent of the social budget in 1950.[71] Nevertheless, after 1950 the expansion of the welfare state continued, albeit at a slower pace than that of one-time welfare state laggards.

Early social and economic policy measures were crucially influenced by the legacy of World War Two. In the wake of the war, German social policy was only gradually replaced. Old age pensions for blue-collar workers implemented under totalitarian rule remained in force, giving the federal government new social policy responsibilities. Supported by the Social Insurance Transition Act (*Sozialversicherungs-Überleitungsgesetz* 1947), corporatist self-administration within social insurance institutions was re-established and certain First Republic social security laws were re-enacted.

---

[70] See Gerhard Lehmbruch, *Parteienwettbewerb im Bundesstaat. Regelsysteme und Spannungslagen im Institutionengefüge der Bundesrepublik Deutschland* (Opladen: Westdeutscher Verlag, 1998).
[71] Tálos and Wörister, *Soziale Sicherung im Sozialstaat Österreich*, p. 36.

In 1946–47 large parts of heavy industry and the large banks were nationalized in order to avert expropriation by the Soviet Union. Nationalized industry was an engine of economic development and a stronghold of labour hoarding in subsequent years. In the late 1940s about 20 per cent of the total industrial labour force was employed in this sector.

Provision for victims of war and fascism played a central role in the immediate post-war years, as is evident in the 1947 Assistance to Victims of War and Fascism Act (*Opferfürsorgegesetz*) and the 1957 War Veterans' Compensation Act (*Kriegsopferversorgungsgesetz*). Both programmes were and remain entirely funded by tax. Family allowances were introduced in 1948 on a provisional basis. This latter programme clearly demonstrates the new corporatist style of policy-making, with transfer payments to employees with dependent children being offset by trade union wage restraint. However, jurisdiction was unclear and the Constitutional Court was asked to decide which tier of government was responsible in this area. The court ruled that federal jurisdiction existed only within the framework of population policy enshrined in section 12 [2]. To clarify the situation, a constitutional amendment was passed in 1955 which assigned the powers of regulation in legislation and enforcement in matters of family support to the federal government.[72] In the same year family allowances were restructured and extended to the self-employed.

The reinstatement of full sovereignty in 1955 signalled the triumph of the welfare state on all fronts. First and foremost, mention should be made of the 1955 General Social Insurance Act (*Allgemeines Sozialversicherungsgesetz*), which combined health and accident insurance and old age pensions for blue- and white-collar workers in a single system. The expansion of the welfare state from 1955 onwards had two sources. First, new programmes such as family allowances, maternity leave and long-term care allowances were established, while existing programmes were steadily improved. The retirement age was significantly reduced, pensions were adjusted to the dynamics of wages and a means-tested minimum pension (*Ausgleichszulage*) was introduced in the 1960s. Contribution-free periods were credited for calculation of old age pensions in periods of military or war service, tertiary education and periods of child-rearing. Sickness cash benefits were extended and new kinds of services such as preventive health checks were introduced. As regards unemployment insurance, benefits were improved and new schemes tailored to cater to the needs of the long-term unemployed. Second, there was a substantial broadening of

---

[72] Section 10 [1], Z 17 Federal Constitutional Law.

social insurance coverage. The share of the employed labour force covered by old age, health, accident and unemployment insurance increased from 50 per cent in 1950 to 82 per cent in 1975.[73] While social insurance in the First Republic was tailored to the needs of blue- and white-collar workers, old age, health and accident insurance have now been expanded to include all professions, students and pupils (accident insurance) and family members. With the General Social Insurance Act as a model, farmers, entrepreneurs, artists and freelance professions were gradually integrated into the social insurance system.[74] A similar process took place within the unemployment insurance system, when land and forestry workers were included in the 1950s. The social insurance system now effectively encompasses all groups of employees and the self-employed.

The increasing inclusiveness and expansion of social policy, as well as changing demographics, was paralleled by an increase in public social expenditure from 12.4 per cent of GNP in 1950 to 24.8 per cent in 1989.[75] The bulk of social expenditure is devoted to social insurance. Social insurance related expenditure as a percentage of GDP (excluding unemployment insurance) increased from 7.4 in 1956 to 15.9 in 1989, and reached an all-time high of 16.4 per cent of GDP in 1999.[76] The increasing weight of the welfare state in public policy becomes evident when social insurance expenditure is compared with the federal budget over time. This ratio increased from 24 per cent in 1948 to 49.1 per cent in 1980. The ratio in 1997 remained exactly the same.

The increasing reach of the welfare state was paralleled by a centralization of government. Federal powers in social policy were further enhanced throughout the 'golden age'. Relying on a two-thirds majority in parliament, the Grand Coalition could change the constitution as and when it pleased. Redistribution of competencies (all of them shifting social policy jurisdictions to the federal level)[77] during this period was often pushed through by means of constitutional provisions. The motives involved in expanding federal government powers were multi-layered. They followed from 'the political needs of the day',[78] were a reaction to Constitutional Court judgements and were aimed at preventing judicial review of social

[73] Alber, *Vom Armenhaus*, p. 152.
[74] The Farmers' Welfare Act (BSGV 1978), Self-Employed and Freelancer's Welfare Act (SFVG 1978), Traders' Welfare Act (GSVG 1978).
[75] See Schmidt, *Sozialpolitik in Deutschland*, p. 198.
[76] Hauptverband der Österreichischen Sozialversicherungsträger, *Statistisches Handbuch der Sozialversicherung für das Jahr 1999* [*Jahrbuch der österreichischen Sozialversicherung*, vol. II] (Vienna: Hauptverband der Österreichischen Sozialversicherungsträger, 2000), table 5.06.
[77] Werndl, *Kompetenzverteilung*.   [78] Ermacora, *Österreichischer Föderalismus*, p. 80.

Table 5.1 *Vetoes of the Federal Council against National Council legislation (1920–2002)*

Legislative period	Vetoes of the Federal Council	National Council insisting on vote	Legislative amendments by the National Council	No reaction from the National Council
I (1920–23)	19 (1)	3 (0)	11 (1)	5 (0)
II (1923–27)	6 (2)	2 (1)	3 (1)	1 (0)
III (1927–30)	6 (0)	2 (0)	4 (0)	0 (0)
IV (1930–34)	7 (0)	5 (0)	2 (0)	0 (0)
V (1945–49)	10 (0)	4 (0)	5 (0)	1 (0)
VI (1949–53)	2 (1)	0 (0)	0 (0)	1 (1)
VII (1953–56)	0 (0)	0 (0)	0 (0)	0 (0)
VIII (1956–59)	4 (0)	1 (0)	3 (0)	0 (0)
IX (1959–62)	0 (0)	0 (0)	0 (0)	0 (0)
X (1962–66)	0 (0)	0 (0)	0 (0)	0 (0)
XI (1966–70)	12 (0)	9 (0)	0 (0)	3 (0)
XII (1970–71)	3 (0)	3 (0)	0 (0)	0 (0)
XIII (1971–75)	4 (2)	4 (2)	0 (0)	0 (0)
XIV (1975–79)	14 (3)	14 (3)	0 (0)	0 (0)
XV (1979–83)	13 (5)	11 (5)	0 (0)	2 (0)
XVI (1983–86)	47 (24)	44 (23)	2 (0)	1 (1)
XVII (1986–90)	1 (0)	0 (0)	1 (0)	0 (0)
XVIII (1990–94)	1 (0)	0 (0)	0 (0)	1 (0)
XIX (1994–96)	0 (0)	0 (0)	0 (0)	0 (0)
XX (1996–99)	0 (0)	0 (0)	0 (0)	0 (0)
XXI (1999–2002)	0 (0)	0 (0)	0 (0)	0 (0)
Total	149	102	31	15
Social policy	38	34	2	2

Note: Vetoes of the Federal Council and reactions of the National Council (vetoes against social policy bills bracketed).
Source: Parlamentsdirektion; Günther Hummer, 'Der Bundesrat und die Gesetzgebung', in Herbert Schambeck, ed., *Bundesstaat und Bundesrat in Österreich* (Vienna: Verlag Österreich, 1997), pp. 367–98.

policy legislation by virtue of a two-thirds majority. The Länder were unable to oppose the enlargement of federal powers. One indicator of the weak influence of the Länder on the federal policy-making process is the number of vetoes the Federal Council submitted against legislative decisions made by the National Council (see table 5.1).

Of the 149 vetoes submitted in the period 1920–2002, thirty-eight were aimed at social policy laws, the vast majority of which were against social policy bills launched by the National Council under Social Democratic leadership in the period 1971–86. Thirty-four social policy-related vetoes were overruled by an insisting vote of the National Council. In two cases, the law was changed and in another two the National Council failed to react (health insurance for entrepreneurs; introduction of child care leave for fathers). In the case of the veto against health insurance for entrepreneurs, the Federal Council criticized a lack of consultation with those affected.[79] Child care leave for fathers initially failed because the SPÖ–FPÖ coalition broke down shortly after the Federal Council veto. It was then enacted in 1989 as part of parental leave.[80]

As regards the numerous shifts in jurisdiction, Felix Ermacora[81] claims that, since 1945, the Federal Council had not fought any of the numerous infringements of Länder rights, and was thus 'a useless instrument for representing Länder interests'. Irmgard Kathrein offers a similarly scathing judgement on the First Republic.[82] However, the weak position of the Federal Council is a necessary, but not a sufficient condition for the chamber's lack of influence on the 'old politics' of the welfare state. Germany provides the relevant counter-factual (see chapter 6 below). Party politics is the relevant sufficient condition. The drive to centralization and towards a unitary structure of provision was largely a result of partisan competition between two major pro-welfare state parties. Despite isolated but at times serious conflict during periods of single party government, expansion took place on a compromise basis because it was largely based on policies that were drawn up in social partnership between the state and the interest organizations of labour and capital – a partnership that had its heyday in the 1960s and 1970s. Measures to make the welfare state more encompassing were an essential source of credit-claiming in the context of a *de facto* two-party system. Social policy initiated by the Grand Coalition largely proceeded through log-rolling and package deals. New benefits for blue-collar workers (a core Social Democratic clientele) were buffered by increased benefits for ÖVP constituencies of support, such as farmers or civil servants. Important economic and social reforms were informally initiated by the social partners and subsequently sanctioned by parliament. In particular, in the area of

---

[79] Günther Hummer, 'Der Bundesrat und die Gesetzgebung', in Herbert Schambeck, ed., *Bundesstaat und Bundesrat in Österreich* (Vienna: Verlag Österreich, 1997), pp. 367–98, p. 383.
[80] Ingrid Mairhuber, *'Die Regulierung des Geschlechterverhältnisses durch sozialstaatliche Maßnahmen in Österreich'*, Ph.D. dissertation, University of Vienna, 1998, pp. 154–55.
[81] Ermacora, *Österreichischer Föderalismus*, p. 85.
[82] Kathrein, *Bundesrat in der Ersten Republik*, p. 57.

labour law, parliament acted as an extended and willing arm of the social partners.[83]

In addition to the impetus towards a strong welfare state resulting from partisan politics, the Länder also had a vital interest in welfare state expansion. The welfare state reduces regional disparities and stabilizes demand in regions affected by high unemployment and structural economic problems. Since the bulk of social security is financed from contributions and federal tax revenues, the Länder have opportunities for free-riding. The most recent major expansion of the welfare state, the introduction of a long-term care allowance (*Bundespflegegeld*) in 1993, is a case in point. This initiative was largely due to the activities of the Länder, which – in a manner similar to that of the municipalities in Germany – hoped that a federal law would relieve them of the financial burden of welfare and social services.[84] This clearly illustrates that the Länder can become petitioners of the federal state under circumstances of fiscal stress. Under a state agreement made according to section 15a of the Federal Constitutional Law, the Länder did however agree to the establishment of an all-encompassing minimum provision of social welfare services and to subsidiary care allowances based on the same objectives and principles as the federal legislation for people not classified as being in need of care under federal law.

Given the expansion of social security schemes regulated by the federal state, only a few social policy programmes are regulated by the Länder, social assistance being the most important. Means-tested social assistance is a safety net of last resort and provides a minimum income to needy people to secure the conditions of a decent life. Because a federal skeleton law on social assistance was lacking when the Federal Constitutional Law was re-enacted in 1945, the Länder have enacted those welfare provisions of the First Republic as modified under German rule (i.e. the provision of assistance is now a responsibility of the place of residence rather than the place of birth). Attempts by the federal government in 1951, 1958 and 1967 to exploit its powers to create a skeleton law on social assistance were successfully opposed by the Länder. In 1968 the federal government formally abstained from framework legislation, thus giving the Länder more opportunities to regulate social assistance.[85] The great variation in benefit levels among the Länder can be explained as an outcome of 'federalist-motivated strong

---

[83] Emmerich Tálos and Bernhard Kittel, *Gesetzgebung in Österreich. Netzwerke, Akteure und Interaktionen in politischen Entscheidungsprozessen* (Vienna: Wiener Universitätsverlag, 2001).
[84] Tálos and Wörister, *Soziale Sicherung im Sozialstaat Österreich*, p. 237.
[85] Walter Pfeil, *Österreichisches Sozialhilferecht* (Vienna: ÖGB-Verlag, 1989), p. 37.

headedness'.[86] In effect, provincial jurisdiction in the area of social assistance empowers the Länder to manipulate the reservation wage. Benefit levels are flat rate and amount to 45–60 per cent of the lowest net earnings of a full-time worker.[87]

Apart from social assistance and the Land care allowance, two additional social policy responsibilities for the Länder are youth welfare and disability benefits. Disability benefit is partly regulated by separate laws of the individual Länder and partly by social assistance laws. As regards youth welfare, the power to enact skeleton legislation has been a federal responsibility since 1920. A federal law passed in 1989 and amended in 1998 outlines minimum standards in infant, maternity and youth welfare that are accompanied by appropriate Länder laws. Social policy-related powers of the Länder also encompass the nursery school and day care systems.

The expansion of the welfare state from 1945 onwards – with only a few exceptions such as the care allowance, family allowances and income support for victims of war and fascism – took the form of an extension of the social insurance state as it was initially established in the late nineteenth century. Social assistance, by contrast, has played a marginal role. Spending on social assistance amounted to 5 per cent of total social expenditure in the late 1990s. Social security transfers clearly outweigh the expenditure devoted to social services. Moreover, social security spending is largely concentrated on a few programmes. In 1998 almost 50 per cent of the social budget, equivalent to 28.5 per cent of GDP, was devoted to old age pensions and survivors' benefits, whereas the share of health expenditure was only 25.8 per cent.

A high degree of path dependency is also evident in the occupationally fragmented organization of social insurance (twenty-eight social insurance carriers) and a financing system that is still largely based on employer and employee contributions. However, the state portion of funding for social policy has substantially increased over time,[88] so that today the state funds around one-third of total social expenditure. The state portion increased, in particular, following the introduction of benefits that were non-insurance related (e.g. minimum pensions) and the expansion of social insurance to include the self-employed and farmers. The state's growing financial involvement has, increasingly, produced an

---

[86] Kurt Pratscher, 'Sozialhilfepolitik der österreichischen Bundesländer', Österreichische Zeitschrift für Politikwissenschaft, vol. 26 (1997), no. 1, pp. 41–55, p. 51.
[87] Tony Eardley, Jonathan Bradshaw, John Ditch, Ian Gough and Peter Whiteford, Social Assistance in OECD Countries, vol. II, Country Reports (London: HMSO [Department of Social Security Research report no. 46–47], 1996), p. 47.
[88] Alber, Vom Armenhaus, p. 65.

intertwining of federal, Land and municipal budgets and social insurance. Today, a fifth of public expenditure and almost a half of total tax revenue is shunted back and forth in the form of inter-governmental grants between the different levels of government and the agencies of social insurance. The Länder act as a sort of hub in all of this. They derive about half their total revenue from transfer payments and the social insurance system draws more than a quarter of its total revenue of 36.1 billion euro from inter-governmental transfer payments. Examples of these complex financial interlocking arrangements include the federal contribution to old age pensions and accident insurance for farmers, federal and municipal contributions to unemployment benefit and the *Familienlastenausgleichsfond* (Compensation Fund of Family Expenses), which is partly funded by employers' contributions and partly by payments from the federal government and the Länder.

Considerable financial interdependence also exists between different tiers of government and the social insurance system in respect of hospital funding, where the federal government only has powers of skeleton legislation. There is also substantial financial interdependence between the Länder and the municipalities in respect of social assistance and disability benefits, the Land care allowance and funding for hospitals and nursery schools. This involves the municipalities funding a fixed portion of expenditure, although the standard of benefits and services is left to the discretion of the respective Länder.[89] Finally, the so-called *Landesumlage* – payments by the municipalities to the Länder – contribute to horizontal financial interdependence.

The interlocking of finances and the centralization of taxation powers have significantly changed the incentive structures for the spending behaviour of subordinate governments. Today, the Länder derive a large portion of their revenues from federal taxes, so that they are spending revenues collected by a different tier of government. They therefore face an incentive to 'overfish' common pool resources. This may lead to inefficient investment, duplication of effort and the generation of excess capacity. In terms of social policy, the cost explosion in the hospital sector deserves particular mention.[90] Even more important, the Länder benefit from federal social policy because the welfare state serves to remove regional economic disparities and stabilizes demand in regions suffering

---

[89] Gerald Lehner, 'Finanzwirtschaftliche Verflechtungen zwischen Ländern und Gemeinden im Überblick', in Helfried Bauer, Robert Hink, Bertram Hüttner and Österreichischer Gemeindebund as well as Österreichischer Städtebund, eds., *Finanzausgleich 2001. Das Handbuch für die Praxis* (Vienna: KDZ Managementberatungs- und Weiterbildungs GmbH, 2001), pp. 201–17, p. 212.

[90] Tálos and Wörister, *Soziale Sicherung im Sozialstaat Österreich*, pp. 249–50.

from severe unemployment. In addition, the expansion of social insurance has reduced their expenditure on social assistance. Since the bulk of social spending is covered by social security contributions and the federal budget, the Länder have no genuine interest in undermining the federal social policy effort. Moreover, para-fiscalism provides an exit option that is available for avoiding policy stalemate in inter-governmental fiscal relations, because, by raising social security contributions, the costs of social security can be offloaded to third parties not involved in the multi-level bargaining game.

The Austrian fiscal constitution not only creates incentives favouring a strong welfare state, but also serves to limit the possibility of social dumping. The fiscal equalization scheme helps to level out differences in spending power between regional entities and thus reduces horizontal competition and the danger of a race to the bottom in benefit provision. Two additional factors have a similar effect. On the one hand, strong restrictions on taxation powers set narrow boundaries for horizontal tax competition between the Länder, which could bridle increases in state expenditure. On the other hand, given their limited social policy competencies, the Länder are unable to offer alternative social policy packages that could spark significant labour or capital mobility and, hence, a race to the bottom.

Federalism and the 'new politics' of the welfare state

A slow-down in the growth trajectory of the Austrian welfare state occurred later than in many other countries. This was the consequence of the efficacy of macro-economic management in the crisis of the 1970s, based on strong co-operation between government and the 'social partners' around a set of policies labelled as Austro-Keynesianism (anti-cyclical fiscal policy, co-ordinated wages policy, establishing a peg to the Deutschmark and labour hoarding in state-run industry and the public sector).[91] Both unemployment figures and inflation rates stabilized at relatively low levels. Deficit spending had its price, however. Between 1970 and 1985 the national debt increased from 20.4 per cent to almost 50 per cent of GDP.[92] High real interest rates in the 1980s and a decline in economic growth increasingly curtailed the federal government's fiscal leeway and increased pressures to stabilize state finances. Changing

---

[91] Fritz W. Scharpf, *Sozialdemokratische Krisenpolitik in Europa* (Frankfurt-on-Main: Campus, 1987).
[92] Eduard Fleischmann, 'Öffentliche Haushalte in Österreich im Überblick', in Gerhard Steger, ed., *Öffentliche Haushalte in Österreich* (Vienna: Verlag Österreich, 2002), pp. 7–26, p. 9.

demographics and labour shedding via early retirement programmes worked in the same direction, given the prominent role of the state in funding old age pensions. Soaring public debt, the liberalization of capital markets in the 1980s and early 1990s, as well as accession to the European Union in 1995, brought Austro-Keynesianism policies to an end. Moreover, the state-run industry disaster of the 1980s not only caused the crumbling of yet another pillar of traditional employment policy, but also led to an enormous demand for state funding and redundancy payments for thousands of workers.

The Social Democrats ended their coalition with the Freedom Party (FPÖ) in 1986, when right-wing populist Jörg Haider took over as chairman of the FPÖ. In the same year a new Grand Coalition was formed that saw itself as a 'restructuring partnership' for taking the country into the European Union. The governing parties – SPÖ and ÖVP – underwent a programmatic change of course at around this time. The pragmatic modernizers led by Chancellor Vranitzky got the upper hand in the Social Democratic camp, while the People's Party increasingly advocated neo-liberal ideas. With the advent of the new coalition government, the stabilization of the welfare state was put firmly on the policy agenda, while at the same time the rise of Jörg Haider began in earnest, his party achieving 9.7 per cent of the vote in that year.

The argument advanced here is that recent social policy development in Austria can be explained by an interaction between 'new politics' and 'old politics' in which the latter retains the upper hand. Some of the determining factors for the expansion of the welfare state outlined in the previous section – a permissive constitution and the dominant role of political parties – go a long way in explaining recent social policy developments. As a consequence, welfare state retrenchment was quite moderate during the period of the SPÖ–ÖVP coalition governments, from 1986 to 2000, with more substantial benefit cuts imposed by the centre-right government that took office in 2000. However, the collapse of the ÖVP–FPÖ coalition in September 2002 also lends support to a core hypothesis of the 'new politics' account,[93] which posits that welfare state retrenchment involves a substantial risk of electoral punishment for incumbent parties. Federalism has played only a subordinate role in these developments, while recent welfare state developments have not really changed the face of federalism. Nevertheless, I shall also argue that there are respects in which federalism does constitute a ratchet mechanism operating to limit radical welfare state retrenchment.

---

[93] Paul Pierson, ed., *The New Politics of the Welfare State* (Oxford: Oxford University Press, 2001).

Judged by aggregate spending data, there is no evidence of any substantial process of welfare state retrenchment in Austria in recent decades. On the contrary, total social expenditure as a percentage of GDP increased from 26.3 in 1980 to 29.2 per cent in 1995 and then declined only marginally to 28.5 per cent by 1998.[94] To conclude that the welfare state was largely unaffected by governmental austerity policies, however, is misleading because benefit cuts may take effect in the long run, especially in the realm of old age pensions. Indeed, a rather different picture emerges when we examine programme-related reforms in the core areas of social insurance.

Social policy development since 1986 can be separated into three phases. This distinction helps us to avoid undifferentiated judgements positing a neo-liberal turn-around in economic and social policy since the 1980s.[95] In the first period between 1986 and 1994, the politics of compensation was on the agenda and expansion measures outweighed benefit cuts. Examples include the establishment of a long-term care allowance in 1993 and the extension of parental leave from one to two years in 1991. The pension reform launched in 1993 was more balanced. Benefits were indexed to net wages, the basis for calculating pensions was changed from ten highest earning years to fifteen, and a credit equivalent to four years of work was allowed for child-raising. The intended budget stabilization totally backfired in this phase: national debt went up from 49.8 (1985) to 69.2 per cent of GDP in 1995.

The second phase (1995–99) is connected with accession to the EU and the associated imperative of budget consolidation in the shadow of the Maastricht Treaty. As the largest component of the federal budget, the welfare state increasingly became the object of cost containment. In this second phase, benefit cuts clearly outweighed enhancement of benefits. Two so-called austerity packages (officially labelled as Structural Adaptation Acts, *Strukturanpassungsgesetze*) launched in 1995 and 1996 led to substantial cutbacks in social policy and public sector spending. The *Strukturanpassungsgesetze* were umbrella laws by which a total of 138 federal laws were amended. Some of the measures were enacted through constitutional provisions (*Verfassungsbestimmungen*) and thus removed from Constitutional Court review. Co-payments have been

---

[94] Bundesministerium für soziale Sicherheit und Generationen, *Bericht über die soziale Lage* (Vienna: Bundesministerium für soziale Sicherheit und Generationen, 2001), p. 40.
[95] Brigitte Unger, 'Österreichs Beschäftigungs- und Sozialpolitik von 1970 bis 2000', *Zeitschrift für Sozialreform*, vol. 47 (2001), no. 4, pp. 340–61. For a more balanced and comprehensive analysis, see Emmerich Tálos and Karl Wörister, 'Soziale Sicherung in Österreich', in Emmerich Tálos, ed., *Soziale Sicherung im Wandel* (Vienna: Böhlau, 1998), pp. 209–88.

introduced for schoolbooks and school transport and parental leave was reduced from 24 to 18 months in 1996. Cash transfers for such provisions as birth allowances and death benefits covering funeral expenses were abolished. Higher pension contributions for farmers, civil servants and the self-employed were imposed. The 1997 pension reform aimed to curtail early retirement and increase the effective retirement age, while eligibility to invalidity pensions was tightened. The ceiling for contributory payment was lifted and the calculation of pensions for civil servants was to some extent harmonized with that based on the General Social Insurance Act. Reform of unemployment insurance was characterized by modest cuts in the replacement rate for high income groups, reduced family supplements and stronger sanctions in cases of unwillingness to work. Special support for the older long-term unemployed (*Sonderunterstützung*) was abolished. Hospital funding was also overhauled in 1997, with hospital funding reorganized by a treaty between the federal government and the Länder, and health insurance now required a new quarterly co-payment of 3.60 euro for doctors' visits.

Despite selective enhancement in benefits and harmonization with more stringent EU occupational health and safety standards, these reforms, together with privatization revenues, resulted in a reduction in public debt. Major strikes were avoided since many of the expenditure measures were, albeit reluctantly, backed by the social partners. Nevertheless, tensions between the social partners increased and spilled over to the coalition. In 1995 the coalition split during negotiations on the federal budget as a result of severe partisan conflict over the austerity measures. The Grand Coalition was immediately restored after the general election in December, in which the Social Democrats gained seats, but the coalition partners became increasingly obstructive – something the general public increasingly viewed as producing a 'reform jam' (*Reformstau*). The elections of 1999 brought painful losses for the major parties, while Jörg Haider's FPÖ gained almost 27 per cent of the vote. In the spring of 2000 a coalition of ÖVP and FPÖ took office, while the Social Democrats went into opposition for the first time in thirty years.

The third phase, which began with the change of government in 2000, was initially identified by what was a unique attempt in the history of the Second Republic to effect radical cuts and restructuring of the welfare state. Given Austria's permissive constitution, the centre-right government, formed by two parties with rather similar preferences in social and economic policy,[96] was largely unhindered in pursuing and achieving its

---

[96] Wolfgang C. Müller and Marcelo Jenny, 'Abgeordnete, Parteien und Koalitionspolitik: Individuelle Präferenzen und politisches Handeln im Nationalrat', *Österreichische Zeitschrift für Politikwissenschaft*, vol. 29 (2000), no. 2, pp. 137–56, pp. 144–46.

neo-liberal political objectives. However, the new course of policy turned out to be costly in the longer run: 'Speed kills', the *Leitmotiv* for rapid policy change coined by ÖVP party whip Andreas Khol, ironically contributed to the collapse of the coalition itself.

The ÖVP–FPÖ coalition stepped into the arena with an ambitious government agenda of bourgeois focus and aiming at a paradigm switch in social and economic policy in order to 'halt a misunderstood Keynesianism, presented as Austro-Keynesianism, that had served as a smokescreen for soaring national debt and to free the nation of debt altogether'. The government agenda in social and economic policy comprised (welfare) state retrenchment down to 'core functions',[97] a downsizing of public administration, securing jobs and investment by reducing non-wage labour costs, deregulation and 'flexibilization', a largely expenditure-based restructuring of state finances (based on a balanced budget), more stringent eligibility conditions and combating abuse of welfare benefits.

This agenda was aggressively sold to the public and there was no attempt to hide benefit reductions nor effort to avoid confrontation with employee organizations. The planned restructuring and retrenchment of the welfare state and the reshaping of state finances were soon put into action. Pension reform is the most prominent example. In an effort to bring the actual age of retirement (which was on average 57.6 years in 1999) closer to the threshold of 65 years stipulated by law, early retirement pensions based on invalidity were abolished and eligibility for early retirement was tightened by imposing benefit deductions. The minimum floor for widow's/widower's pensions was abolished, while a ceiling was established where a person was entitled to receive both an individual and a widow's/widower's pension. Pension contributions for public sector employees and pensioners have been raised. A reform of the system of severance payments in 2002 has encouraged private and occupational retirement plans to play a greater role in the provision of pensions, which will, ultimately, lead to a fully-fledged two-tier pension system. Employers are now obliged to deduct 1.53 per cent of an employee's monthly salary and to transfer this money to an individual account. The accumulated capital may be used in different ways, but converting capital into pension investment funds or occupational pension funds is the most attractive option, since no taxes are levied. This reform was negotiated by the social partners and is one of the few examples of a continuation of corporatist policy-making. Not surprisingly, parliament approved with unanimity.

[97] On the government agenda see *Zukunft im Herzen Europas – Österreich neu regieren. Das Regierungsprogramm 2000* (Vienna: Bundeskanzleramt, Bundespressedienst, 2000).

Retrenchment soon spilled over to other social insurance branches. Unemployment benefits were cut: family supplements for the unemployed were reduced by around one-third (with the partner's income no longer taken into account). This was paralleled by a general reduction of the net replacement rate. Eligibility to unemployment assistance (*Notstandshilfe*) was made more stringent by measures involving workfare elements. Free health co-insurance for childless couples was abolished (with the exceptions of recipients of care allowance and carers of disabled relatives). User charges for hospital treatment and prescription charges were raised, and a new user charge for out-patient treatments in hospitals (*Ambulanzgebühr*) was established. Care allowances were not indexed for inflation for several years, and accident insurance pensions have been made subject to taxation. The latter measure has led to benefit reductions of up to 30 per cent. Privatization also occurred in education, with the introduction of higher education tuition fees, a move strongly opposed by the left.

There were, however, a few areas in which benefits were increased. These involved an equalization of sickness cash benefits between blue-collar and white-collar workers, a slight increase of family allowances and the introduction of a child care benefit for a period of three years as a universal payment rather than the existing insurance-based parental leave. Social Democrats and the Green Party opposed the universal child benefit, because, it was argued, it would discourage female labour market participation.

There were also far-reaching changes in terms of the organization of welfare provision. The ministries of labour and economy were merged and the Federation of Austrian Social Insurance Carriers (*Hauptverband der österreichischen Sozialversicherungsträger*) was restructured to ensure that the FPÖ had an influential role in its administration. The Social Democratic president of the federation was replaced in spectacular circumstances and social insurance institutions were reorganized. However, in October 2003 this reform was annulled by the Constitutional Court, which argued that it has hollowed out the democratically legitimized self-administration of social insurance bodies.

What is truly unique about the above reforms is the way in which the measures were implemented and sometimes almost literally rushed through. The interest organizations of labour were deliberately circumvented and the traditional system of social partnership, with its informal veto position for the trade unions, was deliberately obstructed. In all, a trend that had already become established in the 1990s now appears to be a permanent feature of the policy landscape: the government has become the key actor in policy-making, determining the pace, direction and increasingly the content of reforms, and repeatedly confronting the interest organizations of labour with a series of *faits accomplis*.

The Social Democratic opposition was left with the Constitutional Court as the sole potential instrument with which to confront unpopular political reforms. The SPÖ, supported by its strong National Council mandate, took the pension reform, taxation of accident insurance benefits as well as out-patient charges to the court. Success was mixed. Whereas taxing pensions from accident insurance was declared unconstitutional by a court decision in December 2002, the pension reform passed constitutional review in 2003. Out-patient charges were abolished in 2003 by the government itself.

Welfare state clienteles and the opposition also made use of the popular initiative, which while ineffective as a means of reversing policy nevertheless lends itself to political mobilization against the government and to policy agenda-setting. In April 2002 a popular initiative took place with the aim of anchoring the welfare state as a stated objective of the constitution. This popular initiative, inspired by private groups and subsequently supported by all the opposition parties and the unions, obtained some 717,000 signatures, which was more than enough to require parliamentary consideration. A year earlier, a popular initiative launched to challenge academic tuition fees could only mobilize some 173,000 supporters.

Despite the new style of social politics since 2000, the majority of changes over the last two decades have been about cutting benefits, reducing entitlements and increasing contributions. They have not challenged the structure of provision. Indeed, the contribution–benefit nexus has been strengthened and the pressure for labour market participation has been intensified. There were, however, a few measures indicative of new departures. They included an attempt to level out the profession-specific differences between blue-collar and white-collar workers and to harmonize old age pensions for civil servants with the corresponding provisions of the General Social Insurance Act. The introduction of a tax-financed long-term care allowance for the permanently disabled in 1993 created an additional, structurally unique 'pillar' in the Austrian social security system – an addition to the older pillars of contribution-financed social security, tax financed welfare and tax-financed compensation for war victims and others who are placed at risk in situations that are of relevance to the public interest (*Versorgung*). Finally, the new child care benefit marks a break with the employment-centred design of the welfare state, because its approach is universal and no longer linked to earlier employment.

Federalism has played a marginal role in recent social policy, at least as far as formal influence of the Länder on public policy-making is concerned. Since 1986 each government has had a majority in the Federal Council. In consequence, no use has been made of vetoes in social policy legislation. With the introduction of the care allowance in 1993, the federal government's social policy powers were expanded even further. Co-operative federalism based on informal institutions became even more important. The Länder and the municipalities were sworn to the austerity course during informal negotiations. Evidence of this can be found in the state agreement under section 15a of the Federal Constitutional Law to reduce the cost explosion in the health sector (1997), an agreement between the federal government, the Länder and the municipalities to co-ordinate budgetary policies (the so-called *Stabilitätspakt*, 1999) and the new fiscal equalization scheme agreed in 2001. In this latter case, the Länder have agreed to generate a budget surplus of 0.75 per cent of GDP and to assist the federal government in its austerity course by means of structural reforms. The Länder governments have backed these efforts. Seven out of the nine Länder governments were headed by provincial governors affiliated to the coalition parties.

Nevertheless, there are some limits to radical welfare state retrenchment of a kind suggested by the 'new politics' paradigm. One ratchet effect against radical dismantling of the welfare state arises from the territorial aspects of social policy. Since the welfare state reduces regional socio-economic disparities,[98] the Länder have strong incentives to block radical austerity policies. Substantial retrenchment of social insurance automatically leads to higher spending for needs-based programmes such as social assistance, which are the responsibility of the Länder.

A second important 'ratchet effect' is constituted by partisan competition and the higher frequency of elections in federal states. The 'new politics' paradigm suggests that the popularity of the welfare state and the dependence of large segments of the population on state welfare benefits is the main reason why the political elite, focussed on re-election, rejects drastic benefit reductions and instead operates a policy of obfuscation, compensation and blame avoidance. The centre-right government ignored 'new politics' strategies, openly advocating retrenchment and showing little hesitation about coming into conflict with the trade unions. However, they paid a heavy price for their directness. For federal states such as Austria, where the Länder parliaments are directly elected and where party systems are vertically integrated and congruent, it can be argued that the frequency of elections at the regional level may contribute to a scaling down of retrenchment efforts, since voters express opinions

---

[98] To give an example, the share of pensioners receiving minimum pensions (*Ausgleichszulage*) varies from 8.2 per cent in Vienna to 19.6 in Carinthia.

not only about the Länder government's policy but also about that of the federal government. Hence, electoral outcomes of regional elections regularly favour the opposition at federal level. Indeed, the *Landtag* elections held since the political turnaround in 2000 have signalled how unpopular retrenchment actually is. The FPÖ ended up the loser in the elections in Vienna, Burgenland, Styria, Lower and Upper Austria, Salzburg and Tyrol. This outcome is closely connected to the present configuration of the party system. With the Social Democrats, the biggest pro-welfare state party, in opposition, retrenchment initiatives involved a high electoral risk for the ÖVP–FPÖ coalition, given their constituencies and organizational make-up. The FPÖ came to power on a platform of appealing to the losers of globalization and disgruntled former socialists. In a similar vein, the ÖVP consists of three occupationally organized sub-groups, of which the League of Workers and Employees (ÖAAB) is the most important. In addition, the civil servants' trade union is traditionally closely affiliated with the Christian Democrats. Hence, the party lacks internal cohesion around the issue of reform, which makes welfare state retrenchment difficult to achieve.

At the beginning of its first term the new coalition took the risk of being seen as a whole-hearted adherent of welfare retrenchment, assuming that the stabilization of state finances and the breaking-up of the traditional distributional coalitions (and containing trade union veto power in particular) would be accepted by the voters. Moreover, in accordance with political business cycle theory, tax cuts were to be implemented at the end of the legislative term. In the long run this assumption turned out to be a strategic misinterpretation that led to the breakdown of the coalition. The austerity measures significantly hit the constituents of the governing parties and it was the fear of an electoral backlash in the upcoming 2003 general election that led Jörg Haider to pull the plug on the coalition in early autumn 2002. From his Carinthian bastion, he openly obstructed the austerity course of the federal cabinet, especially the cabinet's decision to postpone tax reform. Having staged an internal putsch at an extraordinary party meeting, three ministers of the Freedom Party quit the federal government, leading to collapse of the ÖVP–FPÖ government and the calling of fresh elections. The general elections on 24 November 2002 led to a resurgence of the two big parties, whereas the Freedom Party experienced electoral defeat on a scale never hitherto experienced in Austrian politics.

Despite that, the ÖVP–FPÖ coalition was restored. As in its first term of office, the coalition drafted a restrictive pension reform immediately after it came to power. This draft was unprecedented in terms of the intensity of the benefit cuts suggested. The government proposed to calculate pensions on the basis of an employee's full employment record, instead of the fifteen years of highest earnings as under the previous system. This proposal was equivalent to a benefit cut of up to 30 per cent. In addition, the government increased its efforts to restrict early retirement by cancelling early retirement pensions for employees with long contribution records and for the long-term unemployed.

This draft was strongly opposed by the Social Democrats and even the governing coalition was divided on the issue. Pension reform 2003 was not only criticized by the FPÖ governor of Carinthia, Jörg Haider, but also by the ÖVP governors of Salzburg and Lower Austria and the party's employee faction (ÖAAB).[99] Given the widespread opposition to the pension reform, Federal President Klestil initiated round-table talks between the federal government, the opposition, social partners and Länder representatives. No agreement was reached and the government went ahead with its legislation. However, compared with the first draft launched by the government, the reform was watered down. The Freedom Party (especially MPs from Carinthia), bearing the stigma of several electoral defeats at Länder level, successfully demanded special regulations for workers in heavy industry. Moreover, a special fund was established to cushion cases of hardship and maximum losses connected with the new mode of benefit calculation were not to exceed 10 per cent for people older than 35 years. This compromise was bundled as an umbrella law (*Budgetbegleitgesetz*) that amended in total ninety-one federal laws. This strategy of pooling many reforms into a single bill of 700 pages proved to be advantageous for the government. Political debate focussed on pension reform and distracted attention from other retrenchment measures contained in the umbrella law, such as the introduction of new co-payments in health insurance.

Resistance against the bill shifted to the streets when trade unions organized the biggest strike since 1945 in June 2003. Though strikes have been a virtually unknown phenomenon in post-war Austria, the government was not impressed and used its parliamentary majority to pass the *Budgetbegleitgesetz* on 11 June. Subsequent occurrences impressively demonstrate the weakness of the opposition's veto powers. In the National Council, Social Democrats demanded an optional referendum

---

[99] Developments in Salzburg and Carinthia early in 2004 nicely demonstrate how the proliferation of elections in federal states may contribute to moderate welfare state retrenchment. The governors of Salzburg and Carinthia, both facing elections in March 2004, announced that they would compensate low income pensioners for losses resulting from increased health insurance contributions for pensioners, imposed on them by federal pension reform in 2003, with Länder funds. This discussion spilled over into the federal arena and ended up with a federal bill making up pension losses to approximately 500,000 pensioners.

on pensions reform, but were overruled by the coalition's majority. In the Upper House, Social Democratic federal councillors proposed a veto on the bill, but the governmental parties rejected this initiative.[100] The Federal President's signature is the final step in law-making. Thomas Klestil had serious doubts as to whether the voluminous umbrella law was constitutional. However, after consulting a former President of the Constitutional Court, he finally signed the bill, which became law on 1 January 2004.[101]

Conclusion

Over the past 130 years Austria has experienced public sector growth on a vast scale, as have all countries of the West. Government spending as a percentage of GDP has risen from 12 per cent prior to the First World War to 57.2 per cent in 1995.[102] A significant factor in this development was the triumph of the welfare state. This chapter has focussed on the question of whether and to what extent the establishment of the federal state structure in 1920 influenced the developmental dynamics of social policy. The key findings indicate that there is little evidence that federalism exercised any marked restraining effect. OECD comparisons show that Austria was an expenditure leader until well into the 1970s, and even by the late 1990s public social expenditure as a percentage of GDP was above the OECD and EU15 averages. The limiting effects of federalism can only be seen in the delayed integration of farm and forestry workers into social insurance before World War Two, and in the federal government's timid post-war attempts to intervene in the areas of social assistance[103] and welfare support for the disabled.

Why did federalism not contain the reach of the welfare state, as one might expect from the findings of econometric research? There are many answers, with three factors deserving particular emphasis.

The first and unquestionably the most important factor is the politically motivated early policy pre-emption by the central state. Thus, the

---

[100] However, the FPÖ fraction in the Federal Council also rejected an initiative of the ÖVP, which proposed not to veto the bill. This schizophrenic behaviour had no consequences except that the bill was delayed for eight weeks as it is stipulated in the Constitution.
[101] All that was left for the Social Democrats to do was to oppose the bill through political mobilization and the Constitutional Court. Consequently, the party launched a people's initiative against pension reform and demanded judicial review of the *Budgetbegleitgesetz* 2003 in March 2004.
[102] Fleischmann, 'Öffentliche Haushalte', pp. 8–9.
[103] In early 2004, however, the federal government and the Länder agreed to formulate a state treaty establishing nation-wide minimum standards for Social Assistance. If this state treaty becomes a reality, this would remove the last salient federalist trait of the Austrian welfare state.

dispute over which tier of government should take action on social policy was decided at an early stage, against any serious decentralization of powers. The democratic federal state, established only in 1920, inherited a welfare state that had already been established on effectively unitary lines by the monarchy and the successor German-Austrian Republic (1918–19). Social insurance established under the monarchy was funded exclusively through contributions. Hence, the early emergence of parafiscalism created opportunities to externalize welfare state costs on to the shoulders of employers and employees.

Second, along with social policy legislation under the autocratic monarchy, National Socialist totalitarian rule further strengthened the social policy powers of the central state. The world wars created not only a considerable need for social policy intervention, but also necessitated large-scale economic restructuring, in turn requiring a state that was both fiscally strong and with the power to act. Significant centralizing thrusts thus took place under autocratic conditions or in reaction to the resulting imperatives of these developments. Social policy legislation enacted during authoritarian phases of government, and social policy programmes that have emerged from critical junctures were, apart from racist Nazi German provisions, not replaced when the country became a democratic federation in 1920 and in 1945 resumed that status. Hence, we can observe substantial displacement effects associated with regime breakdowns and the critical junctures which were the not infrequent fate of Austrian social, political and economic development in the first half of the twentieth century.

Finally, the lack of formal opportunities for the Länder to exercise vetoes and to influence the federal decision-making process and the duopoly of pro-welfare state parties account for the largely unhindered expansion of the welfare state. The SPÖ and the ÖVP, both inclined to statist policy options, were able, where they were in agreement, to ignore the will of the Länder, to change the constitution at will and – thanks to their two-thirds majority – at the same time, to neutralize the Constitutional Court's veto power. In other words, the veto points which theory suggests are likely to be the basis of federalism's impeding effect are more or less absent in the Austrian case.

It has also been demonstrated that federalism presents itself as a political laboratory for experimentation with new ideas and alternative solutions. An important institutional requirement for such decentralized social policy experiments obviously assumes a certain amount of tax autonomy on the part of the federal Länder. Thus, the socialist experiment of Red Vienna, which was largely made possible by Länder powers to create new taxes in the First Republic, was historically unique.

The feedback effects of the welfare state on the structure and dynamics of federalism are of great importance. The evolutionary processes in and the expansion of the welfare state fostered developments towards centralization and unitary federalism. In addition, the take-off of the welfare state led to the interlocking of public budgets at different levels of government. While social insurance budgets and the state budget were separate under the monarchy, the expansion of the welfare state in the republic led to a massive expansion of inter-governmental grants. This required new and more informal forms of governance and co-operation beyond the formal constitution that compensated the Länder for their weak formal influence on federal policy-making.

Efforts aimed at welfare state retrenchment occurred later than in other OECD countries. Initially, substantial social policy changes did not occur because the Grand Coalition could not agree on joint courses of action. Policy reforms in this period entailed a mix of benefit enhancement and retrenchment. The Maastricht Treaty increased the pressure to rein in budgets and led to progressively larger benefit cuts in the 1990s. Since the restrictive social policy prevailing since 2000 can to a large extent be explained by partisan control within the context of a permissive constitution, middle-range theories of the 'old politics' of the welfare state contribute more to the explanation of recent social policy developments in Austria than do the mechanisms of the 'new politics'.

Nevertheless, there is some evidence to support the 'new politics' approach. Increasing the speed of policy-making ('speed kills'), packing reforms into umbrella laws to obfuscate opponents by making policy reform more complex, and the fact that major restrictive measures were implemented immediately after general elections are all cases in point. Moreover, federalism and partisan competition had a sort of indirect backlash in the long run. Partisan competition and the high frequency of elections in a federal state, not to mention a territorial distribution of power in which the constituent units themselves benefit markedly from federal social policy, are all mechanisms that limit the short-term capacity of reforming politicians to do more than tinker at the edges of more than a century of Austrian welfare state expansion.

6 Germany
Co-operative federalism and the overgrazing of the fiscal commons

PHILIP MANOW*

Introduction

Conventional wisdom strongly suggests that federalism is inimical to high levels of social spending. Two arguments are prominent in this context: a veto point thesis and a 'competition of jurisdictions' thesis. The veto point thesis is quite straightforward: federal systems have more veto points than unitary systems *ceteris paribus*.[1] This increases the probability that groups opposed to welfare state expansion can exert some influence in the legislative process. Veto points would then give these groups the opportunity to block or substantially water down redistributive legislation.[2] 'Competition of jurisdiction' arguments hold that welfare redistribution is limited in federal systems because those who would pay more than they would gain in a given jurisdiction (high income earners, 'capital') can credibly threaten to exit highly redistributive jurisdictions and join those that are

---

* I am grateful to the editors, in particular to Francis G. Castles and Stephan Leibfried, to Christine Trampusch, Gerhard Lehmbruch and Steffen Ganghof for critical comments. Editorial assistance by Annika Schulte is gratefully acknowledged.
[1] George Tsebelis and Jeanette Money, *Bicameralism* (Cambridge: Cambridge University Press, 1997); George Tsebelis, 'Decision Making in Political Systems: Veto Players in Presidentialism, Parliamentarism, Multicameralism and Multipartyism', *British Journal of Political Science*, vol. 25 (1995), no. 3, pp. 289–326.
[2] Evelyne Huber, Charles Ragin and John D. Stephens, 'Social Democracy, Constitutional Structure and the Welfare State', *American Journal of Sociology*, vol. 99 (1993), no. 3, pp. 711–49; Theda Skocpol and Edwin Amenta, 'States and Social Policies', *Annual Review of Sociology*, vol. 12 (1986), no. 1, pp. 131–57; Fiona Ross, 'Cutting Public Expenditures in Advanced Industrial Democracies: The Importance of Avoiding Blame', *Governance*, vol. 10 (1997), no. 2, pp. 175–200.

less *égaliste*.³ At the same time, those who gain more than they would pay (e.g. low income earners) are attracted to regions with higher levels of redistribution and these would therefore develop into 'welfare magnets'.⁴ Thus, a redistributional policy stance is self-defeating in a federal context.

Indeed, many econometric studies of the determinants of welfare state spending have found that federalism exerts a statistically significant, stable and negative influence on social spending.⁵ Prominent country cases are Switzerland and the United States, both strongly federalist countries and historically, prominent welfare 'laggards' (although since 1980 Switzerland has moved rapidly from laggard to leadership status). Other cases providing support for these arguments would be Australia and Canada, again federal countries that, for much of the post-war period, have had well below average levels of social spending. Germany, however, is a federal polity, which combines big government with generous social expenditure. This 'anomaly' may motivate us to take a closer look at the postulated inverse relationship between federalism and welfare state development. Is Germany the exception that proves the rule, or does the German case provide unsettling counter-evidence to the federalism thesis? In this chapter I argue that the German case alerts us to the fact that the dampening impact of federalism on welfare state spending is likely to hold only under special circumstances. Two considerations seem to be of particular relevance in this respect.⁶

First, the federalism hypothesis critically depends on the sort of federalism that prevails in a given country: is it one that establishes separate jurisdictions between the central and the regional level (interstate federalism, *Trennföderalismus*), or is it one of interlocked or joint

---

³ Geoffrey Brennan and James Buchanan, *Besteuerung und Staatsgewalt* (Hamburg: Steuer- und Wirtschaftsverlag, 1988); Barry Weingast, 'Constitutions as Governance Structures: The Political Foundations of Secure Markets', *Journal for Institutional and Theoretical Economics*, vol. 149 (1993), no. 1, pp. 286–311; Barry Weingast, 'The Economic Role of Political Institutions: Market-Preserving Federalism and Economic Development', *Journal of Law, Economics and Organization*, vol. 11 (1995), no. 1, pp. 1–31; Robert P. Inman and Daniel L. Rubinfeld, 'The Political Economy of Federalism', in Daniel Mueller, ed., *Perspectives of Public Choice* (Cambridge: Cambridge University Press, 1997), pp. 73–105.
⁴ Paul Peterson and Mark C. Rom, *Welfare Magnets. A New Case for a National Standard* (Washington, DC: Brookings Institution Press, 1990).
⁵ See chapter 1 for references.
⁶ A third qualification to the 'federalism as an impediment to welfare state growth' thesis is worth mentioning, but is not exemplified by the German case (see Giuliano Bonoli, *The Politics of Pension Reform. Institutions and Policy Change in Western Europe* (Cambridge: Cambridge University Press, 2000) and chapters 7 and 2 of this volume). Federalism only appears to have the postulated blocking effect in times of welfare state expansion (the 'old politics of the welfare state'), but not in periods of retrenchment (the 'new politics of the welfare state'). See also chapter 1 of this volume.

jurisdictions (intra-state federalism, *Verbundföderalismus*, of co-operative rather than competitive federalism)? Where federal institutions establish joint jurisdiction over social policy, federalism does not necessarily have a constraining impact on welfare state growth. 'Race to the bottom' dynamics or 'beggar your neighbour' politics, greater political accountability and limited opportunities for blame avoidance – the mechanisms said to constrain welfare state growth in federal polities – all seem to have much less bite in the case of intra-state federalism. Intra-state systems do not establish clearly separated spheres of fiscal responsibility, legislative competency and political accountability between different layers of government, but rather mesh them between the regional and national units. In this case, the conventional 'competition of jurisdictions' arguments do not apply.[7] On the contrary: Because legislative and fiscal responsibilities do not fully overlap, although neither are they clearly separate, the incongruence between 'having a say' and 'having to pay' provides incentives for shifting costs and responsibilities between the different levels of government and between the different budgets of the central state, of the regional states and of the welfare state. This mismatch results in a lack of political transparency. It may, for instance, provide incentives to claim political credit for new spending programmes, while at the same time avoiding the blame for corresponding increases in taxation or public debt. This puts a premium on 'fiscal irresponsibility', which may become manifest in the form of *higher* than average expenditure growth dynamics or the 'political overgrazing of the fiscal commons'.[8] Alternatively, intra-state federalism may make legislating new (joint) taxes extremely difficult, so that a demand for increased state spending is met through the mechanism of para-fiscalism or contribution-based welfare financing – German unification would be a good case in point (see below). In both instances, expenditure *increases* resulting from the common pool resource dilemma inherent in co-operative federalism run directly counter to the veto point hypothesis.

Second, the veto point argument crucially depends on the assumption of significant differences in policy preferences between the different veto players/parties. Yet, this cannot be taken for granted, as again the German case exemplifies. The 'policy distance' between Christian

---

[7] Weingast, 'Constitutions as Governance' and 'Economic Role of Political Institutions'; also Brennan and Buchanan, *Besteuerung und Staatsgewalt*.

[8] Cf. Erik Wibbels, 'Federalism and the Politics of Macroeconomic Policy and Performance', *American Journal of Political Science*, vol. 44 (2000), no. 4, pp. 687–702; Jonathan Rodden, 'The Dilemma of Fiscal Federalism: Grants and Fiscal Performance around the World', *American Journal of Political Science*, vol. 46 (2002), no. 3, pp. 670–87; and Jonathan Rodden and Erik Wibbels, 'Beyond the Fiction of Federalism. Macroeconomic Management in Multitiered Systems', *World Politics*, vol. 54 (2002), no. 3, pp. 494–531.

democracy and social democracy has never been very marked on questions of social policy.⁹ This means that Germany's multi-veto point polity cannot have exerted the hypothesized restrictive influence on government spending during the era of the 'old politics' of the welfare state, at least with respect to partisan-political sources of 'gridlock'. It also means that, in the era of the 'new politics' of the welfare state, Christian Democrats and Social Democrats can either diverge in concert from the 'high redistribution' status quo or not at all. Under these circumstances, what hinders reform efforts is not so much the blocking effect of federal structures, but rather the dynamics of inter-party competition.¹⁰

In what follows I will trace the German welfare state's history of institutional development, starting with Bismarckian social legislation, continuing with the division of social policy competencies between the central government, the states and the localities in the Weimar Republic and, finally, analyzing the interplay between the federal government, the states and the welfare state in the Federal Republic of Germany. On the negative side, my main arguments are that federalism did not function to block welfare expansion, because the policy preferences of the main actors were similar and pro-welfare, and that the dynamics of co-operative federalism served to prevent any kind of inter-regional 'race to the bottom' in social policy. On the positive side, I argue that co-operative federalism actually encouraged expenditure growth, since unclear demarcation lines between the central government and the states and localities positively invited politicians to adopt credit-claiming and blame avoidance strategies with expansionary consequences. In particular, I argue that given the states can veto tax legislation, but cannot prevent increases in social insurance contributions, federal veto structures in the German case translated into welfare state growth. The final section of the chapter summarizes the argument and discusses some implications for a comparative perspective.

Bismarckian social legislation as a federalist compromise

Usually the foundation of the German welfare state is understood as having involved a carrot-and-stick strategy. Repression of the working class through the Anti-Socialist Law (1878) and the imperial edict

---

⁹ Ian Budge, Hans-Dieter Klingemann, Andrea Volkens, Judith Bara and Eric Tanenbaum, *Mapping Policy Preferences. Estimates for Parties, Electors and Governments 1945–1998* (Oxford: Oxford University Press, 2001).
¹⁰ Herbert Kitschelt, 'Partisan Competition and Welfare State Retrenchment. When do Politicians Choose Unpopular Policies?', in Paul Pierson, ed., *The New Politics of the Welfare State* (Oxford: Oxford University Press, 2001), pp. 265–302.

of 1881, in which the forthcoming social legislation was announced, were indeed closely linked. Less well known is the fact that the foundation of the German welfare state between 1883 and 1889 was also a large-scale exercise in nation- and state-building. Germany, along with Austria, was at the time a 'constitutional-dualistic monarchy', in which a modernizing bureaucratic state elite could respond to industrialization and working-class mobilization with the early adoption of social insurance.[11]

In nation-building terms the welfare state was designed to provide momentum for the internal foundation of the Reich after the German–French war of 1870–71 had brought external 'territorial consolidation'. The welfare state offered the social-democratic and the Catholic camps an opportunity for social integration, after both had been stigmatized as enemies of the Reich during the *Kulturkampf* era and in times of political repression under the Anti-Socialist Law. Bismarckian social legislation was targeted at workers, especially at the better-off strata of the working class. And the party that was second most successful in mobilizing voters and members among the working class besides the Social Democratic Party was the Catholic Zentrum or Centre Party.

The new social insurance schemes, with their proto-democratic structures, provided new avenues for political participation and social integration for workers.[12] Clearly, the new social rights were meant as partial substitutes for the absence of democratic rights – general suffrage in the national election was not worth much given the powerlessness of the Imperial Diet, and state elections were often still based on a plutocratic *système censitaire*.[13] But it is also important to highlight that social insurance itself – through the democratic system of workers' self-administration – offered workers important new electoral-participatory rights in areas of direct interest for them. State-building, on the other hand, meant that social reform offered the central government a new arena of political activity and a genuine legislative responsibility. Social reform established a new administrative domain for the central state, it established the need for a new bureaucratic apparatus, and it promised to open up new sources of revenue for the Reich. All this was an impressive exercise in state-building and meant that, from the outset, Bismarck's social legislation had a strong anti-federalist momentum. For instance, an

---

[11] Peter Flora and Jens Alber, 'Modernization, Democratization, and the Development of Welfare States in Western Europe', in Peter Flora and Arnold J. Heidenheimer, eds., *The Development of Welfare States in Europe and America* (New Brunswick, NJ: Transaction Books, 1981), pp. 70–72.

[12] Philip Manow, 'Social Protection, Capitalist Production: The Bismarckian Welfare State and the German Political Economy from the 1880s to the 1990s', habilitation, University of Konstanz, 2001, chapter 2.

[13] Cf. Flora and Alber, 'Modernization, Democratization'.

immediate consequence of the central state's assumption of welfare obligations through Bismarckian social legislation in the period 1883 to 1889 was the need to establish a central bureaucracy charged with the oversight of the new welfare system.[14]

Much of the need for social reform and of the central government's more or less undisputed dominance in this new policy domain can be explained by the apparent inadequacy of the old local support systems for the poor and destitute. The regionally scattered system of social assistance had proved inadequate when confronted with steeply increasing worker mobility in the wake of Germany's feverish industrialization in the last quarter of the nineteenth century. Previously, state aid to the poor and destitute had been provided either according to the principle of origin or according to the principle of current residence. Neither principle proved adequate in coping with the new challenges posed by rapid industrialization. The principle of origin meant that poor rural districts, from which workers had left for the big cities, had to subsidize the new industrial centres of the Reich. Moreover, the principle hindered worker mobility in the first place and aggravated severe labour shortages in the new industrial centres. The residence principle, on the other hand, obliged these new industrial centres to support the poor. Yet, this in turn resulted in fiscal problems as soon as locally concentrated industries faced a business cycle downturn. Thus, the need for a national responsibility in social reform and for risk pooling beyond the regional districts was widely accepted by informed opinion in the 1870s and 1880s.

The organizational principles according to which the new social insurance was designed differed from branch to branch, but nowhere did they exactly mirror the federalist structure of the German Reich. True, Bismarck's initial attempt to give the new welfare state a distinct centralist character by establishing a central state agency staffed by civil servants (and financed not by contributions, but out of the central state's budget; see below) failed due to the resistance of the states (*Länder*) in the *Bundesrat*, the federal chamber. But nor did the new social insurance follow a purely federalist design.[15] Accident insurance was organized along industrial lines, since firms within the same industry were understood to constitute a distinct risk class. The health insurance funds, on the other

---

[14] Friedrich P. Kahlenberg and Dierk Hoffmann, 'Sozialpolitik als Aufgabe zentraler Verwaltungen in Deutschland – ein verwaltungsgeschichtlicher Überblick 1945–1990', in Bundesministerium für Arbeit und Sozialordnung and Bundesarchiv, eds., *Geschichte der Sozialpolitik in Deutschland seit 1945*, vol. I, *Grundlagen der Sozialpolitik* (Baden-Baden: Nomos, 2001), pp. 103–82.

[15] As claimed by Hans Henning, 'Sozialpolitik, Geschichte III', *Handwörterbuch der Wirtschaftswissenschaften*, vol. 7 (1977), pp. 85–110, p. 95. See also Gerhard A. Ritter, *Sozialversicherung in Deutschland und England* (Munich: Beck, 1983), p. 73.

hand, either started as regional organizations (with further differentiation for specific occupations), as company funds or as institutions of collective self-help for certain professional groups. Sickness funds quickly grew in number, but soon problems stemming from their small size made themselves painfully felt. A major overhaul of the system in 1911 reduced the number of funds by more than half from more than 20,000 to less than 10,000. In the case of invalidity and old age insurance, thirty-one regional insurance agencies ran the system.[16]

Almost nowhere did the administrative units of the welfare state correspond with state boundaries. Moreover, when the white-collar movement succeeded in 1911 in obtaining an exclusive old age insurance branch of their own, this introduced an important element of competition between the thirty-one regional insurance offices and the new single national insurance agency for white-collar employees. This competition became one of the most important catalysts for a uniform legal and centralist institutional development of old age insurance. Similarly, sickness funds for white-collar workers were organized as supra-regional, sometimes even nation-wide organizations. Naturally, these funds were of much larger size than the average local or company sickness fund. In 1925 five white-collar funds counted an average membership of 224,500, a number about a hundred times as large as the average membership in one of the statutory, local or company funds. Again, this exerted a unifying effect in the health care insurance system, since contributions could be lower in larger funds thanks to administrative economies of scale and the advantages of risk pooling. The unemployment insurance system, which was founded as the last of the classical social insurance schemes in 1927, was organized on strictly centralist lines. A central agency with thirteen regional sub-branches took over responsibility from the 22 state and 869 municipal employment offices that, previously, had been in charge of unemployment support and labour market policies.[17]

This process of concentration and centralization continues up to the present day and demonstrates the underlying mechanism that has driven much of the institutional development of the German welfare state towards ever higher degrees of uniformity and centrality: the advantages of larger over smaller risk pools. This combined with the central state's

---

[16] Ten additional insurance agencies took care of seamen, railroad workers and miners. See Johannes Frerich and Martin Frey, *Handbuch der Geschichte der Sozialpolitik in Deutschland*, vol. I, *Von der vorindustriellen Zeit bis zum Ende des Dritten Reiches* (Munich: Oldenbourg, 1993), p. 101. See also vol. III, *Sozialpolitik in der Bundesrepublik Deutschland bis zur Herstellung der Deutschen Einheit*.

[17] Peter Lewek, *Arbeitslosigkeit und Arbeitslosenversicherung in der Weimarer Republik 1918–1927* (Stuttgart: Steiner, 1992); Carl Christian Führer, *Arbeitslosigkeit und die Entstehung der Arbeitslosenversicherung in Deutschland 1902–1927* (Berlin: Gruyter, 1990).

interest in the extension of risk pools in order to minimize fiscal liability for 'bad risks'. Thus, it is clear that questions of organizational design were simultaneously issues of considerable financial substance.

According to Bismarck's initial plans, the new social insurance schemes were supposed to be, prominently if not entirely, financed by taxes. This would have granted to the new central state a right of taxation that only existed previously in vestigial form. Bismarck planned to use revenue from a newly established state monopoly for tobacco to finance the new social programmes. That the Reich possessed only a small revenue-raising capacity was a consequence of the fact that the German Constitution of 1871 had resulted from a political compromise, which had centralized legislative powers but had delegated the responsibility for administrative implementation and enforcement to the Länder governments. The upshot was that policies had to be agreed upon jointly by the German central state and the states, effectively granting the states a veto on all political decisions.[18] Yet, implementation was the responsibility of the states and this meant that most of the tax revenue remained in state hands, while the Reich possessed no substantial sources of taxation of its own. The Reich could raise revenue from state-owned enterprises (like the post office), and from tariffs and indirect taxes (on sugar, salt, beer, matches, liquor, etc.). However, to cover its expenses the German central state of the late nineteenth century was also dependent on Länder contributions. Initially, in the 1870s such contributions amounted to 15 to 20 per cent of all revenue, although later – especially after the Reich embarked upon protectionism via high tariffs – the central budget became more independent of state subsidies. Yet, Reich tax revenues remained small.[19] In this period central taxes as a percentage of GDP were around 2 per cent, the smallest figure for countries for which we have comparable data.[20] With respect to the ratio of central to general taxes, only the Swiss central government was weaker than its German counterpart (39.3 per cent of overall taxation in 1886 compared to 49.2 per cent in 1881[21]).[22] In Germany, the central state possessed no large administrative apparatus of its own, with

---

[18] Cf. Gerhard Lehmbruch, *Parteienwettbewerb im Bundesstaat. Regelsysteme und Spannungslagen im Institutionengefüge der Bundesrepublik Deutschland* (Opladen: Westdeutscher Verlag, 1998), chapter 6.
[19] Peter-Christian Witt, *Die Finanzpolitik des Deutschen Reiches von 1903 bis 1913* (Lübeck and Hamburg: Matthiesen, 1970), pp. 378–79.
[20] See Peter Flora, Franz Kraus and Winfried Pfenning, *State, Economy and Society in Western Europe, 1815–1975. A Data Handbook*, vol. I, *The Growth of Mass Democracies and Welfare States* (Frankfurt-on-Main: Campus; London: Macmillan; Chicago: St James Press, 1983), p. 268.
[21] Ibid.
[22] Interestingly, this picture largely continues to hold true. In the 1980s and 1990s Germany still ranked among the OECD countries with the highest degree of fiscal decentralization

the Reich spending most of its revenues on the army and the fleet and, to a small but increasing extent, on the newly established welfare state.[23] The inadequacy of the Reich's tax base meant that an increasing part of total spending was financed out of a rapidly increasing public debt.[24]

Bismarck hoped that the central state's new responsibility for the social security of German citizens would legitimize tapping new sources of direct tax revenue for the Reich. Yet, as in the case of the institutional design of the welfare state, its final financial architecture was once again a compromise between the Reich and the Länder. Central tax financing was not to play a dominant role in the funding of the German welfare state, but nor did the fiscal structure take on federalist characteristics (which would have introduced the potential for 'competition of jurisdiction' dynamics into the system). Instead, social security contributions became the dominant source of revenue. The welfare state grew rapidly and its increasing fiscal and macro-economic importance is demonstrated by the fact that, already by 1904, overall welfare state revenue amounted to more than two-thirds of the central state's general tax revenue. This means that there was always a temptation to tap the financial resources of the welfare state for particularistic fiscal purposes – as the Reich did for the first time on a massive scale in World War One, when it used the financial assets of the social insurance funds to finance the war. Similarly, the autonomous financial status of the welfare state has also tempted politicians to achieve fiscal relief by shifting costs out of the public budget onto the special budgets of the welfare state. I will return to the nature of German para-fiscalism and the determinants of the long-term erosion of the central state's financial involvement in social spending later.

The federalist character of the German Reich not only had a profound impact on the institutional architecture and financial basis of the German welfare state, but also on the substantive nature of national and

and the lowest degree of fiscal centralization (see, also for definitions, Francis G. Castles, 'Federalism, Fiscal Decentralization and Economic Performance', in Ute Wachendorfer-Schmidt, ed., *Federalism and Political Performance* (London: Routledge, 2000), pp. 177–95, here at pp. 179–81, table 8.1), but also as the OECD country in which the share of federal grants and revenue sharing receipts of total provincial revenue was highest. (See Rodden and Wibbels, 'Beyond the Fiction', p. 504, table 1.) A third aspect is also important. Local plus central revenue make up only about two-thirds of total revenue, which hints at the enormous fiscal importance of the welfare state in Germany and of the central role of its para-fiscal mechanisms.

[23] Thomas Nipperdey, 'Machtstaat vor der Demokratie', in Thomas Nipperdey, *Deutsche Geschichte 1866–1918*, vol. II (Munich: Beck, 1992), pp. 166–82; and Witt, *Finanzpolitik des Deutschen Reiches*, p. 380.

[24] Peter-Christian Witt, 'Finanzen und Politik im Bundesstaat – Deutschland 1871–1933', in Jochen Huhn and Peter-Christian Witt, eds., *Föderalismus in Deutschland* (Baden-Baden: Nomos, 1992), pp. 75–99.

regional social protection. The division of labour between the Reich and the Länder, according to which the central state was now responsible for *Arbeiterpolitik* (social insurance for workers), while the Länder and the municipalities remained responsible for *Armenpolitik* (traditional social assistance for the non-working poor and destitute), helped to free the new social insurance from Poor Law traditions. The social protection system could focus exclusively on the social risks and vagaries stemming from industrialization and could be targeted primarily at workers, in fact mostly at the 'labour aristocracy' of trained and politically active workers, leaving local communities to take care of the poor in the traditional way. This dualism, which is most obviously manifest in the largely arbitrary demarcation between social assistance (covered by the municipalities and states) and the lower layers of social insurance, becomes most contested in the case of the long-time unemployed and remains a highly controversial feature of the German welfare system to the present day.[25]

In summing up, one can say that central institutional characteristics of the German welfare state were essentially the outcome of a compromise between the Reich and the states. The compromise had three distinguishing features: first, the centralization/nationalization of the legislative responsibility for social policy; second, an independent organizational design of the welfare state which was neither national nor federalist in character;[26] and finally, third, the financial autonomy of the new schemes (their para-fiscal status – already relatively high from the schemes' inceptions, but steadily increasing in following decades). These features played a decisive role in the further development of the German welfare state, which involved a steady process of coverage extension plus organizational concentration and centralization.

Weimar and the conflict over resources and competencies

Social policy moved to centre stage in the Weimar Republic. For the first time social rights became constitutionally guaranteed (especially Articles 157, 159, 163 and 165 of the Weimar Constitution). Their prominent status in the Weimar Constitution reflected the fact that the 'coalition of

---

[25] Christoph Sachße and Florian Tennstedt, *Geschichte der Armenfürsorge in Deutschland*, vol. I, *Vom Spätmittelalter bis zum ersten Weltkrieg* (Stuttgart: Kohlhammer, 1980), vol. II, *Fürsorge und Wohlfahrtspflege 1871–1929* (Stuttgart: Kohlhammer, 1988), and vol. III, *Der Wohlfahrtsstaat im Nationalsozialismus* (Stuttgart: Kohlhammer, 1992).
[26] Michael Stolleis, 'Historische Grundlagen. Sozialpolitik in Deutschland bis 1945', in Bundesministerium für Arbeit und Sozialordnung and Bundesarchiv, eds., *Geschichte der Sozialpolitik in Deutschland seit 1945*, vol. I, *Grundlagen der Sozialpolitik* (Baden-Baden: Nomos, 2001), pp. 199–332, p. 265; now revised as *Geschichte des Sozialrechts in Deutschland* (Stuttgart: Lucius & Lucius, 2003).

Weimar' – formed by the Social Democratic Party, the Catholic Centre and the liberal DDP – was crucially based upon the parties' common interest in the domain of social policy. Social policy was a natural point of agreement, especially between the two big mass membership parties, the Social Democrats and the Zentrum, since both parties had to please their substantial worker electorate, both possessed close links to the socialist and Catholic unions respectively, and both had established extensive networks with either politically or religiously motivated collective self-help organizations during the time in which they had been excluded from political power. Yet, push factors rapidly began to join these pull factors in the aftermath of the Great War, as Germany found itself coping with a social and economic crisis of massive proportions. The steeply increased number of war invalids, of widows and orphans, of those suffering from malnutrition, of refugees coming from lost territories, of the impoverished elderly and of 6 million soldiers who returned from the front, added to the serious economic problems stemming from the abrupt transition from a war to a peace economy. The number of persons dependent on welfare roughly quadrupled from 1914 to 1924 and per capita welfare expenditure increased nearly eightfold during the same period.[27]

The severe social and economic problems of post-war Germany amplified the need for profound reform and substantial reinforcement of the existing social protection system. In face of these problems the central state's political responsibility for the war combined with the problem overload of state and local authorities to give a strong centralist momentum to Weimar's welfare state development. This trend can be clearly read from the data. Whereas only 5.3 per cent of all central government expenditure was devoted to social spending in 1913/14, in 1925/26 the share was already at 35.8 per cent – only to rise further to almost 50 per cent at the peak of the economic crisis in 1932/33.[28] Similarly, central government social spending plus social insurance expenditure made up a steadily increasing part of total social spending – from 53 per cent in 1913/14 to 69 per cent in 1932/33.[29]

The war economy itself had already had a strong centralizing impact, and to some extent the Weimar Constitution as well as the important tax reform of 1920 only ratified the new power balance between the Reich and the Länder. Centralization of legislative, financial and

---

[27] Sachße and Tennstedt, *Geschichte der Armenfürsorge in Deutschland*, vol. III, p. 81.
[28] Frerich and Frey, *Handbuch der Geschichte der Sozialpolitik*, vol. I, p. 175, table 20; cf. Hans Bürger, *Sozialversicherung und Reichshaushalt. Darstellung und Kritik* (Berlin: Heymanns, 1930).
[29] Frerich and Frey, *Handbuch der Geschichte der Sozialpolitik*, vol. I, p. 175, table 20, own calculations.

administrative responsibilities, harmonization of regulation and homogenization of administrative design, increased generosity and extended coverage of social benefits – in all these respects the war had figured as an important 'pace-setter' of national welfare state development.[30] The same held true for federalism. Already in 1914, in the wake of the start of World War One, all legislative responsibilities had been delegated from parliament to the federal chamber, but this led not – as one might have assumed – to a stronger role for the states in policy-making, but rather to a hegemony of the central administration due to the dominance of Berlin's central Prussian bureaucracy. Once the war was over there was no going back to the federalist *status quo ante*.

After the war the political and financial balance tilted even more clearly towards the Reich. The states' chamber, the *Reichsrat*, was weakened, since under the Weimar Constitution it enjoyed only the right to a so-called 'suspending veto', which could be overridden by the *Diet* or popular house of parliament, and it lost its former exclusive right of legislative initiative. In fact, an effective veto of the Reichsrat remained a rare event, since the political alignment of the central and Länder governments was quite close throughout much of the 1920s. In particular, Prussia, by far the largest and the most important state (with two-thirds of the territory, two-thirds of the population, and with 26 of the 66 seats in the upper house), generally supported or at least tolerated Weimar governments throughout the 1920s.[31]

Compared with both the pre-World War One Reich and the post-World War Two Federal Republic, the constitutional foundations of federalism were less strongly developed during the inter-war years.[32] Under the previous imperial constitution, the federal chamber had possessed an absolute veto on all legislation and an exclusive right to initiate legislation. Today the federal chamber can use its veto to suspend around 45 per cent of all legislation (*Einspruchsgesetze*) and has an absolute veto on the other circa 55 per cent of legislation (*Zustimmungsgesetze*).[33] In the Weimar Republic, the federal house only had the suspending veto – still a powerful instrument given that the override required a two-thirds majority.

---

[30] Ludwig Preller, *Sozialpolitik in der Weimarer Republik* (Düsseldorf: Athenäum, 1978), p. 85; cf. Richard Titmuss, *Social Policy* (London: Allen & Unwin, 1976); Theda Skocpol, *Protecting Soldiers and Mothers: The Political Origins of Social Policy in the United States* (Cambridge, MA: Harvard University Press, 1992); and Gregory J. Kasza, 'War and Comparative Politics', *Comparative Politics*, vol. 28 (1996), no. 3, pp. 355–74.
[31] Lehmbruch, *Parteienwettbewerb*, pp. 70–77.
[32] That parties of the extreme right and left used their power positions in the states, as for instance in Bavaria or Thuringia, to follow secessionist strategies, is another story.
[33] Peter Schindler, *Datenhandbuch zur Geschichte des Deutschen Bundestages* (Baden-Baden: Nomos, 1999), p. 2430, table 3.

Table 6.1 *The position of the federal chamber in Wilhelmine Germany, the Weimar Republic and the Federal Republic*

Imperial Constitution, 1871	Weimar Constitution, 1918	Basic Law, 1949
Bundesrat has absolute veto (Article 5 of the imperial constitution)	Reichsrat has only suspending veto (Article 74 of the Weimar Constitution). To overrule the veto, a two-thirds majority in parliament is required	Bundesrat has absolute veto in matters that affect regional administration ($\approx$55% of all laws); in all other matters only a suspending veto (Article 77, 84, 85 and various other articles of the Basic Law). [A suspending veto with a two-thirds majority in the federal chamber can be overruled with a two-thirds majority in parliament as a whole; Article 77, paragraph 4]
25 states (26[a]) Total of 58 seats/votes (61[a]) • Prussia 17 • Bavaria 6 • Württemberg and Saxony each 4 • Baden and Hessen each 3	18 states Total of 66 seats/votes (68[b]) • Prussia 26 (27[c]) • Bavaria 10 (11[c]) • Saxony 7 • Württemberg 4 • Baden 3	11 states (16[d]) Total of 41 seats/votes (68[d]) • North Rhine-Westphalia, Bavaria, Baden-Württemberg and Lower Saxony each 5 (6[d]) • Hessen, Rhineland-Palatine, Berlin and Saxony each 4[d]
Members are delegates of the regional governments; no free mandate	Members are delegates of the regional governments; no free mandate	Members are delegates of the regional governments; there is no free mandate
States receive all direct taxes, the central state all indirect taxes. Tax laws need the consent of the states	Taxation completely a responsibility of the central state. Income and sales tax are shared between Reich and	Basically the same as under the Weimar Constitution. Extensive fiscal equalization scheme, which

Table 6.1 (cont.)

Imperial Constitution, 1871	Weimar Constitution, 1918	Basic Law, 1949
	states. The central government has *Kompetenzkompetenz*, i.e. it can decide who can levy which taxes. The fiscal equalization scheme is only moderate.	guarantees that no state has a per capita tax revenue lower than 95% of the national average
The right to legislate lies with the federal chamber	The right to legislate lies with the Diet or popular house of parliament	The right to promulgate laws lies with the Bundestag or popular house of parliament, yet laws need the consent of the federal chamber
The federal chamber has the *exclusive* right to initiate legislation	The federal chamber has the right to initiate legislation (co-legislation)	The federal chamber has the right to initiate legislation (co-legislation)

Notes: [a] from 1911; [b] between 1926 and 1928; [c] since 1926; [d] since 1990.
Source: Ernst Rudolf Huber, 'Die Weimarer Reichsverfassung', in *Deutsche Verfassungsgeschichte seit 1789*, vol. VI (Stuttgart: Kohlhammer, 1981), p. 378; Ernst Rudolf Huber, 'Bismarck und das Reich', in *Deutsche Verfassungsgeschichte seit 1789*, vol. III (Stuttgart: Kohlhammer, 1988), p. 855 *et passim*; Stefan Oeter, *Integration und Subsidiarität im deutschen Bundesstaatsrecht* (Tübingen: Mohr Siebeck, 1998), p. 63; Thomas Nipperdey, 'Machtstaat vor der Demokratie', in Thomas Nipperdey, *Deutsche Geschichte 1866–1918*, vol. II (Munich: Beck, 1992), pp. 166–82; Peter Schindler, *Datenhandbuch zur Geschichte des Deutschen Bundestages* (Baden-Baden: Nomos, 1999), p. 2447; and Wolfgang Renzsch, *Finanzverfassung und Finanzausgleich* (Bonn: J. H. W. Dietz, 1991), pp. 11–26.

This reshaping of political power came hand in hand with a loss of fiscal privileges. The tax reform of 1920 gave the central government access to its own substantial tax revenues for the first time (see table 6.2), while the constitution equipped the Reich not only with the autonomy to legislate in full sovereignty all tax laws it deemed necessary for its own revenue needs (Article 8), but also to regulate the states' taxation. Table 6.1 identifies and contrasts the essential features and rights of the federal chamber under the Reich, the Weimar Republic and in the post-war Federal Republic of Germany.

However, it is also necessary to emphasize that the centralist momentum of the Weimar years was not just an outcome of war and economic crisis, but was also an expression of a more secular trend. In this context, it is important to note that fiscal federalism and strict inter-state federalism have never been distinguishing features of the German polity.[34] From the very start, German federalism had a strong bias in favour of national unity and legislative centralization – even if this tendency remained short of administrative centralization. To establish strict inter-state federalism was never seriously contemplated outside the southern Catholic camp, with its fear of Prussian-Protestant hegemony. Revealingly, in the constitutional debates of the second half of the nineteenth century the United States and Switzerland served as negative reference points to exemplify how German federalism should not develop.[35] But what, then, explains the German federalist compromise? The federalist structure of the 'belated German nation' was simply an acknowledgement of the fact that the German states were already autonomous, sovereign entities. Therefore, the constitution was clearly meant to be an institutional structure that would allow and foster national integration and help overcome federalist fragmentation.[36] In other words, federalism was not designed as a constitutional safeguard for regional particularism, but rather as the best available instrument for achieving the goal of national unification – given that German unification could realistically only happen through the delegation of power from the already firmly established and sovereign states to the Reich.[37] It was in line with this underlying unitary tendency that the states under the Weimar Constitution enjoyed only a diminished veto power in the second chamber and lost some of their former fiscal privileges.

The tax reform of 1920 finally provided the material basis for the integrative goals that all the major political actors shared. In all matters of taxation, the Reich could now exert influence through its right of concurrent legislation (*konkurrierende Gesetzgebung*), which stated that the states could regulate their tax affairs autonomously only insofar and only as long as the central government abstained from enacting nation-wide standards (Article 8 of the Weimar Constitution).[38] Furthermore, the tax

[34] Gerhard Lehmbruch, 'Der unitarische Bundesstaat in Deutschland: Pfadabhängigkeit und Wandel', in Arthur Benz and Gerhard Lehmbruch, eds., *Föderalismus. Analysen in entwicklungsgeschichtlicher und vergleichender Perspektive* (Opladen: Westdeutscher Verlag, 2002; special issue *Politische Vierteljahresschrift* 32/2001), pp. 80–83.
[35] Stefan Oeter, *Integration und Subsidiarität im deutschen Bundesstaatsrecht. Untersuchungen zu Bundesstaatstheorie unter dem Grundgesetz* (Tübingen: Mohr Siebeck, 1998), pp. 32, 34, 40; Lehmbruch, *Parteienwettbewerb*, pp. 80–83.
[36] Konrad Hesse, *Der unitarische Bundesstaat* (Karlsruhe: C. F. Müller, 1962).
[37] Oeter, *Integration und Subsidiarität*, pp. 29–52.
[38] Therefore the term 'concurrent legislation' is misleading. The central government has the *prerogative* of legislation, thus the German term *Vorranggesetzgebung* might be more precise.

Table 6.2 *Percentage tax revenue shares of national, regional and local government (1885–1970)*

Year	National government	States	Municipalities
1885	18	57	25
1913	30	29	41
1925	38	26	36
1936	66	10	24
1950	52	31	17
1970	54	34	11

Source: Jürgen Hidien, *Der bundesstaatliche Finanzausgleich in Deutschland* (Baden-Baden: Nomos, 1998), table 18, pp. 338 and 460. See also OECD, *Revenue Statistics* (Paris: OECD, http://www.sourceoecd.org)

reform prohibited the localities from levying additional charges in addition to direct taxation. This not only levelled the enormously varying tax burdens between the different regions, but also had an important welfare side effect: it made local social policy (i.e. social assistance) less dependent on the local tax power, and this, in turn, eased nation-wide regulation of local social policy and the standardization of benefits. However, at the same time the reform intensified the fiscal interdependencies between the central state, the Länder and the localities. It radically changed the relationship between the central state and the Länder: whereas previously the Reich had depended on Länder transfers, now the states became dependent on transfers from the general budget.[39] As table 6.2 shows, by the mid-1920s the central government became, for the first time, the biggest recipient of tax revenues.

As in the field of tax law, the central government now, for the first time, also enjoyed the privilege of concurrent legislation in the domain of social assistance. These new powers were soon used to harmonize widely differing standards and levels of local support for the poor and needy. This was not the only proof of the close nexus between tax and social policy. In the case of social assistance, earmarked financial transfers were the government's initial 'foot in the door' in a policy domain in which it had not previously enjoyed much influence. Financial transfers out of the national budget often came with quite precise policy directives. Therefore, it was not accidental that the central state enacted a tax emergency decree at the same time as the important decree on welfare early in 1924.[40] Whereas the tax decree increased the states' share of personal income taxes from

---

[39] Sachße and Tennstedt, *Geschichte der Armenfürsorge in Deutschland*, vol. I, pp. 176, 178.
[40] Cf. Stolleis, *Historische Grundlagen*, p. 280.

75 to 90 per cent, the welfare decree for the first time substituted uniform national legislation for the various state laws that previously had existed in this policy sector. But legal harmonization and central standard-setting went hand in hand with administrative reform. Devolution (of central government responsibilities) and centralization (of local responsibilities) conspired to assign most of the administrative and financial responsibilities attached to the provision of welfare to the Länder or regional level.

The central state's intrusion into the states' own policy territory met with little resistance so long as it relieved local authorities of some of the pressing financial stress resulting from mass poverty and well-nigh permanent economic recession. Prescriptive notions of uniform living conditions and, hence, uniformity of provision also played an extremely important legitimizing role for central policy initiatives in the welfare sector. Different rules and regulations, tariffs and laws had been the prime target of a forceful bourgeois-liberal critique, castigating them as indicators of outdated parochialism and as barriers to national market integration, which it was the true mission of German national unification to overcome.[41] An encompassing national system of taxation reinforced centralist tendencies in the development of the German nation state, and also ruled out all 'competition of jurisdictions' dynamics in all the tax-financed areas of the welfare state. For instance, tax-financed local social assistance largely followed nation-wide rules and was largely financed from the national budget by way of earmarked direct transfers to the states' budgets. In Germany, social legislation was *deliberately* used as an instrument of national unification and was explicitly designed to prevent a federalist fragmentation of living conditions.

Nor was this unifying effect of social policy an issue of much political dispute. Conservatives, liberals and Social Democrats alike were in favour of national unification led by a strong central state and leading to 'uniform living conditions'. Social democracy had been anti-federalist ever since universal and equal (male) suffrage had been granted in 1871 for national level elections to the imperial Diet, while eligibility to vote in most regional elections before 1918 (especially in Prussia) was on the basis of property qualification. The Catholic Zentrum was not as single minded in its support for central state responsibility. The party represented both federalist and centralist currents, with the faction representing the latter closely linked to the powerful movements of Social Catholicism. In the first decade of the twentieth century social Catholicism had developed into a powerful nation-wide interest group independent of the official

[41] Lehmbruch, 'Der Unitarische Bundesstaat in Deutschland', pp. 80–83.

church bureaucracy, with its still regional structures.[42] Despite the high degree of party fragmentation in the Weimar Republic, no major party voiced decisively regional interests or favoured the organizational devolution of the welfare state.

This preference for a common national response to the 'labour question' resonated well with the ministerial bureaucracy. Both civil servants and German legal thought clearly favoured nation-wide uniform regulation. Social policy was no exception. Contemporary observers characterized the Weimar Labour Ministry as revealing 'markedly centralist tendencies'.[43] This centralism brought the ministry into conflict with the Länder and the local authorities. Yet the substance of their objection did not concern a loss of policy discretion, but rather involved disagreement over the basis for allocating costs between the central government and the states. The resolution of this conflict by an increasing reliance on contribution financing became something of a natural option within Germany's federal polity. This suggests that the German welfare state's substantial dependence on contribution finance should not solely be interpreted as the institutional embodiment or expression of 'conservatism'.[44] To a very important extent it was the political solution to a conflict between the central government and the states and municipalities over how best to minimize their financial involvement, while leaving their rough fiscal balance of power untouched.

The one major social policy innovation in the Weimar Republic was the establishment of unemployment insurance in 1927.[45] This, too, was indicative of the centralizing tendencies of the era. Here, the Reich finally established its dominance by integrating existing local and regional labour agencies into a centralist administrative structure with the status of dependent *Reichsunter-* and *Reichsmittelbehörden* (local and intermediate state agencies). This was the end point of a long and protracted battle between the central state and the localities over administrative competencies and financial responsibilities. The unemployment insurance scheme of 1927 finally established a hierarchical chain of delegation and largely left states and communities without discretion in a domain in which they formerly had enjoyed dominant influence. The administrative structure thus became a prominent example of a deliberate break with the old federal compromise by which legislative responsibilities had been centralized and

---

[42] Dirk H. Müller, *Arbeiter, Katholizismus, Staat. Der Volksverein für das katholische Deutschland und die katholischen Arbeiterorganisationen in der Weimarer Republik* (Bonn: Dietz, 1996).
[43] Preller, *Sozialpolitik in der Weimarer Republik*, p. 290, translation mine.
[44] Gøsta Esping-Andersen, *The Three Worlds of Welfare Capitalism* (Cambridge: Polity Press; Princeton: Princeton University Press, 1990).
[45] Führer, *Arbeitslosigkeit und Entstehung*; Lewek, *Arbeitslosigkeit und Arbeitslosenversicherung*.

nationalized, while the Länder retained the prerogative for administrative execution and programme implementation. To the present day, the labour office and the tax administration remain the two most important deviations from the established federalist 'division of labour' between the centre and the regions. In the Federal Republic, a quarter of all labour office employees are civil servants, the unemployment insurance is run by one central agency with regional branches and, in the governing bodies of the labour office, the government represents a third of all delegates, whereas in the sickness, accident and pension insurance schemes there is equal representation of worker delegates and employer delegates. Moreover, the financial nexus between the unemployment insurance scheme and the public budget is quite close, given that the central state is obliged to cover all deficits of the Labour Office (sickness funds are almost completely financially autonomous, while the government covers a fixed share of total pension spending).

Yet, even this strictly hierarchical design of the unemployment insurance scheme could not end conflicts between the centre and the localities in this sector. Since the localities remained responsible for local welfare (social assistance), conflicts between the local authorities and the central government were far from settled with the enactment of the unemployment insurance law in 1927. The central points of conflict were the length of time that the unemployed should receive benefits on an insurance basis and the basis on which the localities could use insurance funds for active labour market policies. Given the legislative and tax levying powers of the central government, states and municipalities were disadvantaged in the distributive conflict over who should bear the costs of the economic recession that hit Germany extremely hard in 1928 and subsequent years. Both with respect to taxes and the fiscal mix in the welfare sector, the central government used its privileged position to burden the states and localities with welfare tasks without equipping them with the necessary financial means. Compensatory direct financial transfers to the communities out of the public budget remained an insufficient remedy in times of weak economic growth and general fiscal stress. Whereas prior to World War One the central government lacked the resources to match its increased responsibilities, now states and municipalities were the levels of government with inadequate financial means.

Weimar's politics of welfare were driven by (mainly financial) conflicts between centre and periphery and these conflicts were nurtured by the mismatch between fiscal, legislative, administrative and political responsibilities within the German 'co-operative' federal system. This made the 'struggles over resources and competencies between Reich and communities . . . an essential feature of the social policy dynamics of the Weimar

Republic'.[46] In this conflict the states, in turn, were not always acting as the true advocates of the interests of the localities and the municipalities. These, as the 'protectors of last resort', were increasingly left alone in their struggle against the consequences of the economic crisis, as the phrase '*Kommunalisierung der Armut*' (freely translated: devolution of poverty) suggests. Often, central government and the states could compromise within Germany's system of co-operative federalism only at the expense of a third party. At times, contributors lost out; at other times, the local authorities. Shifts between state-financed unemployment aid and locally financed social assistance were indicative of the increasingly fierce distributive conflicts between the different layers of the German state.[47]

The struggle between the centre and the localities over the devolution or centralization of policy responsibilities had an important partisan-political aspect. The centralization of policy responsibilities was part of a political attack against Germany's (allegedly red) municipalities. The Catholic Zentrum, the bourgeois parties and the bourgeois and religious voluntary welfare associations all tried to instil fears of so-called 'creeping socialism' (*Munizipialsozialismus*) at the local level, and corporatist co-operation between the Labour Ministry and welfare peak associations was understood to be an antidote to this allegedly perilous trend.[48] The centralization of social assistance and the integration of voluntary associations as components of the national welfare state were thus part of an attempt to contain the local influence of Social Democrats in the larger cities and industrial centres. Once again, it is apparent that a central distinguishing feature of the German welfare state, the dualism between public *financing* and state *regulation* of the welfare sector and semi-private welfare *provision* by 'third sector' organizations, has been, in large part, an outcome of federalist struggles between the Reich and the localities.

Finally, it is worth asking how the German welfare state compared with others of the same era. Comparative data for this early period are fragmentary, but according to the available evidence, the Weimar welfare state was the most developed in western Europe in respect of both spending and programme coverage.[49] Obvious reasons include the relative maturity of German insurance programmes initiated in the late nineteenth century and the extreme levels of need characterizing inter-war Germany.

Summing up, one can say that the dynamics of German social policy in the inter-war period essentially reflected the conflicts between the

---

[46] Sachße and Tennstedt, *Geschichte der Armenfürsorge in Deutschland*, vol. II, p. 89.
[47] Ibid., vol. III, pp. 57–70.   [48] Ibid., vol. II, pp. 152–72.
[49] Flora *et al.*, eds., *State, Economy and Society*, pp. 460–61 and 355–449; Jens Alber, *Vom Armenhaus zum Wohlfahrtsstaat* (Frankfurt-on-Main: Campus, 1982), p. 152.

central state and regional and local authorities. Both financial issues and partisan conflict between the different layers of government loomed large in the social policy debates of the time, but the most important conflicts were not between the national government in Berlin and the states, but between central and local governments. A genuine federalist dimension of political conflict was not strongly developed in the inter-war years, given that the states were less powerful than they had been before World War One, and given that conflicts were muted by a high degree of partisan-political alignment between central and state governments. Conflicts were also less fierce because the Berlin government and the states could often compromise at the expense of third parties – primarily the insured contributors and the localities. Yet overall, the Weimar period saw the substantial centralization and nationalization of social policy. This was due partly to the extraordinary socio-economic challenges with which the first German republic was confronted. It was also due to the overall centralist tendencies of German federalism itself.

Ultimately, however, the republic and the welfare state both broke down when confronted with social, political and economic problems of enormous proportions. Arguably, no welfare state, however designed, would have been able to cope with the economic catastrophe and social dislocations of the late 1920s and the early 1930s. The advent of National-Socialist rule marked the end of federalism and its replacement by a 'dual state' (Fraenkel, *The Dual State*, 1941) constituted of parallel and often redundant central state bureaucratic structures and of their Nazi Party organizational counterparts.

The Federal Republic's welfare state and fiscal joint decision traps

I turn now to the development of the German welfare state in the post-1945 era, asking initially how the Nazi interregnum influenced the structure of the welfare state that post-war Germany inherited. The answer is that the direct impact was surprisingly small and the lasting influences relatively subtle, with the literature substantially agreeing on the lack of success of the radical reform vision of the National-Socialists in the social welfare field.[50] A powerful coalition of forces, comprising the conservative ministerial bureaucrats of the Labour Ministry, the

[50] Karl Teppe, 'Zur Sozialpolitik des Dritten Reiches am Beispiel der Sozialversicherung', *Archiv für Sozialgeschichte*, vol. 17 (1977), no. 1, pp. 195–250; Sachße and Tennstedt, *Geschichte der Armenfürsorge in Deutschland*, vol. III, and Wolfgang Scheur, '*Einrichtungen und Maßnahmen der sozialen Sicherheit in der Zeit des Nationalsozialismus*', Ph.D. dissertation, University of Cologne, 1967).

administrative apparatus of the social insurance branches, business interest groups and competing party and executive factions, struggling for influence within the chaotic regime, effectively delayed the enactment of grandiose Nazi reform plans until the war began. After 1939 the government shied away from fundamental reforms, because it feared such reforms would endanger social peace and would stand in the way of the smooth working of the war economy by opening a home front. In organizational terms, the 'classical' core of the German welfare state, the social insurance schemes, thus remained to a remarkable extent untouched.

Yet, by abolishing most elements of joint union–employer administration of the social insurance schemes, especially by destroying the unions, and by integrating the social insurance schemes into the state apparatus, the National-Socialists gave an already centralist organizational development a further strong *étatiste* momentum. Moreover, with the abolition of the Länder in 1934, German federalism officially ceased to exist. However, since the German welfare state possessed an organizational structure that was largely independent of the structures of German federalism, the end of federalism had no important direct impact on the welfare state itself. That said, the long-term consequences were quite substantial. Once the states were reconstituted after World War Two, they were confronted with a Bismarckian system that in the meantime had become more centralized and autonomous, more uniform, more encompassing, more bureaucratic and less politicized.[51]

These tendencies may be best exemplified with respect to the old age insurance system. Here the fact that the fundamental reform plan of the Nazis (e.g. the introduction of a uniform, tax-financed people's insurance that would have fused the white-collar and blue-collar branches) was never enacted should not distract from the fact that subtle but long-lasting modifications did take place under the Nazi regime. In this respect, we may mention the following five changes. First, the Nazis started to pay one global (augmented) state subsidy for the pension insurance scheme instead of the fixed subsidy per individual pension paid previously. Second, they issued a central state guarantee for the pension insurance, thereby taking over fiscal responsibility from the Länder and the communities that previously had guaranteed pension payments. Third, for the first time contribution payments were automatically deducted from wages as an exact and equal percentage share for both blue-collar and

---

[51] Stephan Leibfried and Florian Tennstedt, 'Sozialpolitik und Berufsverbote im Jahre 1933', *Zeitschrift für Sozialreform*, vol. 25 (1979), no. 3, pp. 129–53; no. 4, pp. 211–38.

white-collar workers[52] (previously, payments had to be paid in personally at a post office and were differentiated according to different wage groups and with different contribution rates for blue-collar and white-collar workers). Fourth, during the Nazi era social insurance for handicraft workers became obligatory (1938). And fifth, pensioners were integrated into the health insurance scheme (1941). Thus, much of what happened in organizational terms between 1933 and 1945 can be summarized as rationalization, membership extension and further centralization but did not qualify as a radical break with traditional organizational principles. All of these changes survived the Nazi regime and became part of the refounded social protection system of the Federal Republic after the war.

When it comes to the post-war period, the most revealing observation about the relation between the federal *Bundesrepublik* and the reconstituted welfare state is of the 'why the dog did not bark' variety: why did the states not protest about their loss of policy responsibilities in the social policy sector, when the central state reclaimed political responsibility for social policy between 1949 and 1953, after the immediate post-war years had witnessed a significant organizational devolution of the German welfare state? This lack of conflict is, on the one hand, strong evidence for the tacit consensus among the major political camps and between the states and the central government about the national role – promoting unity and equality – that the German welfare state was supposed to play. On the other hand, it was also a matter of necessity. States differed too much with respect to economic starting conditions and were too differently affected by the war (by destruction and the refugee problem) to make welfare state decentralization a feasible option.[53]

The process of administrative and territorial consolidation of the states had ended by mid-1947. The first states were constituted as early as September 1945, only half a year after the military surrender.[54] The states were thus at least two years ahead of the Federal Republic, which

---

[52] In their effort to create *völkische* unity (unity of the German people), the Nazis also fought against what they perceived as outdated *ständische* (status in the sense of social estates) welfare privileges. Their main target was the hitherto privileged status of white-collar workers. See Michael Prinz, *Vom neuen Mittelstand zum Volksgenossen. Die Entwicklung des sozialen Status der Angestellten von der Weimarer Republik bis zum Ende der NS-Zeit* (Munich: Oldenbourg, 1986).

[53] See on this especially Fritz W. Scharpf, 'Der Bundesrat und die Kooperation auf Dritter Ebene', in Bundesrat, ed., *Vierzig Jahre Bundesrat* (Baden-Baden: Nomos, 1989), pp. 121–62.

[54] Heidrose Kilper and Roland Lhotta, *Föderalismus in der Bundesrepublik Deutschland* (Opladen: Leske & Budrich, 1996), p. 83; Hans Boldt, 'Die Wiederaufnahme der deutschen föderativen Tradition im Parlamentarischen Rat 1948/49', *Zeitschrift für Staats- und Europawissenschaften*, vol. 1 (2003), no. 4, pp. 505–26.

was reinaugurated late in 1949. Once again, as in 1871, the states were already in place before the nation state formed. During this time the states became responsible for those social protection programmes that had formerly been run at the national level, that is, especially for the white-collar workers pension and unemployment insurance schemes.[55] For all other programmes, they preserved the right of administrative and legal oversight (but not of legislation) that they had under Weimar. The by and large non-contentious redelegation of organizational responsibilities from the regional level to the national level after 1949 was legitimized by the commonly accepted idea that all Germans should enjoy 'uniform living conditions'.[56] As was true of the period of initial Bismarckian social legislation, after World War Two, nobody forcefully campaigned for an organizational or fiscal devolution of the German welfare state.

When the German Bundestag convened for the first time after the first free post-war elections in the three western military zones in 1949, it had to decide on the future of the German welfare state, while the division of powers between the central state and the Länder had already been part of the constitutional compromise that had preceded the elections. The preliminary constitution, the West German Basic Law, which was supposed to last until the French, British and American zones – constituting the Federal Republic – reunited with the Soviet zone constituting the German Democratic Republic, deliberately refrained from prescribing the institutional detail of the future welfare state. Only a vague reference to Germany being a 'democratic and social federal state' (Article 20) could be found in the Basic Law. Yet, with respect to the design of German federalism, the Basic Law was much more concrete. Essentially, it prolonged, with small but important modifications, the Weimar balance of powers. For all legislative initiatives that affected administration at the state level, the second chamber, the Bundesrat, as the representative of the states at the federal level,[57] possessed an absolute veto (see table 6.1 above). For all other legislation, the second chamber possessed only a suspending veto. Thus, the states had regained some of the political influence they had lost in the Weimar years.

The same picture emerges in the area of taxation. The Catholic 'southwest' current of German Christian democracy, which became dominant in the West after Germany was divided into two nations, had always been in favour of federalist devolution – mainly motivated by its opposition

---

[55] Kahlenberg and Hoffmann, 'Sozialpolitik als Aufgabe zentraler Verwaltungen', p. 118.
[56] Oeter, *Integration und Subsidiarität*, pp. 532–42.
[57] The German Bundesrat does not follow the Senate model, with elected senators, but is composed of delegates of the state governments, with votes weighted differently according to population size.

to the centralist hegemony of Protestant Prussia. These preferences for greater regional autonomy had been reflected in proposals at the constitutional convention to return to the fiscal status quo of Imperial Germany. According to these proposals, the central government would have again become totally dependent on transfers from the states' budgets.[58] Yet, the German Social Democratic Party – not least because of its expectation of winning the first national election in 1949 – struggled vehemently for a more centralist distribution of revenue, while the pro-federalism stance of the Christian Democratic Party (CDU) was, in turn, motivated by the very same expectation that the first democratic government of the Federal Republic would be led by the Social Democrats. But resistance to a decentralized solution also cut across party lines. Substantial differences in size between city states such as Hamburg or Bremen on the one hand, and states such as Bavaria on the other, different economic starting conditions as well as the varying extent to which states were affected by the war (Schleswig-Holstein was flooded with refugees from the east; the city states of Bremen, Hamburg and Berlin had been heavily destroyed by Allied bombing) rendered strict fiscal devolution almost impossible. Under these circumstances, and given that the states resisted all attempts to rearrange the borders or to fuse West Germany's eleven states into a few viable entities, federalist principles could only be defended through a regime of centralized but joint taxation. Therefore, the welfare state and the compromise over federalism can be seen as two sides of the same coin. Given varying degrees of expenditure need, welfare state devolution was highly problematic. The differing revenue potential of the states meant that fiscal federalism was not a realistic option. This led to the paradoxical institutional set-up of the Federal Republic. Autonomy of the states could only be secured by strengthening their influence on *nationally uniform* legislation and by establishing complex *national* tax-and-spend arrangements.

When the CDU formed the first German government under Chancellor Konrad Adenauer, the basic compromise between the 'centralists' and the 'federalists' was already in place. The most important taxes, including value-added tax (VAT), income tax and corporate income tax, were either shared between the central state and the states (income and corporate tax) or were the exclusive province of the central government (VAT). All in all, a rough and relatively stable 55 per cent (central government) to 45 per cent (states) distribution of total tax revenue was established.[59]

---

[58] Cf. Wolfgang Renzsch, *Finanzverfassung und Finanzausgleich. Die Auseinandersetzungen um ihre politische Gestaltung zwischen Währungsreform und deutscher Vereinigung (1948 bis 1990)* (Bonn: J. H. W. Dietz, 1991), pp. 55–74.
[59] Ibid., p. 13.

Today the federal government, the states and local authorities share the personal income tax according to a 42.5/42.5/15 per cent formula and corporate income tax and VAT are split between central and regional governments according to 50/50 and 51/47 ratios respectively (with local authorities receiving 2 per cent of the VAT). Regional differences in tax revenue due to differences in economic development are equalized by a complex system of vertical transfers from the central state to 'needy' states combined with horizontal transfers from rich to poor states.[60] These fiscal equalization schemes guarantee that no state has a per capita tax revenue below 95 per cent of the national average. With respect to tax legislation, the Weimar status quo remained in place: for taxes comprising 30 per cent of total revenue, either central government, the states or the municipalities can claim exclusive responsibility. For the remaining 70 per cent of joint taxes, legislation is national, but states have a quite powerful right of co-legislation due to their position in the Bundesrat. In fact, since no major tax – other than social insurance contributions – falls into the exclusive competence of either the central government or the regional governments, the central government's tax policy is dependent on the consent of the states – and, in times of 'divided government', also on the consent of the opposition.[61]

The fact that political decisions concerning the fate of the German welfare state came much later than the fiscal compromise between the central government and the states again demonstrates that the states conceived of social policy as not being genuinely part of their own policy domain. In the early 1950s, with a couple of rather unspectacular legislative measures, the Adenauer government reclaimed central authority for the social insurance schemes that before 1945 had been organized at the national level. In 1951 the accident insurance scheme was reintegrated into the administrative domain of the Federal Labour Ministry; in 1952 a national labour office was constituted, and in 1953 the national white-collar worker pension scheme was re-established in Berlin as the successor of the former Imperial Insurance Office for white-collar workers.[62] While there was conflict concerning all three measures – mainly over questions concerning the representation of employers and unions on the administrative bodies of the schemes ('self-administration') – a manifest

---

[60] Ibid.; Jürgen Hidien, *Der bundesstaatliche Finanzausgleich in Deutschland* (Baden-Baden: Nomos, 1999).
[61] Steffen Ganghof, *Wer regiert in der Steuerpolitik? Einkommensteuerreform in Deutschland zwischen internationalem Wettbewerb und nationalen Verteilungskonflikten* (Frankfurt-on-Main: Campus, 2004).
[62] Kahlenberg and Hoffmann, 'Sozialpolitik als Aufgabe zentraler Verwaltungen', pp. 118–19; also Frerich and Frey, *Handbuch der Geschichte der Sozialpolitik*, vol. III, pp. 43, 84.

centre–periphery conflict dimension was largely absent from the agenda.[63] True, in the case of accident insurance, the states warned that centralization of responsibilities would lead to a further 'puffing up of the federal bureaucracy',[64] and in the case of the unemployment insurance system, they favoured a more decentralized solution, in which independent regional labour offices would only be engaged in a loose working co-operation at the national level. However, as soon as the federal state promised to take over the entire administrative staff of the regional labour offices, resistance to centralist solutions quickly evaporated.[65] Apparently, the Länder were not very principled in their pro-federalism position.

The successful claim of the Adenauer government for supremacy in the field of social policy was not a consequence of a weakened position of the Länder after 1949. Indeed, the opposite was the case. Partly as a consequence of their institutional primogeniture, but also in terms of constitutional authority, the states were in a seemingly powerful position. This was especially due to their right to an absolute veto on all legislation with an impact on Länder administration or finance. Initially the veto was thought to apply to no more than 10 per cent of all legislation, but today – as a result of extensive legal and political interpretations – about 55 per cent of all laws are seen as requiring the consent of the second chamber.[66] In other words, if no compromise can be found between parliament and the second chamber a law cannot be enacted. True, Article 72 of the Basic Law establishes far-reaching legislative competencies for the central government, but these are balanced by no less far-reaching rights of co-legislation for the states.[67] Now that hegemonic Prussia had ceased to exist, this right of co-legislation was of much greater potential significance. For the government, it became harder to form majorities in the upper chamber and the possibility of veto in the Bundesrat became more real.

With respect to social policy, the late 1940s and early 1950s essentially saw the refounding of the German welfare state along traditional Bismarckian lines, with obligatory social insurance, employment-based membership, contribution finance, organizational fragmentation and so

---

[63] Hans Günter Hockerts, *Sozialpolitische Entscheidungen im Nachkriegsdeutschland. Alliierte und deutsche Sozialversicherungspolitik, 1945–1957* (Stuttgart: Klett-Cotta, 1980).

[64] Kahlenberg and Hoffmann, 'Sozialpolitik als Aufgabe zentraler Verwaltungen', p. 118.

[65] Christine Trampusch, *'Arbeitsmarktpolitik, Gewerkschaften und Arbeitgeber. Ein Vergleich über die Entstehung und Transformation der öffentlichen Arbeitsverwaltungen in Deutschland, Großbritannien und den Niederlanden zwischen 1909 und 1999'*, Ph.D. dissertation, University of Göttingen, 2000.

[66] Schindler, *Datenhandbuch zur Geschichte*, pp. 2430–31.

[67] Oeter, *Integration und Subsidiarität*, pp. 123–24.

forth.[68] Many perceived this as a scandalous anachronism. While contemporaneous reforms in Britain and Scandinavia established allegedly 'modern', uniform and universal central tax-financed systems of social protection, the defeated and economically weak Germany obviously thought it could afford to stick with the old, expensive Byzantine system, with all its outdated status differentiation and bureaucratic overkill. Especially contentious was the restoration of the 'feudal' differentiation between blue-collar and white-collar worker insurance branches (both in the pensions and the health insurance schemes). From early on, two modifications of the pre-war status quo emerged as a kind of institutional response to this critique. First, although organizationally separated, entitlements in both schemes became legally 'assimilated',[69] and, second, internal fiscal transfers, as well as transfers between the different schemes, were introduced to ensure that equal welfare entitlements would not translate into varying contribution levels between regions or social insurance schemes. Initially these financial transfer schemes were voluntary; later they became obligatory.[70]

The financial transfer schemes proved to be of special importance for the further development of the relationship between German federalism and the Bismarckian welfare state, since uniform entitlements and equal contributions backed by fiscal transfers that levelled regional or economic disparities largely ruled out 'race to the bottom' dynamics in the social policy arena. A nationally uniform contribution rate for the pension insurance scheme made fiscal transfers between pension funds necessary. Finally, in 1969, in the wake of Germany's first post-war recession, the 'good' risk pool of the white-collar workers' insurance fund was fully fiscally fused with the comparatively 'bad' blue-collar workers' insurance scheme.[71] Another motive complemented the 'equal contribution rate' argument. Fiscal pooling was introduced largely to provide

---

[68] Hockerts, *Sozialpolitische Entscheidungen*.
[69] It is, therefore, wrong to ascribe to the Adenauer pension reform the intention to 'restore status differences'. See Esping-Andersen, *Three Worlds*, p. 25. In a number of respects, blue-collar workers were, for the first time, put on an equal footing with white-collar workers. See Michael Prinz, 'Die Arbeiterbewegung und das Modell der Angestelltenversicherung. Zu einigen Bedingungen für die besondere Bürgerlichkeit des Wohlfahrtsstaates in der Bundesrepublik', in Klaus Tenfelde, ed., *Arbeiter im 20. Jahrhundert* (Stuttgart: Klett-Cotta, 1991), pp. 435–60.
[70] For an overview, see Winfried Schmähl, 'Finanzverflechtung der gesetzlichen Rentenversicherung: interner Finanzausgleich und Finanzbeziehungen mit dem Bund sowie anderen Sozialversicherungsträgern', in Klaus-Dirk Henke and Winfried Schmähl, eds., *Finanzierungsverflechtung in der sozialen Sicherung* (Baden-Baden: Nomos, 2001), pp. 9–37; Klaus-Dirk Henke, 'Der parafiskalische Finanzausgleich, dargestellt am Beispiel der Gesetzlichen Krankenversicherung', in ibid., pp. 77–93.
[71] Frerich and Frey, *Handbuch der Geschichte der Sozialpolitik*, vol. I, pp. 52–53.

financial relief for the central state, because transfers from the relatively well-off white-collar workers' pension fund to the deficit-ridden blue-collar workers' scheme reduced the need for state subsidies from the general budget. Similar fiscal interests motivated the integration of miners' pension schemes.[72] Thus, the apparent picture of institutional fragmentation conceals an almost complete pooling of financial resources. With nationally uniform contribution rates, however, social insurance contributions developed more and more into national quasi-taxes. The high political barriers for tax legislation in Germany can then explain why subsequently much of Germany's fiscal adjustment to a more unfavourable economic environment after the first oil crisis in 1973 occurred through the adjustment of welfare state revenue and spending.

The most striking example of the often problematic interplay between the regulative idea of nationally uniform living conditions, the high degree of financial autonomy of the German welfare state and the particularistic fiscal interests of both central and state governments was provided by German unification in 1990.[73] On the one hand, German unification exemplified how the German 'unitary welfare state easily overcomes federalist dividing lines',[74] given the fact that much of the East's rapid catch-up in terms of living conditions and income has to be attributed to the operation of the German welfare state. On the other hand, German unification also demonstrated the price that had to be paid for this rapid catch-up, namely, a vast expansion of social spending.

Massive disparities existed between wages and labour productivity in the area of the 'old' Federal Republic and of the five new eastern Länder. However, the electoral appeal of a quick fix for eastern living standards without substantial tax increases or a significant growth in public debt made it more politically attractive to impose 'hidden' tax increases by way of substantial increases in social insurance contributions. But burdening the social insurance funds with the costs of German unification was not only the result of a populist 'read my lips' strategy on the part of a Kohl government motivated by an exceptional density (seventeen national, regional and local) of elections in the decisive year of unification, 1990.[75] The other side of the story is that in the process of unification the western Länder were quite successful in protecting their fiscal

---

[72] Ibid., vol. I, p. 51.
[73] Roland Czada, *Der Kampf um die Finanzierung der deutschen Einheit* (Cologne: MPIfG Discussion Paper, 1995).
[74] Oeter, *Integration und Subsidiarität*, p. 534, translation mine.
[75] Oliver Schwinn, *Die Finanzierung der deutschen Einheit* (Opladen: Leske & Budrich, 1997); Roland Sturm, 'Die Wende im Stolperschritt – eine finanzpolitische Bilanz', in Göttrik Wewer, ed., *Bilanz der Ära Kohl. Christlich-liberale Politik in Deutschland 1982–1998* (Opladen: Leske & Budrich, 1998), pp. 183–200; Roland Czada, 'Der Kampf

Table 6.3 *West–East transfers in billion DM, central and regional governments and social insurance funds (1991–1999)*

	1991	1992	1993	1994	1995	1996	1997	1998	1999	1991–99
Federal government	75.1	90.0	115.7	115.9	136.7	136.7	129.7	130.8	136.3	1066.9
States	5.3	5.7	10.3	13.5	11.2	11.3	11.6	11.5	11.6	92.1
Social insurance	18.7	34.2	23.0	29.8	33.3	30.9	34.7	31.9	36.0	272.2
Net total transfers	109.9	133.5	150.6	148.8	141.3	137.7	135.1	132.6	140.3	1229.9
Social insurance[1]	17.0	25.6	15.3	20.0	23.5	22.5	25.7	24.1	25.7	22.2

Note:[1] As percent of net total transfers
Source: With respect to transfers to the East, data differ. Table 6.3 relies on rather conservative estimates, taken from Joachim Ragnitz, 'Wie hoch sind die Transferleistungen für die neuen Länder?' (Halle: Institut für Wirtschaftsforschung, 2003). Stefan Bach and Dieter Vesper, 'Finanzpolitik und Wiedervereinigung – Bilanz nach 10 Jahren', *DIW Vierteljahreshefte* [special issue *Zehn Jahre deutsche Währungs-, Wirtschafts- und Sozialunion*; Berlin: Duncker & Humblot], vol. 69 (2000), no. 2, pp. 194–223, p. 203, report slightly higher numbers; again slightly different estimates are provided by the Deutsche Bundesbank 'Zur Diskussion über die öffentlichen Transfers im Gefolge der Wiedervereinigung', *Monatsbericht*, vol. 48 (1996), no. 10, pp. 17–31.

interests.[76] As table 6.3 shows, according to conservative estimates roughly a quarter of all financial West–East transfers in the wake of German unification had to be borne by the social insurance schemes, that is, ultimately, by the western contributors. West–East welfare transfers were more than three times higher than transfers out of the western states' budgets. This is a spectacular instance of the way in which federalist veto structures in taxation and revenue sharing (through the *Finanzausgleich*, the fiscal equalization scheme) translated directly into 'welfare state growth'.

As a consequence, contribution rates to social insurance schemes steeply increased and welfare state spending revealed a strong upward trend. Whereas the combined social insurance contribution rates of employers and employees amounted to around 35.6 per cent of net wages (up to an upper limit) in 1990, today they are at a substantial 42 per cent.[77] When it comes to real financial burdens, not nominal rates,

um die Finanzierung der deutschen Einheit', in Gerhard Lehmbruch, ed., *Einigung und Zerfall. Deutschland und Europa nach dem Ende des Ost-West-Konflikts* (Opladen: Leske & Budrich, 1995), pp. 73–102; Reimut Zohlnhöfer, *Die Wirtschaftspolitik der Ära Kohl* (Opladen: Leske & Budrich, 2001).

[76] Jens Altemeier, *Föderale Finanzbeziehungen unter Anpassungsdruck. Verteilungskonflikte in der Verhandlungsdemokratie* (Frankfurt-on-Main: Campus, 1999).

[77] Bundesministerium für Gesundheit [BMG], *Statistisches Taschenbuch* (http://www.bmgesundheit.de or since 2002 www.bmgs.bund.de), table 7.7.

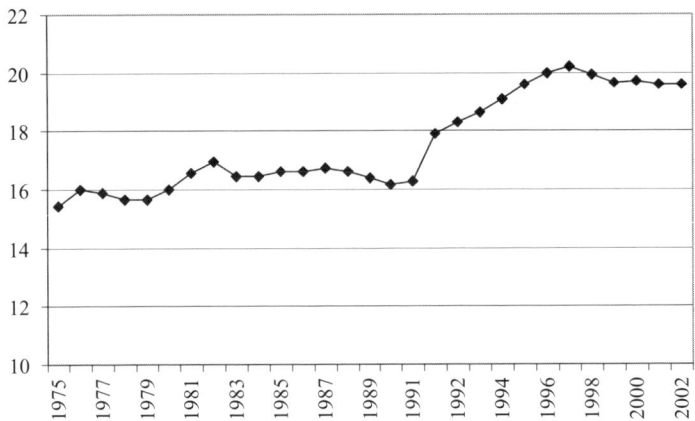

Source: BMG [Bundesministerium für Gesundheit], *Statistisches Taschenbuch* (Bonn and Berlin: BMG, http://bmgesundheit.de; since 2002 www.bmgs.bund.de), table 7.6.

Figure 6.1 Absolute volume of contribution payments of employers and employees as a percentage of GDP (1975–2002)

figure 6.1 shows that the overall financial welfare burden on employers and employees remained fairly stable over the 1980s, with even a small downward trend at the end of the decade, whereas after unification in 1990 employers and employees had to bear steeply increasing costs.

Yet, this is only a particularly flagrant example of what has been a much more long-term trend of political cost externalization at the expense of the contribution-financed welfare state – a trend that can be already observed in the Weimar period. In fact, since the worsening of general economic conditions after the first oil shock, German governments invariably have sought to shift costs on to the contribution-financed welfare state rather than taking the electorally unpopular and politically complicated step of raising taxes or of cutting expenditures.[78] From 1965 to 2002 combined revenue from taxes and social insurance contributions rose from 32.8 to 38.2 per cent of GDP, but whereas tax revenue decreased from

---

[78] Frank Nullmeier, 'Der Zugriff des Bundes auf die Haushalte der Gemeinden und Parafisci', in Hans Hermann-Hartwich and Göttrick Wewer, eds., *Regieren in der Bundesrepublik*, vol. IV, *Finanz- und wirtschaftspolitische Bestimmungsfaktoren des Regierens im Bundesstaat – unter besonderer Berücksichtigung des deutschen Vereinigungsprozesses* (Opladen: Leske & Budrich, 1992), pp. 147–80; Philip Manow and Eric Seils, 'The Employment Crisis of the German Welfare State', *West European Politics*, vol. 23 (2000), no. 1, pp. 137–60; Christine Trampusch, *Ein Bündnis für die nachhaltige Finanzierung der Sozialversicherungssysteme*, discussion paper (Cologne: Max Planck Institute for the Study of Societies, 2003).

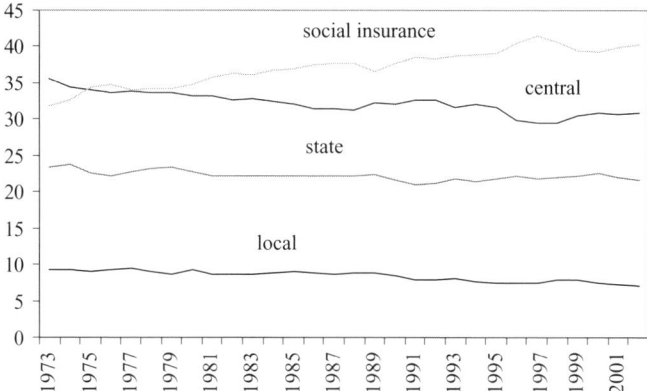

Source: OECD, *Revenue Statistics* (Paris: OECD, http://www.sourceoecd.org)

Figure 6.2 Total tax revenue, relative shares of central, state, local government and social security funds, Germany (1973–2002)

23 to 20.8 per cent during this period, revenue from social insurance contributions increased from 9.8 to 17.4 per cent, or nearly doubled.[79] As figure 6.2 reveals, the tax revenue of local and regional governments has remained relatively stable over the last thirty years. The major revenue shifts have taken place between the central state and the social insurance funds: 'insurance-based programmes . . . have absorbed a steadily growing share of social expenditures since 1970 . . . entirely tax-funded programmes . . . lost a lot of ground'.[80] German unification accelerated, but did not initiate, this process.

As figure 6.2 makes clear, there is indeed ample evidence of *expansionary* expenditure tendencies in German-style 'co-operative' federalism. These findings with respect to welfare state finance mirror the more general point that federalism can 'exacerbate collective action problems' and 'might undermine fiscal discipline' if the fiscal and political responsibilities of the different layers are not clearly separated from each other.[81] It is, therefore, hardly surprising that the veto point hypothesis, so strongly emphasized in the literature concerning the political consequences of

---

[79] Cf. Philip Manow and Thomas Plümper, *The Opportunity Costs of Welfare Reform: Fiscal Adjustment in the OECD 1972–1995* (Cologne: Max Planck Institute for the Study of Societies, 2003).

[80] Stephan Leibfried and Herbert Obinger, 'The State of the Welfare State: German Social Policy between Macroeconomic Retrenchment and Microeconomic Recalibration', *West European Politics*, vol. 26 (2003), no. 1, pp. 199–218.

[81] Rodden and Wibbels, 'Beyond the Fiction', pp. 495, 496.

federalism, does not seem to fit the German case very well. This is so despite the fact that Germany can be considered a 'critical case' for the veto point thesis, with a strong second chamber and the frequent occurrence of countervailing majorities.[82]

From 1972 to 1994 only thirty-four laws have been successfully blocked by the federal chamber, either because the majority in the Bundesrat exercised an absolute veto (N = 29) or because parliament abstained from overruling the federal chamber's suspending veto (N = 5). Only ten of the thirty-four laws had something to do with social policy, and none of them represented a major reform act.[83] This is not a particularly impressive demonstration of federalism's veto power. Of course, looking at outright legislative failure gives us only a small part of the picture. Since the impact of federal veto structures presumably lies in the fact that they have the capacity to 'water down' substantive reforms and force a government to agree on lowest common denominator policies, it is clearly not enough to focus exclusively on failed legislative initiatives. Even with only little strategic capacity, a government can anticipate resistance in the second chamber and will draft legislation accordingly, in order to avoid complete political stalemate. Therefore, any 'evidence' for the veto point thesis must be based on hard to prove and hard to falsify counter-factual reasoning of the kind: 'would government x have proposed a bill substantially different from the bill it introduced had it acted in a unicameral rather than a bicameral system?'

Stalemate politics can be motivated either by calculations of partisan advantage or by states' special interests. If we take into account the fact that the two mass-member parties, the German Social Democratic Party (SPD) and the Christian Democratic Party (CDU) are programmatically quite close to each other on questions of social policy,[84] the rarity of partisan-motivated policy blockade is not that surprising. In fact, almost all major social policy reform acts since 1949 have been enacted with the support of the major opposition party, regardless of whether this was the SPD or the CDU. This might not be seen as particularly surprising in the case of the generous expansion laws of the 1950s and

---

[82] Arend Lijphart, *Democracies. Patterns of Majoritarian and Consensus Government in Twenty-One Countries* (New Haven: Yale University Press, 1984), pp. 99–105; Money and Tsebelis, *Bicameralism*. In Germany the central government has enjoyed a political majority in the federal chamber for only nine of the thirty-two years since the end of the 'golden age' of the welfare state, from 1972 to the present. These 'happy years' of political alignment of the first and second chambers fell basically within the first two (and a half) terms of the Christian Democratic government under Chancellor Kohl, from 1982 to 1991.

[83] Schindler, *Datenhandbuch zur Geschichte*, pp. 2434–36.

[84] See for instance Budge *et al.*, eds., *Mapping Policy Preferences*, p. 235.

1960s. However, there was also a broad consensus between the SPD and the CDU in respect of many of the major retrenchment laws in the years following 1980, including the health reform of 1988, the pension reform of 1990 and the health reform of the second Schröder government. Moreover – and contrary to the 'new politics' of the welfare state thesis – the introduction of a completely new social insurance branch, the Long Term Care Insurance (LTCI) in 1994, two decades after the 'golden age' of welfare state expansion was over, also relied on consensus between Christian Democrats and Social Democrats. Indeed, in the case of long-term care, the conservatives were the initiators of expansionary reform.[85]

True, as Jens Alber has shown, broad political consensus is less likely if welfare cuts are on the agenda than if the legislation is expansionary,[86] a finding that appears trivial only as long as one does not fully recognize how much this tells us about the non-trivial fact that Social Democrats and Christian Democrats largely share a general pro-welfare state attitude. However, it is also the case that major legislative cost containment efforts have frequently been enacted by super-majorities. In international comparison, Germany is a country in which welfare retrenchment started early – already under social-democratic chancellor Schmidt in the second half of the 1970s – and where retrenchment 'actually was quite substantial'.[87] The health care sector and the pension insurance sector were both subjected to continuous cost containment measures.[88] As a welfare state spender, Germany had receded from a leading position to the middle-field by the late 1980s. German unification, then, once again supplied a strong expansionary momentum, but both before and after 1990 successful cost containment was thwarted by two other countervailing trends.

[85] The introduction of the LTCI is another example of cost-externalizing social policy at the expense of the welfare state. Financed in traditional Bismarckian fashion through contributions paid by employers and employees, the LTCI brought substantial financial relief to the budgets of the municipalities and states, since support for the handicapped, frail or elderly that previously had been financed by tax-financed social assistance was now to be covered by the new, 'fifth' social insurance branch. See Ulrike Götting, Karin Haug and Karl Hinrichs, 'The Long Road to Long-Term Care Insurance in Germany', *Journal of Public Policy*, vol. 14 (1994), no. 3, pp. 285–310.
[86] Jens Alber, *Der Sozialstaat in der Bundesrepublik 1950–1983* (Frankfurt-on-Main: Campus, 1989), p. 262, table 43.
[87] Leibfried and Obinger, 'State of the Welfare State', p. 214. See for further evidence, among many, Nico Siegel, *Baustelle Sozialpolitik. Konsolidierung und Rückbau im internationalen Vergleich* (Frankfurt-on-Main: Campus, 2002), chapter 9; Jens Alber, 'Der deutsche Sozialstaat im Licht international vergleichender Daten', in *Leviathan*, vol. 26 (1998), no. 2, pp. 199–227; Jens Alber, 'Recent Developments of the German Welfare State: Basic Continuity or Paradigm Shift?' (Centre for Social Policy Research, University of Bremen, ZeS Working Paper 6/2001).
[88] See also Sven Jochem, 'Reformpolitik im deutschen Sozialversicherungsstaat', in Manfred G. Schmidt, ed., *Wohlfahrtsstaatliche Politik. Institutionen, politischer Prozeß und Leistungsprofil* (Opladen: Leske & Budrich, 2001), pp. 193–226.

First, high and persistent mass unemployment, costly medical progress and – most recently – also the first impact of rapid population ageing have together operated to significantly increase the demand for social spending. Hence, cost containment was successful only in reducing the growth rate of expenditure. Second, and more important in the context of this analysis, cost-cutting had its main effects on the tax-financed state share of total social spending, but had much less impact on the contribution-financed share. In fact, the importance of contributory finance increased, since the central government sought to ease its own fiscal stress by shifting social spending obligations out of the public budget and into the special budgets of the social insurance funds, and by accepting (automatic) contribution hikes as substitutes for legislating unpopular and politically deadlocked tax hikes.

This last point is of particular importance since it highlights the important nexus between taxation and welfare state finance. The linkage helps to explain the otherwise puzzling combination of relatively successful cost containment before 1990 and significant cost increases thereafter. In principle, in response to fiscal stress the German government could either increase debt, cut costs or increase revenue. The strong Bundesbank and, after 1992, the Maastricht criteria have set quite clear limits to the debt option.[89] On the other hand, legislating tax hikes in order to raise revenue is not only notoriously unattractive in electoral terms, but, in the context of the German federalist system of joint taxation, strong bicameralism and frequent divided government,[90] also extremely complicated in partisan political terms. Welfare retrenchment did occur to some degree, but it was never sufficient to close the ever-widening revenue–expenditure gap. The welfare state provided a fiscal pressure valve in two respects. First, public budget cuts plus task delegation at the expense of social insurance funds reduced the fiscal involvement of the central state. Second, semi-automatic increases in social insurance contributions substituted for legislated tax hikes. This further diminished the importance of tax-financed social spending, with strongly regressive consequences. Social contributions are already levied from low incomes, and given that welfare transfers are either not taxed at all or if so, only at a very low level, income taxation does not correct for the regressive effects of the Bismarckian system. In terms of *net* social spending, Germany – on a par with Sweden – is still one of the world's most 'generous' welfare states

---

[89] See for the general argument Manow and Plümper, *Opportunity Costs of Welfare Reform*.
[90] In this context it seems worth mentioning that, only shortly after unification in October 1990, the Kohl government lost its majority in the upper house because of the Hessen elections in April 1991.

and yet is, at the same time, one of the world's least redistributive social policy systems.[91]

Inter-party consensus with respect to steady incremental retrenchment has not prevented fierce clashes between the government and the opposition on issues with a high electoral salience. The massive campaign of the Christian-democratic opposition against pension cuts in 1976 is an example, as is the campaign of the SPD against the retrenchment proposals of the Kohl government in 1996 (reduction of sick pay, a lowering of employment protection for small firms, pension cuts by the introduction of a 'demographic formula', an increase in retirement age, etc.). In 1976, as in 1996, electoral motives were clearly dominant. In 1998 the Social Democrats benefited from the fact that finally the Christian Democratic–liberal coalition had begun to engage in more than incremental tinkering with welfare state costs. For the first time, the Social Democrats' continuous lament that the Kohl government was following a neo-liberal course of deregulation could point to at least some evidence. Achieving office with the promise to modernize *Modell Deutschland* without a neo-liberal neglect of equality and social security, the Schröder government quickly delivered the promised 'counter-reform', that is, it undid the few retrenchment measures of the previous Christian Democratic–liberal administration.[92] It soon became clear, however, that this was not enough. Space prohibits a thorough description of all the reform measures, but it is fair to say that, taken together, the tax, pension, health and labour market reforms of the first and second Schröder governments cut much deeper into the existing structures of the German welfare state and political economy than did all the reforms enacted during the sixteen years of CDU–FDP rule.

If at all, only a modified version of the veto point theory is compatible with this finding, given that the red–green coalition only enjoyed a six months' majority status in the Bundesrat compared with the nine years of concurrent majorities in both houses during the Kohl

---

[91] Willem Adema, 'Net Social Expenditure', Labour Market and Social Policy Occasional Papers, no. 39 (Paris: OECD, 1999; http://www.olis.oecd.org./OLIS/1999DOC. NSF/LINKTO/DEELSA-ELSA-WD(99)3-CORR1). See Ganghof, *Wer regiert in der Steuerpolitik?*.

[92] For a (highly critical) overview of the welfare reforms of the first Schröder government, see Manfred G. Schmidt, 'Rot-Grüne Sozialpolitik (1998–2002)', in Christoph Egle, Tobias Ostheim and Reimut Zohlnhöfer, eds., *Das Rot-Grüne Projekt. Eine Bilanz der Regierung Schröder 1998–2002* (Opladen: Westdeutscher Verlag, 2003), pp. 239–58; see also the contributions by *Rose* (labour law), *Heinelt* (labour market), *Buhr* (social assistance), *Nullmeier* (pensions), *Bleses* (family), *Brandhorst* (health), *West* (education), *Leitner* (gender) and *Vogel/Wüst* (immigration) in Antonia Gohr and Martin Seeleib-Kaiser, eds., *Sozial- und Wirtschaftspolitik unter Rot-Grün* (Opladen: Westdeutscher Verlag, 2003).

chancellorship, from 1982 to 1991. Since April 1999 the Schröder government has been confronted with a hostile upper house, as had been the Kohl government from 1991 to 1998. How, then, can one explain their different reform records? Intense political competition between the two mass-membership parties, both of which had attempted to woo the pro-welfare median voter, would lead one to expect at best incremental changes, and more often, perhaps, simply political stalemate. Furthermore, one would expect governments to shy away from harmful measures or to take action only when the opposition can be brought on board, given that the many state elections (sixteen) spread over the parliamentary term provide strong political disincentives to any programme of painful reforms. Governments try to avoid unpopular cutbacks since they fear electoral punishment, which might result in the loss of power at the state level and, as a consequence, in an oppositional majority in the upper house.[93] Differences in reform intensity must therefore be mainly attributed to the changed party constellation: the Christian Democrats in government were electorally more vulnerable to the charge of being the 'grave-digger' of the welfare state. Now, in turn, the SPD is forced to be an initiator of reform, while the bourgeois parties find it difficult to 'leap-frog' the left by protecting the status quo.[94] What before 1998 was a situation of mutual stalemate has turned into an overbidding game in which the CDU attempts to top the reforms of the red–green coalition with ever more radical proposals.

Compared to antagonistic party competition, political gridlock in the federal chamber as a result of special Länder interests seems to occur more often. Case studies often stress that the veto power of the regional governments in the upper house has regularly prevented more far-reaching reform measures from being enacted. The health care sector in particular has regularly been mentioned as exemplifying this tendency.[95] However, even here, the empirical evidence is not particularly strong. Neither is it true that health sectors in which the states have direct interests

---

[93] Lehmbruch, *Parteienwettbewerb*; Simone Burkhart, *Parteipolitikverflechtung: der Einfluss der Bundespolitik auf Landtagswahlentscheidungen von 1976 bis 2002*, MPIFG Discussion Paper 2004/1 (Cologne: Max Planck Institute for the Study of Societies, 2004); Reiner Dinkel, 'Der Zusammenhang zwischen Bundes- und Landtagswahlergebnissen', *Politische Vierteljahresschrift*, vol. 18 (1977), nos. 2/3, pp. 348–59.
[94] Kitschelt, 'Partisan Competition and Welfare State Retrenchment'.
[95] Douglas Webber, 'Krankheit, Geld und Politik. Zur Geschichte der Gesundheitsreformen in Deutschland', *Leviathan*, vol. 16 (1988), no. 2, pp. 156–203; Douglas Webber, 'Zur Geschichte der Gesundheitsreformen in Deutschland, Teil II: Norbert Blüms Gesundheitsreformen und die Lobby', *Leviathan*, vol. 17 (1989), no. 2, pp. 262–300; Bernd Rosewitz and Douglas Webber, *Reformversuche und Reformblockaden im deutschen Gesundheitswesen* (Frankfurt-on-Main: Campus, 1990).

(hospital sector, pharmaceutical industry) have seen fewer cutbacks than other sectors, such as physicians' reimbursement, where the states' interests are weaker.[96] Nor is there much of a difference between social insurance branches in which the states have a veto position and those in which they have none. With respect to the first point, one can observe that in the hospital sector, sickness funds spent 29.4 per cent of their total outlays on hospitals in 1974, at the onset of the 'period of permanent austerity'. In 2000 they spend only slightly more, 32.2 per cent. Change in the pharmaceuticals sector is even less evident, with the share of total expenses remaining more or less stable with 23.2 per cent in 1974 and 24.7 in the year 2000.[97] As to social insurance branches, much the same picture emerges. In respect of most laws in the health care sector, the states have an absolute veto, since here legal measures usually affect regional administrative responsibilities in one way or another. This is typically not the case in the pension insurance scheme. Yet, if we compare the spending dynamics of these two sectors (both similarly affected by demographics), we cannot see much of a difference. The ratio of pension to health care expenditure in 1974 was 1.8. In 2000 it was at 1.73.[98] Thus, health care costs grew relative to pension costs, but not strongly enough to justify a convincing argument about the influence of federal veto points.

In more general terms, federalism as a veto point thesis has substantial problems in accounting for Germany's post-war welfare state development, given the fact that federal state structures seem to not have hindered Germany from becoming the most generous welfare state in western Europe in the 1950s and 1960s[99] (see table 6.4), and did not stand in the way of quite substantial retrenchment relative to other OECD nations in the period 1970–1990.

The overall German spending trajectory – first fast growth and very high spending levels, then moderate growth at medium spending levels and, finally, again strong expansion in the wake of German unification – is not well accounted for by the veto point thesis, which would predict below average growth in the golden times of welfare state expansion up to the mid-1970s, but, from that time onwards, above average growth rates due to the political difficulty of effecting substantial welfare retrenchment in federal polities.

[96] Cf. Marian Döhler and Philip Manow, *Strukturbildung von Politikfeldern. Das Beispiel bundesdeutscher Gesundheitspolitik seit den fünfziger Jahren* (Opladen: Leske & Budrich, 1997), pp. 60–72.
[97] *Statistical Yearbook, Federal Republic of Germany*, various years.   [98] Ibid.
[99] Alber, *Vom Armenhaus zum Wohlfahrtsstaat*; Alber, 'Der Deutsche Sozialstaat'.

Table 6.4 *Total social expenditures as a percentage of GDP in eleven countries (1950–1970)*

	Austria	Denmark	Finland	France	Germany (W)	UK	Italy	Netherlands	Norway	Sweden	Ireland
1950	12.57	7.84	6.64	n.c.d.	15.34	10.93	8.73	8.65	5.70	8.72	7.32
1955	15.76	9.40	6.77	n.c.d.	14.81	11.23	n.c.d.	9.55	7.44	9.89	n.c.d.
1960	15.74	11.09	8.55	n.c.d.	n.c.d.	12.53	12.22	11.93	9.35	10.94	9.00
1965	18.35	11.20	10.33	16.56	17.93	13.87	17.99	16.00	10.95	13.67	10.10
1970	17.86	15.69	12.48	n.c.d.	18.35	15.80	17.69	20.89	15.46	18.63	14.32

Source: ILO, *Costs of Social Security* (Geneva: ILO, various years).
Legend: n.c.d. = no comparable data for these years provided.

Conclusion

'Decentralized redistribution is self-defeating.'[100] In this sense, it is true that federalism and welfare states represent potentially antagonistic institutional settings (see the introductory chapter to this volume). Federalism can be a powerful institutional impediment to substantial redistribution. And this is exactly how federalism seems to have impacted on welfare state development in the English-speaking liberal nations that have systems of inter-state federalism. Yet, as the German case has made clear, as soon as political actors pursue extensive redistributive aims by superimposing nation-wide tax and transfer systems on still federally fragmented political accountability structures, the strategic logic of the interplay between federalism and the welfare state may change profoundly. Here instead, the diffusion of responsibilities and the incentives for shifting costs between central government, the states and the welfare state are conducive to an 'overgrazing of the fiscal commons', especially if the welfare state is – as is the case in Germany – largely financed by contributions. Instead of the restrictive influence predicted by the standard versions of veto player theory, under these circumstances federalism leads to expansionary spending dynamics and a low degree of fiscal discipline. I have argued that federalist veto structures have played a role in Germany's welfare state development in the period of retrenchment, but in a way not foreseen in

---

[100] Rémy Prud'homme, 'The Dangers of Decentralization', *World Bank Research Observer*, vol. 10 (1995), no. 2, pp. 201–20, p. 202.

Germany: co-operative federalism and overgrazing the commons   261

the literature. Given that the German states have a powerful veto position when it comes to legislation on joint taxes, which account for 70 per cent of total tax revenue, but have no say in matters of social insurance contributions, increasing welfare state revenue offered relief in a situation of severe fiscal stress – particularly, but not exclusively, in the wake of German unification.

Founded with the aim of furthering national unification, the German welfare state indeed has become the great national unifying institution. The feedback effects of the welfare state on both living conditions in Germany and on the functioning of German federalism itself are enormous. The welfare state, together with the national tax system, has effectively prevented inter-regional economic competition. These national achievements have been so successful that proposals to reverse the trend and to introduce what has been called federalist competition not only in education and taxation but also in the welfare state arena have become ever more articulate.[101] Competition would also – so it is hoped – reintroduce experimentation and learning into German federalism, two things that are now largely absent because of nation-wide regulation and encompassing fiscal balancing schemes.[102] However, political support for these calls for welfare state devolution is weak and will remain so in the future, given that the relevant actors are fully aware of the distributional consequences. The new eastern states, as well as the less affluent northern states, can only lose from political and fiscal devolution. Thus, even if, in Germany, federalism does not hinder welfare retrenchment, it still makes it difficult to effect major structural reforms. In Germany's 'grand coalition state',[103] there is still no alternative to 'negotiated' change.

If we refer back to the two 'points of qualification' noted in the introduction, the preceding paragraphs have shown that neither of the implicit

---

[101] Cf. Ursula Münch, 'Entflechtungsmöglichkeiten im Bereich der Sozialpolitik. Zur Diskussion um eine Föderalisierung der Sozialversicherung', in Ursula Männle, ed., *Föderalismus zwischen Konsens und Konkurrenz* (Baden-Baden: Nomos, 1998); Rainer Pitschas, 'Regionalisierung der Rentenversicherung aus verwaltungswissenschaftlicher Sicht', *Neue Zeitschrift für Sozialrecht*, vol. 3 (1994), no. 7, pp. 289–96; Hans Jürgen Papier, 'Die Regionalisierung der gesetzlichen Rentenversicherung aus verfassungsrechtlicher Sicht', *Neue Zeitschrift für Sozialrecht*, vol. 4 (1995), no. 6, pp. 241–44.

[102] Hence it is not surprising that the only instances of policy experimentation and mutual learning are to be found *outside* the traditional social insurance framework, especially in local care for the elderly and local social assistance. See Josef Schmid, *Die CDU, Organisationsstrukturen, Politiken und Funktionsweisen einer Partei im Föderalismus* (Opladen: Leske & Budrich, 1990); Jens Alber and Martin Schölkopf, *Seniorenpolitik. Die soziale Lage älterer Menschen in Deutschland und Europa* (Amsterdam: Fakultas, 1999).

[103] Manfred G. Schmidt, 'Germany – The Grand Coalition State', in Joseph M. Colomer, ed., *Political Institutions in Europe* (London: Routledge, 2002), pp. 57–94.

assumptions of 'inter-state competition' or 'incongruence of political preferences' have had much bite in the German case. It is, therefore, hardly surprising that German federalism has not prevented the Bismarckian welfare state from becoming one of the world's most expensive, generous and encompassing systems of social provision and its favoured revenue-collecting mechanism a para-state within the state. Correspondingly, and contrary to the received wisdom of the federalism thesis, federalism has also not prevented substantial retrenchment in the era of the 'new politics' of the welfare state.

7 Switzerland
The marriage of direct democracy and federalism

HERBERT OBINGER, KLAUS ARMINGEON, GIULIANO
BONOLI AND FABIO BERTOZZI

Introduction

Swiss federalism shares attributes with both United States and German federalism. As in the United States, an essential goal of the federalist project is to allow for differences in living conditions among the constituent territorial units. When the Swiss cantons formed a federal state in 1848, they did so on the basis of a constitutional structure that was designed to allow for diversity of social, economic and political organization at the cantonal level. On the other hand, Swiss federalism is hardly competitive. As in Germany, cantons co-operate with each other, and above all the federal government co-operates with the cantons because it relies on their administration for the implementation of most policies. Finally, as in both the US and Germany, the emergence of national social security systems has shifted power and resources from the local and the state to the federal level.

Unsurprisingly, this peculiar institutional context has contributed to the shaping of social policy over the years. Overall, we can identify three different forces underlying the territorial dimension of the Swiss welfare state and working in different directions: first, a unifying and centralizing force related to the rise of the national welfare state in response to the imperatives of industrialization and societal modernization in the nineteenth and twentieth centuries; second, a unifying – but not centralizing – force arising from the co-operation of cantonal and local administrations with a fiscally and politically weak central government; and, third, a force of diversity and decentralization stemming from the combination of cantonal competencies with different resources, polities, politics and policies.

Analyzing these forces helps us to address key questions concerning the impact of federalism on the development of federal social policy. Did Swiss federalism hinder the rise of the national welfare state, and has it had an influence on the retrenchment or consolidation of Swiss social policy in recent years? And what have been the repercussions of federal social policy reform on cantonal social policy? In Switzerland, compared with other federations, the scope of social policy at a sub-national level is considerable. Cantons and municipalities still have important social policy responsibilities and federal schemes are implemented by state and local administrations. Hence cantonal and local welfare state policies can have a major effect on public welfare, in particular, for those in dire need and requiring social assistance. Thus, it is necessary to address a second set of questions. How big are the differences in cantonal and municipal social policy and how can these differences be explained?

The first set of questions are those explored by this volume as a whole and, for this reason, are our primary concern also. These questions require a historical approach, and our analysis commences with the passing of Switzerland's first federal social policy legislation – the Federal Factory Act of 1877 – and takes us up to the late 1990s, which saw an unprecedented level of activity in the social policy arena. In contrast, questions concerning cantonal differences require a cross-sectional approach. Space limitations make it impossible to do more in this instance than provide a summary description of cantonal differences and discuss statistical findings that have attempted to account for such variation. Our study is guided by two hypotheses, which can be integrated into a more general proposition. According to the first hypothesis, federalism has served as a long-term counterweight to the trajectory of national welfare state development in Switzerland: it has hindered both the growth and the retrenchment of the welfare state. The second hypothesis is that within the interstices of the social security system so created, federalism has contributed to the emergence of a rich regional diversity of welfare state provision. The general proposition is that federalism matters not only for the development and structural make-up of welfare state schemes, but also for the welfare of citizens – particularly in areas where the cantons have a degree of autonomy in policy development.

Switzerland: a multi-tiered welfare state

As in other advanced industrial countries, the core programmes of the welfare state in Switzerland are decided upon and administered at the national level. In the key areas of pensions, health care, accident insurance and unemployment insurance, the federal government plays by far

Table 7.1 *Responsibilities of the cantons and the federation for social security*

Programme	Type of programme	Legislation	Funding	Implementation
Old age and survivors insurance	Universal insurance	Federation	Federation (Cantons)	Federation and cantons
Disability insurance	Universal insurance	Federation	Federation (Cantons)	Federation and cantons
Supplementary benefits	Universal insurance/ means-tested	Federation	Federation (Cantons)	Cantons
Unemployment insurance	Social insurance	Federation	Federation (Cantons)	Federation and cantons
Accident insurance	Social insurance	Federation	Federation (Cantons)	Federation
Health care insurance	Universal insurance	Federation	Federation and cantons	Federation and cantons
Family allowances	Social insurance	Cantons (Federation)	Cantons (Federation)	Cantons (Federation)
Unemployment assistance	Means-tested	Cantons	Cantons	Cantons
Social assistance	Means-tested	Cantons	Cantons	Cantons

Source: Herbert Obinger, *Politische Institutionen und Sozialpolitik in der Schweiz* (Frankfurt: Lang, 1998).

the most prominent role both in terms of funding and decision-making. Most funding is contributory, but tax income, in particular revenue from value-added tax, is also used to finance federal schemes. Even though the cantons contribute to the implementation and funding of these programmes, their direct involvement in these policy areas is rather limited (tables 7.1 and 7.2). These programmes constitute the core of Swiss social policy, both from a historical perspective and with regard to the sheer size of transfer payments. One would, therefore, imagine that the emergence of the modern welfare state would have created similar conditions of living across all the twenty-six federated states and the approximately 3,000 municipalities in Switzerland.

However, a closer examination of Swiss social policy, including those programmes – such as social assistance or family allowances – directly controlled by the cantons, reveals a rather different picture. Cantons and communes pursue welfare policies of their own, adding to and interacting

Table 7.2 *Social expenditure by administrative level as a percentage of total spending for each category (1990–1998)*

Category	Year	Federation	Cantons	Municipalities
Total social expenditure	1990	55.0	28.7	16.3
	1995	57.7	26.0	16.3
	1998	58.4	27.3	14.3
Old age insurance[a]	1990	83.8	12.7	3.5
	1995	83.4	13.5	3.0
	1998	84.5	12.4	3.1
Disability insurance[a]	1990	75.3	19.9	4.8
	1995	73.1	22.1	4.8
	1998	75.0	19.8	5.3
Health care insurance	1990	63.6	30.8	5.6
	1995	86.8	9.6	3.5
	1998	64.4	29.2	6.4
Other social insurances[b]	1990	32.7	42.1	25.2
	1995	23.9	42.2	33.9
	1998	42.3	40.8	16.9
Social assistance 1 (wide definition)[c]	1990	25.2	44.5	30.3
	1995	27.1	37.9	35.0
	1998	31.0	35.5	33.5
Social assistance 2 (narrow definition)[d]	1990	0	70.1	29.9
	1995	0	41.8	58.2
	1998	n.d.[e]	n.d.[e]	n.d.[e]

[a] Public contributions, without employers' contributions.
[b] Includes old age and disability complementary benefits, unemployment insurance, accident insurance and family benefits funds.
[c] Includes assistance to old people, help to the needy, labour offices, help to Swiss in foreign countries and other assistance tasks.
[d] Includes only help to the needy.
[e] n.d. = no data available.
Source: Bundesamt für Sozialversicherung, *Schweizerische Sozialversicherungsstatistik 1999 und 2001* (Berne: Eidgenössische Drucksachen-und Materialzentrale).

with federal social policy. Due to these sub-federal policies, living conditions and social security schemes differ across cantons and even communes within a state. The importance of sub-federal policy arises from four strongly institutionalized features of the practice of Swiss federalism.

The first key feature is that the federal state is not entitled to legislate in an area of policy unless it is explicitly permitted to do so by the federal constitution. Inclusion of new federal competencies in the federal constitution, especially in the field of welfare, has proved to be a difficult political process. Any proposal to extend federal powers must be accepted in a nation-wide referendum and in a majority of the cantons, that is, in a majority of cantons there must be majorities in favour of the amendment. In the past, this constitutional provision has frequently frustrated social reform. Moreover, even where the federal state has obtained the right to legislate in a new (social) policy area, unsatisfied voters can still use the referendum to challenge the policy initiatives of the federal government.[1] As a result of the weak institutional capabilities of the federal government, it was the communes and the cantons that first established social security safety nets, rather than the federal state.[2]

A second feature, contrasting with practice in both Austria and Germany, is that the Swiss constitution allows for substantial regional differences in income tax levels and in the delivery of public services. Hence, it is up to cantonal and communal governments to decide whether to provide benefits above and beyond those available to all citizens through the federal social security system.

The third feature is the strong bias in favour of a lean federal state. Swiss voters have always been very reluctant to give fiscal powers to the federal state. Apart from the contributions of the various social security schemes regulated at the federal level, the federal state has no permanent income from direct taxes. There is a federal income tax, but this is only temporary and dependent on the periodic approval of parliament and voters.

The fourth and final distinctive feature of Swiss federalism is that the federal government is very largely dependent on cantonal and communal public administrations, since cantonal and communal public offices implement the vast bulk of federal social policy. The reliance on local administrative bodies to implement federal policies is to a large extent due to the absence of a large federal administration.[3] In implementing such policies, sub-federal administrations have little leeway. Still more important is the fact that they are the interface between citizens and the welfare

---

[1] Giuliano Bonoli, 'Switzerland: Institutions, Reforms and the Politics of Consensual Retrenchment', in Jochen Clasen, ed., *Social Insurance in Europe* (Bristol: Policy Press, 1997), pp. 107–29; Giuliano Bonoli, 'Switzerland: Stubborn Institutions in a Changing Society', in Peter Taylor-Gooby, ed., *Welfare States under Pressure* (London: Sage, 2001), pp. 123–46.

[2] As will be argued below, pre-existing forms of social protection at the local level have had a strong impact on the development of the federal welfare state. Local bodies have often exerted strong opposition to the transfer of competencies to the federal level; therefore, local interests have had to be appeased in order to buy off opposition. See also Herbert Obinger, *Politische Institutionen und Sozialpolitik in der Schweiz* (Frankfurt: Lang, 1998).

[3] Hanspeter Kriesi, *Le Système politique suisse* (Paris: Economica, 1995).

state. Often there is close collaboration – or even identity – between those parts of the administration implementing, respectively, federal or sub-federal policies. Moreover, cantons are also involved in the financing of federal schemes.

As a result of this very unusual institutional set-up, differences across cantons can be substantial in many aspects of social policy. Health insurance is a case in point. In Switzerland, health care coverage is not provided directly by the state or another public body, but by a large number of private health insurance funds. The legal framework within which these funds operate is provided by federal law. Since 1994 affiliation to a health insurance fund has been compulsory, and insurance premiums, which are not income-related, cannot differentiate according to risk levels. Furthermore, the funds are not allowed to make a profit. But the funds do operate on a cantonal basis, so there is substantial cantonal variation in premium levels. In 2001 the average monthly premium for exactly the same level of coverage ranged from CHF 145 in Appenzell Inner Rhodes to CHF 336 in Geneva.

Differences exist in other fields of social policy, too. In respect of social assistance, student grants and child benefits, the cantons are the major providers. In the latter case, the federal government has the power to provide benefits, but only exercises it in respect of child benefits to farmers. For the rest of the population, each canton is entirely responsible for the administration of this programme, and, as one would expect, there are significant inter-cantonal variations in the coverage and level of benefits. In all but one canton (Valais), child benefits are provided on a contributory basis. The self-employed are included in only ten cantons. In addition, nine cantons supplement the federal child benefit provided for farmers. Benefits levels also vary considerably: in 2001 the maximum monthly benefit available ranged from CHF 150 in Zurich and in Argovia to CHF 378 in Valais.

The result of this complex multi-tiered web of welfare provisions is that the relationship between individuals and the welfare state occurs on different levels. Every Swiss person, throughout his or her life, will almost certainly experience contact with both the cantonal and the federal tier of the welfare state. Another consequence of multiple tiers is that the life experiences of some Swiss citizens – given the extent of cantonal differences – can vary substantially from one canton to the next insofar as their access to non-employment-based income streams and social services is concerned. Indeed, it is possible to argue (see below) that, at a cantonal level, Switzerland is unique in possessing a range of different welfare state regimes. Cantonal welfare regimes are a consequence of the interaction between federal legislation and cantonal provision. Although the federal provision of core social programmes and federally regulated labour law provides strong elements of uniformity, these differences are real enough. As will be seen, the distinctiveness of cantonal welfare state regimes is at its greatest in the areas of family policy and poverty alleviation, where a federal presence is conspicuous by its absence.

The long road to a federal welfare state

Constitutional framework

North-eastern Switzerland was an area of early industrialization. Socio-economic transformation occurred in the context of a political system that was distinguished by a substantial fragmentation of power. Switzerland's political system, as enshrined in the Federal Constitution of 1848, was initially a majoritarian democracy with institutional checks and balances built in. Parliament was strictly bicameral and constitutional amendment required a mandatory referendum. Parliament and the federal government were dominated by the Radical Party until 1918. Political authority was shared between a weak central state and twenty-five (today twenty-six) cantons. The Federal Constitution of 1848 did not provide the federal government (Federal Council) with a mandate for social policy legislation. Though committed to liberal ideas, the Radicals, the dominant party of the era, advocated strong federal government, while the Catholic Conservatives favoured subsidiarity and opposed Radical initiatives for greater secularization.

In 1874 the Federal Constitution was revised and federal powers were slightly enhanced. In addition, an optional referendum and federal judicial review of cantonal laws were introduced. By collecting 30,000 (today 50,000) signatures, petitioners could automatically subject any parliamentary bill or decree to a referendum. In 1891 a constitutional initiative was introduced by which 50,000 (today 100,000) citizens can propose an alteration to the federal constitution. The optional referendum proved to be a powerful instrument for vested interests and political minorities, such as the Catholic Conservatives, to attack legislation initiated by the incumbent Radicals, who advocated a strong federal government. To prevent a referendum battle, political minorities and organized interests of business and labour were either formally or informally incorporated into the federal decision-making process. Hence the optional referendum has gradually changed the nature of Swiss politics, with the initially prevailing majoritarian democracy gradually replaced in piecemeal fashion by consociational practices, which became developed to their fullest extent in the years following World War Two.[4]

One element of consensus democracy is federalism. The cantons have several formal and informal means of exerting influence on the federal policy-making process. First, they are frequently consulted during the pre-parliamentary decision-making process. Initially a rather informal procedure, this consultation has been enshrined in the Constitution since 1947 and gives the cantons a voice at the early stages of policy formation. Second, both houses of parliament have equal powers. However, bicameralism is incongruent, since the houses are elected in different ways. In contrast to the National Council, which has been elected according to proportional principles since 1918, the Council of States is composed of forty-six delegates, who are directly elected on a majority basis. The Senate principle leads to an overrepresentation of small and mostly rural cantons, which are overwhelmingly strongholds of the Catholic Conservatives. Bicameral disagreements in law-making are, first and foremost, due to differences in the partisan complexion of the two houses, and are a consequence of different electoral systems and the associated strategic behaviour of the bourgeois parties. Thus, the Council of States' preference for more liberal economic and social policies[5] is largely attributable to the overrepresentation of bourgeois parties. Finally, direct democracy substantially strengthens the power of veto available to the constituent units. Constitutional initiatives as well as the mandatory referendum require the approval of voters nationally *and* in a majority of the cantons. Again, the small and mainly conservative Catholic cantons in the German-speaking parts of the country benefit greatly from this rigid constitutional amendment procedure.[6] Although the provision has so far been used only once, in principle as few as eight cantons can choose to initiate an optional referendum opposing federal bills.

Advancing from defeat to defeat: Swiss social policy, 1874–1939

According to the Federal Constitution as amended in 1874, the cantons were responsible for almost all matters of social policy. In addition, the central state had very limited taxing powers. Until the outbreak of World

---

[4] Wolf Linder, *Schweizerische Demokratie. Institutionen-Prozesse-Perspektiven* (Berne: Haupt, 1999); Leonhard Neidhart, *Plebiszit und pluralitäre Demokratie. Eine Analyse der Funktion des schweizerischen Gesetzesreferendums* (Berne: Francke, 1970).
[5] Annina Jegher, *Bundesversammlung und Gesetzgebung* (Berne: Haupt, 1999).
[6] Wolf Linder and Adrian Vatter, 'Institutions and Outcomes of Swiss Federalism: The Role of the Cantons in Swiss Politics', *West European Politics*, vol. 24 (2001), no. 1, pp. 95–122, p. 98.

War One, its revenues were based mainly on tariffs, while the cantons had the power to levy direct taxes. Under section 34 of the Federal Constitution of 1874 the federal government was only empowered to regulate working conditions in factories. The federal government immediately made use of federal jurisdiction in this field and enacted a series of federal laws that made Switzerland a pioneer in terms of labour protection. Based on the 1877 Federal Factory Act, the working day for industry was restricted to eleven hours and child labour was prohibited. A liability law was enacted in 1881 and extended in 1887. This obliged employers to pay compensation to injured factory workers. In 1911 the Code of Obligations established a base for collective labour agreements.

In spite of these early advances, from the time of the enactment of the Federal Factory Act, it took the federal state another seventy years to acquire the constitutional mandate for legislating in respect of all branches of social security. The federal government was first entrusted with the right to enact health and accident insurance in 1890. Thirty-five years later, in 1925, it was given the right to legislate on old age, survivors' and disability insurance. In 1945 the federal government was empowered to regulate maternity insurance as well as family allowances. Finally, unemployment insurance became a central state responsibility in 1947. The pace at which benefits were centralized made the country a welfare state laggard compared to the majority of other western nations.

In what follows, we argue that early local policy pre-emption and the interaction of direct democracy with fragmented policy authority were crucial determinants of Switzerland's belated social policy centralization. Federal institutions substantially increased the number of actors involved in social policy-making, while the mechanisms of direct democracy provided opportunities for anti-welfare interests to challenge expansive social policies. As a result, policy-making in Switzerland is characterized by a protracted decision-making process, since compromise among many interests is necessary in order to avert a referendum.

This time lag built into the Swiss policy process was further extended where a referendum could not be prevented. Between 1874 and 2000 Swiss voters had to decide on sixty-four social policy proposals, including twenty-seven optional referenda.[7] This latter instrument decisively blocked the early take-off of the Swiss welfare state. Exclusively launched by parties of the right and/or interested business organizations, the optional referendum blocked or delayed core programmes such as health

---

[7] Herbert Obinger and Uwe Wagschal, 'Zwischen Reform und Blockade: Plebiszite und der Steuer- und Wohlfahrtsstaat', in Manfred G. Schmidt, ed., *Wohlfahrtsstaatliche Politik* (Opladen: Leske & Budrich, 2001), pp. 90–123.

insurance and old age pensions before World War Two. By contrast, the political left failed in its attempt to catalyze social policy via constitutional initiatives. All nineteen initiatives launched by the Social Democrats and trade unions between 1891 and 1999 were rejected, although some of them have indirectly accelerated programme adoption in the post-war period, when the booming economy enabled the authorities to respond to bottom-up initiatives.[8] Direct democracy has also influenced the shape of the Swiss welfare state. Given that the absence of comprehensive federal social policy resulting from these referendum defeats was compensated for by private welfare and occupational benefits, the evidence supports the view that the use of the referendum procedure has crucially reshaped the public–private divide in benefit provision and geared social policy towards a liberal trajectory.

Local policy pre-emption
In the absence of federal jurisdiction in the 1880s, social security programmes at the local level were established both by the cantons, cities and municipalities and by friendly societies, trade unions and entrepreneurs. Local policy pre-emption led to a patchwork of decentralized social security arrangements, which differed markedly from one another in terms of funding, organization and levels of benefit provision. The regulation of working time and working conditions was the first realm of the local social policy initiative. The canton of Glarus had regulated working hours for adults as far back as 1846. In the 1860s the more industrialized cantons – Argovia, Glarus, Schaffhausen and Basle – established Factory Acts that paved the way for the Federal Factory Act in 1877. Since the federal state had only the power to regulate working conditions in factories, the cantons were responsible for all other categories of employees. Between 1887 and 1912 almost all the cantons enacted labour protection legislation.[9]

In the late nineteenth century Swiss cities established the first public unemployment compensation funds in Europe. The capital Berne established a non-compulsory unemployment compensation fund in 1893. Similar initiatives occurred in Zurich, St Gall and other Swiss cities.[10] Berne was also first in establishing a public employment agency in 1888.

---

[8] Herbert Obinger, 'Federalism, Direct Democracy, and Welfare State Development in Switzerland', *Journal of Public Policy*, vol. 18 (1998), no. 3, pp. 241–63, p. 256.

[9] Erich Gruner and Hans-Rudolf Widmer, 'Arbeiterschutz', in Erich Gruner, ed., *Arbeiterschaft und Wirtschaft in der Schweiz, 1880–1914*, 3 vols. (Zurich: Chronos, 1987–88), vol. I, pp. 445–64, p. 462.

[10] Georg Zacher, *Die Arbeiter-Versicherung in der Schweiz* (Berlin: Verlag der Arbeiterversorgung, 1899); Naum Reichesberg, *Die Arbeitslosenversicherung in der Schweiz* (Berne: Scheitlin, Spring & Cie, 1906).

The cities of Basle, Schaffhausen, Biel and Winterthur followed in the 1890s. An early health initiative was the establishment by the city of Lucerne of a compulsory sickness fund for workers. The city of Basle also provided old age pensions to civil servants, while the cantons of Neuchâtel and Vaud established non-mandatory universal old age pension schemes in 1898 and 1907 respectively. Glarus created the first mandatory cantonal pension scheme in 1916. However, many cities and cantons remained inactive; they either lacked the incentive to act because workers at the end of their working lives were entitled to receive welfare in their home cantons, or they felt too weak to do so.[11] In still other cantons, social policy initiatives were frustrated by the use of the referendum procedure. The people rejected public unemployment insurance in the city of Basle in 1900, old age pensions were rejected in Geneva in 1910 and the introduction of minimum wages failed in both Berne (1898) and Zurich (1899).

Nevertheless, the number of mutual compensation funds increased from 652 in 1865 to 2,006 in 1903, covering almost 500,000 people at the turn of the twentieth century. These mostly local social security institutions faced similar problems. Most of them suffered from insufficient membership, so that a pooling of risk was not guaranteed. In 1886 every second sickness fund had less than 100 members; as of 1903, Berne's unemployment compensation fund had only 543 members. Adverse selection and the collapse of unemployment compensation funds were natural consequences. This was the starting point for a greater cantonal role in social policy: cantons gradually began to provide subsidies to existing private and occupational funds in order to put the schemes on a sounder financial footing.

Reining in the social insurance state
In the 1880s the malfunctioning of the Federal Liability Act – many injured workers did not receive compensation or did not claim it, in order to avoid dismissal – together with the exemplary effects of German and Austrian social insurance legislation had convinced the exclusively radical-democratic federal government to adopt a new approach to social policy by advocating health and accident insurance. However, federal social policy intervention faced various problems. Given the federation's lack of social policy competence, the legislation process was necessarily split into two stages. The first step was to pass constitutional amendments empowering the federal authorities to undertake social security

[11] Tonio Bödiker, *Die Arbeiterversicherung in den Europäischen Staaten* (Leipzig: Duncker & Humblot, 1895).

legislation. This reallocation of jurisdiction proved to be difficult because each amendment was subject to an obligatory referendum, and the Swiss have always been hesitant to entrust the federal government with new powers.[12] Moreover, the political actors negotiating the constitutional changes attempted to predetermine the basic design of the proposed social insurance schemes, at least in respect to coverage, funding and organization. As a result, the first phase of legislation was furiously contested and often extended over several years. Nevertheless, these protracted negotiations proved to be successful: none of the six mandatory referendums associated with the reallocation of jurisdiction in social insurance failed.[13]

However, acceptance of a constitutional amendment in a mandatory referendum did not automatically result in a new federal policy. In order for this to occur, the government needed to adopt so-called 'implementing legislation'. This second stage of social policy legislation was even more contested. Early policy pre-emption at the local level was a major impediment to achieving far-reaching policy changes. Given the 'patchwork quilt' nature of local social security schemes, the federal government had a limited degree of freedom to replace these arrangements. Since many interests had already crystallized around the existing decentralized social programmes, and because local social policies were associated with sunk costs and created a source of political support and legitimacy, the providers of these programmes were reluctant to accept federal policy intervention.[14] The optional referendum proved to be a powerful veto point through which vested interests were able to influence the federal policy-making process. Consequently, the federal government was forced to take into consideration the design of local social security arrangements and had to adjust federal programmes to prevailing patterns of social policy. This policy feedback resulted in the adoption of lowest common denominator solutions.

A case in point is the Federal Health and Accident Insurance Act. After the federal government obtained the power to enact health and accident insurance in 1890, the liberal Federal Councillor Ludwig Forrer submitted a bill, the *Lex Forrer*, which was strongly influenced by Bismarckian health and accident insurance.[15] Forrer's draft suggested a mandatory and

---

[12] Arnold Saxer, 'Die Entwicklung der Sozialversicherung in der direkten Demokratie', in Walter Rohrbeck, ed., *Aus der Privat- und Sozialversicherung des In- und Auslandes* (Berlin: Duncker & Humblot, 1951), pp. 222–51; Linder, *Schweizerische Demokratie*.
[13] Obinger and Wagschal, 'Zwischen Reform und Blockade', p. 110.
[14] Paul Pierson, 'Fragmented Welfare States: Federal Institutions and the Development of Social Policy', *Governance*, vol. 8 (1995), no. 4, pp. 449–78.
[15] Kurt Krumbiegel, *Die schweizerische Sozialversicherung insbesondere das Kranken- und Unfallversicherungsgesetz vom 13. Juni 1911 verglichen mit der entsprechenden deutschen Gesetzgebung* (Jena: G. Fischer, 1913).

predominantly contribution-based scheme of workers' insurance, which would be organized around public and semi-public sickness funds. A public accident insurance company was to be put in charge of mandatory accident insurance. The bill passed both houses of parliament almost unanimously.[16] Yet, existing private sickness funds argued that competition by public sickness funds would jeopardize business. Industry, small businesses and farmers opposed increasing non-wage labour costs, liberals rejected compulsory insurance, while workers disapproved of state supervision of self-administered mutual compensation funds. A referendum was launched by Catholic groups and right-wing forces, with the former strongly inclining to the subsidiarity principle and the latter branding the bill as both centralist and collectivist. In 1900 the *Lex Forrer* was rejected by the voters. The bourgeois federal government was fully aware of the interests backing the referendum.[17]

Six years after the *Lex Forrer* was rejected a second bill was drafted, which made far-reaching concessions to the opponents of the *Lex Forrer*: employers no longer had to pay contributions, the insured had to pay per capita premiums and farmers as well as small businesses were excluded from coverage. Compulsory insurance was abandoned, although the cantons were empowered to introduce compulsory insurance for certain groups. The federal government confined itself to providing positive incentives. The existing private sickness funds received federal subsidies if they guaranteed the minimum standards outlined in federal legislation. With respect to accident insurance, employers were released from contributory payments for non-occupational accidents. However, in order to prevent 'cream skimming' by private insurance companies, the monopoly of the Swiss National Accident Insurance Institute was preserved. This gave rise to a second referendum launched by a business interest organization. Nevertheless, the redrafted bill was adopted by voters in 1911. Health insurance commenced in 1914, while accident insurance became a reality in 1918.

This brief account of the adoption of health and accident insurance shows how policy change was not only delayed for nearly two decades, but also fundamentally affected by direct democracy. Specifically, the defeat of the *Lex Forrer* opened the way for a liberal framework law with universal coverage instead of an imitation of mandatory and class-based health insurance along Bismarckian lines. Employers were exempted from contributory payments so that the cost burden was shifted to the insured, who now had to pay per capita premiums and not the earnings-related contributions initially proposed. The defeat of the *Lex Forrer* crucially shaped

[16] Jürg H. Sommer, *Das Ringen um soziale Sicherheit in der Schweiz* (Diessenhofen: Rüegger, 1978).
[17] *Bundesblatt* 1906, vol. VI, p. 252.

subsequent policies. The emerging compromise, which was regarded as a provisional solution by the Federal Council at the time, built on the established patterns of health insurance, namely 'head premiums' and non-obligatory insurance, which furthered increasing returns,[18] and reinforced the legacy of locally generated social policies. Apart from one minor reform in 1964, all efforts to restructure health insurance were either stymied by conflicts between doctors and sickness funds on the one hand, or by leftist and bourgeois parties on the other.[19]

A further example of the mechanisms by which democratic federalism has impeded and delayed the adoption of social policy programmes is unemployment insurance. This delay can be explained by four factors: the absence of federal jurisdiction, strong policy feedback from local social security arrangements, institutional factors, and a lack of political will. Already in 1893, the Swiss labour movement launched a constitutional initiative to improve the position of the unemployed, either through federal unemployment insurance or by subsidizing existing private funds from the general budget. Yet, this initiative was decisively rejected by voters in 1894. In subsequent years the bourgeois federal government blocked federal unemployment insurance on the grounds of cost. Given the politics of non-decision at the federal level, the cantons began to provide subsidies to the existing unemployment compensation funds. By 1914 seven cantons had adopted the so-called Ghent system, that is, they provided public subsidies to privately run unemployment insurance schemes.[20] Initially on a provisional basis (until 1924), the central state stepped in and provided subsidies from 1916 onwards. Severe social tensions in the aftermath of World War One culminated in a general strike, which increased the pressure for political action.

In 1924 the first federal law dealing with unemployment compensation was enacted. Given limited federal powers in this field, the Federal Council enacted a framework law that anchored the Ghent system at the federal level. At this point the federal government limited its intervention to regulating minimum standards and to providing

---

[18] Increasing returns is a technical term in economics. It was adopted by the path dependency literature in political science to characterize a sequential policy process in which the costs of a policy change increase over time. See Paul Pierson, 'Increasing Returns, Path Dependency, and the Study of Politics', *American Political Science Review*, vol. 94 (2000), no. 2, pp. 251–67.

[19] Sommer, *Ringen um soziale Sicherheit*; Tony Erni, *Die Entwicklung des schweizerischen Kranken- und Unfallversicherungswesens* (Freiburg: Universitätsverlag Freiburg, 1980); Ellen M. Immergut, *Health Politics: Interests and Institutions in Western Europe* (Cambridge: Cambridge University Press, 1992).

[20] Hermann Dommer, 'Arbeitslosenfürsorge und Arbeitslosenpolitik, 1880–1914', Gruner, ed., *Arbeiterschaft und Wirtschaft*, vol. III, pp. 689–776, p. 767.

subsidies to the existing unemployment funds, expecting that federal subsidies would stimulate the creation of new unemployment funds at the local and cantonal level. However, the system was inadequately equipped to cope with soaring unemployment rates during the Great Depression. Hence a new constitutional initiative was launched to give the federal government powers to enact unemployment compensation, but like all social policy related constitutional initiatives this was rejected by voters in 1935.[21] A further initiative launched by the Swiss Trade Union Federation in 1936 was opposed by the government and was finally withdrawn in 1947.[22]

Decision-making with respect to the introduction of old age, survivors' and invalidity insurance reveals a somewhat different picture. As in the case of health insurance, federalism and direct democracy played a significant role in determining the policy output. Specifically, this example demonstrates not only how the federation's tax base was constrained by these institutions, but also how this, in turn, led to delays in and a reshaping of the relevant social policy legislation.

At the turn of the twentieth century, both the Radicals and Social Democrats had put the introduction of a general pension scheme on the political agenda. This proposal was rejected by the Federal Council on the grounds of cost.[23] However, facing social tensions in the wake of World War One, the government promised to introduce old age pension insurance. The proposed scheme involved mandatory old age, survivors' and invalidity insurance with universal coverage. However, the federal government tied both the introduction and the generosity of the programme to enhanced federal taxing powers.[24] Specifically, the federal government demanded new taxes on tobacco and beer, a federal inheritance tax, and the extension of the alcohol monopoly. Facing the recession of the early twenties, parliament cancelled the beer tax to protect the breweries. The enlargement of the alcohol monopoly was rejected at the ballot box in 1923,[25] while the cantons refused to cede jurisdiction of the inheritance tax to the central state. Given this situation, the federal government had to scale down the proposed project, and, instead, proceed with a piecemeal development of social insurance.[26] As a result, invalidity insurance was split off from old age and survivors' insurance to ensure that a minimum federal mandate for legislation could be adopted.

---

[21] Obinger, 'Federalism, Direct Democracy', p. 256.
[22] Oswald Sigg, *Die eidgenössischen Volksinitiativen 1892–1939* (Berne: Francke, 1978), p. 199.
[23] *Bundesblatt* 1919, vol. IV, p. 38.   [24] *Bundesblatt* 1919, vol. IV, p. 127 and pp. 149–50.
[25] Tobacco and beer tax were introduced in the early 1930s.
[26] *Bundesblatt* 1924, vol. II, p. 685.

After six years of discussion, the constitutional amendment, which empowered the federation to enact old age insurance, passed the obligatory referendum stage in 1925. The implementing bill, the *Lex Schulthess*, was submitted to pre-parliamentary consultation in 1928. Owing to insufficient tax revenues, benefits were watered down compared to a first draft of 1919. Contributions as well as benefits were flat-rate and significantly lower than the benefits provided by the existing private and public occupational pensions funds. These occupational pension funds date back to the late 1880s and experienced a substantial expansion in the 1920s, when approximately 150 new pension funds were established each year. In 1925 about 17.4 per cent of the labour force were covered by occupational pension schemes. Moreover, about 800,000 persons had life insurance at the time.[27] Hence, occupational pensions and private insurance were already well established when the *Lex Schulthess* was submitted to parliament for deliberation.

Like the *Lex Forrer*, the bill was easily approved by the two houses of parliament.[28] Despite this, right-wing groups, most of them located in the French-speaking cantons, launched a referendum against the *Lex Schulthess*. The Liberal and Catholic Conservative groups backing the referendum opposed compulsory insurance, which was characterized as *étatiste*, centralist and a step towards socialism. Since the *Lex Schulthess* was not designed to replace occupational pensions, employees who were already covered by occupational pensions also opposed the bill in order to avert 'double insurance'.[29] The Social Democrats supported the bill in order to salvage a solution of some kind, while the Communists joined the referendum committee because they considered the benefits on offer to be entirely inadequate. As a consequence, the referendum was backed by the extreme poles of the political spectrum. To provide an alternative to the *Lex Schulthess*, the right-wing opponents launched a constitutional initiative demanding the extension of public assistance rather than social insurance. This move forced the voters to choose between social insurance and social assistance. A majority favoured the latter and rejected the *Lex Schulthess* in 1931.

This defeat had two major consequences: first, the introduction of old age and survivors' insurance was delayed until 1948, while invalidity insurance was postponed even longer, until 1960. Second, social

---

[27] Martin Lengwiler, 'Das Drei-Säulen-Konzept und seine Grenzen: Private und berufliche Altersvorsorge in der Schweiz im 20. Jahrhundert', *Zeitschrift für Unternehmensgeschichte*, vol. 48 (2003), no. 1, pp. 29–47.
[28] Sommer, *Ringen um soziale Sicherheit*, p. 151.
[29] In particular, this held true for employees who were covered by public pension funds providing more generous benefits. See Lengwiler, 'Drei-Säulen-Konzept', pp. 37–41.

policy in the 1930s followed the trajectory outlined by the proponents of the constitutional initiative. During the Great Depression, the federal government provided grants to social assistance programmes and subsidized charitable foundations such as Pro Senectute, Pro Juventute and Pro Infirmis. This was one of the starting points for the peculiar public–private mix in Switzerland's social security system.[30] The defeat of the *Lex Schulthess* also had long-lasting implications for the public–private divide of benefit provision, because the lack of public pensions increasingly stimulated the growth of privately organized pension schemes. Once in place, occupational pensions filled the void ever more successfully and comprehensively, making for increasing returns and also encouraging lock-in effects. This process was accelerated when public old age insurance was rejected in 1931. The number of employees covered by occupational pension schemes increased from 258,000 in 1925 to 1,342,000 in 1966. From 1931 onwards it therefore became increasingly evident that public old age insurance would never be able to replace the manifold forms of pension provision that preceded state provision. Hence the 1931 referendum was a pivotal step in the progress towards the Swiss multi-pillar approach in pension policy that emerged in the 1970s (see below).

Into the 'golden age'

A different backdrop

The take-off of the Swiss welfare state took place against a political backdrop markedly different from that of the nineteenth century. As the previous section has shown, political minorities as well as vested interest groups were able to veto many reforms proposed by the Radicals. To prevent referenda and to avert policy stalemate, political minorities were gradually incorporated into the federal government (see table 7.3). This 'process of paradigmatic integration'[31] culminated in the 'magic formula' of 1959, which became the cornerstone of Switzerland's consensus democracy and which remained unchanged until 2003.

A similar process of integration occurred in the arena of industrial relations. The strong role of interest organizations in public policy-making dates back to the late nineteenth century. Facing a weakly developed federal bureaucracy, the federal government endorsed co-operation with business associations and delegated administrative tasks to the domain

---

[30] Danielle Butschi and Sandro Cattacin, 'The Third Sector in Switzerland: The Transformation of the Subsidiarity Principle', *West European Politics*, vol. 16 (1993), no. 3, pp. 362–79.
[31] Karl W. Deutsch, *Die Schweiz als ein paradigmatischer Fall politischer Integration* (Berne: Haupt, 1976).

Table 7.3 *Partisan complexion of the federal government (1848–2004)*

Party	1848–91	1891–1919	1919–29	1929–43	1943–53	1953–54	1954–59	1959–2003	Since 2003
Radicals (FDP)	7	6	5	4	3	4	3	2	2
Catholic Conservatives/ Christian Democrats (CVP)	–	1	2	2	2	2	3	2	1
Swiss People's Party (SVP)	–	–	–	1	1	1	1	1	2
Social Democrats (SPS)	–	–	–	–	1	–	–	2	2

Source: Quelle: Bundesamt für Statistik, *Statistisches Jahrbuch der Schweiz* (Berne: Verlag Neue Zürcher Zeitung, 1996), p. 369; updated by the authors.

of interest organizations.[32] Moreover, it was necessary to incorporate big business organizations and trade unions into the pre-parliamentary decision-making process in order to avoid referendum deadlocks. Since 1947 the interest organizations of capital and labour and the twenty-six cantons have had a constitutionally guaranteed right to be heard in the pre-parliamentary consultation process (*Vernehmlassungsverfahren*). In addition, experts affiliated to these interest organizations play an important role in drafting federal bills. As a result of the referendum threat, decision-making by majority rule was replaced one step at a time by consensual practices[33] and by a liberal version of corporatism.[34] More specifically, public policy-making in the post-war period has been shaped by the three highly interconnected bargaining arenas in which it takes place: a negotiation arena between the cantons and the federation, a bargaining arena comprising the political parties – the consociational forum – and, finally, the corporatist arena encompassing the interest organizations

---

[32] Leonhard Neidhart, *Plebiszit und pluralitäre Demokratie: Eine Analyse der Funktion des schweizerischen Gesetzgebungsreferendums* (Berne: Francke, 1970).

[33] Ibid.; Yannis Papadopulous, 'How Does Direct Democracy Matter? The Impact of Referendum Votes on Politics and Policy-Making', *West European Politics*, vol. 24 (2001), no. 1, pp. 35–58.

[34] Gerhard Lehmbruch, 'Die korporative Verhandlungsdemokratie in Westmitteleuropa', in Klaus Armingeon and Pascal Sciarini, eds., *Deutschland, Österreich und die Schweiz im Vergleich* (Zurich: Seismo, 1996), pp. 19–41; Klaus Armingeon, 'Swiss Corporatism in Comparative Perspective', *West European Politics*, vol. 20 (1997), no. 4, pp. 164–79. Note, however, that corporatist bargains did not include trade-offs between the 'social wage' and earnings growth. This pattern of corporatist deals, indicative of a system of social partnership, was not a feature of the Swiss consensus system.

of business and labour and the executive arm of government. Since a negotiation-based, decision-making logic applies to all three arenas, Switzerland is unlikely to suffer a policy stalemate stemming from clashing decision-making rationales in the federal and partisan arena.[35]

The take-off of the Swiss welfare state
Social policy during the immediate post-war years was crucially shaped by war-related policies. Facing the military threat of Nazi Germany and relying on extraordinary war powers, the federal government set up a contributory scheme for servicemen to compensate for their loss of earnings in periods of military service. In 1944 the federal government introduced family allowances for farmers. The unemployment compensation system was revised in 1942, since a substantial increase in unemployment was expected after the end of the war. Finally, federal taxing powers were enhanced during the war. The federal government for the first time gained, albeit on a temporary basis, a mandate to levy direct taxes. In 1941 an income tax and a federal sales tax were introduced.

Immediately after the end of the war the federal government obtained the power to legislate on family allowances and maternity insurance (1945) as well as unemployment insurance (1947). Facilitated by a war-induced wave of solidarity, the federal government quickly enacted old age pensions in 1946. The adoption of the Old Age and Survivors' Insurance Act was accelerated because the income compensation scheme for servicemen lost relevance after the war. Consequently, the revenues, funding principles and organization of the servicemen's programme were used to run the old age and survivors' insurance. Although right-wing groups launched a referendum, the bill was approved by the voters and came into force in 1948. Cantonal pension schemes, especially that of Glarus, together with Britain's Beveridge Plan, served as blueprints for federal legislation. Swiss old age and survivors' insurance is designed to be a compulsory general public insurance (*Volksversicherung*). Initially, the insurance only provided flat-rate benefits. The scheme is funded by employer and employee contributions and is highly redistributive. The central state and to a lesser extent the cantons provide subsidies that are based on revenues from tobacco and alcohol taxes. Pushed by several constitutional initiatives,[36] benefits were considerably enhanced during the 1950s and 1960s, and the retirement age for women was lowered in 1963. Indeed,

---

[35] Klaus Armingeon, 'Renegotiating the Swiss Welfare State', in Gerhard Lehmbruch and Frans van Waarden, eds., *Renegotiating the Welfare State* (London: Routledge, 2003) pp. 169–188.
[36] Hans Werder, *Die Bedeutung der Volksinitiative in der Nachkriegszeit* (Berne: Francke, 1978).

in contrast to the era of welfare state formation,[37] post-war welfare state development was catalyzed and reinforced by constitutional initiatives. Although all initiatives were either rejected or withdrawn, mobilization from the bottom up had an indirect impact, since the federal government adopted some of the initiators' proposals and integrated them into their own legislation.

The 1972 reorganization of the pension system provides an instance of this indirect push-effect.[38] In the late 1960s three constitutional initiatives called for a restructuring of the pension system. The Social Democrats launched an initiative aimed at creating a two-pillar system based on public and occupational pensions. The Communists advocated public pensions aimed at maintaining the previous standard of living of pensioners. Faced with these initiatives from the political left, the bourgeois parties submitted a third initiative that advocated a three-pillar pension system. Confronted with three heterogeneous initiatives, the federal government decided on a three-pillar system based on public pensions, mandatory occupational pensions and private insurance. The three-pillar system was adopted by the people in a mandatory referendum and enshrined in the Federal Constitution in 1972. Based on this multi-pillar conception, Swiss pension politics shifted focus from poverty alleviation to status preservation. The implementing law on occupational pensions was enacted in 1982 and came into force three years later. The reorganization of the pension system illustrates the importance of policy feedback resulting from past political decisions and social security arrangements that have emerged beyond the state. After the defeat of the *Lex Schulthess* in 1931, the lack of a public pension system meant that occupational pensions became increasingly important. In 1941 there were already 3,467 funds with about 365,000 members.[39] Patterns that emerged in an evolutionary way were preserved under the federal law on occupational pensions enacted in 1982. Again, this bill is a framework law that determines minimum regulations and was superimposed on existing social security arrangements.

Disability insurance was adopted in 1959, with a structure that borrowed heavily from the principles underpinning old age pensions. Fifty per cent of total expenditures are covered by cantons and the central state on a cost-sharing basis. Retrospectively, the delayed adoption of disability insurance has proven to be advantageous, allowing it to be designed according to modern principles, with a strong emphasis on rehabilitation.

---

[37] Oswald Sigg, *Die eidgenössischen Volksinitiativen 1892–1939* (Berne: Francke, 1978).
[38] Werder, *Bedeutung der Volksinitiative*; Hans-Peter Tschudi, *Entstehung und Entwicklung der schweizerischen Sozialversicherungen* (Basle: Helbling & Lichtenhahn, 1989).
[39] Peter Binswanger, *Geschichte der AHV* (Zurich: Pro Senectute Verlag, 1986), p. 24.

To provide a decent standard of living for needy old age and invalidity pensioners, means-tested supplementary benefits were introduced in 1966. Supplementary benefits are regulated by the central state, while implementation has been delegated to the cantons. The programme is entirely tax-funded. The central state provides grants to the cantons depending on their fiscal capacity.

Family allowances for agricultural workers and farmers introduced in wartime became part of ordinary legislation in 1952. Although the federal government has been empowered since 1945 to introduce family allowances for all employees, the federal power has never been used. In 1959 the federal government's attempt to provide family allowances to non-agricultural workers was successfully vetoed by the cantons and employers during pre-parliamentary consultation. The cantons stepped in themselves and enacted cantonal family allowance schemes. Cantonal legislation resulted in heterogeneous regulations governing benefit provision and coverage. At present there are forty-nine different schemes, since some cantons have extended family allowances to the self-employed and to non-employed persons.

In 1947 a new constitutional article was adopted that empowered the federation to establish a federal unemployment insurance scheme. However, this article obliged the federation to adhere to the Ghent system and prohibited compulsory unemployment insurance.[40] Facing these constraints, the federal scheme enacted in 1951 largely built on provisions established during World War Two. Given the exceptional labour market performance of the post-war period (see figure 7.1), voluntary unemployment insurance never gained great importance. Unemployment figures remained at a very low level, while the employment to population ratio was extraordinarily high by international comparison. However, the oil shocks of the 1970s caused a temporary increase in unemployment, which provided the impetus for making unemployment insurance compulsory by a provisional decree in 1976–77.[41] In 1982 the provisional regulation was replaced by the Federal Unemployment Insurance Act. This bill, which is still in force, combines tight controls with relatively generous benefits, which were originally contingent on sufficient previous contribution payments. The insurance is funded by equal contributions from employers and employees, without public subsidies. Since the

---

[40] Hans-Peter Tschudi, *Die Sozialverfassung der Schweiz* (Berne: Schriftenreihe des Gewerkschaftsbundes, 1986), p. 18.
[41] Manfred G. Schmidt, *Der schweizerische Weg zur Vollbeschäftigung* (Frankfurt-on-Main: Campus, 1985); Manfred G. Schmidt, 'Vollbeschäftigung und Arbeitslosigkeit in der Schweiz. Vom Sonderweg zum 'Normalfall'', *Politische Vierteljahresschrift*, vol. 36 (1995), no. 1, pp. 35–48.

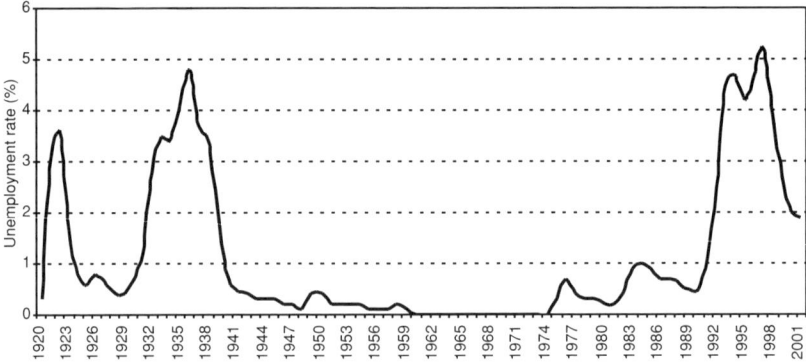

Source: Bundesamt für Statistik, *Statistisches Jahrbuch der Schweiz* (Neuchâtel: Bundesamt für Statistik, various years).

Figure 7.1   Unemployment rate in Switzerland (1920–2001)

unemployment rate was less than 1 per cent during the 1980s, the new law worked well. However, the situation changed appreciably in the early 1990s, with an increase in unemployment to around 5 per cent.

In contrast to social policy development before 1945, none of the post-war social security programmes discussed so far were successfully vetoed by the optional referendum mechanism during the post-war period. Social insurance expenditure as a percentage of GDP increased from 4 per cent in 1948 to 13.2 per cent in 1980 (see figure 7.2). This development was paralleled by substantial public sector growth.[42] Economic prosperity and fully-fledged consensus democracy are the main factors underpinning this pattern. As has already been noted, the Social Democrats as well as the interest groups of business and labour now became embedded into the decision-making process. Hence, social policy-making was now based on comprehensive formal and informal bargaining between the interest organizations of labour and business and all the major political parties, representing about 80 per cent of the electorate. Rapid economic growth provided sufficient resources to expand the welfare state and facilitated log-rolling and compromise-building among conflicting interests. As a result, the number of referenda seeking to frustrate social policy reform significantly diminished, the only exceptions being in the areas of health and maternity insurance.

From the outset, health politics were a Sisyphean endeavour. Until 1994 all attempts to overhaul the 1911 Sickness Insurance Act were

---

[42] Jan-Erik Lane and Reinert Maeland, 'The Growth of the Public Sector in Switzerland', *West European Politics*, vol. 24 (2001), no. 1, pp. 169–90.

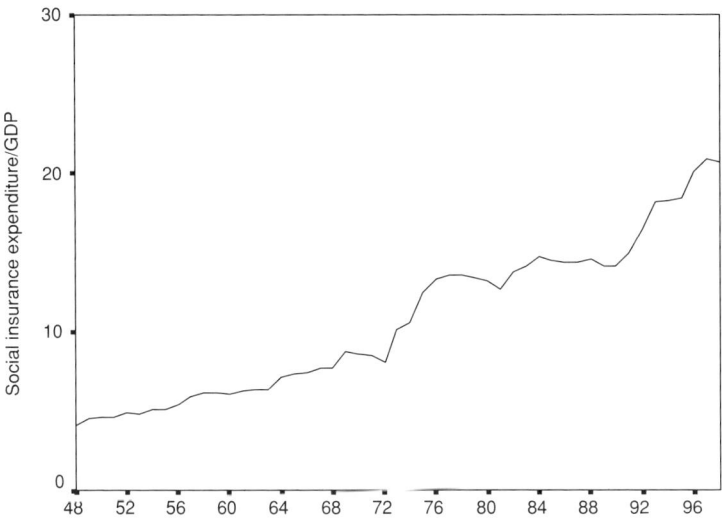

Source: Bundesamt für Statistik, *Statistisches Jahrbuch der Schweiz* (Neuchâtel: Bundesamt für Statistik, various years).

Figure 7.2 Social insurance expenditure as a percentage of GDP (1948–1998)

frustrated as a consequence of severe conflicts between the doctors and sickness funds on the one hand, and the diverse policy options of the leftist and bourgeois parties on the other. In 1954 an expert commission drafted a bill which proposed a compulsory, contribution-based maternity insurance scheme as well as a revision of the Federal Sickness and Accident Insurance Act. Facing the resistance of some cantons and of employers', farmers' and doctors' interest organizations,[43] the federal government did not submit this draft to parliament. In 1964 a minor revision of the health insurance provisions passed parliament for the first time since the law was enacted in 1911. However, all other efforts aimed at introducing compulsory, earnings-related health insurance failed at the ballot-box. In 1974 a constitutional initiative launched by the Social Democrats, and a more liberal and compromise-based, counter-proposal submitted by the Federal Council, were rejected by the people. A further attempt to revise health insurance and to introduce maternity insurance backfired in 1987 after a business association had launched an optional referendum. Similarly, mandatory, contribution-based maternity insurance failed at the ballot-box in 1999. Given this situation, the cantons remained the sole occupants of this policy area. Geneva put in place cantonal maternity insurance in

---

[43] Neidhart, *Plebiszit und pluralitäre Demokratie*, pp. 336–37.

2000; other cantons, such as Vaud, will follow in due course. In 2004 a somewhat minimalist version of maternity insurance was at last adopted in a referendum.

Until the 1990s the way in which health insurance was developed provided a classic example of how the optional referendum can freeze the status quo. Although the Health and Accident Insurance Act of 1911 was conceived of as a provisional solution, the parameters of health and accident insurance remained more or less unchanged until the 1990s. This policy stalemate was caused by a dense web of veto points, which allowed doctors and sickness funds on the one hand, and employers, trade unions and political parties on the other, to successfully defend their interests.

Policy-making in an age of austerity: the 1990s

Compared with earlier years, social policy-making in the early 1990s has been characterized by a shift in policy direction. Until the late 1980s welfare reform generally meant expansion in the coverage or generosity of social programmes. In some respects the Swiss welfare state was still catching up with its European counterparts in those areas in which it was underdeveloped. The 1990s, largely because of a dramatic increase in unemployment, were instead characterized by constant tension and, consequently, an increasing number of referenda. On the one hand, financial constraints and economic concerns pushed policy makers in the direction of austerity and retrenchment measures. On the other, voters, through referenda, supported the maintenance of current levels of protection.[44]

The 1990s also saw a major increase in the proportion of GDP taken up by social expenditure (see figure 7.2). Spending on social programmes rose from 19.8 per cent of GDP in 1990 to 28.3 per cent in 1998.[45]

---

[44] Klaus Armingeon, 'Institutionalising the Swiss Welfare State', *West European Politics*, vol. 24 (2001), no. 1, pp. 145–68; Giuliano Bonoli and André Mach, 'Switzerland: Adjustment Politics within Institutional Constraints', in Fritz W. Scharpf and Vivien Schmidt, eds., *Welfare and Work in the Open Economy* (Oxford: Oxford University Press, 2000), pp. 131–73; Bonoli, 'Switzerland: Institutions, Reforms'; Herbert Obinger, 'Soziale Sicherung in der Schweiz', in Emmerich Tálos, ed., *Soziale Sicherung im Wandel. Österreich und seine Nachbarn* (Vienna: Böhlau, 1998), pp. 31–102; Herbert Obinger, 'Wohlfahrtsstaat Schweiz: Vom Nachzügler zum Vorbild?', in Herbert Obinger and Uwe Wagschal, eds., *Der gezügelte Wohlfahrtsstaat* (Frankfurt-on-Main: Campus, 2000), pp. 245–82.

[45] See OECD, *Social Expenditure Database*, CD-ROM (Paris: OECD, 2001). In the late 1990s the OECD changed the rules for estimating Swiss public expenditure by including mandatory spending on pensions and health insurance under 'public social expenditure'. Both figures (for 1990 and 1998) use the new method and are therefore fully comparable. The nearly 10 percentage point increase of social expenditure reported in the database is, therefore, not a statistical artefact, but represents a real change in the magnitude of spending (and is confirmed by national statistical sources).

Even more strikingly, during the 1990s Switzerland moved from being the fifteenth biggest spender on welfare to the fourth rank in 1998 (after Sweden, Denmark and France). This was not, however, the result of any conscious policy of welfare state expansion. Rather, it is to be explained with reference to a number of non-policy related factors and previous decisions.

About half (44 per cent) of the relative increase in Swiss social spending is explained by the dismal record of the country in terms of economic growth. Between 1990 and 1998 real GDP grew on average 0.5 per cent per year in Switzerland, whereas the (unweighted) average for the older established countries of the OECD was 2.1 per cent. Had the Swiss economy grown in line with other industrial economies, social expenditure would not have exceeded 23.5 per cent of GDP, leaving Switzerland in a very middling position in the social spending league table. The rest of the increase can be explained with reference to increasing numbers of beneficiaries, in particular in the unemployment, invalidity insurance and pension schemes. Since old age pensions came into force as recently as 1948, full programme maturation was postponed to the late 1980s. Public health expenditure also grew during the 1990s by nearly two percentage points to 7.6 of GDP. With the exception of health care policy, which was transformed by the 1994 reform, the dramatic increase in social expenditure in the 1990s did not result from any significant expansion of the Swiss welfare state. It simply reflected a weak economy and decisions taken in the previous decade in the fields of unemployment insurance and pensions.

The first of a series of cost containment measures was the health insurance reform of 1994. In previous years health expenditure and health care insurance premiums had been increasing dramatically. In addition, at the time it was rather difficult for an insured person to change mutual funds if he or she was unhappy with premium increases. This meant that the mutual funds had no incentive to try to negotiate lower fees with doctors.

When the health insurance reform was presented in parliament in 1991, its main objectives were to introduce more 'solidarity' – meaning cross-subsidies between age groups and sexes and help for low income people – to introduce mechanisms countering upward trends in expenditure, and to adapt coverage to the changing needs of the population, in particular by including long-term care and home care for elderly people. Perhaps the most remarkable innovation of the new law was the attempt to create a competitive market among health insurance funds by removing all obstacles for insured persons wishing to move from one fund to another. A second important reform dealt with targeting subsidies towards low income people. Under the old legislation, the federal government and the cantons paid subsidies to mutual funds, which as a result were able to offer lower premiums at below market price. In this way the subsidies benefited all insured persons, regardless of income. In the new legislation subsidies were increased and targeted towards those on low incomes. In practical terms, however, the transition from the old system to the new one resulted in the withdrawal of subsidies from mutual funds, making for increased premiums, and the introduction of an individual means-tested 'health insurance' grant. The 1994 reform also made it compulsory for every resident person to be insured.[46]

The reform was challenged in a referendum, but the opponents – some health insurance funds and parts of the medical profession – failed to prevent its implementation. The reform was skilfully put together to attract support from different camps: it combined a liberal approach to cost-containment, based on enhanced competition in the health insurance market, with subsidies targeting the poorest segment of the population. This feature was arguably instrumental in guaranteeing its success.[47]

The 1995 pension reform illustrates the shift in social policy-making that has occurred since the early 1990s. Work on this reform started in 1979, with the intention of introducing gender equality into the basic pension scheme. Under the legislation in force at the time, pensions for couples were calculated on the basis of the husband's contribution record, unless the wife was entitled to a higher pension. Moreover, the scheme made no provision for contribution credits for informal care-givers – generally women – as is common practice in most European countries. The bill reached parliament in the early 1990s, but by then the political climate had changed. As planned, a series of gender equality measures were adopted, but at the same time it was also decided that the retirement age for women should be raised from 62 to 64 – for men, the retirement age is 65. This change was imposed by the right of centre parliamentary majority, against the opposition of both the Social Democrats and the government.

The reform was attacked by the trade unions, which collected the 50,000 signatures needed for a referendum. However, while referenda decide between the adoption and the rejection of a bill, they cannot modify its content. Thus, in opposing a rise in the age of pension eligibility, the unions were forced to oppose gender equality measures for which they had long campaigned. For the broader political left, this constituted a powerful dilemma. The Social Democrats declined to join the unions in supporting the referendum. However, the bill survived the referendum hurdle. This outcome was not accidental. By combining elements of retrenchment with

[46] Bonoli, 'Switzerland: Institutions, Reforms'.
[47] Obinger, 'Soziale Sicherung in der Schweiz', pp. 64–65.

measures that were among the key priorities of the left,[48] the proponents of the bill maximized the chance of division amongst their opponents.

A similar strategy paved the way for the acceptance of the 1995 unemployment insurance reform, adopted in response to a sharp increase in unemployment insurance outlays. The reform was drafted by a joint group of representatives of the employers and trade unions, and passed by parliament without major changes. Like the 1995 pension reform, the new unemployment insurance law included measures with divergent impacts. On the one hand, contribution rates were increased and more funds were made available for active labour market programmes, such as vocational training and job creation schemes. On the other hand, benefits were cut from 80 to 70 per cent of salary, and the entitlement period was reduced to two years, whereas previously benefits could be drawn almost indefinitely if the recipient was prepared to participate in labour market programmes. The 1995 unemployment insurance reform was adopted by parliament and was not challenged in a referendum. The left cared mainly about the introduction of new labour market programmes, whereas the right was satisfied with the two-year limit imposed on benefits. In this respect, the 1995 unemployment insurance reform can be regarded as a legislative package that included a substantial element of retrenchment, yet which nevertheless managed to survive the hurdles of the law-making process in Switzerland.[49]

In 1997, because of the persisting deficits incurred by the unemployment insurance scheme, the government proposed an emergency decree to reduce the level of benefit payments to the unemployed, a 1 per cent or 3 per cent cut depending on the amount of the benefit and family obligations. After the right-wing majority in parliament adopted this proposal, a referendum was called by an association of unemployed people, who were subsequently joined by the trade unions and the Social Democrats. After a confrontational campaign and to the surprise of many observers, the bill was rejected by a small majority in September 1997. Unlike the 1995 unemployment insurance reform, the 1997 decree did not contain improvements in provision or measures to attract the support of the left and of the labour movement.[50]

---

[48] Giuliano Bonoli, 'Pension Policy in Switzerland: Institutions and the Politics of Expansion and Retrenchment', in Ulrich Klöti and Katsumi Yorimoto, eds., *Institutional Change and Public Policy in Japan and Switzerland* (Zurich: Universität Zürich: Institut für Politikwissenschaft/Abteilung für Internationale Beziehungen, 1999), pp. 165–78; Bonoli, 'Switzerland: Stubborn Institutions'.

[49] Pierre-Yves Giriens and Julien Stauffer, 'Deuxième révision de l'assurance chômage: génèse d'un compromis', in André Mach, ed., *Globalisation, néo-libéralisme et politiques publiques dans la Suisse des anneés 1990* (Zurich: Seismo, 1999), pp. 105–44.

[50] Bonoli and Mach, 'Switzerland: Adjustment Politics'.

The reform process of the Federal Labour Law unfolded in a similar way. Work on this reform started in the mid-1980s, as employers argued for more flexibility to hire women for night work in industry, a practice previously prohibited by federal law. A consultation procedure was launched in the late 1980s, but the proposal was severely criticized by both the trade unions and some employers. Moreover, women's night work was also prohibited by an ILO convention to which Switzerland was a party. As a result, the federal government decided to abandon plans to reform the Federal Labour Law.

In the early 1990s, however, after Switzerland denounced ILO convention no. 89, the idea of amending the Federal Labour Law re-emerged on the political agenda. The federal commission on employment prepared the first draft of a bill, which was then subject to a consultation procedure. On this basis, the federal government presented a bill in parliament in 1994. This included the following measures: the legalization of women's night work in industry, a new legal definition of night work – from 11 p.m. to 6 a.m., instead of from 8 p.m. to 6 a.m. – and the obligation to compensate for night and Sunday work with at least 10 per cent extra time off. As in the case of previous reforms, the bill prepared by the federal government contained both deregulation and expansion measures, namely compulsory compensation by means of extra time off.

In parliament the right of centre parties were successful in modifying the bill. In the new version, night work remained possible for both men and women, but was not to be automatically compensated, either with time off or with extra pay. Moreover, the bill allowed for the opening of shops for six Sundays every year. Finally, the maximum annual number of overtime hours was increased from 200–260 under the old law to 500. These measures were strongly criticized by the left and the trade unions, which decided to call a referendum against the bill adopted by parliament.

The labour law reform was subjected to a popular vote on 1 December 1996, and rejected by 67 per cent of voters, a fairly clear result. Before the vote, a number of influential political actors – including the Christian Democrats – had sided with the 'no' camp, which explains its success. The federal government, in addition, did not support the version of the bill that had been adopted by parliament.[51] Soon after the rejection of the 1996 labour bill, work started on a second attempt at reforming the labour law. This time, the most radical measures – Sunday work, the absence of automatic compensation for night work – were excluded. At the same

---

[51] Fabienne De Pietro Fierro, Sergio Laurenza and Virglie Perret, 'Révision de la loi sur le travail: compromis d'intérêt et intérêt du compromis', in Mach, ed., *Globalisation, néo-libéralisme et politiques publiques*, pp. 145–90.

time, the idea that at least 10 per cent of Sunday and night work must be compensated for by means of extra time off was reintroduced. After being adopted by parliament, this new version of the bill was subjected to a referendum vote in November 1998. This time, however, the bill was accepted by 63.4 per cent of voters.

In this new phase of social policy-making, characterized by strong economic and financial pressures, it is direct democracy rather than federalism that seems to have played the most important role. Federalism, however, was not completely absent from social politics in the 1990s. In fact, in the field of social policy the rules governing the division of labour between the federal state and the cantons provided substantial incentives for the cantons to oppose welfare state retrenchment because federal social programmes were mostly beneficial to them. Social insurance benefits – which are overwhelmingly financed from contributions and by the federal state – stabilize regional demand and, more importantly, lower the pressure on canton-administered social programmes, such as social assistance. The cantons, for instance, had a vital interest in the 1995 unemployment insurance reform because increasing numbers of the unemployed had exhausted unemployment cash benefits and were consequently forced to resort to social assistance provided by the cantons. Hence, the cantons backed both the shift towards active labour market policy and the extension of daily allowances to the elderly unemployed.

Direct democracy and federalism, thus, conspire to make retrenchment a particularly difficult exercise in Switzerland. Its fragmented political system means that legislation can only be successful when there is widespread agreement on legislative proposals. Those who lose out under a welfare reform have a series of opportunities to challenge the government and to prevent the adoption of legislation they regard as unsatisfactory. In recent years Swiss policy-makers have developed a strategy to overcome the obstacles represented by institutional power fragmentation, and particularly by the referendum. This entails combining retrenchment and expansion measures within a single piece of legislation. Initiatives lacking such an expansionary component have been systematically rejected by voters. A prominent recent example is the eleventh revision of the Old Age and Survivors' Insurance Act. The federal government proposed another increase in the retirement age of women, cuts for widows' pensions, and a deferment of benefit indexation (to prices) to every third – instead of every second – year. Trade unions, supported by the Social Democrats, successfully launched an optional referendum against this restrictive proposal: in May 2004 some 68 per cent of the voters rejected the bill proposed by the government.

Varieties of cantonal welfare regimes

The focus of our analysis so far has been on the impact the institutions of federalism have had on federal social policy. However, Swiss federalism permits considerable inter-regional differences in direct taxation on income and entitlements to public services and transfers. Federalism in Switzerland tolerates and even encourages diversity. Article 3 of the constitution states that the 'Cantons are sovereign insofar as their sovereignty is not limited by the Federal Constitution; they exercise all rights which are not transferred to the Confederation', and Article 42 makes it clear that the confederation shall accomplish only those tasks which are explicitly attributed to it by the constitution.

Historically, federal social policy was superimposed on existing cantonal and local social policies. Since the federal government does not possess its own administrative units in certain areas, implementation of federal social policy necessarily takes place at cantonal level. Cantons also run their own social programmes. Legislation and implementation of means-tested income support programmes providing unemployment assistance, social assistance and subsidies to health premiums are all cantonal responsibilities. Beyond these means-tested programmes, all cantons provide family allowances to employees. Some cantons also provide family allowances to non-employed persons as well as to the self-employed and to farmers, while Geneva has recently introduced maternity insurance after federal maternity insurance was rejected by referendum in 1999. Another major activity of the cantons is subsidies to hospitals.

Soaring unemployment in the 1990s prompted numerous reforms of unemployment and social assistance at the cantonal tier. The Latin, that is the Italian- and French-speaking cantons, are those most affected by unemployment, and those which have adopted the most thorough-going policy innovation in this area. Unemployment assistance is tailored to the long-term unemployed. After the daily allowances of federal unemployment insurance have been exhausted, the long-term unemployed are entitled to cantonal unemployment assistance. There is no universal unemployment assistance at the federal level, although the federal state acquired the power to legislate in this area in 1947. Unemployment assistance is thus the responsibility of the twenty-six cantons. However, not all the cantons have established means-tested income support schemes for the long-term unemployed. In the mid-1990s, nineteen out of twenty-six cantons had enacted unemployment assistance schemes. These exhibited substantial variation. Sixteen cantons have established earnings-related cash benefits, while Geneva, Neuchâtel and Jura have provided labour market programmes.[52] From the mid-1990s onwards, some Latin cantons started to restructure income support to the long-term unemployed. Most have replaced cash benefits by activation and public works schemes. At present, only two cantons provide monetary support. In contrast, many German-speaking cantons have not adopted such schemes, although some have extended activation programmes in accordance with the revised federal unemployment insurance scheme.

Social assistance serves as a safety net of last resort for those who lack support from their families, receive insufficient income or social security benefits or have exhausted their social insurance rights. Social assistance is regulated, administered and funded by twenty-six cantons and approximately 3,000 municipalities. Apart from deviant inter-cantonal concordats (*Konkordate*), the home municipality and the home canton were responsible for income support until the 1970s. Article 48 of the Swiss Federal Constitution, which was approved by citizens and cantons in a referendum in 1975, shifted the responsibility with regard to income support from the home canton to the canton of residence, which in turn can delegate social assistance to the municipalities. Much of the cantonal legislation – especially in the German-speaking regions – has delegated social assistance to the communes. Federal responsibilities in the field of social assistance are outlined by the Federal Law of Legal Responsibility for Support of the Needy. This law defines neediness, entrusts the canton of residence with responsibility for support and regulates cost-sharing and reimbursement between the home canton and the canton of residence.

The fact that social assistance falls within cantonal jurisdiction leads to huge diversity in eligibility conditions, benefits and procedural rules. The mode of benefit provision and the procedural rules vary substantially between urban agglomerations and rural areas.[53] Swiss social assistance is probably the most fragmented system of social provision within the OECD.[54] Coping with regional disparities is subject to horizontal self-co-ordination rather than standard-setting from the top down. Owing to

---

[52] OECD, *The Battle against Exclusion*, vol. III, *Social Assistance in Canada and Switzerland* (Paris: OECD, 1999).

[53] François Höpflinger and Kurt Wyss, *Am Rande des Sozialstaates. Formen und Funktionen öffentlicher Sozialhilfe im Vergleich* (Berne: Haupt, 1994); Robert Fluder and Jürgen Stremlow, *Armut und Bedürftigkeit. Herausforderungen für das kommunale Sozialwesen* (Berne: Haupt, 1999).

[54] Tony Eardley, Jonathan Bradshaw, John Ditch, Ian Gough and Peter Whiteford, *Social Assistance in OECD Countries*, Department of Social Security Research Report no. 46–47, 2 vols. (London: HMSO, 1996); John Ditch, Jonathan Bradshaw, Meg Huby, Margaret Moodie and Jochen Clasen, eds., *Comparative Social Assistance: Localisation and Discretion* (Aldershot: Ashgate, 1997).

the heterogeneity of social assistance, the Swiss Conference for Social Assistance (SKOS)[55] provides recommendations and guidelines for benefit provision. Hence, a semi-public organization staffed with experts and representatives of the cantonal administration is engaged in setting the standards and general rules in order to improve efforts to harmonize the twenty-six cantonal laws with respect to procedure, scope and level of benefits. Besides the SKOS, social assistance is also subject to formal and informal horizontal co-ordination between cantonal governments.

However, federalism not only contributes to a fragmented social assistance system but is also a source of policy innovation. Facing high unemployment since the early 1990s, many Latin cantons have revised social assistance legislation and adopted new programmes focussed on coping with problems arising as a consequence of long-term unemployment. Geneva and Vaud have introduced special systems aimed at the reintegration of the long-term unemployed. The *revenu minimum cantonal d'aide sociale* (RMACS) in Geneva and the *revenu minimum de réinsertion* (RMR) in Vaud are aimed at preventing long-term welfare dependency. All these new programmes were established in the second half of the 1990s.

In sum, recent reforms of unemployment and social assistance lend support to the hypothesis that constituent units act as laboratories of democracy, where tested and proven policy solutions have a demonstrable effect on other cantons, so that it is possible for cantons to learn from and share experiences with each other. While federalism provides room for manoeuvre, the constitutional units' strong fiscal basis encourages policy experimentation: facing soaring unemployment, the cantons in the western and southern parts of the country have launched more radical reforms than have the German-speaking cantons. Hence, federalism has proved to be not only an engine of innovation, but also an elastic system allowing for flexible problem-solving. However, the price of such experimentation is a territorially fragmented system of unemployment and social assistance. The same is true for the forty-nine different schemes of family allowances. Efforts to harmonize these schemes have taken a different route, since a federal framework law on family allowances is at present pending.

These large differences in cantonal policies and living conditions suggest the possibility that the Swiss cantons may inhabit distinctly different worlds of welfare. This is a possibility that is a current research preoccupation of some of the contributors to this chapter, and here we summarize

---

[55] Schweizerische Konferenz für Sozialhilfe (SKOS)/Conférence suisse des institutions d'action sociale (CSIAS).

findings that appear elsewhere in considerably greater detail.[56] In this research, we assign cantons to liberal, conservative and social democratic regime types on the basis of characteristics of their social security and taxation systems. Types are generated by combining two indicators or sets of indicators denoting two different sub-dimensions (cf. table 7.4). These sub-dimensions have been chosen so that they distinguish one type of welfare regime from the remaining two. By intersecting the two sub-dimensions, we obtain a fourfold classification, where three cells correspond to the three worlds of welfare. The fourth cell is a residual type, which on theoretical grounds one would assume would contain no empirical instances. However, relaxing the assumption of just three worlds of welfare, there might well be different mixes of policies constituting cases that cannot neatly be assigned to one of Esping-Andersen's welfare state types.

Social security The first dimension of social security is the size of the welfare state measured in terms of the number of cantonal social security schemes and the per capita social security benefits paid out of cantonal and local funds. In this regard, lean liberal welfare cantons stand in contrast to conservative and social democratic ones. The second dimension, which distinguishes between social democratic or liberal and conservative welfare schemes, is familialism, understood as the extent to which a welfare regime assumes that families will correspond to the traditional male breadwinner model.[57] We measure familialism by the difference between the effort cantons make to support non-working mothers on the one hand, here by birth grants and the amount of child benefits for the fourth child, and to help mothers reconcile work and family life on the other, here by expenditure on pre-school facilities.[58] Cantons with a liberal welfare regime are assumed to have a non-familialistic and a lean social security system; those belonging to the conservative regime will have extensive and strongly familialistic social security schemes, while, in social democratic welfare states, social security is extensive and

---

[56] For an unabridged version, including education and employment policies in addition to taxation policy and social security schemes, see Klaus Armingeon, Fabio Bertozzi and Giuliano Bonoli, 'Swiss Worlds of Welfare', *West European Politics*, vol. 27 (2004), no. 1, pp. 20–44.
[57] Gøsta Esping-Andersen, *Social Foundations of Postindustrial Societies* (Oxford: Oxford University Press, 1999), p. 45.
[58] The variable has been calculated as follows. The z-values of child benefits for the fourth child and of birth grants have been added and then z-standardized. From these z-scores, z-scores for the variable 'expenditures on pre-school facilities' have been subtracted. The variable as calculated indicates the weight given to the goal of sustaining traditional family forms as compared to the weight given to the liberal and social democratic goals of giving working women the right to combine work and family.

Table 7.4 *Operationalization of variables for the different aspects of cantonal welfare regimes*

	Dimension 1	Dimension 2	Outcomes
Social Security[a]	*Number of cantonal social security schemes and per capita social security benefits paid for by canton and municipalities*	*Degree of familialism* (birth grants, child benefits to fourth child minus expenditure on pre-school facilities)	
	High	Low	Social-democratic
	High	High	Conservative
	Low	Low	Liberal
	Low	High	Unclear (liberal-conservative)
Taxation[b]	*Level of taxation*	*Progressivity of taxation*	
	High	High	Social-democratic
	High	Low	Conservative
	Low	Low	Liberal
	Low	High	Unclear (redistributive-liberal)

Data and sources:
[a] Dimension 1, number of cantonal welfare schemes (max. 7, social assistance excluded), 1998, *source*: Kurt Wyss, 'Aide sociale – un pilier de la sécurité sociale?', *Info:social*, 1/1999 (Neuchâtel: Bundesamt für Statistik, 1999), pp. 5–37, our calculations, and cantonal and municipal social expenditure (in Swiss francs per capita, without federal subsidies), 1997, *source*: Adrian Vatter, Markus Freitag, Christoph Müller, *Politische, soziale und ökonomische Daten zu den Schweizer Kantonen, 1983 bis 1998* (Berne: Institute of Political Science, February 2002). Dimension 2, birth grants (in Swiss francs) and benefits for fourth child (in Swiss francs), 2000, *source*: Bundesamt für Sozialversicherung, *Schweizerische Sozialversicherungsstatistik* (Berne: Bundesamt für Sozialversicherung, 2001), minus pre-school expenditure (in Swiss francs per head) (z-scored values), 1998, *source*: Bundesamt für Statistik, *Öffentliche Bildungsausgaben. Finanzindikatoren 1998* (Neuchâtel: Bundesamt für Statistik, 2000).
[b] Dimension 1, total taxation index on income and assets and general index of taxation level, 1999, *source*: Bundesamt für Statistik, *Statistisches Jahrbuch der Schweiz 2001* (Neuchâtel: Bundesamt für Statistik, 2001). Dimension 2, taxation progression index (index for highest income class/index for lowest income class), 2000, *source*: Vatter *et al.*, *Politische, soziale und ökonomische Daten*.

familialism low. The remaining – residual – case is of lean schemes combined with strong familialism. This latter instance might be seen as a case of 'liberal-conservative' social policy.

Taxation Running a large welfare state implies considerable costs, which have to be covered by taxes or social security contributions. Since cantonal social security schemes mainly depend on taxes, our first dimension is the overall level of taxation. We can expect the tax load to be low in liberal welfare regimes and higher in social democratic or conservative ones. The second dimension is the degree of progressivity of cantonal income tax. While there should be few differences between socialist and conservative welfare states with regard to the distribution of the domestic product between public and private households, the distribution of the tax load over income categories may be very different. In social democratic regimes we would expect more progressive tax rates, seeking to effect redistribution from the top to the bottom end of the income scale, while liberal and conservative political actors are likely to be more sceptical of the virtues of progressivity on a variety of grounds. Hence, in a liberal world of welfare we would expect both tax load and tax progressivity to be low; in conservative worlds, tax loads will be high while progressivity is low, while in social democratic worlds, both the tax load and progressivity will be high. The remaining case is of a low tax load combined with high progressivity ('redistributive-liberal').

This classification makes sense only if the difference in social security effort between cantons is substantial, not only in qualitative terms – as shown above – but also quantitatively. In fact, this is the case. In 1998 about 58 per cent of all social security expenditure was undertaken by the federation, 27 per cent by the cantons and 14 per cent by municipalities.[59] This suggests that the variation of cantonal welfare state effort is of at least the same magnitude as the variation between OECD countries.[60]

Applying our operational rules to the twenty-six cantons, they can be classified as in table 7.5. Taking together both aspects of the welfare state, some cantons are consistently in the same category: Argovia, Appenzell Inner-Rhodes, Glarus and Grisons are liberal, Basle-Town and Geneva are social democratic and Valais and Neuchâtel are conservative. However, there is no strong correlation between the two aspects of the welfare state, suggesting that different factors may shape variation of the tax and social security dimensions. A redistributive social democratic taxation regime can be combined with a conservative system of social security, as

---

[59] Bundesamt für Sozialversicherung, *Schweizerische Sozialversicherungsstatistik* (Berne: Bundesamt für Sozialversicherung, 2001).
[60] For data see complete article (note 56).

Table 7.5 *Worlds of welfare in Switzerland: classification of the twenty-six Swiss cantons by taxation and social security*

List of cantons	Taxation	Social security
AG: Argovia	Liberal	Liberal
AI: Appenzell Inner-Rhodes	Liberal	Liberal
AR: Appenzell Outer-Rhodes	Conservative	Liberal
BE: Berne	Conservative	Liberal
BL: Basle-Country	Redistributive-liberal	Social-democratic
BS: Basle-Town	Social-democratic	Social-democratic
FR: Fribourg	Social-democratic	Conservative
GE: Geneva	Social-democratic	Social-democratic
GL: Glarus	Liberal	Liberal
GR: Grisons	Liberal	Liberal
JU: Jura	Social-democratic	Liberal
LU: Lucerne	Conservative	Liberal-conservative
NE: Neuchâtel	Conservative	Conservative
NW: Nidwalden	Liberal	Liberal-conservative
OW: Obwalden	Conservative	Liberal-conservative
SG: St Gall	Conservative	Liberal
SH: Schaffhausen	Liberal	Social-democratic
SO: Solothurn	Redistributive-liberal	Liberal-conservative
SZ: Schwyz	Liberal	Liberal-conservative
TG: Thurgovia	Social-democratic	Liberal
TI: Ticino	Redistributive-liberal	Social-democratic
UR: Uri	Liberal	Liberal-conservative
VD: Vaud	Social-democratic	Conservative
VS: Valais	Conservative	Conservative
ZG: Zug	Liberal	Conservative
ZH: Zurich	Liberal	Social-democratic

Source: These classifications are derived from a separate empirical study by the authors (cf. Klaus Armingeon, Fabio Bertozzi and Giuliano Bonoli, 'Swiss Worlds of Welfare', *West European Politics*, vol. 24 (2001), no. 1, pp. 145–68).

in Vaud, and a lean public sector goes together with liberal-conservative social security schemes in Schwyz. This finding is in obvious contrast to recent cross-national findings demonstrating a functional nexus between types of social security, employment, taxation and education.[61]

In order to examine whether there are common factors shaping cantonal welfare regimes, we regressed the types on a range of relevant independent cultural, politico-institutional and socio-economic

---

[61] Peter A. Hall and David Soskice, 'An Introduction to Varieties of Capitalism', in Peter A. Hall and David Soskice, eds., *Varieties of Capitalism. The Institutional Foundations of Comparative Advantage* (Oxford: Oxford University Press, 2001), pp. 1–68.

variables.⁶² Examples are the share of Protestants in the population, the importance of direct democracy, the strength of the left in government, urbanisation and levels of unemployment.

Our findings suggest that taxation regimes are influenced significantly by the level of unemployment and by the importance of direct democracy, while social security regimes, in addition to these two variables, are also influenced by cultural (share of Protestants), political (strength of the left and size of coalition) and socio-economic (urbanization, share of foreigners) factors. These findings support the view that the logic of taxation is different from the logic of redistributive social security activities. In the former case, taxation politics seem to be a conflict between citizens and politicians, and the outcome depends on institutions giving the people a large say in tax questions.⁶³ In contrast, social security expenditure differences appear to reflect much stronger societal norms, political power distributions and functional requirements.⁶⁴

Overall, our analysis of the Swiss cantons suggests three conclusions. First, it would appear that in some federal systems there are major differences in sub-national social policy outcomes. This in turn suggests the need for a clear distinction between different types of federalism: countries such as Switzerland, the USA and Canada, where there is real sub-national autonomy, and countries such as Germany, Austria and, in some respects, Australia, where there is much greater social policy uniformity. Our second conclusion follows from the first, suggesting that in federations where there is greater sub-national autonomy, welfare state outcomes will be the result of an interaction between federal and state policies to which state politics will make a genuine contribution. Finally, if the findings of our wider analysis can be generalized, our analysis of regime types among the Swiss cantons suggests that linkages between aspects of the welfare state, such as social security, taxation and, in the wider study, also employment and education, are more loosely connected than is sometimes thought, with diverse patterns of outcomes shaped by different historical developments and contingencies.⁶⁵

---

⁶² For a list of such relevant variables, see Gøsta Esping-Andersen, *The Three Worlds of Welfare Capitalism* (Cambridge: Polity Press; Princeton: Princeton University Press, 1990); Manfred G. Schmidt, 'Die sozialpolitischen Nachzüglerstaaten und die Theorien der vergleichenden Staatstätigkeitsforschung', in Herbert Obinger and Uwe Wagschal, eds., *Der gezügelte Wohlfahrtsstaat* (Frankfurt-on-Main: Campus, 2000), pp. 22–36.
⁶³ Sven Steinmo, *Taxation and Democracy. Swedish, British and American Approaches to Financing the Modern State* (New Haven: Yale University Press, 1993).
⁶⁴ Manfred G. Schmidt, 'When Parties Matter: A Review of the Possibilities and Limits of Partisan Influence on Public Policy', *European Journal of Political Research*, vol. 30 (1996), no. 2, pp. 155–83.
⁶⁵ Jens Alber, 'Sozialstaat und Arbeitsmarkt', *Leviathan*, vol. 28 (2000), no. 4, pp. 535–69.

Conclusion

The preceding analysis suggests that party politics is not enough to explain the belated take-off of the Swiss welfare state. Although the Federal Council was exclusively dominated by bourgeois parties prior to 1943, several major reform initiatives by the federal government were frustrated in the years prior to World War Two. State structures help to explain this policy deadlock and the resulting impact on the trajectory and patterns of Swiss social policy. Specifically, it has been the *interaction* between federalism and direct democracy that has crucially influenced the developmental trajectory of the Swiss welfare state. Both institutions have contributed to a status quo bias in public policy-making and to path dependency.[66] While federalism has created new actors and actor constellations, direct democracy has provided opportunities for subordinate governments, vested interest groups and local social policy providers to defend their interests.

Four findings should be emphasized. First, programme adoption at the federal level was delayed because of an initial lack of federal jurisdiction in social policy. Social policy legislation became a two-stage process and each phase was subject to an obligatory and/or optional referendum. The time lag resulting from this two-stage decision-making process is summarized in table 7.6.

Second, federalism and direct democracy have influenced patterns of social policy development in manifold ways. The absence of policy-making power at the centre opened the door for social experiments at the local tier. Local policy pre-emption caused two different kinds of feedback effects on subsequent federal social policies. On the one hand, policy pre-emption constrained the ability of the federal government to enact social policy autonomously, while on the other hand innovative local social security arrangements served as a blueprint and a pacemaker for federal legislation. An example of the latter effect is the Federal Factory Act, which was strongly influenced by prior cantonal legislation.

Apart from early local policy pre-emption, the weakness of federal parties and the optional referendum are the causal factors underpinning this structural effect. From their cantonal strongholds, sub-groups within the Catholic Conservative Party tried to keep cantonal, social policy responsibilities in line with the subsidiarity principle. Equally, the small Liberal-Conservative Party, which was headquartered in the French-speaking cantons, was strongly committed to anti-centralism and

---

[66] Paul Pierson, 'Increasing Returns, Path Dependence, and the Study of Politics', *American Political Science Review*, vol. 94 (2000), no. 2, pp. 251–67.

Table 7.6 Lag effect of obligatory and optional referenda on the introduction of core branches of social insurance

Social insurance branch	Adoption of constitutional amendment	First draft	Δ^a	Optional referendum	Second draft	Enforcement of law	Lag^b	Timelag due to referendum
Health	1890	1899	9	1900	1911	1914	23	14
Accident	1890	1899	9	1900	1911	1918	28	18
Old age	1925	1931	6	1931	1946	1948	23	17
Disability	1925	1959	34	None	–	1960	35	–
Unemployment	1947	1951	4	None	–	1952	5	–
Family allowances	1945	1952	7	None	–	1953	8	–
Occupational pensions	1972	1982	10	None	–	1985	13	–
Maternity leave	1945	1987	42	1987, 1999, 2004	1998	2005	60	18

Notes:
^{a} Difference between constitutional amendment and first bill.
^{b} Difference between constitutional amendment and enforcement of law.
Source: Data based on evaluation of the legal development by the authors.

individualism.⁶⁷ In close coalition with business interest organizations and existing compensation funds, these political parties of the right successfully vetoed the expansion of federal social security legislation prior to World War Two. The main instrument for their success was the optional referendum. Defeats over health, accident and old age insurance have substantially shaped subsequent patterns of federal social policy. Instead of realizing a class-based social insurance, the federal government had to take into account social policies that had emerged at the local tier and the interest groups that backed them. Facing the rejection of state-interventionist social policy, the federal government was constrained to establish legislative frameworks regulating minimum standards and providing subsidies to the traditional, private and corporatist carriers. Hence, locally conceived policy patterns were largely retained under this mode of governance.

As a result, the referendum has geared the Swiss welfare state towards a liberal trajectory. The institutionally induced policy stalemate has also redirected social security from the state to private carriers, since defeated were federal social policy projects replaced by private welfare organizations and workplace benefits. Because attempts to establish comprehensive federal social policy programmes failed, the central government as well as the cantons began to subsidize those private programmes at the sub-national level. This led to the emergence of a peculiar public–private mix in the field of social policy. In addition, the referendum process favoured the adoption of general public insurance instead of purely employment-related insurance schemes. In particular, it has proved to be difficult in Switzerland's referendum democracy to differentiate between those who have to pay and those who receive benefits, since tax-payers are prone to veto a social security system that is funded from the general budget, but which does not honour the principle of reciprocity. Such considerations were taken into account by the federal government when the old age insurance scheme was drafted.⁶⁸ Together with the fiscal weakness of the federal government, this has contributed to a mode of funding that is largely contributions-based.

The third effect of federalism relates to the fiscal powers of the federal government. Direct democracy and federalism have constrained the federal budget.⁶⁹ Originally, the central state's limited taxing powers severely

---

⁶⁷ Bruno Rimli, *Sozialpolitische Ideen der Liberal-Konservativen in der Schweiz (1815–1939)* (Zurich: Europa Verlag, 1951).
⁶⁸ *Bundesblatt* 1924, vol. II, pp. 731–32.
⁶⁹ Bruno S. Frey and Iris Bohnet, 'Democracy by Competition: Referenda and Federalism in Switzerland', *Publius: The Journal of Federalism*, vol. 23 (1993), no. 2, pp. 71–81; Bruno S. Frey, 'Direct Democracy: Politico-Economic Lessons from Swiss Experience',

restricted its capacity to fund welfare state programmes in a generous and consistent way. Even today, the fiscal powers of the federal government remain weak compared even to other federal OECD countries. The federal government controls about one-third of public revenues, with the largest share of public revenues going to the cantons and municipalities. The ability to fund social policy from the general budget was even more restricted at the end of the nineteenth century, when the fiscal resources of the federal government mainly depended on revenues from tariffs. Thus, as the federation became gradually empowered to legislate on most aspects of social security, fiscal and social responsibility increasingly failed to coincide, because the central state was unable to acquire the power to levy direct taxes before World War Two. Voters not only rejected new taxes in a mandatory referendum, but also have repeatedly vetoed tax increases in optional referenda. The lack of an adequate tax base led to the postponement of social legislation, and also predisposed the federal government to view contributory social insurance as a favoured form of social security funding.

The fourth finding relates to welfare state development in the 1990s. This chapter shows that the interaction between federalism and direct democracy varies according to the time period. Under conditions of austerity and increased demands for welfare retrenchment, direct democracy becomes a much more important explanatory variable than federalism. It was the use of the referendum that contributed to the maintenance of welfare schemes and welfare expenditures, despite having impeded the development of the welfare state prior to 1945. Hence, direct democracy goes hand in hand with a status quo bias in public policy-making. Once in place, social programmes show a remarkable resilience to retrenchment efforts. However, groups backing the referendum have changed significantly over time. While the political right and interest organizations of business successfully employed the optional referendum to challenge expansive social policies before 1945, the use of the optional referendum in times of austerity has been launched by the political left, trade unions and the interest organizations of welfare clienteles with the aim of defending current levels of social provision.[70] Federalism has not had a direct impact on policy during the 1990s, but the incentive structure faced by the cantons in the field of federal welfare reform inclines them to oppose

---

American Economic Review. Papers and Proceedings, vol. 84 (1994), no. 2, pp. 338–42; Lars P. Feld and Marcel R. Savioz, 'Vox Populi, Vox Bovi? Ökonomische Auswirkungen direkter Demokratie', in Gerd Grözinger and Stephan Panther, eds., *Konstitutionelle Politische Ökonomie* (Marburg: Metropolis, 1998), pp. 29–80; Obinger and Wagschal, 'Zwischen Reform und Blockade'.

[70] Obinger, 'Federalism, Direct Democracy', pp. 252–55.

retrenchment, since federal cutbacks could imply more cantonal spending. In contrast, federalism has ceased to restrain the growth of social policy schemes. A major reason for the very substantial increase in social expenditure in the 1990s is that Swiss social programmes were maturing late under circumstances of increased unemployment and extremely low economic growth.

Considering this evidence, how can we respond to the guiding questions of this volume? What are the feedback effects of federalism on welfare state development and how did the welfare state reshape federalism? With regard to the first aspect – how federalism impacts on the welfare state – it is, by and large, possible to endorse the findings of the comparative literature. Federalism has proved to be a brake on welfare state growth, especially in the period until 1945, when struggles over the reallocation of social and fiscal powers substantially delayed programme adoption. However, federalism interacts with other institutions – such as direct democracy – and political power distributions. And finally, its impact is greatly contingent on whether expansion or retrenchment is at stake. Where the feedback effects of social policy on federalism are concerned, there is some evidence that the welfare state has contributed to the emergence of co-operative federalism and consequently to the disappearance of the clear vertical separation of powers, which was the original idea of Swiss federalism in the nineteenth century.[71] The (creeping) reallocation of social policy powers from the cantons to the federal government was compensated for by the shifting implementation of social insurance to the cantons. Moreover, the take-off of the welfare state was paralleled by increasingly complex inter-governmental fiscal relations. In consequence, all federally regulated but not entirely contribution-based social programmes are today co-financed by the cantons and the federal government on a cost-sharing basis, thereby accentuating the already Byzantine system of fiscal relations between the cantons and the federal state.

---

[71] Linder and Vatter, 'Institutions and Outcomes', p. 96.

PART 3
Conclusion

8 'Old' and 'new politics' in federal welfare states

STEPHAN LEIBFRIED, FRANCIS G. CASTLES AND
HERBERT OBINGER*

The twentieth century will herald the age of federations, or humanity will resume its thousand years of purgatory.

Pierre-Joseph Proudhon (1809–1865), 1863**

We began by questioning the widely held premise of econometric research that federalism is generally inimical to the growth of the welfare state in all countries and in all eras. Employing a qualitative comparative approach that Peter Hall calls 'systematic process analysis',[1] we derived our hypotheses concerning federalism's effects on welfare state development from theories of fiscal federalism and political institutionalism. According to theories of actor-centred institutionalism, institutions create opportunity structures for political action by shaping actor constellations, actor preferences and the modes of their interaction. Exploiting these institutionally pre-configured opportunities for public policy-making, then, depends on a number of contextual variables. We have

---

* We would like to thank Arthur Benz, Keith Banting, Susan Gaines and Paul Pierson for their comments, suggestions and amendments.
** 'Le vingtième siècle ouvrira l'ère des fédérations, ou l'humanité recommençera un purgatoire de mille ans.' Pierre-Joseph Proudhon, *Du Principe fédératif et de la nécessité de reconstituer le parti de la révolution* (Paris: Dentu, 1863), p. 109. For a discussion of the French constitutional debate on federalism, cf. Olivier Beaud, 'Fédéralisme et fédération en France. Histoire d'un concept impossible?', *Annales de la Faculté de droit de Strasbourg*, n.s. no. 3, pp. 7–82; Olivier Beaud, 'La fédération entre l'état et l'empire', in Bruno Théret, ed., *L'Etat, la finance et le social. Souveraineté nationale et construction européenne* (Paris: Découverte, 1995), pp. 282–305.
[1] See Peter Hall, 'Aligning Ontology and Methodology in Comparative Research', in James Mahoney and Dietrich Rueschemeyer, eds., *Comparative Historical Analysis in Social Sciences* (Cambridge: Cambridge University Press, 2003), pp. 373–404, p. 391.

used middle-range theories of the determinants of welfare state development to predict the power of these contextual factors to impede or enhance our eight hypothesized effects (table 1.8).

We have also argued that the time dependence of institutional effects[2] should be taken into account. The reasons were several. First, as shown in the path dependency literature, iterative political decision-making involves a sequential process in which earlier decisions strongly influence the trajectory of subsequent policy development. Second, the impact of federalism on social policy is contingent upon the stage of welfare state development, that is, whether social policy is in the process of initiation and expansion, or whether it is undergoing retrenchment. And finally, the institutions of federalism have themselves changed over time, and the welfare state itself may well be a major factor in this process. In order to give appropriate weight to these temporal factors, we have employed Paul Pierson's distinction between the 'old politics' and the 'new politics' of the welfare state, and concentrated on the feedback loop between the development of the welfare state and the evolution of federal institutions. We then presented case studies of the interactions between federalism and welfare state development in the six affluent, long-established OECD federations, using this framework for analysis and for testing our hypotheses.

In this final chapter we discuss and draw conclusions from each of those studies and use them to locate the effects of federal institutions on welfare state development, and vice versa. In this analysis we discover that federalism does indeed have inhibitory effects on welfare state development, but that these effects have crucial temporal and contextual limitations not identified in the econometric research. Indeed, we note that, under certain circumstances, federalism may actually serve to encourage the growth of social expenditure. We also discover that welfare state development can have profound effects on the structure of federalism – again, strongly dependent on the relative timing of events. Welfare state programmes have sometimes been deliberately used by political elites as an instrument of nation-building, and their initiation has often been a trigger for shifts from inter-state to intra-state institutional forms.

What the case studies say

We begin our analysis with summaries of each of the six country chapters, starting with the three New World nations and moving on to the European federations.

---

[2] See Paul Pierson, *Politics in Time. History, Institutions, and Social Analysis* (Princeton: Princeton University Press, 2004).

Australia The Australian development can be summed up in terms of three phases: a late consolidation of programmes prior to World War Two; a delayed expansion of spending in the period of what elsewhere was the 'golden era' of welfare state development; and, finally, in the era of retrenchment, some spirited institutional resistance to government attempts to curtail social spending. Federalism played a major role in both the first and the last of these phases, but had a more muted presence in respect of the second.

Although the Australian federation was seen in its early years as a pioneer of radical social reform, the new constitutional set-up provided the federal government with few explicit welfare powers. Although it had the capacity to settle industrial disputes through compulsory wage arbitration, its other powers were limited to pensions and quarantine. As a consequence, the majority of social policy programmes were established considerably later than in other nations, with the strongest wave of consolidation occurring in the wartime conditions of the early to mid-1940s. At the same time, the use of the arbitration power gave the emergent welfare state a peculiar cast, with wage levels supposedly determined, at least in some part, by social policy considerations. In this sense, the federation's arbitration power was a pre-condition of what has since come to be called 'the wage earner's welfare state'.

After World War Two the great contradiction of Australian development in the era of the 'old politics' of the welfare state was that the federal government now had the constitutional authority to expand spending, but, for the most part, failed to do so. Castles and Uhr's account suggests three main reasons for this paradox. The first was that the party in office for much of the period was ideologically opposed to welfare state expansion. The second was that the means-tested form of social provision that was typical of Australian social policy programmes was intrinsically less expansive than the kinds of welfare state structures found in most other countries. Finally, for much of the 'golden era', in a period when Australia combined exceptionally low unemployment with a youthful age structure, the wage earner's welfare state was widely seen as sufficient protection for the relatively small minority in need. In this era, federalism's only real contribution was a path dependent one as the ultimate cause of late adoption and, hence, of continuingly low expenditure levels.

Finally, in the most recent period, federalism has played an increasingly more important and active part as a bulwark against a decline in welfare standards resulting from the abandonment of the wage earner's strategy of social protection through the control of wage levels. In this struggle the federal upper house – the Senate – has taken a prominent role, using its quasi-permanent anti-government blocking majority to force the government to draw back from a variety of welfare cutback proposals over a period of nearly two decades. This is not a mechanism capable of resisting all incursions. The Senate has not been an effective champion against successive thrusts against the protective efficacy of the arbitration system. It is, however, clearly the opposite face of the inertia that frustrated early programme adoption. Australia, in consequence, stands as a classic case of federalism as a source of resistance to rapid change – whether that change seeks to build a bigger welfare state or to undermine an existing one.

Canada As in the majority of federations, decentralization slowed the early development of the welfare state in Canada. Although a number of welfare initiatives emerged at the local level during the early decades of the twentieth century, provincial politicians clearly felt constrained by fiscal imbalances and the mobility of labour and capital in a federal state, constraints which were especially important in limiting the response to mass unemployment during the 1930s. Major breakthroughs emerged only after a significant centralization of power during World War Two, which ushered in an era of unparalleled political and fiscal dominance by the federal government. The federal government moved quickly to introduce major income security programmes of its own in the 1940s and early 1950s, and led the nation-wide development of provincial health and social services in the 1950s and 1960s.

However, more subtle relationships also emerged in the post-war era. Canada never developed a single model of federal–provincial relations. Indeed, Banting locates three distinct models governing different social programmes: *classical federalism*, with programmes run exclusively by one level of government; *shared-cost federalism*, with the federal government financially supporting provincial programmes; and *joint decision federalism*, where formal approval by both levels of government is mandatory before any action can take place. Each of these models creates different decision rules, altering the mix of governments and ideologies at the bargaining table, redistributing power among those who have a seat at the table, and requiring different levels of consensus for action. The result has been three separate kinds of interactions between institutions and policy during the era of welfare state expansion. In the case of exclusively federal programmes, federal officials acted as they would have done in a unitary state, and their programmes faithfully reflected the currents of national politics. At the same time, a complex system of joint decision-making was slowing the expansion of contributory pensions, while the shared-cost model was giving opportunities to the political left at the regional level to launch health care on more social-democratic premises than those prevailing in income security programmes.

As in the era of expansion, the 'new politics' of social policy in the 'silver age' had to flow through three distinctive institutional filters created by federal institutions, helping to explain the uneven impact of retrenchment in Canada. Exclusively federal programmes were unprotected by inter-governmental relations and fully exposed to shifts in national politics, with dramatic cuts especially in unemployment benefits. In contrast, joint decision federalism helped to protect contributory pensions from radical restructuring, while shared-cost federalism made it possible to preserve the basic model of the health care system, at least in respect of hospital, physicians and diagnostic services, if not always in respect of the generosity of funding. As a consequence, Banting suggests, the liberal and social-democratic worlds of Canadian welfare that had emerged during the course of the post-war decades moved further apart.

The United States US federalism is the oldest model of democratic federalism and constitutes the classic instance of the inter-state type in which the dominant principle remains a deliberate vertical division and separation of powers rather than a complex pattern of overlapping and co-operative relationships across levels of government. Finegold's account stresses the impacts of federalism and the character it imparts to US social policy. Key effects include the variety of policy outcomes across the fifty states, the absence of state-level social policy, the lateness and incompleteness of national-level programmes, the US penchant for state-level policy experimentation (including waivers), the federal governments' proclivity to attach (some) strings to aid to the states, and the use of the federal mechanism to overcome policy deadlocks at the national level. Lack of uniformity, the relative weakness of sub-national spending programmes and the lateness of national programme adoption are all elements in the standard account of federalism as a major factor contributing to the view of the US as a welfare state laggard.

A well-known aspect of the distinctiveness of US social policy is its bifurcation into social security and welfare programmes. Finegold shows that the story is still more complex. Programmes are arrayed along a spectrum from greater to lesser national authority, with Social Security at one end and General Assistance at the other. Programmes for the aged tend to cluster towards the national, institutionalized and legitimate end of the spectrum; so-called welfare programmes catering to the needs of the poor cluster towards the state-provided, less institutionalized and much less legitimate end. As one moves away from the two major national programmes of Social Security and Medicare, catering to the needs of the aged, and from Supplemental Security Income (SSI), again a programme for the aged, and Food Stamps, uniformity of provision disappears rapidly. On closer inspection, though, this disbanding of uniformity mainly holds for only *one* programme, that is, for what used to be Aid to Families with Dependent Children (AFDC) and is now Temporary Assistance to Needy Families (TANF). States offer varying supplements to federally funded or shared-cost programmes and rates of benefit vary widely for what are ostensibly the same programmes. The pattern of social provision is only partly nationalized and the tendency for programmes established at the state end of the spectrum to become radically more centralized or uniform in character stopped after Nixon. The story is different, though, on the tax expenditure side, with the expansion of the Earned Income Tax Credit (EITC), which goes to low income families with at least one parent working.

In terms of feedback effects of the welfare state on government practice, Finegold notes that state participation in federal social programmes has led to the modernization of the states and their professionalization. Social policy also affected the constitutional basis of federalism, namely by court interpretations, permitting the grants-in-aid approach that in turn made room for the categorical and special revenue-sharing (block grants) programmes that play such a central role today. This evolution is typical of the ad hoc bypass structures that have emerged in the US.

The conventional account of the relationship between federalism and social policy in the United States is highly consonant with the standard econometric interpretation: the US is the classic case of strong federalism and the classic case of arrested welfare development. Finegold's counter-factual analysis suggests that such an account misses ways in which federal arrangements may have countered social policy deadlock. This may have been the case both with respect to the New Deal and, more recently, with respect to welfare state reform. Finegold asks whether, in 1935, the blocking effect of the southern veto – which some commentators might argue was in itself the historical product of federalism – could possibly have been removed without devolving authority for unemployment insurance, old age assistance and aid to dependent children to the states. He argues that it could not, and without federal institutions, important parts of the New Deal would not have been adopted. In effect, federalism was the midwife of the New Deal. Similarly, he suggests that Clinton's failed health reform would not have given birth to a programme providing for the health needs of children from families above the Medicaid income limit (State Children's Health Insurance Program; SCHIP) had it not been for federal arrangements. Seeing things from this perspective nuances the conventional account. It suggests that without federalism the 'old politics' of the welfare state in the US might have been even less hospitable to welfare state initiatives than it actually was. By the same token, in the era of the 'new politics', the use of presidential waivers in welfare reform appears to have offered fertile opportunities for sidestepping national-level constituencies of support for existing social policy programmes. Thus, the 'old' and 'new politics' travel via the same bypasses, although, since Nixon, the emphasis has shifted from 'categorical' to 'block' sharing of revenues, thus de-emphasizing 'welfare rights' and underscoring 'states' rights'.

We now turn to the experience of European federalism.

Austria Welfare state consolidation in the Austrian part of the Habsburg Empire took place in a non-federal and authoritarian institutional context. Initiated by a conservative political elite seeking to bolster its political legitimacy and to preserve the existing socio-economic order, the central state made the social policy terrain its own from the late 1880s onwards. Social insurance programmes launched in that period were occupationally fragmented and entirely contribution-based, operating independently of the central government in a para-fiscal fashion. World War One not only brought about the demise of the multi-ethnic Austro-Hungarian Empire, but also led to massive socio-economic turmoil that had to be addressed by the unitary but also decentralized German-Austrian Republic founded in 1918.

The social policy agenda of the first Grand Coalition government from 1918 to 1920 was largely preoccupied with legislation designed to cope with the human aftermath of war. When the country became a democratic federation in 1920, core social programmes such as health and accident insurance, old age pensions for white-collar workers as well as unemployment insurance were already established at the national level. In consequence, federal institutions had no leverage for impeding the adoption of welfare state programmes. From the outset, Austrian intra-state federalism was characterized by a low degree of horizontal and vertical power fragmentation. The federal government possessed comprehensive fiscal and social policy powers and was largely unconstrained by institutional veto players. This, in turn, meant that the developmental trajectory of the welfare state was crucially shaped by the partisan complexion of government. Between 1920 and the demise of democracy in 1933–34, the federal government was composed of Christian Social and Pan-German parties. Welfare state expansion was moderate and was shaped by the ideological doctrines of these parties, while the Great Depression marked the starting point for the first major retrenchment phase of the twentieth century. In opposition, the Social Democrats concentrated their efforts in their Viennese bastion, thereby successfully exploiting the capabilities for political action that federal systems offer to territorially concentrated political or ethnic minorities. The *Anschluss* with Nazi Germany in 1938 terminated the short-lived pre-fascist authoritarian state. With it, federalism as well as a sovereign Austrian state came to an end.

World War Two was an indirect pacemaker for social expenditure growth in the post-war period. Early steps were to extend the powers of the government to cope with war-induced social needs and to coordinate economic reconstruction. When full sovereignty was restored in 1955, a powerful duopoly of welfare state parties operated in the context of consociational democracy and corporatism to introduce new programmes and to extend social insurance coverage to the vast majority of citizens. Federalism was no impediment to welfare state expansion, since the government was able to change the constitution more or less as it pleased, while the Länder backed these policies in order to reduce their social assistance spending.

Favourable economic performance moderated retrenchment pressure on the Grand Coalition of the mid-1980s onwards. The turn-around came in 2000, when a centre-right government took office. With no real institutional veto points and deliberately bypassing the trade unions, the government adopted a new and highly confrontational course in economic and social policy. However, the collapse of the centre-right government in 2002, as well as a series of electoral defeats for the Freedom Party at the Länder level, have demonstrated the risks attaching to all-out welfare state retrenchment. The proliferation of elections in federal systems and the genuine interest of sub-governments in greater spending have acted as buffers against a radical rollback of the welfare state. However, these mechanisms could only moderate but not entirely avert the benefit cuts imposed by a centre-right government operating within a highly permissive constitutional setting.

Germany From its inception in 1871, German federalism was committed to national unity and legislative, although not administrative, centralization. Throughout the 1880s there was continuous feedback between early welfare state consolidation, seeking to standardize living conditions throughout the Reich, and the further elaboration of federal institutions. The welfare state was immediately established as, and continues to be, *the* great national unifying institution of the German state. The Weimar years brought further centralization and institutional uniformity for the state apparatus in general and the welfare state in particular, first in the wake of severe turmoil following World War One, and then in the second half of the 1920s triggered by the mounting economic crisis. Such was the institutional legacy bequeathed to the Federal Republic, which had only a few institutional remnants carried over from the Nazi period.

Federalism did little to dampen post-war welfare state growth in Germany. Indeed, Manow suggests that it provided surprisingly fertile ground for welfare expansion. Interlocked rather than clearly separated jurisdictions obscured political responsibility, offering fruitful opportunities for blame avoidance and credit claiming and leading to a political overgrazing of the fiscal commons. These tendencies have been exacerbated by the para-fiscal opportunity structure built into the German Constitution. This has permitted the passage of contribution-financed measures as well as rate rises by simple parliamentary majority, by indexation and by ministerial edict, all of them mechanisms that sidestep in varying degrees of intensity the veto prone federal route required for tax-based programmes. All social insurance contributions go to the independent agencies administering social security programmes, which are regulated through diverse forms of corporatist self-government. This institutional arrangement is held responsible for the tendency of German federalism to externalize costs to the welfare state, while providing fiscal relief to the municipalities, the states and the federal budget. Instead of blocking social policy expenditures, federalism becomes part of a feedback loop, encouraging buoyant growth of social expenditures, while the welfare state offers the various governments a means of buying themselves out of their politically most pressing problems, from unification to fiscal consolidation, and to the management of the labour market.

Unlike most English-speaking federalisms, Germany is not characterized by the adversarial politics of pro- and anti-welfare state parties. Even without a Grand Coalition in office, an effective double Grand Coalition is produced by a bipartisan pro-welfare stance and by the regular failure of either major party to dominate both houses simultaneously. Theoretically, there is sufficient veto potential in German intra-state federalism to block spending initiatives, despite the existence of the para-fiscal bypass mechanism. In fact, the threat of retrenchment has been contained for a long time by permanent one-upmanship in the tightly contested game of being seen as the 'true' party of the welfare state. Given that much of Germany's peculiar pattern of crisis adjustment is explained by party competition (reinforced by federalism), present reform efforts may be seen as resulting from a transformation of the political landscape. There is now a stalemate in which the Social Democratic opposition, which has previously always opposed the welfare reforms of the conservatives as a neo-liberal onslaught on the welfare state, now finds itself in an overbidding game, in which the conservative opposition criticizes red–green reforms as being insufficiently radical or not profound enough.

The consensus model thus remained dominant well into the era of retrenchment. It now shows signs of erosion, however. Since the welfare state is largely a para-state, the arena of the 'new politics' is shifted away from the state proper, with Germany's fiscal adjustment to adverse economic circumstances taking place primarily through the adjustment of welfare state revenues and spending. Given the dynamics of the system, it should come as no surprise that the two major initiatives to expand the welfare state after 1973 also became part of the '*new* politics'. In the name of unity and equality – the paradoxical maxims of the German welfare state since the 1880s – the West German welfare state was exported holus-bolus to the East. In 1994 Long Term Care Insurance was legislated as a fifth social insurance pillar, stimulated again by cost-externalization, in this case, by the municipalities. Both reforms were CDU-initiated and SPD-supported. Retrenchment in Germany, therefore, is just one aspect of the permanent 'repackaging' of the welfare state, a process that is ill-understood if seen only as an exercise in expenditure clawback.

Substantial cost containment did actually occur in Germany. However, it only becomes visible if expenditures are measured with reference to the old levels of (now cut) entitlements. Cost-cutting has mainly affected the tax-financed share of social spending, which has often subsidized the contribution-financed share. Indeed, contribution increases were actually used to offset cutbacks in tax-financed programmes, a point rarely noted in a federalism literature fixated on the supposedly comprehensive 'blocking' power of institutional veto points.

The German welfare state's feedback effects on federalism are, nevertheless, ecological and pervasive: Together with the similarly shaped tax state, it subverts inter-regional economic competition from the bottom up, effectively blocking any structural reforms which aim at a more competitive federalism. Under these conditions 'negotiated change' remains the only real alternative.

Switzerland   The Swiss case study reveals clearly the braking effect of federalism on early welfare state formation. Since the federal government faced substantial competence constraints in fiscal and social policy, the government could not impose national programmes unilaterally. Given the federation's lack of powers, the effects of industrialization were initially experienced at the local and cantonal level. Local policy pre-emption has, in consequence, been very considerable and has given rise to a heterogeneous web of local social security arrangements. In strong contrast to both Austria and Germany, Switzerland's welfare state consolidation was a bottom-up process extending over a period of around seventy years.

More specifically, delays in programme adoption at the national level were a consequence of a two-stage decision-making process. To obtain the authority to act, the federal government first required a constitutional amendment that was only obtainable by means of a mandatory referendum requiring a majority of both voters and cantons. Though all constitutional amendments ultimately overcame this hurdle, disputes between the different tiers of government over policy jurisdiction and welfare state funding often delayed the reallocation of jurisdiction by many years. Programme adoption was further postponed during the second stage of the decision-making process because opponents of reform were in a position to attack ordinary federal bills by means of the optional referendum, a mechanism giving business interests, regional parties and local interests the leverage to water down federal social policy initiatives.

With veto points so deeply entrenched, the enactment of core social security programmes either failed or was substantially postponed. It was only after World War Two that things changed. War-induced solidarity, emerging consociational practice and continuous economic growth constituted a favourable environment for the enactment of those programmes that had hitherto fallen foul of these obstacles to programme adoption. After 1945, with the exception of health insurance, the optional referendum and federalism ceased to be insurmountable barriers against expansive social policy.

The 1990s witnessed a huge increase in welfare spending that had its main roots in belated programme maturation and a declining rate of economic growth. Spending growth was to a far lesser extent a result of new social programmes or of enhanced benefits. Retrenchment was difficult to achieve because the optional referendum, frequently used by welfare state clienteles, trade unions and leftist parties, proved to be an effective means of defending the status quo. Negotiation-based welfare state restructuring via balanced reform packages was more successful. In sum, the Swiss case illuminates how the complex institutional arrangements of federalism and direct democracy have increased policy stability. This holds true both for the 'old' and the 'new politics' of the welfare state. The emergence of the welfare state modified the functioning of federalism. Inter-state federalism was hollowed out as fiscal and social competencies were shifted to the federal level, which gradually assumed the upper hand in legislation, while cantons were simultaneously entrusted with the administration of federal legislation. A corollary of the emergence of intra-state federal practice has been an ever larger and more complex web of grants distributed across different levels of government.

The impact of federalism in comparative perspective

In the introduction to this volume we noted an apparent correspondence between types of federal arrangement – whether inter-state or intra-state – and the character of the welfare state, and hypothesized that the former might be an important factor in determining the latter. On the basis of this simple typology, one would expect the welfare states of the New World federalisms to conform to one pattern and those of the Old World federalisms to another. But the reality revealed by our six case studies is far less clear-cut. Examined in greater detail, the apparent correspondence of federal and welfare state types largely disappears, with a high degree of variability in both the institutional and the welfare state arrangements of New World and Old World federalisms.

We noted from the outset that several of our countries – Australia, Switzerland and possibly Canada – failed to fit precisely into either the inter-state or intra-state type of federalism. Despite its cantonal diversity, Switzerland has made giant strides towards co-operative federalism over the years. Australia's strong taxing powers and commitment to 'fiscal equalization' in the early 1940s were hardly what one would expect of an inter-state federalism. Half a century later, the growing significance of the Council of Australian Governments is clearly indicative of the continuing evolution of intra-state arrangements, particularly with respect to the provision of welfare state services such as health and education. Canada arguably provides the most dramatic example of the temporal variability and mix-and-match nature of federal arrangements, with different forms of federalism in place for different areas of policy and substantially different federal–state relationships from one programme to the next. These qualitative comparisons of the evolution of the relationships between federalism and the welfare state over time underline the dangers of oversimplification of a complex and changing phenomenon.

The 'old politics' of the welfare state

The above caveats notwithstanding, our findings with respect to the early consolidation stage of the 'old politics' of the welfare state do, indeed, suggest that types of federalism are pertinent to the developmental trajectory of welfare states. However, the crucial distinction is not that between inter-state and intra-state forms, but rather whether federal welfare development took place under democratic or non-democratic auspices. The six-country comparison provided in this volume reveals that, in all those federations which have been *democratic* throughout the course of the twentieth century, welfare state consolidation has taken place later and the pace of social expenditure growth has been slower than in the majority of unitary states at a comparable level of economic development. In contrast, however, the two nations lacking fully responsible and representative institutions of government during the consolidation phase – Austria and Germany – were in the vanguard of programme adoption.

Consolidation in early democratic federalisms

Hence, a major finding of this volume is that the impact of federalism is strongest at the stage of programme consolidation. By identifying *democratic* federalism as a major impediment at the formative phase of welfare state development, our main finding with regard to the 'old politics' of the welfare state dovetails neatly with the evidence from comparative statistical research. It was democratic federations that were in the majority, and it is their retarding effect on programme adoption, and, hence, on the initial stages of programme expenditure growth that has been picked up in the statistical studies. However, in contradistinction to the necessarily undifferentiated conclusions of such studies, our historical, ideographic approach allows us to locate the precise circumstances under which federalism matters and to identify the underlying mechanisms explaining why federalism has been an impediment in some contexts and not in others.

A key consideration in these differential dynamics of federal welfare states is the question of which tier of government first occupied the welfare state terrain. Of central importance, therefore, is the original distribution of jurisdictions among levels of government, which in turn is strongly influenced by the type of federalism under consideration. The programme impeding and expenditure restraining effects of federalism can be seen most clearly in democratic federations with inter-state federal arrangements, where the federal level of government originally had little or no power to take up social policy concerns and the scope for federal fiscal manoeuvre was relatively limited (see table 8.1). In such instances, the take-off of the welfare state was delayed until the necessary powers had been acquired. Because they either lacked or shared social and fiscal policy competencies, federal authorities could not act unilaterally but only in collaboration with the constituent units. Hence, social policy frequently got stuck in the kind of jurisdictional game of hide-and-seek that Banting notes as being typical of the Canadian situation: while the federal level lacked the power to launch national social programmes, constituent units were often hesitant to establish welfare programmes unilaterally as they feared the competitive disadvantage of a pioneer status.

Such considerations were of particular relevance in North America in the period prior to the Great Depression, and were further strengthened by the complete absence or weak development of systems of fiscal equalization. Although fiscal equalization was a stronger theme in the Australian development, the inter-war failure to initiate a scheme of child endowment was a classic instance of jurisdictional hide-and-seek. On the other hand, there were also instances where constituent units and municipalities established social programmes at the local and regional level. Swiss federalism, with its emphasis on local autonomy rather than horizontal competition, is a clear case in point.

As a consequence of limited federal powers and local policy pre-emption, welfare state consolidation took place from the bottom up in all the democratic federations. Prompt upward redistribution of

Table 8.1 Distribution of legislative authority for social provision as between state and central government 1920, 1950 and today

	Australia			Canada			USA			Austria			Germany			Switzerland			Sum		
	1920	1950	Today	1920	1950	Today	1920	1950	Today	1920	1950	Today	1920	1950	Today	1920	1950	Today	1920	1950	Today
Old age, survivors and disability	1	1	1	(0)[1]	1.0	0.5	(0)	0.5	1	1	1	1	1	1	1	0	1	1	3	5.5	5.5
Health	0	0.5	1	(0)	(0)	0.5	(0)	(0.5)	0.5	1	1	1	1	1	1	1	1	1	3	4	5
Work injury	0[1]	0[1]	0[1]	0	0	0	0[1]	0[1]	0[1]	1	1	1	1	1	1	1	1	1	3	3	3
Unemployment	0	1	1	(0)	1	1	(0)	0.5	0.5	1	1	1	1	1	1	0	1	1	2	5.5	5.5
Family allowances[I]	0	1	1	(0)	1	0.5	(0)	(0.5)[2]	(0.5)[2]	(1)[1]	1[1]	1	(1)	(1)[1]	1[1]	0	(1)	1[1]	2	5.5	5
Social assistance[II]	0	1[2]	1[2]	0	0.5[2]	0	0	0.5	0.5	0.5[2]	0.5[2]	0.5[2]	(1)[2]	(1)[2]	1[2]	0	0	0	1.5	3.5	3
Sum	1	4.5	5	0	3.5	2.5	0	2.5	3	5.5	5.5	5.5	6	6	6	2	5	5	14.5	27	27

Legend: 1 = federal jurisdiction, 0 = state or provincial jurisdiction, 0.5 = shared jurisdiction. Bracketed figures (X) denote that a competence was either *explicitly given* or *generally presumed*, but was not (yet) utilized through legislation.
General notes: [I] Family allowances includes all programmes aimed at families, whether means-tested or not.
[II] Social assistance consists of means-tested programmes provided exclusively on the basis of need.
Notes on countries:
Australia: [1] The Commonwealth Workers Compensation system covers only Commonwealth employees. Technically, then, there is a very small degree of federal involvement, but the basic principle is one of state-based provision.
[2] Since all income maintenance programmes are means-tested, it is possible to argue that the entire system is one of social assistance. However, there is also a Special Benefit programme established in 1944 for indigent individuals not qualifying under other programmes. This is very small and in the late 1990s had circa 10,000 beneficiaries across Australia.

Canada:[1] Although social problems were generally seen as local matters and widely presumed to be provincial in 1920, jurisdictional boundaries remained uncertain and contested, with the federal and provincial governments arguing about who was responsible. The constitution was not explicit about jurisdiction over key fields of social security, and the courts had to infer competence from more general grants of power in decisions that came later in the century.

[2] Technically provincial in 1950. In 1956, however, the federal government established a major shared cost programme, which was expanded in 1965, but then eliminated again in 1995. The field was thus shared for four decades.

USA:[1] Most workers are covered by state worker compensation programmes financed by employers. Federal programmes cover only federal employees, some maritime workers, and coal miners with black lung disease.

[2] Neither level of government provides universal cash transfers to families. Some state and national income tax provisions, however, have related effects.

Austria:[1] According to a Constitutional Court ruling, a federal jurisdiction existed only for population policy according to Section 12 [2] of the Constitution. In 1955 a constitutional amendment was passed, which gave the federal government the power to legislate in all matters of family support.

[2] The federal government may enact framework legislation but never did so.

Germany:[1] Since 1919 the Reich government had, according to article 7, no. 7 Weimar Constitution, a concurrent competency (*konkurrierende Gesetzgebung*) for 'demographic policy [*Bevölkerungspolitik*], mother, infant and child and youth care'. But a universal child allowance did not come until 1954, with the first child participating only after 1975. Pension rights solely based on years of child raising were introduced in 1985 and expanded ever since. In addition there are income tax allowances.

[2] Since 1919 the Reich government had the same competence for 'Social Assistance' (article 7, no. 5: *Armenwesen, Wandererfürsorge*). The process of nationalization was slow, starting in 1924 and completed only in 1961 with the *Bundessozialhilfegesetz*, though it already came close to that result by 1950 (cf. the 1954 judgement of the *Bundesverwaltungsgericht*, vol. 1, pp. 159ff.). Nationalization in Germany is functionally incomplete, though, as administration and finance continue to be a local and state government responsibility, though both tiers can rely on pervasive general revenue sharing.

Switzerland:[1] The *federal* government provides family allowances for farmers and agricultural employees only. All other employees are covered by *cantonal* schemes. Some cantons also provide income support to the self-employed.

competencies was blocked through a series of institutional veto points, with multi-tiered negotiations required to remove such obstacles necessarily involving a considerable number of actors with often conflicting interests. Rigid procedures of constitutional amendment and judicial review have repeatedly struck down federal intrusions in social affairs. In cases where reallocation of jurisdictions was unsuccessful, the only way for the federal government to launch social policy initiatives was to provide federal grants to the constituent units. However, such a strategy marked the starting point of a cost-sharing federalism that in most instances was conducive to an ever-increasing fiscal interdependence between different tiers of government.

The creeping nationalization of social policy, therefore, often resulted from federal–state struggles over the acquisition of social and fiscal powers, and this was particularly true if the field had already been, to some extent, pre-empted by a lower tier of government. Since social policy had become an important source of political legitimacy, state-level political actors have, on occasions, been hesitant to let competencies for social and fiscal policies move upward. Apart from the interests of the constituent units in retaining their own powers and in enhancing their own legitimacy, a broad array of private interests have also frequently crystallized around these systems. Institutional veto points built into federal constitutions gave local interests a powerful leverage to oppose shifts in competencies to the federal tier.

The built-in institutional complexity of federal arrangements, the territorial fragmentation of power resources and the great number of actors involved in the decision-making process have together made for a substantial delay in programme adoption at the national level in democratic federations. Health politics is the most prominent case in point. Federalism is indeed part of the answer to the question of why there is no national health system in the United States, and why health systems emerged so late in Australia, Switzerland and Canada. This outcome can be explained by the interaction of several mechanisms. In none of these nations was the federal government initially equipped with the powers required for legislation in this field. The highest courts repeatedly fended off federal incursions into state territory, while the thorny procedures for changing a constitution in a federal system substantially delayed the reallocation of fiscal and social policy jurisdictions. Moreover, interest groups, such as those constituted by the medical profession and private sickness funds, could make use of the many veto points afforded by federal arrangements to obstruct federal initiatives in the health policy arena.

Strong nationally organized interest groups seeking to frustrate change in the context of a decentralized polity clearly have the cards strongly stacked in their favour. The resulting braking effects are rather impressive. A delay of almost exactly a quarter of a century in introducing a national health service in Australia resulted from the High Court's rejection of constitutionality of the federal legislation in 1948. In Switzerland, the lack of federal powers, local policy pre-emption and the proliferation of veto points delayed federal legislation by some twenty years. Attempts to enact health insurance repeatedly failed or were watered down by optional referendum. In Canada, a national health programme only began to emerge with provincial prodding in the late 1950s and was only completed more than a decade later. The United States remains, of course, the only western nation without a comprehensive national health insurance scheme in place.

Health is, moreover, only the most dramatic instance. The veto power of federal institutions is visible in other branches of social policy as well. In Australia in the early years of federation, the High Court frequently ruled in such a way as to limit the scope of the Commonwealth's power of arbitration. In 1937 the Canadian courts struck down the Employment and Social Insurance Act initiated by a Conservative government, while in the US the Supreme Court invalidated the prohibition of child labour as violating the Tenth Amendment.

Local policy pre-emption has not only delayed programme adoption at the federal level, but has also reduced the degrees of freedom available for future federal social policy initiatives by reducing the capacity of the federal government to penetrate locally grown social programmes. Faced with the strong bargaining power of local interests and constituent units mediated by the proliferation of institutional veto points, federal governments have often been forced to incorporate pre-existing, state-level policy solutions in order to accommodate or prevent resistance to federalization by the interests embedded in state-level structures. Such moderation forcing tendencies have often resulted in federal framework legislation at a distance, conserving state-level policies much as they were – a subtly modified version of one of Murphy's sub-laws, which used to be the economists' Edinburgh rule ('leave them as you find them'). In some instances, the federal level has simply subsidized the systems run by the constituent units, marking a further departure for an increasingly complex system of inter-governmental transfers through which different tiers of government became increasingly intertwined. Existing patterns of benefit provision were, therefore, largely retained, but superseded by federal framework legislation that stipulated minimum standards in this field. As a consequence, federalism also had a structural impact on national welfare state architectures. Another instance of such an effect is where competence constraints and institutionally induced inertia have redirected social provision from the state to the private sphere, leading to the reshaping of the public–private mix in benefit provision.

An instance of this is the way in which the failed Swiss health insurance reform of 1900 triggered switches in the developmental trajectory of the public–private mix in social insurance and shifted health politics towards a liberal trajectory of development based on limited forms of federal intervention. A similar pattern occurred in the United States. The federal breakthrough in US social policy in the 1930s occurred in the sphere of pensions and other aspects of social security, but (repeatedly) failed in the sphere of health provision.[3] This has led to highly (tax) subsidized and densely regulated private provision of health insurance through employment-based schemes, which are highly resistant to external, that is governmental, control. In Australia too, the quarter-century hiatus in the emergence of a national health scheme led to the growth of private insurance arrangements, which, despite national legislation in the 1970s and 1980s, remain more entrenched than anywhere else outside the United States, albeit with an increasing degree of subsidization from a Liberal federal government. In Canada, veto-prone decision-making rules also influenced the public–private mix in the retirement income system. By constraining the expansion of contributory pensions, joint decision rules helped to preserve a larger role for the private sector, making for a greater reliance on tax-subsidized private instruments. In contrast, the more flexible rules governing the introduction of federal shared-cost programmes facilitated the expansion of universal public health provision on a national basis from the late 1950s onwards, more or less displacing the role of the private insurance industry in the provision of core medical and hospital services.

A further structural impact, inherent in the logic of federalism, has been the territorial fragmentation of standards of benefit provision, where states rather than the federation are the locus of social provision. The failed nationalization of social programmes automatically led to territorial inequalities in terms of benefit levels and eligibility provisions. By the same token, territorially fragmented problem-solving caused an increasing pressure for horizontal inter-governmental co-operation. This emergent need for horizontal co-ordination was frequently addressed by largely informal co-operation among regional governments, but also sometimes by private organizations, as Swiss social assistance politics illustrate.

To sum up, territorially fragmented powers, institutional veto points and local social policy initiatives defended by vested interest groups all

---

[3] For the US this trajectory of public–private mixes is pursued in detail for health and pension insurance by Jacob S. Hacker, *The Divided Welfare State: The Battle over Public and Private Benefits in the United States* (Cambridge: Cambridge University Press, 2002).

contributed in those democratic federations with inter-state-type federalism to causing a protracted and veto-ridden decision-making process that ultimately ended up in delayed programme adoption and preconfiguring the structural development of welfare states. Party politics is not a sufficient explanation of the delayed enactment of particular social programmes in such nations, since even initiatives launched by bourgeois governments were frustrated by a complex and veto-prone decision-making process.

Consolidation before democratic federalism
While it is quite easy to marshal evidence of the constraining effects on programmes and expenditures in the democratic federations, such forces appear to have been largely absent in Germany and Austria. Neither country was a fully developed democracy until 1918. Moreover, before World War One Austrian institutional forms can, at best, be seen as proto-federal in character. Early and comprehensive policy pre-emption of welfare state territory at the central state level in both countries was the major reason for unhindered and speedy social policy expansion in the years thereafter, as the central government controlled the relevant jurisdictions from the start (see table 8.1). The conservative political elite had little reason to concern itself with institutional veto points, as the judicial review of laws was unknown in either country. Moreover, there was no need to amend the constitution to empower the central state to legislate in the area of social policy. Bismarck's position as Chancellor, Prime Minister of Prussia and Chairman of the Bundesrat gave him considerable authority for agenda-setting, except in respect of programme funding, where the Bundesrat's power of fiscal veto was used to defeat a proposal that programme costs be met from general taxation. Ironically, it was this setback which made Bismarck opt for contribution-based funding, thereby creating a vehicle for the subsequent rapid growth of the welfare state by providing a means of shifting costs to third parties not involved in the bargaining game between the Reich and the states. In Austria, the franchise was even more restricted than in Germany and social reforms could be made into law at the stroke of a pen,[4] thus ensuring that, by the time Austria formally became a federation in 1920, welfare state consolidation was, in many respects, already a reality.

Several contextual factors accelerated welfare state consolidation under both monarchies. An important factor was the legitimacy requirement of a conservative elite that found itself confronted with a growing

---

[4] Subsequently, in the 1920s this was found to be constitutionally invalid, but with almost no effect on continuing practice.

working-class movement demanding more extensive political participation. In addition, a political culture of state-centred reform embedded in an 'enlightened' absolutism sustained a 'top-down' welfare state reform pattern. At the same time, an impetus for national policy intervention also came from the municipalities, which felt fiscally overburdened in coping with the consequences of rapid industrialization through the mechanism of traditional poor relief. These early welfare state building initiatives were, moreover, aspects of state-building and nation-building processes, making social policy a catalyst for the reinforcement of unitary trends in political and administrative development. In Germany, after the founding of the German Reich in 1871 social insurance policy became an important instrument for the consolidation of the new Reich. International competition also contributed to welfare state consolidation, since social policy was, amongst other objectives, seen by Bismarck as a means of competing with Britain in the race for world market leadership. This latter motive was absent in the Austro-Hungarian Empire, where early social policy was launched as part of an attempt to protect the pre-existing economic order by imposing non-wage labour costs on industry, giving social policy an anti-industrial and anti-liberal character. Nation-building was more important in the Habsburg Empire, since the emergence of welfare institutions here was seen as a means of countering the strong centrifugal forces of a multi-ethnic empire.

Germany and, in particular, Austria lend strong *ex adverso* support to the finding that welfare state consolidation was severely constrained in those instances in which democracy was conjoined with inter-state federalism. In consequence, the German and Austrian case studies should not be seen as contradicting the finding of the econometric literature, but rather as qualifying more precisely the ambit within which this finding applies. Early programme adoption in Germany and Austria is largely explained by top-down social policy enacted by semi-democratic or authoritarian regimes. The social policy terrain was comprehensively pre-empted by the central state, while the contribution-based funding of programmes provided a mechanism for continued welfare state growth, given that fiscal conflicts between different levels of government could be neatly sidestepped by externalizing costs to employers and employees.

By the late 1920s a great gulf separated Germany and Austria from the democratic federalist welfare state laggards. In the former, welfare state consolidation was largely accomplished, while, in the latter, it had, in respect of the vast majority of programmes, yet to begin. Over the next two decades external shocks – economic depression and total war – influenced social policy development in both types of federal setting, but in ways that reflected their prior contexts of development. In the long-time democratic federations, external shocks provided an impetus for overcoming entrenched veto point opposition, especially where the party in office was one favouring reform. In the United States, economic crisis was the major catalyst of change, with the Democratic hegemony in government and Congress in the 1930s constituting a window of opportunity for a Big Bang in social policy.[5] In Australia, the wartime crisis provided the occasion for centralization of the tax system and an extension of the social services role of the Commonwealth, with the longest Labor administration since Federation as its agent. In Canada, where the left remained weak, wartime conditions had very similar effects. In consequence, federal governments in all the nations studied had acquired considerable competencies for legislating social policy by the end of World War Two (see table 8.1).

In all these countries, even in neutral Switzerland, as in the vast majority of unitary states, the experience of total war was a catalyst for social expenditure growth, because it was in itself both a source of enhanced social solidarity[6] and of a 'displacement effect' by which post-war social expenditure naturally expanded into the fiscal space left by reductions in military spending.[7] In Austria and Germany, however, both the incentive and the mechanism for enhanced spending were stronger than elsewhere. The consequences of total defeat required massive social intervention by the state and the already consolidated welfare states in these nations provided the means by which such intervention could be accomplished. Hence, despite the removal of roadblocks in the way of programme adoption in former federal welfare state laggards during these years, they were unable to close the expenditure gap on Austria and Germany. On the contrary, these latter countries emerged from these years of crisis as unequivocally the world's biggest welfare states. In the aftermath of war, federal nations again supplied both the leaders and the laggards of modern social policy development, illustrating once more the need for greater historical nuance than can be supplied by the aggregating methods of quantitative analysis.

---

[5] Abram de Swaan, *In Care of the State: Education and Welfare in Europe and the USA in the Modern Era* (Cambridge: Polity Press, 1988), pp. 204ff. On an earlier development of the 'big bang' thesis, see Christopher Leman, *The Collapse of Welfare Reform: Political Institutions, Policy, and the Poor in Canada and the United States* (Cambridge, MA: MIT Press, 1980).

[6] See Robert E. Goodin and John Dryzek, 'Risk Sharing and Social Justice: The Motivational Foundations of the Post-War Welfare State', in Robert E. Goodin and Julian LeGrand, eds., *Not Only the Poor: The Middle Classes and the Welfare State* (London: Allen & Unwin, 1987), pp. 37–73, 48ff.

[7] See Alan T. Peacock and Jack Wiseman, *The Growth of Public Expenditure in the United Kingdom* (Princeton: Princeton University Press, 1961).

Expansion under generalized democratic federalism
After the war Germany and Austria remained the OECD's biggest spenders on welfare until well into the 1960s, when their spending levels began to be overtaken by a number of unitary states in both continental western Europe and in Scandinavia. Catch-up, by contrast, was modest in the English-speaking federations, which, together with Switzerland, lagged well behind German and Austrian social expenditure levels until long after the 'golden age' of social policy had come to an end in the mid to late 1970s. The driving forces behind these divergent patterns of expansion characterizing the later years of the 'old politics' of the welfare state are multifaceted. Three, often operating in conjunction, deserve particular mention.

First, once a full array of programmes was in place, and democratic institutions were fully developed, the welfare state became an important source of credit claiming and partisan competition. Hence, the partisan complexion of government was the primary factor that shaped the trajectory of social expenditure growth in the post-war period, explaining the rapid growth of social policy expenditure in social-democratic Scandinavia. However, the way in which party politics was played out was strongly influenced by the character of governmental (and federal) institutions. Expansion of the welfare state was strongest in those unitary states where major welfare state parties competed for office. In intra-state federations, such as Germany and Austria, the fate of the welfare state also remained highly contingent on the partisan complexion of government and on partisan competition. Arguably itself a feedback consequence of late welfare state consolidation in the long-time democratic federations, the relative weakness or complete absence of pro-welfare state parties in these nations was a major reason why there was no closing of the expenditure gap with Austria and Germany, even though these latter were no longer in the welfare vanguard. Welfare state expansion was muted in North America, where neither the Christian Democratic nor the Social Democratic parties operated at the national level, or, indeed, in the United States, even at the state level.

Moreover, the Canadian case demonstrates clearly that the regional fragmentation of power resources can be a potent barrier to the formation of welfare alliances at the national level. In Canada, class-based politics were also overshadowed by linguistic and regional cleavages. Direct partisan influence was strongest on those programmes that were managed exclusively either by Ottawa or by the provincial governments. Because governments were able to operate within their own sphere of jurisdiction, parties were in a position to shape outcomes according to their own preferences. The health policy innovations of the social-democratic government of Saskatchewan are a case in point. That social policy would have taken a different route in Canada had strong welfare state parties existed at the federal level is proven by the fact that small social-democratic parties such as the NDP were able to force the pace of welfare state expansion quite effectively on those occasions when the Liberals had no majority of their own and needed NDP support.

At first glance, it would seem that the partisanship hypothesis could also account for Australian developments in the 'golden age'. In contrast to the other English-speaking federations, Australia did have a strong party of the left in the Australian Labor Party (ALP), with an electoral record second only to that of the Swedish Social Democrats. Sadly, though, for the ALP, in the Australian context of a non-proportional electoral system votes did not always translate into parliamentary seats and the party was out of federal office from 1949 through to 1972. The question, then, is whether this provides a sufficient explanation of Australia's welfare trajectory during the immediate post-war decades.

Castles and Uhr point to a second driving force behind divergent patterns of expansion. They suggest that partisanship alone does not explain the Australian trajectory, and that it requires some reference to other dynamics to account for a 1960–1980 growth rate of social expenditure that was as low as any in the OECD. Conspicuous in their analysis is reference to the ways in which the legacy of past policy choices shape those of the present. This factor influences post-war policy outcomes in unitary countries as much as it does in federal countries. Different policy instruments – social insurance, means testing and universalism, tax expenditures – have diverse potentials for expenditure growth, and particular policy strategies imply greater or lesser emphasis on social spending as the primary mechanism of social amelioration. Australia is not peculiar in these respects, but because its policy instruments and policy choices have, in some respects, been rather unusual, it demonstrates the role of such legacies from the past rather more clearly than some other countries. Castles and Uhr's argument is not that partisanship was irrelevant in the Australian development, but that the weakness of post-war expenditure growth was also a function of the unusually high degree of welfare state means testing in Australia, together with the use of the arbitration system to secure a social policy minimum through wage control. Under circumstances of full employment, the wage earners' welfare state strategy was widely seen as being capable of dealing with most obvious social policy needs, and successive Liberal governments were happy to go along with policies underwriting a low tax/low public expenditure profile. In Australia, partisan preferences combined with the legacy of past policy choices to keep expenditure growth on the back burner in an era when new and expanded social programmes were the main political currency in most other western nations.

The third factor influencing cross-national expenditure profiles was the influence of federal arrangements themselves. The proliferation of veto points and the high level of consensus required for policy change in multi-tiered settings continued to have delaying effects in several of the federal nations during the course of the 'golden age'. The Canadian experience in the post-war period, that is, in the formative phase of welfare state consolidation, reveals that the impact of federalism on welfare state development is highly contingent upon the prevailing decision-making rules. In Canada, inter-governmental decision rules, which vary from one policy arena to another, can produce quite different programme dynamics. Policy gridlock was most likely to occur in those social policy realms where jurisdiction was divided and where super-majorities were required to alter the status quo (*joint decision federalism*). Heterogeneity in the partisan complexion of executives across different tiers of government and among provinces, together with an absence of federal mechanisms for mediating conflicts (the Senate is an unelected body), made inter-governmental consensus difficult to achieve. In contrast, programmes run by the provinces but to some degree regulated and funded by Ottawa (*shared-cost federalism*) were less prone to policy stalemate. Here, programme development was markedly influenced by the incentive structure provided by federal funding priorities, with programme innovation strongly influenced by federal grants delivered to the provinces. Finally, as noted previously, under the *classical model of federalism*, where jurisdiction is exclusive at either the federal or provincial level, programme content was substantially shaped by the incumbent government of the day.

Health politics in Switzerland provides a further example of the way in which the institutional veto points connected to federalism and direct democracy continued to have a restraining impact on social policy after World War Two and right through the 'old politics' era. Apart from one minor reform enacted in the 1960s, all attempts to restructure health insurance failed in Switzerland until the early 1990s. While party politics and vested interest groups were of the utmost importance in health policy-making, the way in which party conflicts were played out was strongly influenced by the character of governmental institutions. Much the same can be said of the push to social policy reform in the US in the 1960s, where the congruence of Democratic Party control of both Congress and the Presidency can be read simultaneously as evidence for an account premised on the influence of partisanship and as support for the view, that, as in the New Deal era, reform potential was greatest where the number of veto players was least.[8] Policy change was thus most pronounced in settings where reform-minded governments operated in permissive institutional environments.

The fact that both German and Austrian social expenditure levels were surpassed by a number of Scandinavian and other nations in the latter years of the 'golden age' is largely a consequence of programme maturation. Programmes were instituted earlier in these countries and, consequently, matured earlier. The accounts offered in the Austrian and German case studies do not suggest that this relative slow-down in growth was, in any sense, a function of institutionally induced political gridlock. Institutional veto points could be easily bypassed because a central condition for policy stability advanced by veto player theory was not fulfilled in the post-war era: there was no substantial ideological distance between the most prominent political actors, as the major political parties in both countries were unequivocally pro-welfare state in their attitudes. In addition, the structure of provision created opportunities for government to cope with the institutionally in-built complexity of federal arrangements. From the outset, the welfare state was mainly funded via contributions and not through taxes.[9] Multi-level governance problems were avoided by creating a new sub-level (the para-fiscus), regularly also spun off organizationally, creating new exit options for offloading costs from the state or federal level to the para-fiscal level. This strategy of externalizing the costs of welfare state funding was strongly backed by the states, since enhancing federal programmes lowered the costs of running welfare-related schemes and levelled out regional disparities.

Another strategy for bypassing veto players is best illustrated by the Austrian case, where the Constitutional Court, as the only major institutional veto player, was often circumvented by passing laws with supermajorities. As a consequence, such laws became 'constitution proof' and judicial review ceased to be relevant. Nevertheless, the success of such bypass strategies is contingent upon several factors, such as the centralization, congruence and vertical integration of the party system, the strength of the pro-welfare state parties, their ideological distance and the existence of constitutional veto points beyond those enshrined in federal arrangements. Thus, shifting the costs of the welfare state to

---

[8] This is an instance of the absorption rule stipulated by veto player theory. See George Tsebelis, *Veto Players. How Political Institutions Work* (Princeton: Princeton University Press, 2002).
[9] This is an organizational feature common to all German-speaking countries, and at least in the German and Swiss cases was a historical function of the fact that the central state was initially only semi-sovereign in fiscal matters.

employers was much more difficult in Switzerland, because business interests always had the option of launching an optional referendum.[10] As a consequence, both the adoption and the expansion of programmes were more veto-prone in Switzerland than in the other European federal nations.

The 'new politics' of the welfare state

The conclusion of our analysis so far is that federalism had a general inhibitory impact on welfare state consolidation in the early democratic federations, but that, once consolidation was accomplished, cross-national differences in spending trajectories were a function of a range of factors including partisan control, policy legacies and continuing institutional effects. In the present retrenchment phase, the era of the 'new politics', federalism does appear to work more generally as an institution slowing the pace of welfare reform. Although there are instances in individual countries where the existence of federal institutions have actually facilitated retrenchment, for the most part federalism and institutional complexity appear, in comparative perspective, to make expenditure cutbacks more difficult to achieve. Thus, our findings by and large corroborate a basic axiom of veto player theory, which posits that the institutional fragmentation of power reduces the opportunity for altering the status quo. This holds true equally of policies aimed at expanding the reach of the welfare state and of efforts to roll it back. Nevertheless, as in the era of the 'old politics', much depends on context, including country-specific institutional settings, policy structures and actor constellations. The different decision-making rules associated with different models of federalism are also important for understanding the extent of programme-related retrenchment in this more straitened era of welfare state development.

The case studies suggest several ways in which federal mechanisms have reduced the freedom of manoeuvre of those favouring expenditure retrenchment, but also reveal a variety of strategies by which policy stalemate can be averted.

First, economically weaker sub-national governments in multi-level systems have a substantial interest in preserving the social policy status quo. The welfare state is a gigantic machinery for redistribution, in which distribution amongst regions is often more significant than redistribution between classes. Arguably, the most spectacular instance is that of

---

[10] Historically, the introduction of the optional referendum in 1874 was not an element of vertical power sharing.

post-reunification Germany, where unemployment, pension and health insurance schemes redistribute several billion Euros a year from the western to the eastern Länder. However, a similar logic applies in all federations where there is a formal or informal practice of equalizing citizen provision across states. In Canada, political controversy over inter-regional redistribution centres on the explicit system of equalization grants, which narrow the immense gap in the fiscal capacity of provincial governments in rich and poor regions. But as in Germany, large implicit transfers also flow through national social programmes. The populations of poor regions have larger proportions of needy people who receive benefits, whereas tax-payers in those regions pay a smaller proportion of the federal taxes that support them. The dynamic reappears in another form in Australia, where the Grants Commission has a formal duty to equalize the fiscal resources devoted to citizens irrespective of the state in which they live. The instruments of inter-regional redistribution vary from one federation to another. But the common equalizing role of the federal welfare state is a key reason for rejecting simplistic distinctions between the New World and European brands of federalism.

Constituent units are especially interested in upholding national welfare state programmes if they themselves benefit from federal schemes but are not or are only to a limited degree responsible for their financing. Under such circumstances, states have strong incentives for free-riding and overgrazing the fiscal commons. Attempts to roll back federal schemes are, in consequence, likely to provoke the fierce resistance of the constituent units. Australia is again an instance, with Senate opposition to reduced Medicare funding owing much to the unpopularity of these cuts at the state level. Resistance is likely to be stronger where cuts in federal benefits have to be compensated for by social assistance programmes run by regional governments. In Canada, for example, the poorer Atlantic Provinces have protested successfully against cuts in federal unemployment insurance benefits. As a consequence, regional criteria were introduced into the rules governing the eligibility and benefit periods in the programme, making for a strongly increased regional differentiation of insurance transfers. Germany's strategy for avoiding such conflicts has, until recently, been to buy-off Länder opposition by utilizing the *para-state* to take up the slack of cuts in general revenues.

Second, general revenue sharing and a concentration of social policy powers at the central state level in intra-state federal settings has undercut a competitive race to the bottom. In Australia, all federal schemes are funded from the general exchequer, while much of the funding for state services comes from a federally levied goods and services tax. Moreover, Australia has the third most centralized fisc in the OECD world, so that there is presently almost no scope for tax competition.[11] Much the same holds for Germany and Austria, where the federal governments exercise almost exclusive powers of social policy legislation and most schemes are overwhelmingly funded by federally controlled contributions. The bulk of the revenues of constituent units come from federally levied taxes, which are distributed by nation-wide revenue sharing. Constrained tax autonomy at the Länder level in addition to fiscal equalization provide no leverage for competitive fiscal federalism or a race to the bottom in social standards. In Switzerland, despite considerable cantonal tax powers, there is also little evidence of the kind of competitive behaviour supposedly leading to a downward spiral of social provision. Again, the dominant role of the federal government in setting nation-wide social insurance standards and a fiscal equalization scheme are the main factors preventing a competitive race to the bottom, although low levels of inter-cantonal mobility resulting from linguistic and cultural barriers are also an important part of the equation.

Third, while institutional veto points may serve as a brake on retrenchment initiatives, this effect is mediated through political parties, party constellations and ideological preferences. Since the 1980s no government in Australia has had a Senate majority, giving leftist parties and independents a chance to block a variety of proposed cuts in welfare spending. However, in the arena of industrial policy, the government has been more successful in pushing through rationalizing changes inimical to the traditional wage earner's strategy. That is because, for the more bourgeois parties of the Left, such as the Australian Democrats, industrial issues have a lower ideological salience than direct welfare cuts, and because, in any case, their veto position on economic issues is undercut by the commitment of both major parties to a strategy of 'economic rationalization'. As a consequence, the trajectory of Australian welfare expenditure has been upwards over precisely the same period in which Australia's traditional strategy of social amelioration has been progressively dismantled through major party consensus.

Since the change of the Austrian government in 2000, the now oppositional Social Democrats have called on the Constitutional Court to block a number of the retrenchment programmes of the right-wing federal government. Their success, however, has only been partial. In Switzerland, just as in the 'old politics' era, it is not federal veto points as such that are most useful in fighting expenditure cuts, but rather the threat or reality of a

---

[11] The exception proving the rule was death duties, which in Australia were a state tax. As a consequence, when this form of taxation was abandoned in Queensland, all the other states were forced to follow suit.

referendum. Where once entrepreneurs and parties of the right mobilized against welfare state expansion, today in both Austria and Switzerland trade unions, parties of the left and welfare state clientele organizations mobilize successfully against retrenchment.

Fourthly, in intra-state federations with congruent and vertically integrated party systems, the proliferation of elections at the state level may retard retrenchment efforts, since parties considered responsible by voters for unpopular federal policies are frequently punished in state elections. Germany and Austria are prime examples illustrating this mechanism. The junior partner of Austria's centre-right coalition, the populist Freedom Party, suffered dramatic losses in all regional elections except Carinthia from the time of the change in government in 2000. Much the same was true for the last Kohl government, as it now is for the present Schröder cabinet in Germany. Defeats in regional elections have particularly significant consequences for the German federal government's capacity to make policy, since the unique design of the Bundesrat as a body representing the Länder executives provides the opposition with veto powers in the case of divergent majorities in the two houses of parliament. This means that informal grand coalitions are vital to successful cost-containment initiatives. Manow has shown that such broadly backed initiatives have been a relatively common feature of Germany's 'new politics' of welfare state retrenchment.

Because the division of powers and associated decision rules structure federal–state relations and the number of actors involved in policy-making, they provide a crucial context for successful retrenchment initiatives. In nations in which social policy is the exclusive responsibility of the central government, the fate of the welfare state is closely tied to the partisan composition of the federal government. Since the federal government can act more or less unilaterally, what matters is who runs the government. Of course, the apparent autonomy of decision-making in such contexts remains hedged about by other influences, not least the electoral salience of welfare state clienteles, a constraint that is intensified in some federal systems by the frequency of state-level elections, which may be seen as a form of rolling reassessment of federal policies. The salience of such clienteles is, it would appear, the main reason why pensioners in both Canada and the United States have done so much better than the unemployed. In both countries, the size of the pensioner lobby and its national electoral salience have provided it with a clout sufficient to deter any serious reform initiatives. In contrast, less salient and less popularly legitimate unemployment programmes were the subject of both cuts and extensive 'active' labour market experimentation.

Programmes with fragmented jurisdiction exhibit different outcomes depending on whether super-majorities are required to alter the status quo. In Canada, where programmes could not be changed unilaterally but required joint decision processes between the federal government and the provinces, that is, super-majorities, they appear to have been, effectively, retrenchment-proof. A clear instance was the Canadian/Quebec Pension Plan. Negotiated change was extremely difficult, since the different governments at the federal–provincial table had diverse partisan preferences, and several groups of provinces were armed with a veto power. In contrast, the federal government was able to make dramatic changes in shared-cost programmes, as the provinces had no veto power over changes in the level of federal financial support or conditions attached to it. These circumstances provided opportunities for obfuscating accountability and for shifting blame backwards and forwards between the different tiers of government. In the realms of both health and social assistance, the Canadian federal government passed the buck for unpopular policies to the provinces. As federal deficits grew, the federal government cut back the transfers it made to the provinces. In the case of health care, Ottawa still remained in charge of the broad outline of policies, seeking to maintain the principle of universal and equal access to health care which was popular with the voters, while seeking to limit federal exposure to ever increasing health care costs. As a result, the provinces were forced to absorb the pressures on health care budgets. Hence, the basic policy model remained frozen, but cost-containment was facilitated through cost-shifting through the federal mechanism. In the case of social assistance, Ottawa simply reduced its contribution to cost-sharing and abandoned almost all of the conditions attached to the transfer, leading to increasing programme decentralization and what one analyst calls a 'slouch to the bottom' in levels of provision.

The most fundamental policy changes in the US also occurred in those programmes that were characterized by revenue sharing and which were targeted at the poor. Retrenchment in the US is something that takes place mainly in the means-tested welfare realm and not in the realm of Social Security proper, which, as Pierson notes, is protected by the sheer size of welfare state clienteles.[12] Policy change in welfare was launched by a stepwise restructuring of conditional federal grants into bloc grants giving the states greater discretion in resource allocation. Since Reagan, waivers have frequently been used to allow for experiments in policy reform at

---

[12] Paul Pierson, 'Coping with Permanent Austerity: Welfare State Restructuring in Affluent Democracies', in Paul Pierson, ed., *The New Politics of the Welfare State* (Oxford: Oxford University Press, 2001), pp. 410–456, p. 413.

the state level that Congress would have been most unlikely to approve at the federal level. In the 1990s a 'devolution revolution' (Richard Nathan; see above p. 171, note 55) took place in US welfare programmes, despite the absence of the kind of austerity motivation powering reform in the majority of European nations. In the US the incentive to reform appears to have been ideological and not economic. Connected to this fact, and an interesting aside to Pierson's 'new politics' analysis, is that America's retrenchment or 'welfare revolution' of the 1990s, which affected only AFDC, a relatively small portion of its welfare edifice, appears to have been more about claiming credit for *cuts* than about avoiding blame.[13] In the case of EITC, Food Stamps and even SSI programmes, the emphasis was also on claiming credit, in this case for increasing programme generosity rather than budget cuts. Certainly the uniquely American bifurcation of 'social security' and 'welfare' made it legitimate to attack the latter in a way that was not possible in other welfare states.

Finally, there is another development that should be discussed in the context of the 'new politics', one that has only been mentioned peripherally in the case studies. This is the shift to a more regulatory form of provision, usually by obliging private parties to provide public benefits, such as pensions and rights to equal treatment, usually of a kind improving the employment status of workers. A shift of this kind has been noticed as a recent trend of American development,[14] but has a much longer theoretical history going back at least to Titmuss' insistence that a full

---

[13] What seems to have taken place in the US is a radical policy shift from grants to the able-bodied poor *outside* the labour market (typical AFDC) to benefits available *within* the labour market only (for instance, EITC). While means-tested welfare state transfers have actually expanded, certain kinds of benefits ('old welfare') have shrunk or access has been reorganized and made more punitive. Programme *nationalization* has been maintained and developed in labour market related programmes, such as EITC and Food Stamps, while *de*nationalization reigns in the 'old welfare' arena, with the progressive dismantling of programmes such as AFDC/TANF. On these developments, see R. Kent Weaver, *Ending Welfare as We Know It* (Washington, DC: Brookings Institution Press, 2000); R. Kent Weaver, 'Ending Welfare as We Know It: Policy-Making for Low-Income Families in the Clinton/Gingrich Era', in Margaret Weir, ed., *The Social Divide: Political Parties and the Future of Activist Government* (Washington, DC: Brookings Institution Press, 1997), pp. 361–416.

[14] See Pietro S. Nivola, 'American Social Regulation Meets the Global Economy', in Pietro S. Nivola, ed., *Comparative Disadvantages: Social Regulation Meets the Global Economy* (Washington, DC: Brookings Institution Press, 1997), pp. 16–65. As Nivola shows, the emergent US emphasis is on the role of the 'consumer' rather than the 'worker', as in traditional schemes of occupational welfare of the kind discussed by Titmuss. This resonates with nineteenth-century US traditions, where it was not trade unions but rather the protection of an individual's consumption power that was the focus of social and political action. See on this, Elmar Rieger and Stephan Leibfried in *Limits to Globalization: Welfare States and the World Economy* (Cambridge: Polity Press, 2003), chapter 3.

accounting of social provision needs to examine occupational as well as fiscal and expenditure welfare. Regulatory provision has a no less strong empirical pedigree in the form of ostensibly private but, nevertheless, mandatory employer benefits, which have been particularly conspicuous in both Australian and Swiss social policy development, with the Australian 'wage earner's welfare' strategy making extensive use of this device and, more recently, second-tier pensions in both countries being provided through this route. Whether mandated benefits represent an enhancement of provision or an aspect of 'new politics' retrenchment clearly depends on whether such benefits supplement or replace existing direct entitlements. The Swiss and Australian experiences tend to suggest the former, while commentary on recent American development suggests the latter. Either way, the fact that the regulative route seems to be more strongly developed in federal systems than elsewhere argues for this being yet another mechanism devised by political actors in federal systems to bypass the institutional rigidities built into their system of government.

Synthesis

The quotation by Proudhon at the beginning of this chapter constitutes a nineteenth-century warning that, without the adoption of broader federal structures to moderate the conflict amongst nations, Europe and the wider world would be unable to avoid repeating a thousand years of destructive conflict. However, late twentieth-century quantitative research on the expenditure effects of federalism suggests that this form of political rule came at a real price in reduced social protection and, hence, greater social inequality. Taking the two together seemingly confirms a key axiom of federalist theory, that federalism involves a trade-off in which social peace is bought at the cost of permitting some degree of territorial and social diversity.

What the findings of our study suggest is that the terms of this trade-off may be less severe than is implied by quantitative analysis and by theory. The entry price for democratic federalism appears to be a delay in welfare consolidation; an institutional blockage, which, in each of the countries treated here, was overcome only under the emergency conditions of World War Two. The constraint on social policy development proved to be the decentralization of jurisdiction more than federal institutions as such. Once central governments had inserted themselves in a given sector, the barriers fell away. Thereafter, in good economic times, the cost appears to be negligible, with patterns of partisanship moulding and shaping the developmental trajectory of the welfare state in federal and non-federal states alike, and, when times are not so good, may even be positive, with federal institutions serving not only to keep the peace but also to preserve the existing state of welfare.

Our analysis has shown that two dimensions of distributional conflict interact when federalism meets the welfare state:

- the (re)distribution of money and other benefits between social classes
- the distribution of power between tiers of government

The 'old politics' of the welfare state was mainly determined by the extent to which the distribution of power allowed social policy to unfold and that was mainly driven by how conflictual these politics were. Three aspects seem crucial here:

- the level of democratic development at the time when the welfare state emerged
- the type of federalism: *intra*-state (co-operative) federalism allows federal level social policy to flourish early on, as the other tiers may participate in federal decision-making and can pass on some of their social burdens to the central government; in contrast, *inter*-state (dual) federalism rather tends to protect the political status quo, and, thus, to retard welfare state growth
- the way in which social security is financed: contributions are more easily decoupled from multi-tiered government than other forms of taxation

These institutional factors are overlaid by social interest patterns: if there are fewer regional cleavages – in the party system and elsewhere – it is much easier to nationalize power than in strongly regionalized societies.

With the exception of the democratic parameter, which ceased to differentiate these states after World War Two, these differences are also pertinent in the era of the 'new politics' of the welfare state. Recalibrating the welfare state has different socio-economic regional impacts, especially in a federation characterized by strong regional cleavages and the absence (or limited development) of general revenue sharing. The 'new politics' is channelled by

- the veto power of the lower tiers, which may be affected negatively by recalibration of expenditures, be it directly or indirectly;
- the *de facto* power of the lower tiers to pass back added burdens to the upper tier;

- the spill-over potential of regional conflict, driven by the relative power of regional parties and interests, the national relevance of regional elections, and the extent to which social conflict has been concentrated regionally.

It is much harder and less satisfactory to play the game of blame avoidance in *intra*-state (co-operative) federalism marked by strong regional disparities. To a large extent, this explains Germany's present reform problems, although Germany can, at least, shift blame upwards to the EU, a tier which has become quite widely implicated in issues of domestic welfare.

In terms of theory, the findings of our study underscore the analytical utility of a historical institutionalism that focusses on the interrelationship between federalism and social interest formation, thus overcoming the supposed distinction between solely 'state-centred' and 'society-centred' types of federalism.[15]

Beyond 'old' and 'new politics': federalism as a laboratory for social experimentation

Federalism provides a fertile ground for policy experiments. Experiments may result from local policy initiatives, but may also be encouraged by federal governments. However, as has already been noted, the impact of decentralized policy innovation and policy initiatives on *national* welfare state building can be ambivalent. While local policy pre-emption has often limited the degree of freedom for federal policy intervention, policy experiments can also serve as pacemakers and blueprints for national programmes. Indeed, in some instances the development of federal programmes is actually encouraged by decentralized social policy innovation and experience. Local innovation not only spreads new policies from state to state ('horizontal diffusion'), but also produces spill-overs, with bottom-up effects on policy innovation at the federal level ('pacemaker effects').

---

[15] This distinction was first made in the analysis of Canadian federalism, and evolved as an anti-thesis to 'society-centered' arguments in William S. Livingston, *Federalism and Constitutional Change* (Oxford: Clarendon Press, 1956; reprint Westport, CT: Greenwood Press, 1974). The idea of a 'state-centered federalism' was espoused by Alan C. Cairns, 'The Governments and Societies of Canadian Federalism', *Canadian Journal of Political Science*, vol. 10 (1977), pp. 695–726, and by Donald Smiley, 'Federal States and Federal Societies, with Special Reference to Canada', *International Political Science Review*, vol. 5 (1984), pp. 443–54. The concept was then applied to the German case by Lori Thorlakson, 'Government-Building and Political Development in Federations: Applying Canadian Theory to the German Case', *Regional and Federal Studies*, vol. 10 (2000), no. 3 (autumn), pp. 129–48.

Conclusion: 'old' and 'new politics' in federal welfare states 341

In sum, policy initiatives at the regional level have facilitated as well as retarded the expansion of a national welfare state. But federal copying of state programmes has also had major structural effects on national social policy. The Swiss Factory Act of 1877 was built largely on prior cantonal legislation. Since the federal government could rely on cantonal experience, and since factory legislation – due to its regulatory nature – had few fiscal implications, the law could be implemented quite speedily. A most instructive example of the importance of provincial innovation and vertical spill-over is the introduction in 1947 of Universal Hospital Insurance in Saskatchewan. By adopting this model nationally in what was otherwise a typically 'liberal' welfare state, Canadian health policy was channelled in a social-democratic direction. Structural contagion of a similar kind can be found in the Australian pension system, which imported holus-bolus the means-tested but largely non-discretionary mode of provision to be found in the earlier New South Wales Act. This contagion effect extended far beyond age provision, since the Commonwealth Act in turn served as a template for all subsequent Australian social security legislation. These examples all demonstrate strong path dependency effects on the basis of initial federal – or, in the Australian case, pre-federal – experimentation.

The analysis of the case studies constituting this volume suggests five conditions under which state-level policy initiatives are likely. The first condition is the territorial concentration of ethnic or linguistic minorities. Examples here are autonomous social policy programmes in Quebec and recent experimentation in some western Swiss cantons with mothers' allowances and benefit schemes for the long-term unemployed. In both cases, a genuine and territorially concentrated political culture has played a major role. That French-speaking cantons are more inclined to state intervention than German ones is clearly demonstrated by the remarkably distinct voting patterns manifested in the relevant national referenda. At the federal level, the introduction of mothers' allowances was defeated in a 1999 referendum. However, while most French-speaking cantons voted for the bill, it was defeated in the more populous German-speaking cantons. Subsequently, the canton Geneva introduced mothers' allowances in 2000. This is a case that provides support for Finegold's argument that federalism creates opportunities for overcoming policy stalemate at the federal level. However, the delegation of decision-making to the constituent units also necessarily leads to territorial inequalities in benefit provision, and may impede the re-establishment of national standards once the constituent units have occupied the policy terrain.

A second condition for state-level initiatives is the territorial concentration of political minorities. Arguably more influential than the impact of ethnic minorities is the influence of territorially concentrated political forces that are ideologically inclined to big government. The obvious example is Red Vienna in the 1920s and early 1930s,[16] but the pioneer role of Saskatchewan in health policy and the introduction of child allowances in New South Wales and unemployment insurance in Queensland are other instances. The Australian examples, however, demonstrate that policy transfer from the state to the federal level is sometimes impeded by the structure of federalism itself. In neither case did the Commonwealth have the power to adopt such measures. Almost axiomatically, all the instances discussed here were the initiatives of left-leaning governments.

A third institutional precondition for implementing decentralized policy experiments is, of course, that the states retain some autonomy in policy-making. Since the federal governments of both Germany and Austria had acquired most of the important competencies early on, the room for decentralized experimentation was relatively limited, and mostly took place at the local level rather than the state level. Herein lie the origins of municipal socialism (*Munizipalsozialismus*) in the German cities and in Vienna of the inter-war period. The Viennese case is an ambiguous one, since it was a city and a Land all in one, providing the Social Democrats with more leverage on taxation than would normally have been available for municipal experimentation. Since both nations are 'codification' driven, experimentation with new solutions in part of the national territory has not come naturally, although outside the social policy arena some such experimentation has been attempted in recent years.

Nations with a stronger division of powers have seen experimentation from the bottom up, but also, especially after World War Two, from the top down. Experiments encouraged by the federal government have been largely restricted to programmes characterized by shared jurisdiction. To entice constituent units into reform ambitions, the US federal government started financing territorial 'income experiments' and stipulated waivers to try out new social policy approaches and to evaluate their effects. As Finegold notes, national level 'workfare' reforms were made to seem more feasible, since they could be demonstrated to have worked at the state level. Here, Wisconsin, which had been the experimental template for unemployment insurance in the 1930s, once again became a model state,

---

[16] Like the city-state Vienna, the city of Berlin acted as a laboratory for social policy in the Reich and the Weimar Republic. This ended with Nazism, but flared up in the early 1950s, when Berlin became a federal state and a showcase for social capitalism in the midst of the GDR. The capital cities of our other four federal nations never played such a pronounced experimental role in social policy development. Autocratic federalism and the capital city as social laboratory seem to be twinned.

but now in reverse as an exemplar of the virtues of active as compared to passive labour market interventions. In this kind of 'systematic thinking' and experimenting 'for social action' (Alice M. Rivlin),[17] subsidies were often used as a form of leverage to overcome erstwhile policy constraints.

Inter-state equalization or fiscal capacity is the fourth institutional precondition under which state-level initiatives are likely to occur. It is not surprising that the poorest Canadian provinces in Atlantic Canada were seldom innovators; rather, they have been laggards or policy followers for much of the last century. In a similar vein, the weakness of inter-state equalization in the US has constrained the scope for state-led initiatives in many parts of the US.

Finally, and fifth, local experimentation may also be driven by local problem pressure. This explains why risks related to industrialization – for example, accidents at work and health protection in the workplace – were introduced so early in the Swiss canton Glarus and in Ontario, Canada. Both areas were leading industrial regions in their time. Beginning with Ontario in 1914, workers' compensation spilled over to almost all the provinces by the 1940s. More recent reforms in the 'Latin' – French and Italian – parts of Switzerland relating to benefits for the unemployed are also driven by the higher unemployment rates plaguing these regions and not just by differences in political culture. Such reforms also underline the fact that federal arrangements offer a means of providing flexible solutions to regional problems, although once again at the cost of enhancing regional welfare differentiation. Once again, almost axiomatically, territorially fragmented benefit provision is the corollary of federalism's problem-solving flexibility.

Feedback effects: the intended and unintended consequences of the welfare state

In all the countries treated in this volume, federalism and social policy have co-existed for many decades. The emphasis here has been primarily on how federal forms have influenced welfare state development, but the relationship has been far from one way. The growth of the social state has, in turn, had important effects on the mechanisms and routines of government in these countries and on how citizens define their national identity. Such feedback effects have been strongly influenced by the sequencing of political and social development. The more institutionalized federal arrangements were prior to the emergence of the welfare

---

[17] *Systematic Thinking for Social Action* (Washington, DC: Brookings Institution Press, 1971).

state, the less susceptible they have been to fundamental change in their structural forms.

The general notion of feedback effects comes from a systems or cybernetic analogy. The usual implication is that such effects are *unintended* consequences of disturbances to the system, and such is, indeed, the case for many of the changes to federal structure resulting from the development of social policy in these countries. In certain instances, however, welfare state programmes have been deliberately adopted with the intention of achieving these changes, in other words the feedback effects are the *intended* consequence of policy.

Intended effects

Political elites have sometimes used the adoption of welfare state programmes as an instrument of state- and nation-building or have resisted welfare state retrenchment in order to bolster a sense of national identity otherwise threatened by fragmentation.

State- and nation-building have always been regarded as important motivations for early German and Austrian welfare consolidation under non-democratic auspices. The efficacy of such strategies remains an open question. The Habsburg regime did not survive World War One, and German nation-building relied on militarism as much as on welfare solidarity in the latter years of the inter-war period. Perhaps, for such strategies to be fully effective, it is necessary for welfare development to be married to democracy. Certainly, in both post-war Germany and Austria, a strong welfare state, and the social partnership it entailed, contributed in no small way to the disappearance of pre-war political cleavages. Then again, in Switzerland, where these cleavages were even more extensive, the welfare state was never thought of as an instrument of nation-building. Here it was Swiss federalism, with its enthronement of local autonomy and the minority representation requisite in its consensus democracy, that lowered tensions and created – together with direct democracy and neutrality in its foreign policy – the polity that is now the major source of Swiss identity and societal cohesion.

Today, the issue is not one of state- and nation-building, but a matter of preserving national identities against the counter-claims of territorial particularism, with Canada being the most obvious example. Canadian social policy has played a vital, though as yet not fully resolved, role in the definition of community and nurturing of political identities. This process was highlighted by the competitive nation-building agendas of the federal and Quebec governments during the 1960s and 1970s, and by the anxieties triggered by the fading of the federal role in the last twenty years.

Contested identities radically increase the significance of the (otherwise) mundane world of inter-governmental relations. Certainly in Canada, the crisis of political identity has transformed the debate over the division of powers from a discourse on effectiveness into a struggle about community and national unity. In the process, social programmes have become cultural instruments and controversies over jurisdiction have taken on a political symbolism that makes their resolution more problematic.

These are debates about ways and means in which intentions are quite explicit, if very far from agreed. Advocates of programme decentralization see greater provincial jurisdiction as a means of accommodating diversity and eliminating a lingering source of tension between Canada and Quebec. Defenders of a stronger federal role counter that decentralization diminishes the presence of the national government in the daily lives of Canadians and erodes the underlying sense that, at some level, all citizens are part of a common political community with shared commitments to each other and to a collective future. The Canadian debates seem destined for repetition in nations such as Belgium,[18] Spain,[19] and Italy[20] – and even the territorially devolving United Kingdom,[21] where national welfare provision is increasingly viewed in some quarters as a last defence against rising tides of sub-national enthusiasm.[22] The future of

---

[18] Whilst leaving what French-speaking elites consider 'the cement of Belgian national unity' – social security – intact, Belgium has slowly been decentralizing social policy since the 1970s. See Pierre Baudewyns and Régis Dandoy, 'Federalism and Social Security in Belgium', unpublished ms, ECPR Joint Sessions, Edinburgh, 28 March–2 April 2003, published as 'The Preservation of Social Security as a National Function in the Belgian Federal State', in Nicola McEwen and Luis Moreno, eds., *The Territorial Politics of Welfare* (London: Routledge, 2005).

[19] See Luis Moreno, *The Federalization of Spain* (London: Frank Cass, 2001); Luis Moreno, 'Spain, a *via media* of Welfare Development', in Peter Taylor-Gooby, ed., *Welfare States Under Pressure* (London and Thousand Oaks, CA: Sage, 2001), pp. 100–22; Luis Moreno and Ana Arriba, 'Decentralization, Mesogovernments, and the New Logic of Welfare Provision in Spain', ISEA Working Paper 99–01 (Madrid, Consejo Superior de Investigaciones Científicas, Unidad de Políticas Comparados, 1999; http://www.iesam.csic.es/doctrab.htm).

[20] For a first overview on Italian regionalism, see chapter 5 ('Subnational Social Protection: Towards Welfare Regions?') in Maurizio Ferrera, *The Boundaries of Welfare. European Integration and the Territorial Restructuring of National Social Protection* (Oxford: Oxford University Press, 2005); also Valeria Fargion, 'The Regionalization of the Welfare State as a Side Effect of Territorial Politics in Italy (1992–2002)', in McEwen and Moreno, eds., *Territorial Politics*.

[21] For an overview see Richard Parry and Nicola McEwen, 'Devolution and the Preservation of the British Welfare State', in McEwen and Moreno, eds., *Territorial Politics*. On Scotland, cf. Nicola McEwen, 'State Welfare Nationalism: The Territorial Impact of Welfare State Development in Scotland', *Regional and Federal Studies*, vol. 12 (2002), no. 1 (spring), pp. 66–90.

[22] For a recent overview on several mostly European nations, see the contributions in McEwan and Moreno, eds., *Territorial Politics*.

Unintended effects

Unintended effects come in different sizes, in some instances, transforming the conduct of government merely as it pertains to the welfare state and, in others, with broader implications for the conduct of government as a whole. In the first category are what we have described as 'bypass' effects. In the second category are changes marking a shift from inter-state or layer cake federalism to intra-state or marble cake federalism. Where lower-tier governments have been called upon to administer national welfare state programmes on any major scale, shifts of this nature are more or less inevitable.

The emergence of bypass mechanisms results from a functional problem of all evolving democratic federal systems in the modern era: how to get around their own in-built constitutional rigidities to institute and deliver the welfare programmes and reforms demanded by democratic electorates. Federal constitutions are deliberately designed to inhibit change or, at least, to slow down changes that alter the balance of power and responsibility between state and federal jurisdictions. Thus, those who seek to effect change must find a way around existing institutional barriers. Typical bypass strategies differ from federation to federation.

In the strongly institutionalized federalisms of North America, there is no single favoured mechanism of provision, but rather the establishment of each programme takes place as a consequence of a separate agreement between the federal and the state authorities, generally based on a complex one-off deal in which the chips at the bargaining table are federal funding, constitutional competence and the electoral popularity of the programmes on offer. That, of course, is why the mix of state and federal responsibilities differs so widely in US social policy programmes. Both joint decision federalism and shared-cost federalism are ways of bypassing constitutional rules giving lower-tier governments control over certain aspects of policy initiation and implementation and getting them to carry out national programmes. These lower-tier governments can only be persuaded to act where their own electorates favour the programme in question and where agreement can be reached on funding. The result is a *multi-tiered patchwork quilt* of programmes, with no coherent organizing principle of provision and with, in many instances, an in-built potential for different treatment in different jurisdictions.

However, not all bypass mechanisms have to be *ad hoc* in character. Federal nations outside North America have, over time, found routes around the social policy restrictions in their own constitutions that end up giving a particular flavour to wider governmental and societal practices. Arguably, that is because welfare state and federal practices have interacted and evolved together, rather than federal rules simply shaping emergent welfare state practice. Because this is so, bypass structures have been able to acquire their own institutional legitimacy. This is true, for instance, of the widespread use of *regulatory legislation* to mandate employers to provide benefits, which has become a preferred option in Australia and to some extent in Switzerland, and which has the signal virtue of sidestepping the whole issue of which level of government will provide benefits, since benefits are ostensibly not provided by the state at all. In Australia, moreover, the conjuring trick was still more complex. The federal arbitration system used its power to control wages in order to provide a social policy minimum, and, thus, in principle, removed the need for specific poverty alleviation measures. It also served as the legal authority for providing mandated benefits such as sickness expenditure and, initially, second-tier pensions and in the process not merely bypassed the states and federation as providers of benefits, but also the federal executive and legislature as makers of social policy decisions.

Of all the bypass mechanisms identified in this volume, the most strongly institutionalized are the para-fiscal systems of Germany, Austria and, to a lesser extent, Switzerland. German and Austrian *para-fiscalism* bypasses the state and federal budgetary process and channels contributions directly to independent public agencies. These agencies deliver all social insurance benefits and are governed by a mix of representatives from employer and/or employee organizations, and federal, state and local government functionaries[23] often serving as arbiters between and amongst the 'social partners'. After World War Two para-fiscal arrangements expanded radically, at once channelling and obscuring the development of the German and Austrian version of the 'golden age' of the welfare state. These organizational arrangements developed into an all-encompassing system, a virtual state beyond a state, responsible for some half of public expenditures, but beyond the central focus of the public eye.

---

[23] For an overview of such governance structures, see Ulrich Becker, 'Organisation und Selbstverwaltung der Sozialversicherung', in Bernd Baron von Maydell and Franz Ruland, eds., *Sozialrechts-Handbuch*, 3rd edn (Baden-Baden: Nomos, 2003), pp. 225–47. On the distinction between creating independent para-fiscal public agencies and supplying them also with a self-governing power base (*Selbstverwaltung*), see also Reinhard Hendler, *Selbstverwaltung als Ordnungsprinzip. Zur politischen Willensbildung und Entscheidung im demokratischen Verfassungsstaat der Industriegesellschaft* (Cologne: Heymanns, 1984).

In this system, the state frequently makes use of administrative decrees to determine the particulars of social benefits, in the process also bypassing parliament's law-making authority. Although para-*fiscal* arrangements may, initially, be mere legal or administrative technicalities, as they develop and progressively envelop other bureaucratic and political channels and attract a major part of all public finances, they come to constitute what is, effectively, a para-*state*.

Para-fiscalism is, in many ways, an extraordinary bedfellow of federalism, because it directly contravenes and contradicts the principle of a territorial division of powers. Manow, in his chapter, explicitly argues that the excessive use of such mechanisms has led to an overgrazing of the fiscal commons in Germany. Arguably, there is a kind of *ex adverso* support for the case that federalism is a barrier to welfare state expansion in the fact that the federal countries in which this expansion has been most prominent were those in which the territorial division of powers was most directly and immediately bypassed. Arguably, too, the central government's capacity to easily circumvent the spirit of its own federal arrangements was partly a function of the fact that, in both Germany and Austria, the welfare state emerged under non-democratic auspices. Table 8.2 gives a summary of the three bypass structures described.

As members of the European Union (EU), Germany and Austria are in the position of having another, supra-national, tier of governance overlaying their multi-tiered national structures.[24] Like all evolving democratic federal systems, the EU, in attempting to deliver welfare to its electorate – in this case, driven by the Commission's peculiar legitimation needs, and cheered on by member state governments and the European Parliament – has developed its own set of bypasses to fit its own particular constitutional rigidities. As the EU has no power of taxation, it cannot rely on para-fiscalism. Instead, its focus on 'integration through law' made it predisposed to *regulatory* bypasses, in social policy as elsewhere. One of the most prominent examples is the on-going juridification and expansion of constitutionalized equalities, from nationality in the 1960s and gender in the 1970s, to ethnicity, sexual preference, religion and age at the turn of

---

[24] For a recent analysis of the federal analogy for the EU, starting from the US and especially the Canadian case, see Bruno Théret, *Protection sociale et fédéralisme. L'Europe dans le miroir de l'Amérique du Nord* (Brussels: Presses Interuniversitaires Européennes; Berne: Peter Lang; and Montreal: Presses de l'Université de Montréal, 2002), chapters 1 (pp. 41–74) and 12 (pp. 423–564). The patterns of subordination that occurred in the process of federation-building are analyzed by Leslie Friedman Goldstein in *Constituting Federal Sovereignty: The European Union in Comparative Context* (Baltimore, MD: Johns Hopkins University Press, 2001), where she deals with the EU (1958–99), the American Union (1789–1859), the Dutch Union (seventeenth-century) and the Swiss Union (1800–58).

Table 8.2 *Bypass structures*

Bypass	Description	Exemplary countries
Patchwork quilt	An array of discrete agreements between federal and state authorities gives lower tiers of government control over aspects of social policy initiation and implementation, while compelling them to carry out national programmes. Going beyond some conceptions of federalism, where each programme is run and financed by a single level of government, the patchwork quilt may be based on *joint decisions*, whereby agreements require approval by both levels of government, or run on a *shared costs basis*, with the federal government simply providing financial support for multi-tier programmes.	Canada, USA
Regulatory	The state mandates *private* parties to pay for and provide certain benefits, such as pensions, health care, etc. Most regulation concerns *employers'* provisions to employees. Mandates may be hard (*binding*) or soft (*optional*). In the latter case, the effectiveness of regulation is dependent on the largesse of tax deductions or subsidies.	Australia, Switzerland
Para-fiscal (or, when fully developed, para-state)	Institutionalized *independent* public agencies, mandated by the state but with their own tax base (contributions) *outside* of the state's general budget (*para-fiscus*), manage the delivery of benefits. These agencies, in addition, often have *an independent power base* of employer associations and unions, with state representatives from various levels of federalism serving as arbiters between and amongst the 'social partners'. In its most fully developed form, with almost half of public finances dedicated to the *para-fiscus*, independent agencies are so pervasive they form an effective para-state.	Austria, Germany [Switzerland]

the millennium.²⁵ The EU complements this regulatory approach with the *patchwork quilt* type of bypass. As 'joint decision federalism' the EU must satisfy difficult unanimity or, when specially authorized, super-majority requirements. As a result, its bypasses are often merely mandates for information gathering and goal-setting, as exemplified by the Open Method of Co-ordination²⁶ currently in vogue for employment, immigration, health and pensions.

Looking beyond national federalism to the entire multi-tiered EU system, we see that in the case of Austria and Germany the three bypass structures form an ensemble, with the para-fiscal bypass operating at the national level, and the regulatory and patchwork quilt bypasses at the supra-national level. In addition to its upper-tier bypass structures, the EU has also affected member state federalisms from the bottom up. Over the last few decades provincial governments have gradually been finding ways to deal directly with Brussels, jumping immediately from the local or state level to the supra-national tier, thereby bypassing their national governments altogether. Some of these local constituencies have been built into EU programmes and advisory committees, and have even established their own 'embassies'. The sovereignty of the German federal structure was formally overridden in 1992. Article 23 of the constitution was reformulated to allow the states, through the Bundesrat, to co-determine German EU policies within their proper domain (sections 2–6), or even to represent the Federal Republic within their exclusive domain (section 6, first sentence). The federal government's monopoly on

---

[25] Relying on the US experience with the 'regulatory state', Giandomenico Majone argues that the regulatory bypass is the natural developmental trajectory for the EU. See his edited volume *Regulating Europe* (London and New York: Routledge, 1996) and *Dilemmas of European Integration* (Oxford: Oxford University Press, 2005). For a recent treatment of regulatory symmetries in multi-tiered systems that compares the USA, Germany, Australia and Canada to the EU, see R. Daniel Kelemen, *The Rules of Federalism: Institutions and Regulatory Position in the EU and Beyond* (Cambridge, MA: Harvard University Press, 2004).

[26] The pressures for a solution to the common welfare problems facing a joint federalist structure naturally also lead to other forms of circumnavigation. Take the tendency to neutralize these hurdles by way of common EU package deals, by the reinterpretation of unanimity as only super-majority requirements ('the Treaty base game'; see Martin Rhodes, 'A Regulatory Conundrum: Industrial Relations and the Social Dimension', in Stephan Leibfried and Paul Pierson, eds., *European Social Policy: Between Fragmentation and Integration* (Washington, DC: Brookings Institution Press, 1995), pp. 78–122, p. 99), or by their transubstantiation into simple majority requirements (achieved by transforming political issues mainly into juridical Treaty cases to be decided by the European Court of Justice, where a majority of the Court always must decide), through governance by indirection (setting Maastricht criteria, which leave the influence on welfare state development to the national level), etc.

representing the German state in international affairs was thus effectively superseded,[27] although authority for German social policy is now, in many respects, so overwhelmingly national that this only affects the spheres of education, science and domestic security.

Extended discussion of the nature of European integration in the last three decades has identified the EU as a kind of hermaphrodite, part international organization or confederation, part multi-tiered nation state or federation, with traits of both. When we look at the history of federalisms that were not chartered by their mother countries, as Canada and Australia were by the UK, we find that they all went through a similar hybrid period, usually in the nineteenth century. Not until after the American Civil War did it finally become clear that the US would be one nation under law with an internal federal structure, and not just a federation of sovereign states.[28] Germany took more than a century to move from the idea of unification to the democratic federalism of 1919, and during that time it went progressively from a loose federation of German-speaking states (the *Deutsche Bund*, founded in 1815) to visions of 'a new form of federation, somewhere midway between a unitary government and compacts between states as we know them' (Karl Joseph Mittermaier),[29] to the autocratic federalism of 1871. Similar hybrid

---

[27] This revision was part of a package deal: the states agreed not to block ratification of the Maastricht Treaty and its European Monetary Union if Article 23 was so amended and the legal procedures defined as in 'Gesetz über die Zusammenarbeit von Bund und Ländern in Angelegenheiten der EU', 12 March 1993, *Bundesgesetzblatt*, vol. I, p. 313. Helmut Kohl compromised, and this has been a contested issue ever since. Günter Bannas, 'Institutionalisiertes Mißtrauen. Die Föderalismuskommission berät über die Europapolitik', *Frankfurter Allgemeine Zeitung*, 17 May 2004, no. 114, p. 12; Rudolf Hrbek, ed., *Europapolitik und Bundesstaatsprinzip, Die 'Europafähigkeit' Deutschlands und seiner Länder im internationalen Vergleich* (Baden-Baden: Nomos, 2000); Ingolf Pernice, 'Article 23', in Horst Dreier, ed., *Grundgesetz-Kommentar*, 3 vols. (Tübingen: Mohr Siebeck, 1996–2000), vol. II, especially pp. 386–400, paras. 95–121.

[28] See William H. Riker, 'Federalism', in Fred I. Greenstein and Nelson W. Polsby, eds., *Handbook of Political Science*, vol. V, *Governmental Institutions and Processes* (Reading, MA: Addison-Wesley, 1975), pp. 93–172; see also Riker's collection of essays entitled *The Development of American Federalism* (Boston, MA: Kluwer, 1987) and his introductory text in *Federalism: Origin, Operation, Significance*, 4th rpt (Boston, MA: Little, Brown, 1964); cf. also Carl Brent Swisher, *American Constitutional Development*, 2nd edn rpt (Boston, MA: Houghton Mifflin, 1978).

[29] 'Eine neue Bundesform, die zwischen der Einheitsregierung und der bisherigen Form des Staatenbundes in der Mitte steht', a statement by Mittermaier in 1848 in the German National Assembly, cited by Reinhart Koselleck, 'Bündnis, Föderalismus, Bundesstaat', in Otto Brunner, Werner Conze and Reinhart Koselleck, eds., *Geschichtliche Grundbegriffe. Historisches Lexikon zur politisch-sozialen Sprache in Deutschland* (Stuttgart: E. Klett, 1972), vol. I, pp. 582–671, pp. 665ff.

configurations were present in nineteenth-century Austria[30] and in Switzerland prior to 1848.[31]

In the first part of the nineteenth century, therefore, hybrids of confederation and federation were the rule, but by the end of the century a clear distinction had been drawn between the two forms of governance, with clear-cut federalism in place everywhere but Austria, where it only emerged in the aftermath of World War One. Herein lies the major difference between these federalisms and the EU, which may be a true hermaphrodite, permanently confined to its half-confederate, half-federate form.

Another unintended effect of the welfare state on federalism lies in the welfare state's contribution to the subversion of inter-state federalism and its transformation into intra-state or co-operative federalism. Substantial redistribution can be effectively achieved only at the national level. The rise of the welfare state was thus a decisive factor in the centralization of power and policy, including the nationalization of political parties and political conflict. Centralization was initially strongest in those federations where the federal government quickly acquired or inherited social policy jurisdiction and then exploited it comprehensively. In these federations the welfare state was designed to produce homogeneity of living conditions throughout the federation. The absence of territorial homogeneity is, then again, most salient in those federations where the emergence of the welfare state substantially lagged behind the adoption of a federal constitution. In these nations built-in constitutional rigidity has proved a substantial barrier to the enactment of comprehensive nation-wide standards in benefit provision.

Nevertheless, the continuing influence of the development of social policy in all these nations is apparent in the fact that the 'social budget' is now a major component of all public budgets, often documented separately, and that, in the modern era, social policy legislation is a predominantly federal matter in all these nations. An apocryphal story from American criminology tells of an interview with the famous bank robber Willy Sutton, who, when asked why he robbed banks, said, with astonishment that he should be asked such an obvious question: 'Because that's where the money is!' The same reasoning accounts for the centralization of power in the modern welfare state.

---

[30] Hans Peter Hye, *Das politische System in der Habsburgermonarchie. Konstitutionalismus, Parlamentarismus und politische Partizipation* (Prague: Karolinum, 1998).
[31] Wolf Linder, *Swiss Democracy: Possible Solutions to Conflict in Multicultural Societies* (Houndsmills: Macmillan, 1994), pp. 5–6. Koselleck, 'Bündnis, Föderalismus', pp. 627ff. gives an overview of the discussion on all these countries in that time period.

Indeed, there has been no major instance in which social policy competencies have been reallocated downwards to the constituent units of an established federation. Genuine devolution and decentralization have only been seriously contemplated or experimented with – as in the 1996 Clinton–Gingrich welfare reform – in North America, although 'new federalism' has also been an intermittent, but largely rhetorical, slogan in Australia. Also, in the European experience the reform of federalism has been a recurrent theme. But in all such cases the proposals and supposed innovations have fallen back on shared-cost federalism, one version of 'quasi-federalism', rather than reinstating the kind of division of competencies that was the hallmark of classical inter-state federalism. A corollary of centralization and emerging intra-state federalism in a world where federal niceties are still observed is a Byzantine network of interlocking financial relations between different tiers of government,[32] as obvious in the intricacies of debates in the Council of Australian Governments as it is in the workings of German and Austrian para-fiscal institutions. Untying these financial Gordian knots is as difficult as reforming the welfare state itself and, indeed, welfare state reform in federal nations is difficult for precisely that reason, accounting for both the diversity and the complexity of the 'new politics' of the welfare state in the studies constituting this research.

The future of the federal welfare state

What became of Proudhon's fond hopes for a twentieth-century age of federalism that would bring relief from the military and political turmoil of his own era? In many ways the early twentieth century went even beyond Proudhon's worst imaginings. Ultimately, conflict was 'resolved' by two wars 'to end all wars', and federalism was not part of the solution. By 1950 the six federations that had celebrated the birth of a new century in 1901 had been joined by just one new western federal state – the Republic of Austria.

In the first half of the twentieth century those federations were arrayed against one another in an epochal and bloody conflict between democracy and authoritarianism. However, the positive aspect of the 'resolution' wrought by the Second World War was that democracy became the entrenched political form for federal and unitary states alike. And, with the founding of the European Community and its new version of federalism in 1957, it appeared that redemption of the sort Proudhon had

---

[32] If we take Germany as an example, see Klaus-Dirk Henke and Wilfried Schmähl, eds., *Finanzierungsverflechtung in der sozialen Sicherung* (Baden-Baden: Nomos, 2001).

imagined might well, at last, be realized. European integration was superimposed on existing nation-state institutions, gradually altering their status and structure, part of a layering transformation[33] that continues to this day.

These top-down changes were, and are, even more pronounced for the twenty-three member states that were *not* prior federations than they were for Germany and Austria. Most were unitary states learning to live with an institutional layer that went against the grain of pre-established central government traditions. In the final quarter of the century federalism and various other, more limited, forms of political devolution have begun to spread anew, this time within brittle EU nation states such as Belgium, Spain, Italy and the UK. One might argue that it was only beneath the ever expanding protective upper tier of the European Union that these states could afford to loosen their strained national bonds and break up their unitary national shells.

Meanwhile, New World federalisms were experiencing their own version of a top-down versus a bottom-up twentieth-century evolution, though with a different point of departure. Here the British Empire took on the role of a token upper tier from the moment it chartered the federations and relinquished its rule. These top-down, continental creations were flexible, innovative and able to accommodate the challenges of the twentieth century. In contrast, the US created its own federalism by revolution, from the bottom up, and in so doing inaugurated a new moral universe with institutions that were more resistant to constitutional change. This made it virtually immune to the imposition of external institutional layers – from the United Nations to the World Trade Organization, to the Kyoto Treaty – perceived as threats to its sovereignty.

None of the New World federalisms would ever have contemplated membership in a supra-national construction like the EU. International free trade arrangements, such as the North American Free Trade Agreement (NAFTA) of 1992 created by the US, Canada and Mexico, do not constitute a top tier of government, nor, by any stretch of the imagination, do they function as protective umbrellas for the signatories. Indeed, for many Canadians, NAFTA was seen as an outright threat to nationhood. Only in the 1980s did Québécois indépendantistes give serious thought to refashioning Canada as a North American version of the EU that would elevate Quebec from provincial to member state status.

---

[33] On the different types of slow and incremental transformations, see Wolfgang Streeck and Kathleen Thelen, 'Institutional Change in Advanced Political Economies', in Wolfgang Streeck and Kathleen Thelen, eds., *Beyond Continuity: Explorations in the Dynamics of Advanced Political Economies* (Cambridge: Cambridge University Press, 2004), pp. 1–39; Kathleen Thelen, 'How Institutions Evolve: Insights from Comparative Historical Analysis', in Mahoney and Rueschemeyer, eds., *Comparative Historical Analysis*, pp. 208–40.

Many fragmenting nation states have taken the Canada–Quebec experience to heart, and comprehend that, nowadays, the institutional arrangements of the welfare state may be the only glue that holds them together. In the early years of the marriage between federalism and the welfare state, democratic federalism was an impediment to the growth of social solidarity, but now that the relationship has matured, social solidarity has a pivotal role in preserving otherwise fragile national entities. For these states, federalism is a refuge half-way between a no longer feasible unitary state and an intolerable break-up of the nation state. The new role of the welfare state is to be part of that process. As things turned out, the twentieth century was not the age of federalism, although one might argue that it was, in its post-war years, the 'golden age' of the welfare state. What, then, of the twenty-first century? The present era is no less troubled, and no less in need of mechanisms of conflict resolution, than that which preceded it. Indeed, as we enter the 'silver age' of welfare austerity, the need may be greater than at any time since the Second World War.[34]

The relationship between federalism and the welfare state, as we have seen in this volume, has always been close, and now it is more intimate than ever before. According to Michael Greve and the fiscal federalists, this is a marriage made in hell. But in the older tradition that Friedrich Schiller so eloquently articulated, it is a natural union that nurtures brotherhood and solidarity in danger and distress (see pages 1 and 3). Indeed, we see the robust and enduring marriage of social solidarity and decentralization as offering hope and salvation for the nations of our new millennium.

---

[34] Fragmenting nation-states in the European Union have taken refuge in and, in the silver age, can build on almost fifty years of constructing an evolving set of quasi-federal institutions. The lessons that *Federalism and the Welfare State* hold for the EU are explored at length in: Herbert Obinger, Stephan Leibfried and Francis G. Castles, 'Bypasses to a Social Europe? Lessons from Federal Experience', *Journal of European Public Policy*, vol. 12, no. 3 (2005) (forthcoming; Special Issue *Towards a Federal Europe?* Alexander H. Trechsel, ed.).

Index

An index of authors for the citations of literature in the footnotes can be downloaded from http:// www.state.uni-bremen.de/federalism.

Adenauer, Chancellor Konrad 246, 247, 248
age pensions
    contributory pensions 93, 106, 108–09, 114, 120–21, 129, 135, 154, 162
        Canada Pension Plan (CPP) 108, 110, 120, 136, 336
        Quebec Pension Plan (QPP) 106, 108, 120, 336
    Australia 64, 66, 68, 69, 69n.39, 70
    Austria 186, 192, 201, 202, 216n.98
        pension reform 211, 213, 218
    Canada 95, 99–100, 106, 109, 311, 324
        Guaranteed Income Supplement (GIS) 106, 107, 109, 110, 119, 136
        Old Age Security (OAS) 93, 106, 107, 110, 119, 129
        Spouses Allowance 106
    Germany 228, 240, 243, 245, 247, 249, 255, 257, 259
    Switzerland 271, 272, 273, 274, 277, 278, 281–82, 287, 288–89, 302
        Lex Schulthess 278, 282
        occupational pensions 278, 279, 282
        Old Age and Survivors' Insurance Act 281, 291
        public pensions 278, 282
    United States
        Civil War pension 139, 160
        Old Age, Survivors, and Disability Insurance (OASDI) 141, 153, 158, 161, 162
        Supplemental Security Insurance (SSI) 154, 161, 169, 337
allocation of jurisdiction/powers 9, 14, 34, 36, 38, 40, 44, 59, 83, 339
    nationalization of social policy 322, 323, 324, 340

shared responsibilities 10, 30, 84, 224, 270, 342, 345
Australia 52, 53–55, 58, 67, 73, 83
Austria 185, 190, 197, 202, 205, 214, 231
Canada 92, 98, 99, 103, 104, 106, 124, 126
    doctrine of the spending power 93
    Royal Commission on Dominion–Provincial Relations 99
Germany 231, 235, 237, 240, 241, 244, 245, 246, 248
    German unification 236, 238
Switzerland 263, 264, 267, 270, 293, 300, 304
United States 144, 147, 311
see also political institutionalism
Armingeon, Klaus 47

Banting, Keith G. 46, 319
Belkin, Aaron 163, 164
Bennett, Prime Minister R. B. 100
Bertozzi, Fabio 47
bicameralism 10, 17, 35, 36, 254, 256
    Australian Senate 17, 36, 55, 60n.16, 65, 80, 83, 84–86, 87, 309–10
    Austrian Bundesrat 17, 36, 186, 188
    Canadian Senate 17, 94
    German Bundesrat 17, 36, 227, 245, 245n.57, 248, 254, 335, 350
    Swiss Ständerat 17, 36, 270
    US Senate 17, 36, 145, 146, 170, 176
Brennan, Geoffrey 31, 181
Buchanan, James M. 31, 181
Bush, President George 174
Bush, President George W. 156, 168
bypass mechanisms 346–48
    regulatory legislation 347
    see also constitutional rigidities

356

Index   357

Carter, President Jimmy 170
Castles, Francis G. 11, 26, 46, 309,
    329
centralization 33, 352
  fiscal centralization 33, 60, 61, 73, 159,
      196, 198
    Australia 58
    Austria 182, 189, 205
    Canada 130, 134, 135
    Germany 230n.22
  legislative centralization 228, 231,
      232, 236, 244, 314
  local responsibility 238, 241, 242
  Switzerland 271
  see also decentralization
child benefit programmes
  Australia 69, 70, 70n.42, 73
    Child Endowment Scheme 105
  Austria 214, 215
    family allowances 202
    youth welfare 207
  Canada 95, 128
    Family Allowance Programme 98, 99,
        105–06, 107, 129
    Child Tax Credit 107
    Family Income Supplement 107
  Switzerland 268
    family allowances 265, 271, 281, 283,
        292, 294
  United States 145, 160, 171
    Child Care and Development Fund
        (CCDF) 173
classical federalism 95, 104, 118–19, 136,
    310, 330
Clinton, President William J. 147, 156,
    172, 174, 176
Cohen, Wilbur 162
constitutional amendment 14, 322
  Australia 58–59, 62
  Austria 202, 215
  Canada 93, 101, 106, 108, 118, 131
  Switzerland 269, 273, 278, 316
  United States 147–48, 170
    Bill of Rights 148
constitutional rigidities (limits) 14, 34, 42,
    346, 352
  Australia 14, 15, 70n.41
  Austria 15, 183, 186, 190
    Federal Constitutional Law 188,
        190–91, 196, 198, 206, 216
    Fiscal Constitution 188, 189, 191
  Canada 101, 103
    Constitution Act (1867) 92
  Germany 15, 229, 248
    Basic Law 245, 248

  Weimar Constitution 231, 232, 233,
      236
  Switzerland 14, 15, 263, 266, 270, 292
    federal constitutions 269, 270, 293
  United States 14, 15, 139, 143, 151,
      178, 312
co-operative federalism 13, 52, 197, 224
  Germany 225, 240, 253
  Switzerland 304, 318
courts 37, 38, 40
  role of judicial review 15, 17, 37, 190,
      199, 203, 269, 322
  Australian High Court 15, 57, 58, 62,
      67, 69, 72, 83, 83n.65, 84
    Commonwealth Court 67
    Judiciary Act 1903 57
  Austrian Constitutional Court 199, 202,
      214, 220, 331
  Canadian Supreme Court 15, 100, 111
  German Bundesverfassungsgericht 15
  Swiss Bundesgericht 17
  US Supreme Court 15, 40, 143, 145,
      147, 161, 176, 177
    Social Security Act (1935) 144,
        144n.18, 158, 163–66

Davies, Gareth 166
decentralization 2, 30, 31, 33, 34, 323,
    326
  and development of welfare state 338,
      342, 353
  Canada 89, 115, 128, 134, 135, 137,
      310, 345
  Germany 244
  Switzerland 267, 341
  of authority 15, 36, 92, 101, 160, 183
  taxes and expenditures 31, 33, 34, 42,
      229n.22
  see also devolution, centralization
decision rules 9, 111, 129, 135, 139, 281,
    335
  deadlock 10, 280, 300, 311
  joint decision-making
    Canada 95, 104, 108–11, 116, 120,
        136, 310, 324, 330; Social Union
        Framework Agreement 129
  joint decision trap 20, 40, 43
  super-majorities 40, 145, 166, 198, 255,
      330, 336, 350, 350n.26
  unilateralism 95
  see also veto points
Derthick, Martha 166
devolution 43, 229, 238, 244, 245, 261,
    354
  of programmes 154, 267

direct democracy
  Austria 198, 199
  Switzerland 47, 270, 284, 291, 300, 303, 344
    policy stability 271, 272, 275, 277, 317
    pragmatic integration 279
Duchacek, Ivo D. 8, 9

education spending
  Australia 77, 79
  Austria 194–95, 214
  Canada 102
Eisenhower, President Dwight D. 166
Elazar, Daniel 160
Esping-Andersen, Gøsta 11, 187, 295
European Union 20, 210, 340, 348–51, 353
  and Austria 212
  debt option 256
  integration 20, 351
  Maastricht Treaty 211, 221, 256, 350n.26
  sovereignty 20, 350
expansion of welfare state 4, 39, 51, 307, 325, 328, 338, 341
  Australia 52, 53, 62, 63, 64, 75, 78, 87
    under Labor governments 71, 73, 74, 79, 85, 327
  Austria 192, 201, 202, 205–06, 207, 209, 210, 211, 221, 313, 325
  Canada 106, 136, 327
    impact of federalism 95, 118, 131
  Germany 244, 254, 314, 326
    impact of federalism 223n.6, 225, 233, 242, 259, 260, 314
    unification 255, 259
  Switzerland 279, 282, 284, 291, 302
    impact of federalism 264, 277, 291, 299, 300, 304, 316, 317
  United States 140–41, 144, 166, 327
    impact of federalism 139, 140, 143, 153, 174
experimentation 30, 34, 35, 42, 174, 220, 340
  Australia 65, 68
  Germany 261, 261n.102, 342, 342n.16
  Switzerland 294, 300
  United States 139, 144, 173
    presidential waivers 170, 174, 311, 312, 336, 342
  see also public choice, policy innovation

families of nations 10–11, 46
financing the welfare state 25, 27–29, 34, 223, 224, 339, 353
  funding arrangements 26, 30, 33
    Australia 14, 63; Royal Commission on National Insurance (1928) 70
    Austria 14, 192, 194, 208, 210, 215
    Canada 14, 92, 95, 103, 121; shared cost 104, 111, 330
    Germany 232, 241, 243, 253, 256, 259, 315; contribution-based 239, 240, 325
    Switzerland 14, 265, 267, 268, 275, 276, 281, 282, 297, 302
    United States 14, 158, 170, 176
Finegold, Kenneth F. 46, 312
fiscal competition 34, 44, 75
  Canada 98, 116
  Germany 224, 228, 261, 316
  United States 10, 143
fiscal equalization (revenue sharing) 6, 33, 34, 319, 333–34, 343
  Australia 72, 84, 318
  Austria 197, 209, 216
  Canada 93, 93n.5, 102, 125, 131, 135, 333
  Germany 6, 237, 247, 251
  United States 169, 170, 336
fiscal transfers 9, 33, 34, 322, 323
  tax shares 34, 206, 246
    Australia 72, 73, 78
      Australian Loan Council 72
      Commonwealth Grants Commission 72, 76n.53, 333
    Austria 192, 195, 208, 221
    Canada 95, 129, 131, 134, 135, 136, 310
      bloc funding 121–22, 123, 126; Canada Health and Social Transfer (CHST) 122
      Canada Assistance Plan (CAP) 114, 115, 119, 125, 126
      grants-in-aid 100
      shared-cost programmes 93, 100, 104, 114, 121, 324, 336
    Germany 237, 240, 247, 249–50
    Switzerland 265, 283, 297, 304
    United States 144, 160, 161, 174, 177
      block grants 152, 156, 157, 169, 173, 176–77, 312, 336
      Earned Income Tax Credit (EITC) 156, 159, 312, 337
      grants-in-aid 151
Forrer, Federal Councillor Ludwig 274

Index

Galligan, Brian 58
Geiger, Kim 166
Glazer, Nathan 139
Greve, Michael 1, 3
Grodzins, Morton 160

Hacker, Jacob S. 143
Haider, Jörg 210, 217, 218
Hall, Peter A. 307
Hamilton, Alexander 165
Hayek, Friedrich A. 31
health care 322
  Australia 74, 78, 79, 82, 323, 324
  Austria 187, 192n.41, 207, 208, 212
    Health Insurance Act (1921) 190
  Canada 90, 95, 111, 113–14, 124, 125, 131, 134, 135
    Canada Health Act 123, 125
    Canadian Medical Association 112
    hospital insurance 112, 311
    Medicare 112, 113, 135
    private coverage 113
    universal coverage 122, 129, 323, 336
  Germany 228, 244, 255, 258
  Switzerland 268, 271, 275, 276, 285, 287–88, 292, 323
    Health and Accident Insurance Act (1911) 273, 284, 286
  United States 323, 324
    American Medical Association 167
    Commonwealth of Massachusetts v. Mellon 160, 177
    Clinton, Hillary 171
    Clinton health care proposals 144, 171–72
    Health Security Card 172
    Medicaid 154, 156, 157, 167, 173, 175, 176
    Medicare 154, 167
    State Children's Health Insurance Program (SCHIP) 158, 174, 175, 312
Howard, Prime Minister John 57, 86

inter-governmentalism 6, 10, 30
  Australia 81, 84
  Canada 6, 94, 104, 113, 118, 121, 124, 135, 136, 310, 318
inter-state federalism 6, 10, 11, 223, 317, 319, 325, 339, 352
  Australia 84
    Council of Australian Governments (COAG) 84, 318

  Canada 93–94, 103, 104, 124, 135
  United States 47, 145, 148, 152, 156, 160, 166, 170
intra-state federalism 6, 11–12, 224, 336
  Austria 11, 196, 197, 205, 208, 215, 313
  Germany 11, 47, 315
  Switzerland 263, 264, 266, 292, 294, 317
invalidity (disability) pensions
  Australia 65, 86
  Austria 207
  Switzerland 271, 277, 278, 282, 287
  United States 141
  see also age pensions, OASDI

Johnson, President Lyndon B. 167, 169

Katznelson, Ira 166
Keating, Prime Minister Paul 56
Keman, Hans 8
Kittel, Bernhard 4
Klestil, President Thomas 218, 219
Kohl, Chancellor Helmut 250, 257, 335
Kreis, Georg xiv
Kreisky, Chancellor Bruno 201
Kryder, Daniel 166

Laski, Harold 165
Lijphart, Arend 8
Livingstone, William S. 91
Lowi, Theodore J. 139

Mackenzie King, Prime Minister William Lyon 100, 102
Manow, Philip 47, 314, 335
maternity benefits
  Australia 65, 68
  Canada 107
  Switzerland 271, 281, 285, 341
minimum wage
  Australia 67n.30, 67–68, 71, 75, 80
Mitchell, Deborah 26
Mittermaier, Karl Joseph 351

Nathan, Richard 337
nation-building 226, 308, 326, 344
  and social programmes (Canada) 90, 121, 130, 133
    Quebec nationalism 92, 103, 104, 132, 133, 134
'new politics' of the welfare state 3, 5, 43, 210, 216, 217, 255, 335, 339
'silver age' of the welfare state 4, 31, 46, 47
  Australia 51, 53, 87, 309
  Austria 215, 221

'new politics' of the welfare state (*cont.*)
  Canada 97, 101, 117, 128, 311
  Germany 316
  United States 312
Nixon, President Richard 168
Noël, Alain 99

Obinger, Herbert 47
'old politics' of the welfare state 25, 42–43, 81, 210, 339
'golden age' of the welfare state 3, 5, 31, 318, 331
  Australia 51, 62, 64, 76, 309
  Austria 182, 183, 184, 185, 189, 193, 194, 195, 203, 313
    Social Democrats (1919–34) 193, 195
  Canada 96
  Germany 226, 228, 237, 241, 242, 314
    Bismarckian social legislation 225, 226–27, 229, 230, 243, 248, 262
    Social Catholicism 238, 241
    social reform 227, 243
  Switzerland 269, 271, 273, 276
    Code of Obligations (1911) 271
    Federal Factory Act (1877) 264, 271, 272, 300, 341
    Federal Liability Act 273
  United States 312
    New Deal 141, 143, 161, 162, 163, 168, 175, 312
    War on Poverty 167, 168

Pal, Les 101
para-fiscal arrangements 23, 24–25, 26n.58, 43, 138, 331, 337, 347
  Australia 23
  Austria 201, 207, 208, 209, 212, 220
  Germany 227, 230n.22, 231
    contribution-based funds 243, 249, 251, 252–53, 261, 262
    structure 241, 242, 243, 315
  Switzerland 274–75, 279, 287
    corporatism 268, 273, 280
    Ghent system 276, 283
    public–private mix 283, 291, 302, 324
partisan complexion of governments 19, 21, 210, 328
  Australia 21, 36, 329
    Australian Labor Party (ALP) 21, 56, 59, 62, 65–66
    Liberal Party 70, 76, 79, 80, 86, 87
    National Party 70
    United Australian Party 70
  Austria 21, 182, 189, 198, 205, 216, 313

Austrian People's Party (ÖVP) 200, 213, 217, 220
Freedom Party (FPÖ) 212, 213, 216, 217, 219n.100, 314
Grand Coalition 201, 203, 205, 212, 221
New Coalition (ÖVP–FPÖ) 217
Social Democratic Party (SPÖ) 200, 205, 210, 215, 218, 219n.101, 220, 334
Canada 21
  Liberal Party 91, 99
  political left 92; Cooperative Commonwealth Federation (CCF) 92, 101, 105, 112; New Democratic Party (NDP) 92, 102, 105, 329
Germany 21, 224, 231, 255, 258, 315
  Catholic Zentrum 232, 238, 241
  Christian Democratic Party (CDU) 246, 254, 257, 258
  Social Democratic Party (SPD) 232, 254, 257, 258, 315
Switzerland 290, 300
  Catholic Conservatives 269, 270, 300
  Radical Party 269, 277
  Social Democrats 272, 277, 278, 281, 282, 284, 285, 288, 291
United States 21, 148, 330
  Democrats 159, 162, 163, 165, 166, 167, 172, 174
  Republicans 147, 168, 172, 174, 176
path dependency 39–40, 42, 319, 341
  Australia 66, 309
  Austria 207
  Switzerland 276n.18, 300
  see also political institutionalism
Peterson, Paul E. 142
pharmaceutical benefits scheme
  Australia 74, 86
Pierson, Paul 2, 5, 143, 308, 337, 342
policy innovation 30, 34, 42, 135, 185, 186, 192, 294, 328, 341
policy pre-emption 41, 42, 319, 323, 325, 340
  Austria 47, 185, 186, 192, 219
  Switzerland 271, 272, 274, 286, 300, 316
political accountability 43, 224, 336
political institutionalism 35–41, 307, 340
  and political economy/political interests 35–36, 116, 183, 230, 355
  counter-factual analysis (US) 144n.18, 163–66, 312
  fragmentation of power 36, 322, 328, 332
  Canada 118, 136

Index 361

Germany 250
Switzerland 269, 271, 291, 293
imbalance of fiscal powers 41, 60, 97–98, 233, 240, 310
joint decision systems 37, 324
ratchet effect 38; Australia 51, 86–87; Austria 210, 216
see also path dependency, policy pre-emption and veto players and points
Porter, Ann 107
presidential regimes 19, 146–47, 178
Prince, Michael 6
Proudhon, Pierre-Joseph 353
public choice theory: federalism and constraints on government growth 31–35
  exit options 32–33, 44
  welfare-induced mobility 32, 33, 126, 128, 143, 223, 310
  competitive federalism 13, 40
  see also fiscal competition, race to the bottom, policy innovation and experimentation

race to the bottom 30, 33, 34, 126, 139, 142–43, 209, 224, 249
Reagan, President Ronald 156, 169, 170, 174
  Omnibus Budget Reconciliation Act (1981) 169
referenda 37
  constitutional amendment
    Australia 52, 58, 59, 70, 74
    Austria 15n.41, 198–99, 218
    Switzerland 267, 269, 271–72, 273, 284, 286, 288, 289, 290, 291, 300, 302; mandatory 270, 303, 316; optional 274, 286, 291, 300, 303, 317, 332
  procedures 36
  Quebec sovereignty 117, 133, 134, 135
regionalism 14, 19, 119–20, 339, 341
  redistribution 332, 336
  Canada 14, 91, 107, 131
    economic divisions 91, 117
    geographic divisions 91, 92, 103, 118, 121
    language divisions 91, 103; Quebec 90, 91, 93, 132–33, 134
  Switzerland 10, 14, 19, 264, 267, 268, 293
  United States 139, 141
retrenchment 2, 38–39
  welfare state 5–6, 43, 46, 128, 332

Australia 309, 333
social expenditure retrenchment 53, 85, 87
Austria 195, 210, 211, 213–14, 216, 217, 218n.99, 221, 314, 334
Great Depression 313
Canada 90, 118, 121, 122, 125, 129, 134, 135, 311
Germany 255, 256, 257, 259, 260, 315, 316
Switzerland 264, 286, 289, 291, 303, 317
United States 171, 336
see also 'new politics'
Riker, William S. 9
Rivlin, Alice M. 343
Robertson, David Brian 142, 144
Rodden, Jonathan 33, 34
Roosevelt, President Franklin 141, 151, 162

Saint-Martin, Denis 132
Schiller, Friedrich 1, 355
Schmidt, Chancellor Helmut 255
Schröder, Chancellor Gerhard 255, 257, 335
secondary institutions of federalism 38, 75
see also veto points
Simeon, Richard 108
Skocpol, Theda 139
social assistance
  Australia 69, 74, 78, 341
  Austria 191, 192, 193, 194, 198, 206–07, 219n.103
  Canada 96, 97, 100, 111, 114–15, 125–26, 129, 336
  Germany 227, 231, 236, 237, 238
  Switzerland 265, 267, 268, 273, 292, 293, 294
    cantons 295–97, 299
    Swiss Conference for Social Assistance (SKOS) 294
  United States 154, 158, 173, 312, 337n.13
    Aid to Families with Dependent Children (AFDC) 159, 161, 168, 337
    Food Stamps Program 141, 156–57, 167, 171, 173, 177, 337
    Personal Responsibility and Work Opportunity Reconciliation Act (PRWORA) 157, 158, 173–75
    Temporary Assistance for Needy Families (TANF) 141, 157–58, 311

362   Index

social programmes
  generosity of coverage 31, 75, 139, 159, 177, 192, 203, 211, 233, 277
  income security programme (Canada) 26, 90, 95, 104, 105, 114, 115, 129, 133, 135, 310
  selectivity 87, 97
    Austria 186, 212
    Switzerland 283, 292
    United States 154, 156, 157, 159, 162, 169
  social insurance 3, 69, 130, 211, 226, 231
    Austria 187, 190, 209, 215, 219, 220, 313, 314; Federation of Austrian Insurance Carriers 214; General Social Insurance Act (1955) 202, 203, 212, 215; long-term care allowance (1993) 206, 211, 215
    Germany 247, 257, 259, 326; contribution-based 244, 250, 251, 256, 315; Long Term Care Insurance 20, 255, 255n.85, 316; programme design 227–28, 231, 241, 243
    Switzerland 274, 275, 277, 284, 291, 303
  social spending 38, 329
    Australia 63–64, 67, 71, 73, 76, 77, 79, 81–83, 309; Joint Parliamentary Committee on Social Security (1941) 73; social protection spending 77
    Austria 201, 203, 207, 209, 211
    Canada 90, 94, 102, 129, 130; national programmes 90, 100, 103, 112, 117, 130–31, 132, 133–34
    Germany 232, 250, 251, 256, 316; unification 250–51, 252
    Switzerland 11n.30, 269, 274, 286n.45, 286–87
    United States 151, 152, 162; national programmes 154, 159, 169, 175, 311
Sombart, Werner 139
St Laurent, Prime Minister Louis 112
state-building 12, 40, 41, 42, 226, 344–45
  United States 12, 165, 312, 346
  see also nation-building, political institutionalism

taxation
  horizontal tax competition 33, 209
  income taxation 73, 78, 141, 151, 168, 247, 256, 297
  inter-state tariffs 32, 229, 271, 303
  taxing authority 33, 42, 191
    Australia 60, 73, 75, 76, 78, 84
    Austria 198, 208, 220
    Canada 93, 130, 135
    Germany 229, 230, 235, 238, 245, 246, 256, 261
    Switzerland 267, 270, 277, 281, 292, 299, 302
    United States 150, 162
Tetlock, Philip E. 163, 164
Tiebout, Charles M. 32
trade unions/labour 23, 343
  Australia 61, 87, 309, 310, 334
    arbitration 62, 64, 87, 323, 329, 347
  Austria 200, 202, 206, 214, 215, 218
    labour law 196, 232
    League of Workers and Employees (ÖAAB) 217, 218
  Canada 96, 101, 116, 323
  Germany 227, 232, 239, 247
  Switzerland 288, 290–91
    labour market programmes 292, 294
  United States 139, 147, 167, 168, 323, 337n.14
    Taft-Hartley Act (1947) 166
  see also para-fiscal arrangements
Trudeau, Pierre, Prime Minister 133
Tsebelis, George 36
Tuohy, Carolyn 111

Uhr, John 46, 309, 329
unemployment insurance
  Australia 68, 69, 71, 72
  Austria 192, 202, 203, 212, 214
    Red Vienna 194–95, 220, 337, 342
    White-Collar Workers' Insurance Act 191
  Canada 93, 95, 99, 105, 107, 119, 119n.49, 131, 333
    Unemployment Assistance Act (UAA) 114
  Germany 228, 239, 240, 245, 248
  Switzerland 271, 272, 273, 276, 281, 283–84, 287, 292, 294
    Federal Unemployment Insurance Act (1982) 283
    reforms 289, 291
  United States 144, 158, 161, 342
unitary federalism 8n.18, 37, 47, 104, 236, 310, 329

veto players 36–37, 38, 39, 146, 331
  Australia 55, 56, 57

Index

Austria 199
Germany 229, 233–35, 251
see also veto points, political institutionalism
veto points 36, 38, 41, 43, 44, 322, 330, 339
  Australia 55–56, 74–75, 85, 334
  Austria 201, 220, 314
  Canada 108, 336
  Germany 222, 225, 236, 248, 254, 257, 258, 259, 260
  Switzerland 270, 274, 286, 317, 322, 330–32
  United States 145, 166
  see also veto players
Von Taaffe, Prime Minister Graf 184, 185, 187

welfare regimes 10, 29–31, 223, 231, 323
  regime status / hybrid welfare regime 12
    Australia 26–27, 52, 67, 68, 71, 323; National Welfare Scheme 74, 75
    Switzerland 12, 27, 268, 275, 286, 294, 299

conservative welfare regime 12, 13
  Austria 12, 187
  Germany 12, 228, 230, 248, 261
  'worker question' 26
  see also intra-state federalism
liberal welfare regime 12, 13, 26
  see also inter-state federalism
social-democratic welfare regime 26, 112, 341
Whitlam Labor government (Australia) 56, 76, 78
Wildavsky, Aaron 140
Wilensky, Harold 31
workers' compensation
  Canada 95, 97
World Wars 13
  impact of war 21, 66, 68n.36, 70, 72, 102, 220, 281, 327, 353
  World War One 230, 233; social/economic tensions 276, 277, 313
  World War Two 148, 202, 335, 338; economic effect 75, 76, 151, 201, 232, 244, 246, 317; veterans' pensions 99